# Travels in the two Sicilies, by Henry Swinburne, Esq. In the years 1777, 1778, 1779, and 1780. ... Volume 1 of 2

## Henry Swinburne

ECCO

PRINT EDITIONS

*Travels in the two Sicilies, by Henry Swinburne, Esq. In the years 1777, 1778, 1779, and 1780.*
*... Volume 1 of 2*
Swinburne, Henry
ESTCID: T088881
Reproduction from British Library
Vol.II. bears the imprint: "London: printed by J. Davis, for P. Elmsly".
London : printed for P. Elmsly, 1783-85.
2v.,plates,table : map ; 4°

## Gale ECCO Print Editions

Relive history with *Eighteenth Century Collections Online*, now available in print for the independent historian and collector. This series includes the most significant English-language and foreign-language works printed in Great Britain during the eighteenth century, and is organized in seven different subject areas including literature and language; medicine, science, and technology; and religion and philosophy. The collection also includes thousands of important works from the Americas.

The eighteenth century has been called "The Age of Enlightenment." It was a period of rapid advance in print culture and publishing, in world exploration, and in the rapid growth of science and technology – all of which had a profound impact on the political and cultural landscape. At the end of the century the American Revolution, French Revolution and Industrial Revolution, perhaps three of the most significant events in modern history, set in motion developments that eventually dominated world political, economic, and social life.

In a groundbreaking effort, Gale initiated a revolution of its own: digitization of epic proportions to preserve these invaluable works in the largest online archive of its kind. Contributions from major world libraries constitute over 175,000 original printed works. Scanned images of the actual pages, rather than transcriptions, recreate the works *as they first appeared.*

Now for the first time, these high-quality digital scans of original works are available via print-on-demand, making them readily accessible to libraries, students, independent scholars, and readers of all ages.

For our initial release we have created seven robust collections to form one the world's most comprehensive catalogs of 18<sup>th</sup> century works.

*Initial Gale ECCO Print Editions collections include:*

### History and Geography
Rich in titles on English life and social history, this collection spans the world as it was known to eighteenth-century historians and explorers. Titles include a wealth of travel accounts and diaries, histories of nations from throughout the world, and maps and charts of a world that was still being discovered. Students of the War of American Independence will find fascinating accounts from the British side of conflict.

### Social Science

Delve into what it was like to live during the eighteenth century by reading the first-hand accounts of everyday people, including city dwellers and farmers, businessmen and bankers, artisans and merchants, artists and their patrons, politicians and their constituents. Original texts make the American, French, and Industrial revolutions vividly contemporary.

### Medicine, Science and Technology

Medical theory and practice of the 1700s developed rapidly, as is evidenced by the extensive collection, which includes descriptions of diseases, their conditions, and treatments. Books on science and technology, agriculture, military technology, natural philosophy, even cookbooks, are all contained here.

### Literature and Language

Western literary study flows out of eighteenth-century works by Alexander Pope, Daniel Defoe, Henry Fielding, Frances Burney, Denis Diderot, Johann Gottfried Herder, Johann Wolfgang von Goethe, and others. Experience the birth of the modern novel, or compare the development of language using dictionaries and grammar discourses.

### Religion and Philosophy

The Age of Enlightenment profoundly enriched religious and philosophical understanding and continues to influence present-day thinking. Works collected here include masterpieces by David Hume, Immanuel Kant, and Jean-Jacques Rousseau, as well as religious sermons and moral debates on the issues of the day, such as the slave trade. The Age of Reason saw conflict between Protestantism and Catholicism transformed into one between faith and logic -- a debate that continues in the twenty-first century.

### Law and Reference

This collection reveals the history of English common law and Empire law in a vastly changing world of British expansion. Dominating the legal field is the *Commentaries of the Law of England* by Sir William Blackstone, which first appeared in 1765. Reference works such as almanacs and catalogues continue to educate us by revealing the day-to-day workings of society.

### Fine Arts

The eighteenth-century fascination with Greek and Roman antiquity followed the systematic excavation of the ruins at Pompeii and Herculaneum in southern Italy; and after 1750 a neoclassical style dominated all artistic fields. The titles here trace developments in mostly English-language works on painting, sculpture, architecture, music, theater, and other disciplines. Instructional works on musical instruments, catalogs of art objects, comic operas, and more are also included.

**The BiblioLife Network**

This project was made possible in part by the BiblioLife Network (BLN), a project aimed at addressing some of the huge challenges facing book preservationists around the world. The BLN includes libraries, library networks, archives, subject matter experts, online communities and library service providers. We believe every book ever published should be available as a high-quality print reproduction; printed on-demand anywhere in the world. This insures the ongoing accessibility of the content and helps generate sustainable revenue for the libraries and organizations that work to preserve these important materials.

The following book is in the "public domain" and represents an authentic reproduction of the text as printed by the original publisher. While we have attempted to accurately maintain the integrity of the original work, there are sometimes problems with the original work or the micro-film from which the books were digitized. This can result in minor errors in reproduction. Possible imperfections include missing and blurred pages, poor pictures, markings and other reproduction issues beyond our control. Because this work is culturally important, we have made it available as part of our commitment to protecting, preserving, and promoting the world's literature.

**GUIDE TO FOLD-OUTS MAPS and OVERSIZED IMAGES**

The book you are reading was digitized from microfilm captured over the past thirty to forty years. Years after the creation of the original microfilm, the book was converted to digital files and made available in an online database.

In an online database, page images do not need to conform to the size restrictions found in a printed book. When converting these images back into a printed bound book, the page sizes are standardized in ways that maintain the detail of the original. For large images, such as fold-out maps, the original page image is split into two or more pages

Guidelines used to determine how to split the page image follows:

• Some images are split vertically; large images require vertical and horizontal splits.
• For horizontal splits, the content is split left to right.
• For vertical splits, the content is split from top to bottom.
• For both vertical and horizontal splits, the image is processed from top left to bottom right.

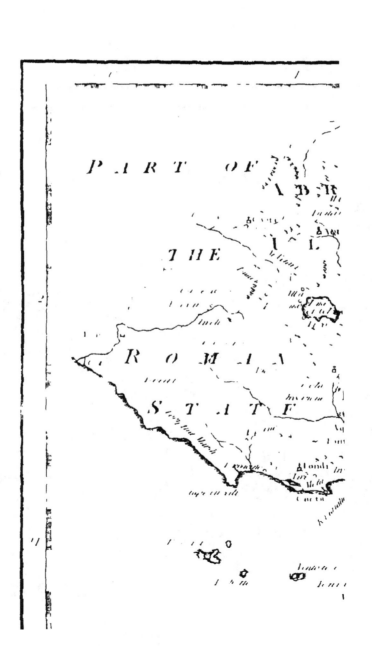

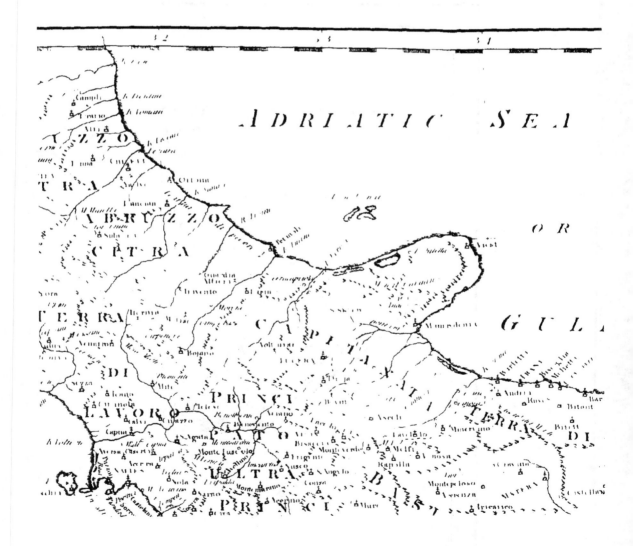

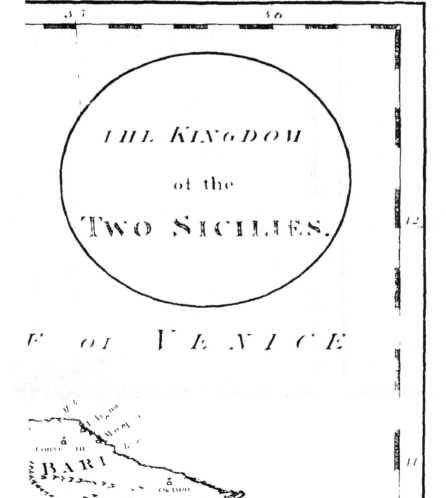

THE KINGDOM

of the

TWO SICILIES.

E of VENICE

BARI

TERRA DI

Ostuni

Taranto

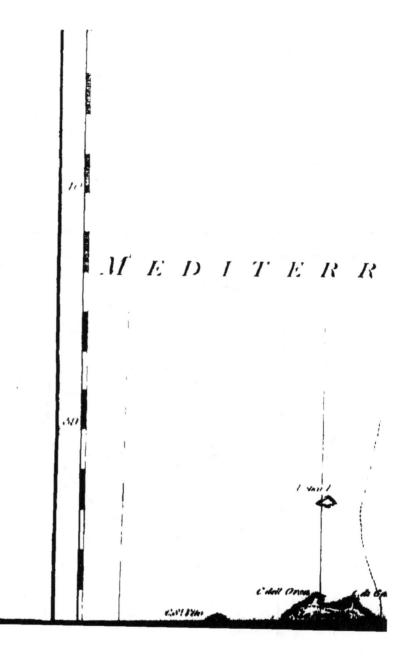

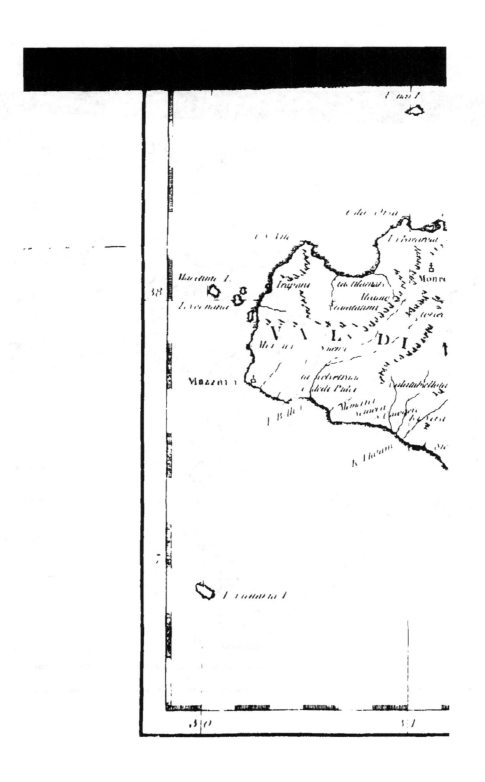

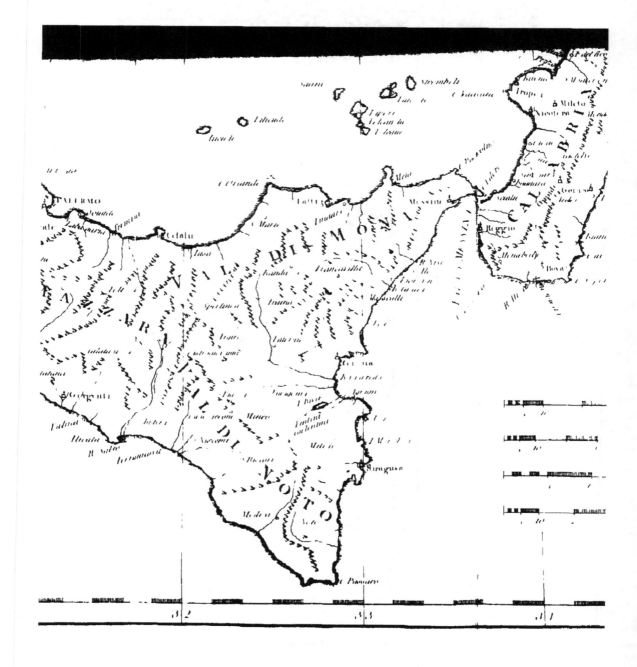

SQUILLACE     SEA

Stelleti

# TRAVELS

### IN THE

# TWO SICILIES,

BY

HENRY SWINBURNE, Esq.

IN

The Years 1777, 1778, 1779, and 1780.

## VOL. I.

---

QUID VERUM ATQUI DECENS CURO—— Hor.

---

LONDON

PRINTED FOR P. ELMSLY, IN THE STRAND

M.DCC.LXXXIII.

# PREFACE.

I CANNOT presume to print a Tour through the Two Sicilies, without offering an apology for its appearance. They have been so often described, that nothing but novelty of matter can excuse a fresh attempt. Our earliest education has made us acquainted with those classic regions; Poetry and History have rendered their topography familiar to us, and every school-boy can point out the ruins of Magna Græcia and Sicily. No country, Latium alone excepted, has so frequently employed the pen of the antiquary; and the observations made by travellers of a political turn may be supposed to have canvassed sufficiently the advantages as well as the inconveniences of its present situation.

Under the discouragement arising from this anticipation, and the unpromising circumstance of painting over ground often and nicely examined, I yet do not despair of conveying such information on many heads, as may justify my boldness to the Reader, if, from a laudable desire of improvement, any will venture with me along so beaten a track. Part of my route is fresh land; and where I shall be under the irksome necessity of treading in the footsteps

of

of preceding authors, I hope something will be struck out that has escaped their penetration. Far be it from me, wantonly, to impugn their authority, or detract from their merits; I only wish to insinuate, that, as two persons seldom consider an object in the same point of view, and are still more rarely led by their perceptions to a combination of ideas exactly similar, it is but reasonable to hope that many openings may be left for the remarks of subsequent observers*. When allowances are made for difference of seasons, diversity of studies, occasional information, and many other accidental helps, we shall find an ample field still remain for our curiosity to range in: to say nothing of the revolutions, moral, physical and political, effectuated by the hand of Time, which, however slowly and imperceptibly it may perform its operations, acts with irresistible force upon the state both of nature and of man. In the southern parts of Italy, where the elements torment with more than ordinary violence, where changes in government have succeeded each other with uncommon rapidity, the variations are more precipitate, the effects more striking.

In the course of seventeen centuries, the face of things has been so much altered, that the descriptions given by the ancient classics can seldom interfere with those of a modern writer. The later Latin and Italian authors, who

* Jamais deux hommes ne jugerent pareillement de mesme chose. Il est impossible de voir deux opinions semblables exactement, non seulement de divers hommes, mais en mesme homme a diverses heures.

have treated these subjects, are but little known or read in
England, and most of them are rather discussers of detached points of history and geography, than general
circumambulatory observers. They were too little acquainted with the laws and customs of foreign nations, to be able
to form just criticisms upon those of their own country,
and without some solid grounds for comparison, a writer
will bewilder himself in his reasonings, and betray in each
page that he is blinded and misled by ignorance and
vanity.

How far my endeavours to instruct may be rendered
superfluous by any recent accounts is a point which the
voice of the Public has alone a right to determine. I wait
the decision with respect, but without fear, conscious of
having done my utmost to deserve its indulgence, for to
my own observations, and the information derived from
books, I have added many interesting details communicated
to me by learned and curious persons of the kingdom of
Naples [*].

Whatever my opinions deviate from those of my predecessors, I have studied to convey my dissent in such
diffident terms, as may avoid all appearance of an attack on
the literary reputation of those from whom I presume to
differ in sentiment; but this delicacy does not prevail so

* I am particularly indebted to Monsignor Capecelatro, Archbishop of Taranto, Counsellor Monsignor Grimm, D. Filippo Briante Patriarch di Gallipoli, D. Pasquale Bath, D. Domenico Curdo, George Hurt, Esquire,
Padre Antonio Minch, of the order of St. Dominick, D. Domenico Minch,
Arciprete of Molocchio, and D. Giovanni Pretti of Gallipoli.

a

far as to obstruct the liberty of judging for myself; the maxim of *nullius jurare in verba*, constitutes the very spirit of my undertaking. In this freedom, and a scrupulous attention to truth, consisted the chief, perhaps the only merit of my Spanish Tour. The same principle shall direct my pen throughout the present work. By thus pursuing the dull plain track of truth, I shall, no doubt, run the risk of displeasing some of my Readers; but, I confess, I cannot condescend to keep their attention alive with fiction, be it ever so agreeable. According to my plan, the effusions of imagination are debarred all share in the composition: I deny myself the usual privilege of working up a trivial event into a sentimental or laughable adventure; the lively dialogue with persons who never honoured me with their confidence, is excluded; nor do I allow myself to dress up the trite story of an old book of jests, and pass it off for the scandalous chronicle of the day.

By refusing the assistance of such ready auxiliaries, I am aware that I weaken my force, and contract the circle of entertainment to a degree many people will disapprove of; but I intreat them to consider, that I am writing the account of a real Tour, and not an imitation of Sterne's Sentimental Journey.

Some Critics, I am told, have imputed as a blemish to my Letters on Spain, that I was rather an exact describer of still life, than an acute delineator of characters and manners. To this charge I can only answer, that having detected former writers in many errors, which they had

fallen

fallen into through haftinefs, mifconception, or credulity, it was natural I fhould give into the oppofite extreme, and, by advancing nothing but what I had vouchers for, lay myfelf open to an accufation of excefhive caution, and confequently dulnefs.

I am apprehenfive the fame cenfure will be paffed upon my prefent publication; but I choofe to imitate the fatif-factory drynefs of an authentic Gazette, rather than, like a fprightly Morning-Paper, amufe and miflead, by inter-weaving a thoufand pleafing impoftures with half a dozen real facts.

The longer any man of candour refides in a foreign country, the greater difficulty he finds in giving a character of its inhabitants. He perceives fo many nice varieties, fo many exceptions to general rules, as almoft deftroy his hopes of drawing up one comprehenfive defcription of them: he every day becomes more confcious of the prefumption of thofe who run and read; and, what is worfe, write Unfortunately, it is from fuch rapid obfervations, that moft people are to derive their knowledge of foreign nations; and I leave it to the impartial to decide upon the probability of any refemblance exifting in fuch portraits. I have read the travels of one of thefe dafhing writers *, who allots a whole chapter, with a title in capitals, to the character and manners of the Neapolitan, which paints he

---

* Voyage de France, d'Efpagne, de Portugal, & d'Italie, par Mr S——
(Silhouette) in 1730.

handles

handles with as much decisiveness, as if he had resided forty years at Naples in quality of spy. Upon comparing the dates of his Journal, it appears, that his whole stay in that city was exactly five days and a half, part of which was spent upon Mount Vesuvius, and among the curiosities of Puzzuoli.

My style has been by some thought deficient in elegance and refinement, but until the positive ideas we are to attach to these words be ascertained and generally agreed upon, I shall not attempt to emerge out of my humble sphere. They have of late been much used, perhaps mis-applied, and many persons of taste and knowledge in our language are of opinion, that the terms elegant and refined have been frequently employed in speaking of writings, where the epithets, fustian and affected, wou'd have been more applicable. They pretend, that many of our modern compositions verge to that simpering style known in France by the name of *preceux*, which breaks out in an unne-cessary adoption of foreign and learned phrases, a fondness for founding words to express common ideas, and a con-tinual round of metaphorical and bombastical imagery. I do not know how far these critics may have reason on their side, but as I feel no ambition to try any daring flights, I shall rest contented, if I am allowed in this work the same merits that were granted me in my Spanish Tour, viz. truth, perspicuity, and common sense.

# TABLE OF CONTENTS

## OF THE

## FIRST VOLUME.

## A SHORT SKETCH of the HISTORY of the KINGDOM of NAPLES.

A VOYAGE

# CONTENTS

SECT.

# C O N T E N T S.

SECT.

## TARANTO and its ENVIRONS.

SECT.

## JOURNEY from TARANTO to REGGIO.

# CONTENTS.

## JOURNEY from REGGIO to NAPLES.

SECT.

# I R R A T A

Page 80, line 21, for *ponti* ‡ *Ingenii celfa* read *ponti ingenii* ‡ *Celfa*

101, ———— 7, for *bella* read *illia*

106, ———— 20, for *spoil, has* read *spoil had*

1 7, ———— 13, for *rife, at* read *rife a*

136, ———— 6, for *arbor juda* read *arbor Juda.*

1 0, ———— 27, for *fupplies of corn from other countries* read *other countries for a fupply of corn*

193, ———— 3, for *brut* read *Albert*

215, ———— 5, for *indifferent, to about* read *indifferently, about*

222, ———— 7, for *this side* read *this fide*

226, ———— 5, for *at the high* read *at the end of the high.*

245, ———— 10, for *Lu rene* read *Lucrine*

258, ———— 17, for *veffels fly* read *veffels could fly*

260, ———— 23, for *Tarentum* read *Tarentinorum*

201, ———— 16, for *aquo* read *equo*

274, ———— 5, for *properly* read *profufely*

274, ———— 21, for *Metapontorum* read *Metapontinorum*

277, ———— 19, for *a few off in her* read *a few mile off*

299, ———— 23, for *Carigliano* read *Coriglino*

3 , ———— 25, for *traffic* read *traffic*

312, ———— 9, for *Philochus* read *Philoctetes*

321, ———— 11, for *high, rocks coarse* read *high, the rocks coarfe.*

321, ———— 16, for *faten* read *d'Preſed*

325, ———— 6, for *lib can* read *libacan*

325, ———— 16, for *Ibra* read *Ithaca*

330, ———— 24, for *Palermo After* read *Palermo, after*

34 , ———— 5, for *tufted* read *lutel*

3 , ———— 9, for *rind* read *rind*

395, ———— 6, for *leg* read *legs*

409, ———— 6, for *break on all* read *break out on all*

# A GENEALOGICAL TABLE of the SOVEREIGNS of the TWO SICILIES

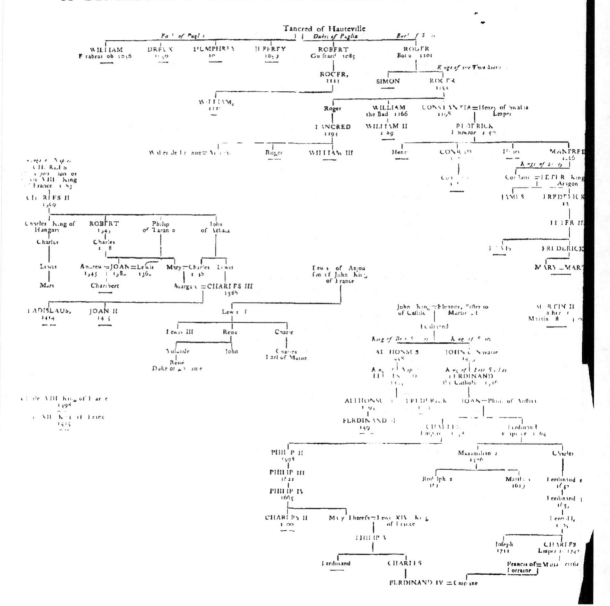

# TABLES OF COINS, &c.

## GOLD COINS.

1. Piece of fix ducats.
2. Piece of four ducats.
3. Piece of three ducats, or, Oncia, a Sicilian coin.
4. Piece of two ducats.

## BRASS COINS.

The piece of 1 grano and 6 calli *, called the Publica †.

| | |
|---|---|
| ——— 1 ——— | 0 |
| ——— 0 ——— | 9 |
| ——— 0 ——— | 6 The |

Tornefe ‡.

| | |
|---|---|
| ——— 0 ——— | 4 |
| ——— 0 ——— | 3 |

## SILVER COINS.

Piece of 13 carlini & 2 grana.

| | | |
|---|---|---|
| 12 | 0 | |
| 10 | 0 | The ducat, very scarce |
| 6 | 6 | |
| 6 | 0 | Very common |
| 5 | 0 | The patacca, scarce |
| 4 | 0 | Common |
| 3 | 0 | Common |
| 2 | 6 | |
| 2 | 4 | |
| 2 | 0 | The Neapolitan |
| 1 | 3 | |
| 1 | 2 | |
| 1 | 0 | { The carlino of Nap , and tari of Sicily |
| 0 | 5 | |

| | | | |
|---|---|---|---|
| 1 Oncia | | 3 ducats. | |
| 1 Ducat | contains | 10 carlini. | Accounts are kept at Naples in ducats, carlini, and grana, but regular merchants keep theirs in two columns only, viz. ducats and grana. |
| 1 Carlino | | 10 grana. | |
| 1 Grano | | 12 calli. | |

The Neapolitan ducat, upon the fuppofed par with England, is worth forty-five pence, or 3 s. 9 d. fterling, and the carlino 4½ d but this is no fixed rule, as exchange is continually varying, and occafionally makes a difference of ten or fifteen per cent higher or lower, and fometimes even more.

* Calli ought to be written Cavalli, from the horfes ftamped on the coin of Ferdinand the Firft, who, by a wretched quibble, put on it the legend, *Æquitas regni*
† Publica is fo named from its motto, *Publica commoditas*
‡ A word taken from the French *Tournois*

WEIGHTS

# WEIGHTS and MEASURES.

| 1 Cantaro | | | 100 rotoli | | N. B The Neapolitan cantaro is equal to 196 English ℔ of Averdupois weight, and the rotolo to 2 English ℔. The pound is a trifling fraction above 11 oz. English. |
| 1 Rotolo | contains | | 33½ ounces | | |
| 1 Pound | | | 12 ounces. | | |

## LONG-MEASURE.

1 Cana contains 8 palmi.——It is computed that $2\frac{1}{3}$ yards English make a Neapolitan canna, and that a palmo is equal to $10\frac{1}{4}$ inches English

## LAND-MEASURE.

Land is measured by the moggia, a superficial quantity containing 900 passi, each passo containing $7\frac{1}{3}$ palmi.

## LAND-MEASURE in Puglia.

| 1 Caro | | | 20 versure |
| 1 Versura | contains | | 6 catene |
| 1 Catena | | | 10 passi |
| 1 Passo | | | 7 palmi. |

## DRY-MEASURE.

Wheat is measured by the tomolo, of which $5\frac{1}{3}$ are equal to an English quarter

## WINE-MEASURE.

Wine is measured by the barrel, containing 66 caraffi, equal to $9\frac{1}{4}$ English gallons ——In the city of Naples, the barrel contains only 60 caraffi.

## OIL-MEASURE.

| 1 Salma | | | 16 stars |
| 1 Star | contains | | 10½ rotoli |
| 1 Rotolo | | | 33½ ounces, equal to 2 ℔ English. |

A salma contains about 40 English gallons.

ROADS

# ROADS of the Kingdom of NAPLES.

**Post-Road from Rome to Naples.**

From Rome to Terracina

| | |
|---|---|
| Fondi | 1 |
| Itri | 1 |
| Mola | 1 |
| Garigliano | 1 |
| S. Agata | 1 |
| Francolisi | 1 |
| Capua | 1 |
| Aversa | 1 |
| Naples. Post royal. | |

**Post-Road from Naples to Caserta.**

From Naples to Caivano, post royal.

| | |
|---|---|
| Caserta | 1 |

From Caserta to S. Luci    $\frac{1}{2}$

From Caserta to the Aqueduct    1

From Caserta to Capua    0 $\frac{1}{2}$

From Naples to Puzzuoli, post royal

**Post-Road from Naples to Manfredonia**

From Naples to Marigliano, p. r. & $\frac{1}{2}$

| | |
|---|---|
| Cardinale | 1 $\frac{1}{2}$ |
| Avellino | 1 $\frac{1}{2}$ |
| Dentecane | 1 $\frac{1}{2}$ |
| Grottaminarda | 1 |
| Ariano | 1 |
| Savignano | 1 |
| Ponte di Bovino | 1 $\frac{1}{2}$ |
| Lucera | 2 |
| Foggia | 2 |
| Manfredonia | 3 |

**Post-Road from Naples to Lecce.**

From Naples to Ponte Bovino   10 $\frac{1}{2}$

| | |
|---|---|
| Ordona | 1 |
| Cerignuola | 1 $\frac{1}{2}$ |
| S. Cassano | 1 |
| Barletta | 1 |
| Bisceglia | 1 |
| Giovenazzo | 1 |
| Bari | 1 $\frac{1}{2}$ |
| Mola | 0 $\frac{1}{2}$ |
| Monopoli | 1 $\frac{1}{2}$ |
| Iasano | 1 |
| Ostuni | 1 $\frac{1}{2}$ |
| S. Vito | 1 |
| Mesagna | 1 $\frac{1}{2}$ |
| Cellino | 1 $\frac{1}{2}$ |
| Lecce | 1 $\frac{1}{2}$ |

**Post-Road from Naples to Persano.**

From Naples to La Nunziata, p r. $\frac{1}{2}$

| | |
|---|---|
| Nocera | 1 |
| Salerno | 1 |
| Vicenza | 1 |
| Evoli | 1 |
| Persano | 1 |

From Naples to Pesto.

| | |
|---|---|
| To Evoli | 5 $\frac{1}{2}$ |
| Pesto | 1 $\frac{1}{2}$ |

Price. 11 Carlini each pair of horses, and 5 $\frac{1}{2}$ more at the post royal. 3 Carlini are the due of the postillion for each pair of horses.

Post-

| Post-Road from Naples to Reggio. | | To Pantoni | 1 | |
|---|---|---|---|---|
| | | Cofenza | 1 | |
| To Evoli | 5½ | Rogliano | 1 | |
| La Ducheffa | 1 | Seigliano | 1 | |
| Auletta | 1 | S Biafe | 1 | * |
| Sala | 1 | Fondaco del Fico | 1 | |
| Cafalnuovo | 1 | Monteleone | 1 | |
| Lagonegro | 1 | S Petro de Melito | 1 | |
| Lauria | 1 | Drofi | 1 | |
| Caftelluccio | 1 | Seminare | 1 | |
| La Rotonda | 1 | Paffo di Solani | 1 | |
| Caftrovillari | 1 | Fiumara di Muro | 1 | |
| Efero | 1 | Catona | 1 | † |
| Celfo | 1 | Reggio | 1 | |

# R O U T E S  of  C A L E S S I,  Muleteers  and  Vetturini.

**From Naples to Reggio, by Puglia.**

1 Day, dinner at Cardinale, fup-
   at Avellino.
2. Mirabella——Ariano.
3. Ponte di Bovino——Ordona.
4 Canofa——San Cofimo.
5. Fontana d'Ogna——Gravina.
6. Matera
7. Vallecupa——Torre di Mare.
8. Policoro——Rocca Imperiale.
9. Caftel Rofeto——Trebifaccia
10. Madonna dell' Arma——Bufa-
    lara di Caffano
11 Torre de Paolini——Mirti.
12. Cariati——Capo d'Alice.
13. Fafano——Cotrone.
14 Cutri——Megliacane.
15. Taverna Nova——Cafine di
    Catanzaro. Carriages can go
    no further, and litters are ufed
    from hence
16 Borgia——Fondaco del Fico.

17. Monteleone——Seminara.
18. Scilla.
19. Reggio.

**From Naples to Reggio, by Salerno.**

1. Nocera——Salerno.
2. Vicenza——Evoli.
3. La Ducheffa——Polla.
4. Sala——S. Lorenzo
5. Cafalnuovo——Lagonero.
6 Lauria——Caftelluccio.
7. La Rotonda——Murano.
8 Oria——Corigliano
9. Roffano——Mirti.
10. Cariati——Capo d'Alice.
11. Foffaro——Cotrone.
12. Cutri——Megliacane.
13. Catanzaro.
14 Borgia——Aqua che Favella
15 Pizzo——Monteleone.
16 Seminara.
17 Reggio.

**From Naples to Aquila in Abruzzo.**

| To Clavi | 23 miles | Caftel del Sangro | 21 | Novelli | 14 |
|---|---|---|---|---|---|
| Tiverno | 23 | Sulmona | 20 | Aquila | 14 |

Here is a road of communication to Catanzaro.——1 40 pofts.
† Here one embarks for Meffina.

A

# GEOGRAPHICAL VIEW

OF THE

# KINGDOM OF NAPLES.

THIS Kingdom occupies the moſt ſouthern extremity of Italy, Situation and extends from latitude 42° 50′ to latitude 37° 50′; and and Extent from longitude 14° to longitude 19° Eaſt from London. Its greateſt length 450 Italian miles; breadth 140; circumference 1,468. Its ſurface contains 3,500 ſquare leagues, or, as ſome geographers compute, 14,508,973 Moggie, each of which is a ſquare of 30 paces on each ſide, every pace of ſeven palms and one-fifth:—but theſe are rough calculations.

The Apennine runs through it from North to South, a branch of Mountains the Apennine runs Weſt, to form the promontory of Sorrento Monte Gargano is a promontory on the Adriatic Sea; Monte Barbaro, Miſeno, and Veſuvius, are inſulated mountains.

Garigliano and Voltorno, navigable; Tronto, Aterno, Sangro, Rivers Fortore, Ofanto, Baſiento, Agri, Ciati, Metramo, Amato, Silari, and Sarno.

Celano

Lakes.   Celano, Agnano, Averno, Licola, Fusaro, Patria, Lesina, Fondi.

Islands   In the Mediterranean, Ponza, Ventotiene, Ischia, Procida, Nisida, Capri, Galli, Licosa, Dino.

In the Ionian, the island of Calypso, Monte Sardo, S. Andrea, and S Pelagia.

In the Adriatic, Tremiti and Pelagosa.

Number of Inhabitants   In 1669, it amounted to 2,500,000; in 1765, to 3,953,098; in 1773, to 4,249,430; and in 1779, to 4,641,363, exclusive of the army and naval establishment.

Provinces.   Twelve; viz. Terra di Lavoro, Principato citra, Principato ultra, Basilicata, Capitanata, County of Molise, Terra di Bari, Terra di Otranto, Calabria citra, Calabria ultra, Abruzzo citra, and Abruzzo ultra. These contain 2,067 universita, under the denomination of cities, towns, and villages.

Tribunals   At Naples,—Camera di Santa Chiara, S. R C di Santa Chiara, Sommaria, Vicaria, Del Almirante, Consolato, Della Lana, Della Seta, Giunta de' Poveri, Degli Allodiali, Del Lotto, Di Sicilia, Di Stato, Del Montiero, Proto Medicato, Azienda, Dé Presidij, Udienza dell Esercito, De Castelli, Di Marina, Zecca dé Pesi, &c.

Terra di Lavoro is governed by Sopra Intendenti, royal governors of towns, and judges

The other provinces have presidents, viz. Principato citra, Principato ultra, Basilicata, Bari, Otranto, Abruzzo citra, Calabria citra, and Calabria ultra, have one each; Abruzzo ultra has two, and Capitanata and Molise one between them.

At Foggia is the tribunal Della Dogana.

Ecclesiastical government   Twenty-one archbishoprics, and one hundred and ten bishoprics: of which, eight archbishoprics, and twenty bishoprics, are in the King s gift, the rest in the Pope's.

Arms   Azure, femee of fleur de luces, or, with a label of five points, gules

Orders of Knighthood   Order of St Januarius, bishop and martyr,—instituted by Charles, now King of Spain, in 1738. The number of Knights not positively fixed.

2

fixed. They wear a red ribbon, and a ſtar on the left breaſt, with the image of the Saint in the centre; and the motto, *In Sanguine Fœdus* The King confers the Croſs of the Conſtantinian Order, as Duke of Parma

Ferdinand the Fourth, by the Grace of God, King of Both Sicilies, Jeruſalem, and Infant of Spain; Duke of Parma, Placentia, Caſtro, &c; and hereditary Great Prince of Tuſcany, &c &c.

Titles of the King

---

## 1. TERRA DI LAVORO;
### *anciently*, *Campania Felix*

Derived from its fertility, or from the ancient *Campi Leborini*.
Azure, over 2 cornucopias, a crown, or.
1,530,964 Moggie
In 1779, 1,210,989.
Garigliano, Voltorno, Saone, Clani, Sebeto.
Agnano, Averno, Fuſaro, Licola, Patria, Fondi.
Iſchia, Procida, Ponza, Ventotiene, S. Maria, Botte, Niſida.
Naples, Baia, Gaeta.
Veſuvius, Epomeo, Camaldoli, Barbara, Nuovo, Tifata, Mattcſe, St Leo, St. Salvatore, Cecubo, Auronco, Ofelſio, Maſſico, Caſſino, Attico, Nivoſo, Cairo, Ceſino, Seli, Ortaſio, and Aſo.

Name

Arms

Extent

Inhabit.

River

Lake

Iſland.

Seapor.

Mountain.

1 Naples capital, archbiſhopric.
2 Capua fortreſs, archbiſhopric.

Principal Place

3. Biſhoprics. Sora, Aquino, reduced to a hamlet, the biſhop reſides at the united ſee of Pontecorvo, Fondi, Alife, the biſhop lives at Piedimonte, Venafro, Seſſa, Calvi, Telele, the biſhop reſides at Cerieto, Teano, Caiazzo, Gaeta, a fortreſs; Caſerta, the biſhop lives at Caſerta Nova, where the King has a palace, Averſa Acerra, Nola; Pozzuoli, Iſchia, Carinola.

4. Monte

4. Monte Casino, the head convent of the Order of St. Benedict.

5. Portici, St. Leuci, Cacciabella ; royal residences.

6. Pompeii, Herculaneum, Cuma, Baiæ, Capua, Formiæ, Minturnæ, Sinuessa ; ruined cities.

7. Vesuvius, Solfatara ; mountains emitting smoke or flame.

---

## 2. PRINCIPATO CITRA; or,

*Principality of Salerno, anciently inhabited by the Picentini and Lucani.*

Name
In the year 851, the possessions of the Lombards were divided into two parts ; one of which obeyed the Prince of Salerno ; the other was subject to that of Benevento.

Arms
Party per fess, argent and sable , a sailor's compass with 8 wings, argent , in chief, a mullet, or.

Extent
1,175,994 Moggie.

Inhabitants
447,465

Rivers
Sarno, Sele, Battipaglia, Alento, Busento, Calore, Bianco, Negro, St. Gregorio.

Islands
Capri, li Galli, Piana di Lacosa.

Seaports
Castelamare, Salerno.

Mountains
Toro, Canutario, Majano, Collo, Aquarro, Lattario, Sarno, St. Donato, Calpazzo, Lucano, Nero, Alburno, Civita, Calimarco, Cantena, Stella, Novi, Cavallara, Antillia, Bulgaria, Maddalena, Balzater, St Onofrio, Aquila, Motulo, Cervati, Navarra, Petraro, Centaurino, Lagorosso.

Principal Places
1. Salerno presidency, archbishopric.

2. Amalfi, archbishopric.

3. Sorrento, archbishopric.

4. Bishop-

4. Bifhoprics :—Nocera, Sarno, Vico, Maffa, Capri, Cava, Let-
tere, Caftelamare, Acerno, Campagna cum Satriano, Capaccio, Poli-
caftro, Scala cum Ravello, Minori, Marfico Novo.

5. Pæftum, Stabia, Velia; ruined cities.

6. Perfano, Caftelamare; royal feats.

---

### 3  PRINCIPATO ULTRA; or,
*Principality of Benevento —Samnites, Hirpini.*

| | |
|---|---|
| Party per fefs, gules and argent ; on the 1ft, a crown. | Arms. |
| 664,280 Moggie. | Extent |
| 250,136. | Inhabitants. |
| Calore, Sabato, Tamoro. | Rivers |
| Virgine, Taburno, Sabletta, Agnone, Termolo, Guleto, Paflagone, Irpino, Rumulo, Jarminio, Divoto, Voltore. | Mountains |
| Anfanto. | Lake |
| 1. Benevento, archbifhopric ; belongs to the Pope | Principal Places |

2. Conza, archbifhopric.

3. Bifhoprics :—St. Agata de' Goti ; St. Angelo de' Lombardi, cum
Bifaccia, Ariano ; Trevico, cum Vico della Baronia ; Avellino, cum
Frigento ; Nufeo ; Montemarano, Lacedogna ; Monteverde, united
to Canne and Nazareth.

4. Montevergine, chief convent of the Verginian order

5  Montefufcolo, prefidency.

6. Lculanum, a ruined city.

---

### 4  B A S I L I C A T A.
*Lucania.*

| | |
|---|---|
| From the Greek Emperor Bafil II. | Name |
| Barry wavy, of fix, argent and azure ; in chief, an eagle's head crowned, gules. | Arms. |

　　　　　　　c　　　　　1,605,047

| | |
|---|---|
| Extent | 1,605,047 Moggie. |
| Inhabitants | 325,682. |
| Rivers | Bradano, Basiento, Salandrella, Acri, Sinno. |
| Lakes | Lagonegro, Olmo. |
| Mountains | Calale, Croce, Funicchio, Pomazzo, Muro, Acuto, Rivezzone, Fondone, Maruggio, St. Martino, Carrafo, Vefpe, Alpi, Raparo, Melaggioto, Sirino, St Brancato, Noce Trecchina. |
| Principal Places | 1 Acerenza, archbifhopric, united to Matera, where the prefidency is held. |

2. Bifhoprics :—Melfi cum Rapolla, Montepelofo, Tricarico, Potenza, Anglona cum Turfi, Venofa, Muro.

3. Metapontum, Heraclea ; ruined cities.

---

## 5  C A P I T A N A T A.
### *Apulia, Daunia, Frentani.*

| | |
|---|---|
| Name | A corruption of Catapanata (the diftrict under the Catapan, or Greek viceroy). |
| Arms | Azure, on a mount, St. Michael, or. |
| Extent | 1,141,622 Moggie. |
| Inhabitants | 491,255. |
| Rivers | Bifrno, Fortore, Candelaro, Carapelle, Ofanto, Cervaro |
| Lakes | Lefina, Varano, Bataglia, St. Giovanni, Salpi |
| Islands | St Domino, St Nicola, Caprara, Cretaccio, Mergoli. |
| Seaports | Manfredonia, Viefti. |
| Mountains. | Granato, Secco, Corvino, Pagano, Auro, Chilone, Bucculo, Liburno, Origine, Calvo, Sagro, Saracino, Barone, Condizzo. |
| Principal Places | 1. Manfredonia, archbifhopric. |

2 Bifhoprics.—Luccera, prefidency, Viefti, San Severo, Larino, Troja, Termoli, Bovino, Volturara cum Monte Corvino, Afcoli.

3. Foggia, tribunal for duties on cattle.

4  Bofco

4. Bosco di Bovino, royal seat.
5. Monte St Angelo di Gargano, a pilgrimage.
6. Sipontum, Arpi, Salapia, Herdonia, ruined cities.

---

## 6. COUNTY OF MOLISE.
### *Samnium and Pentri.*

| | |
|---|---|
| From a castle. | Name |
| Gules within a garland of ears of corn, or, a bearded comet, argent. | Arms. |
| 484,898 Moggie. | Extent |
| Included in the enumeration of Capitanata. | Inhabitants |
| Biferno, Fortore, Trigno. | Rivers |
| Sangra, Janipro, Vallone, Rotaro, Biferno, Caprara, Bisano, Albano. | Mountains. |
| 1. Bishoprics —Bojano, the prelate resides at Campobasso, Guardia, Alfiera, Isernia, Trivento. | Principal Places |
| 2. Campobasso, chief place of the county; Molise, a burgh, from whence the county takes its name. | |

---

## 7. TERRA DI BARI.
### *Apulia, Peucetia, and Padiculi.*

| | |
|---|---|
| From the principal city. | Name. |
| Party per saltire, azure and argent; over all, a crozier, or. | Arms |
| 869,097 Moggie. | Extent |
| 281,048. | Inhabitants |
| Ofanto, Cane | Rivers |

Barletta,

Seaports Barletta, Trani, Bari, Molfetta.

Mountains Sanazzo, Femina Morta, Lupulo, Franco, St. Agoſtino.

Principal Places
1. Bari, archbiſhopric.
2. Trani, archbiſhopric and preſidency.
3. Barletta, reſidence of the archbiſhop of Nazareth.
4. Biſhoprics —Andria, Biſceglia, Ruvo, Bitonto, Monopoli, Gravina, Giovenazzo cum Terlizzi, Bitetto, Converſano, Molfetta, Polignano (the biſhop's reſidence is at Mola), Minervino.
5. Egnatia and Canne, ruined cities.

___

## 8. TERRA DI OTRANTO.
### *Meſſapia or Japigia, Calabria, Salentini.*

Arms Paly of 8, gules and or; over all a dolphin, with a creſcent in his mouth, proper.

Extent 1,377,102 Moggie.

Inhabitants 290,915

River Bradano, Patimiſco, Lieto, Chiatano, Tara, Galeſo, Hidro.

Lake Limina.

Seaports Brindiſi, Otranto, Taranto.

Mountains Hidro, Scotano.

Iſland St. Andrea, St Pelagia, Iſola de Brindiſi.

Principal Places
1. Taranto, archbiſhopric.
2. Brindiſi, archbiſhopric.
3. Otranto, archbiſhopric.
4. Biſhoprics —Lecce, preſidency, Caſtellaneta, Gallipoli, Motula, Ugento, Caſtro, Nardo, Oria, Oſtuni, Aleſſano.
5. Manduriæ, Dupiæ, Rudii, Salentum; ruined cities.

___

9. CALA-

## 9. CALABRIA CITRA

*Lucania and Brutium.*

Given by the Greek Emperors, to perpetuate the memory of Name. ancient Calabria, which they had loft.

Argent, a crofs potent, fable. Arms.

1,605,463 Moggie. Extent

315,330. Inhabitants.

Calandro, Cerfhiara, Raccanello, Cofcile, Crati, Efaro, Moccono, Rivers Lucino, Celano, Celenito, Trionto, Fimarello, Aquanile, Fiomenica, Lipuda, Nieto, Savuto, Cleta, Solio, Bato, Lao

Mauro, Provizia, Pollino, Cilifterno, Malafpina, Saffo, Caritore, Mountains. Muta, Ifauro, Coruzzo, Calaferna, Gigante, Macalla, Bovi, Scaccia Diavolo, Fumiero, Negro, del Calabrefe, Patiati, Caperofa, Januario, Goliero, Porcina, Ilia.

1. Cofenza, archbifhopric and prefidency. Principal Places
2. Roffano, archbifhopric.

3. Bifhoprics :——Cariati cum Gerenza, Martorano, St. Marco, Bifignano, Umbriatico, Strongoli, Caffano.

4. Sibaris, Pandofia, Petilia ; ruined cities.

---

## 10. CALABRIA ULTRA.

*Brutium.*

Gironnce of 4 ; 1 and 4 Aragon , 2 and 3 argent , a crofs potent, Arms fable.

1,901,878 Moggie. Extent

460,392. Inhabitants.

Nieto, Efaro, Pilaca, Diagone, Tacina, Nafcaio, Acone, Litrello, Rivers Alli, Corace, Allefi, Beltrana, Ancinale, Alaca, Calipari, Bruda,

Pacanito,

Pacanito, Affa, Stilaro, Alaro, Calamizzi, Locano, Novito, Merico, Ciamuti, Bova, Alice, Gallico, Allecio, Sfalaffa, Metauro, Metramo, Mefima, Angitola, Amato.

| | |
|---|---|
| Seaports | Cotrone, Reggio. |
| Mountains | Afpro, Zefirio, Pittaro, Sagittario, Sacro, Efope, Caulone, Sagra, Jeio, Clibano, la Sibilla, Corvaro, Neibo, Ordica, Pettinella. |
| Principal Places | 1. Reggio, archbifhopric. |
| | 2 Santa Severina, archbifhopric. |
| | 3 Bifhoprics:—Catanzara cum Taverna, prefidency; Belcaftro, Ifola, Bova, Oppido, Nicotera, Tropea, Gerace, Squillacce cum Stilo, Mileto, Cotrone, Nicaftro. |
| | 4. Locri, Hippona, Terina, Caulon, Croton, ruined cities. |

---

## 11. ABRUZZO CITRA.

*Samnium, Peligni, Marrucini, Frentani, Caraceni.*

| | |
|---|---|
| Name | From the city of Aprutium, the Prætutii, or the afperity of the country. |
| Arms | Or, a boar's head with a yoke, gules. |
| Extent | 917,052 Moggie. |
| Inhabitants | 232,256. |
| Seaport | Ortona. |
| Rivers | Pefcaia, Lenta, Foro, Moro, Feltrino, Sangro, Sente, Afinella, Trigno, Merola. |
| Mountains | St. Nicolà, Majella, Cavallo, Frminio, Piata, Morone, Argatone, Iongo, Schienaforte, Marfo, Caraccio, Capraro, Sorbo, Scollofo, Pallana, Policorno. |
| Principal Places | 1. Chieti, archbifhopric and prefidency. |
| | 2. Lanciano, archbifhopric |
| | 3. Bifhoprics.—Sulmona cum Valve, Ortona cum Campli. |
| | 4. Corfinium, ruined city. |

---

## 12. ABRUZZO ULTRA.

*Marsi, Vestini, Prætutii.*

Azure, an eagle displayed, or, on 3 hills, vert.    Arms.

1,311,476 Moggie.    Extent.

345,825    Inhabitants.

Tronto, Librata, Salinello, Trontino, Vomana, Piomba, Salino,  Rivers.
Pescara, Salto, Velino.

Celano.    Lakes.

Velino, Elvino, Fiore, Corno, Pietra Fiorita, Pietra Solida, Can-  Mountains.
dido, Nitella, Pietra Gentile, Calvo, Carofa, Peschiolo, Saffuolo,
Gurguri, Rofetta, Mofcie, Seno, Luco, Corbaro, Ducheffa, Accerella,
Carbonara, Grottolo, Turchio, Lampallo.

1 Bifhoprics ·—Aquila, prefidency; Teramo, prefidency; Pef-  Principal
cina, refidence of the bifhop of the Marfi; Civita Ducale, Atri cum  Places.
Penne.

2. Amiterno, Aveia, ruined cities.

# A
# SHORT SKETCH
OF THE
# HISTORY
OF THE
# KINGDOM OF NAPLES.

---

### I.

THIS Country has been celebrated from the earlieft dawn of Grecian literature, and illuftrated by many achievements of gods and heroes: fome authors even lay the fcene of the Giants' War in Campania, and prove their affertion by the fable of the Titans, who were buried under the neighbouring iflands. As it is not likely that thefe ftories fhould have originated entirely in the imagination of the poets, we may reafonably fuppofe fome hiftorical event afforded a canvas for them to work upon; and the moft natural conjecture is, that the firft adventurers, on their

B landing

landing in Italy, met with a vigorous oppofition from men of an extraordinary ftature. From their taking refuge in fulphureous vallies and gloomy caverns, among burning mountains, the difcoverers called them fons of the earth, and their abodes the mouths of hell.

All accounts of thefe primordial inhabitants are extremely imperfect; moft probably the invaders drove them into the inland mountainous regions, where they became the parents of the Lucanians and other warlike nations.

Greeks.

Divers tribes of Greeks planted colonies along the fhores of the Adriatic and Mediterranean feas. Diomed is faid to have founded Arpi, and Idomeneus Salentum, immediately after the Trojan war; and fo many Greek fettlements were made in the fouthern part of Italy, that it acquired the name of Magna Græcia.

Thefe commonwealths experienced a variety of fortunes; fometimes they gave law to the people of the midland countries, at others were obliged to receive it from them. Alexander, king of the Moloffians, paffed over into Italy to fupport the caufe of his countrymen; but, after a few brilliant campaigns, loft his life in a battle againft the Lucanians. Not long after, the Bruttians, a people fprung from a fet of outlaws, carried all before them, and gave their name to the province which is now called Farther Calabria. At length Rome turned her ambitious eye towards this extremity of the peninfula: in vain did the Bruttians refift her arms with obftinate valour; in vain did

Pyrrhus

Pyrrhus from Epirus, and Hannibal from Carthage, check her progress at different periods; in the course of a few years, the fortunes of Rome prevailed over all opposition, and these countries submitted to the yoke of bondage with the rest of Italy.

Romans.

## II.

As the Romans divided this district according to the various nations that composed it, the forms of government were as different as its inhabitants, some cities were made colonies, others ruled by magistrates sent from Rome, and a few indulged with their old republican constitution, subject to a tributary acknowledgment; but, sooner or later, the mode of deputing governors from the Capital was universally adopted.

Hadrian made a great change in the distribution; and, having divided Italy into provinces, formed four of them out of the present kingdom of Naples.

Some alterations took place under Constantine, but none very material.

After enjoying longer and greater tranquillity than any other department of the Roman empire, this country was over-run by the Visigoths, in the reign of Honorius. Upon the retreat of the invaders, who made no settlement here, these provinces were found to have suffered so excessively from the devastation, that it became necessary to remit their usual tribute. They had scarce recovered their losses, when

After Christ 400

Genseric

Genferic the Vandal laid them wafte, and deftroyed many of their moft flourifhing cities.

### III.

The final diffolution of the Roman empire now drew near, and the convulfions that fhook it, in the laft moments of its exiftence in the Weft, were too violent not to be feverely felt in parts fo near the centre. They accordingly fhared largely in the common calamity.

Goths.

The long profperous reign of Theodoric, the Oftrogoth, allowed fome refpite to their mifery, and was a period of happinefs in the annals of Italy. After many viciffitudes of fortune, the Gothic fceptre was broken at the battle 553. of Nocera ; and Naples, with the adjacent provinces, returned to the obedience of the emperors of Conftantinople.

### IV.

Lower Greek Empire.

In the courfe of the century that followed the deftruction of the Goths, a very material change took place in political nomenclature, the fource of many modern names and fubdivifions of countries. In fome degree, the foundation of the feudal fyftem was laid by Longinus the Exarch, who, after abolifhing the dignity of Confulars and Prefidents, appointed in each city a Duke, and in every caftle a Warden.

V. In

## V.

In 558, the eunuch Narſes, a diſcontented general of the
Emperor Juſtin, invited the Lombards into Italy, where they
made themſelves maſters of thoſe rich plains, to which they
gave their own name. They did not penetrate into the
Neapolitan ſtate till the year 589, when their king Autharis
marched down the heart of the country, as far as Rhegium,
and founded the duchy of Beneventum. The reaſon of his
making his invaſion along the range of mountains that
divides Italy into two parts, was, the invincible averſion his
nation at all times betrayed for maritime enterprizes.

Lombards

The Dukes of Beneventum became formidable potentates,
and extended their dominion over all the ſouthern provinces,
except a few ſea-ports, that remained faithful to the Greek
Emperor, and governed themſelves like commonwealths,
under his protection. Beneventum ſurvived the downſal of
the Lombards in 774, when their monarchy was annihilated by Charlemagne, and two hundred and twenty-eight
years after that event, princes of Lombard blood were ſtill
ſeated on the thrones of Capua, Salerno, and Benevento:
But Puglia and Calabria obeyed the mandates of the Emperor of Greece.

## VI.

About the beginning of the eleventh century, forty
Norman gentlemen, returning from the Holy Land, a
pilgrimage

1002
Normans

pilgrimage then coming into fashion, stopped at Salerno, where they were received with great hospitality by Guaimar, a prince of the Lombard line. During their stay at his court, a fleet of Saracens appeared off the harbour, and sent in a threatening message, to intimate that, unless they were immediately supplied with a large sum of money, they would land, sack the city, and lay the territory waste, as they had often done before. These Mahometan rovers were at that time the scourge of Italy: from strong settlements, formed by them on the river Garigliano, and in Sicily, they were wont to issue forth, in powerful fleets, to pillage and lay under contribution all the maritime places of a country too little united, and consequently too weak to make a proper resistance. Guaimar, conscious of his inability to repel them, set about collecting the ransom; and the pirates landed on the beach, where they abandoned themselves to every species of riotous intemperance. The Normans, unaccustomed to behold such insults tamely submitted to, and esteeming it an eternal stain upon their honour, dastardly to stand by, and see their benefactors plundered by a set of ruffians, snatched up their arms, rushed out of the gates, and fell upon the Infidels with such impetuosity, that they put the greatest part of them to the sword; the remainder fled to their ships, cut their cables, and immediately ran out to sea.

The grateful Salernitans would gladly have detained their gallant deliverers in Italy, but perceiving them bent upon

returning

returning to their native country, difmiffed them loaded with valuable prefents.

The fight of thefe treafures, and the rapturous defcription given by the travellers of the Italian climate, excited the cupidity of other Normans, and tempted many to fteer their courfe that way, in fearch of fortune. Ranulph headed the firft emigration; and, having rendered many fignal fervices to the Greek and Lombard princes, was allowed, for his recompence, to build and fortify Averfa, a fmall town in Campagna. This was the firft fettlement his nation made in thefe provinces, and ferved for many years as a rendezvous and refuge for the Normans on every emergency.

After him came the fons of Tancred of Hauteville, who in military renown left all their countrymen far behind them. Invincible wherever they lent their aid, and terrible to the effeminate Greeks and Italians, they were careffed and fought after by the petty fovereigns, whofe diffention, then diftracted this country. Maniaces, generaliffimo of the Grecian forces, courted their friendfhip, and engaged them to affift him in the invafion of Sicily, at that time in the hands of the Saracens. With their help he obtained a complete victory over the Muffulmen, and might have atchieved the conqueft of the ifland, had he checked his national avarice and perfidy; but, while the Normans were intent upon the purfuit of the routed enemy, the Greek feized on all the fpoil, and divided it among his own idle

5                                                              foldiers,

soldiers, without reserving any share for those who had earned it at the hazard of their lives. The Normans sent Ardwin to expostulate with him on the injustice of his mode of proceeding; but the messenger met with most ignominious treatment from him, was whipped round the camp, and sent back bleeding to his friends. At the sight of his wounds, the adventurers were worked up to a pitch of madness, and with loud cries were about to rush upon the Greeks, when Ardwin, whose deep-rooted resentment disdained a transient revenge, curbed this violence, and having explained his projects to their chiefs, persuaded them to withdraw secretly across the Faro of Messina. They were no sooner landed in Calabria, than they attacked the principal cities and castles of the Imperial province. In order to pursue their plan with regularity, they elected a chief, and united into one compact confederation. Their first leaders were of Lombard extraction, but they afterwards placed themselves under the direction of William Fierabras, the eldest of Tancred's sons.

After his death, they were governed successively by his brothers Dreux and Humphrey, who extended the Norman dominions very considerably; but the great founder of this dynasty was Robert, the fourth brother, surnamed Guiscard, or Wiscard, from his great skill and cunning. His conquests were rapid, and conducted with judgment; nor was his policy in the cabinet inferior to his valour in the field.

VII. To

## VII.

To Robert, Pope Nicholas II. granted what it is hard to prove he had any right to difpofe of, viz. the title of Duke of Puglia, with the perpetual fovereignty of that country; and alfo of Sicily, if he could conquer it. The truth is, thefe princes ftood fo much in need of each other's affift-ance, to enable them to refift the power of the Emperors, that it is no wonder they endeavoured to fecure their mutual attachment by fo many reciprocal conceffions. Robert, who could not divine the fatal confequences his treaty was to have in future times, promifed to the See of Rome an obedience and homage, which he had no intention of pay-ing any longer than it might fuit the fituation of his affairs: and Nicholas found no difficulty in granting inveftitures of countries he had never been in poffeffion of, and which he knew muft fall into the hands of the Normans, whether he oppofed or authorifed their ufurpation. Emboldened by the papal fanction, Robert and his younger brother Roger invaded Sicily, expelled the Saracens, and foon after com-pleted the conqueft of what is now called the kingdom of Naples. A family quarrel* with the Emperor of Conftan-tinople opened a new fcene of action for Guifcard's reftlefs fpirit. After repeated victories, he penetrated into the very

Robert, firft
Duke
1059.

* His daughter Helen, married to Conftantine, fon of the emperor Michael Ducas VII, had been fent back, and her hufband fhut up in a convent, by Nicephorus III.

C                                                              heart

heart of Greece, and threatened the throne of the eastern Cæsars with immediate destruction, when he was suddenly recalled to Italy by the danger of his friend the Pope. Robert flew to Rome, defeated and drove away the Emperor Henry IV., by whom the Pontiff had been reduced to the utmost distress, and having secured his ally from future insults, resumed his favourite scheme of subduing Greece; but there, in the height of his most promising

1085.          success, his glorious career was cut short by a malignant fever.

Roger.          Roger, his son by a second wife, succeeded to his dominions, notwithstanding the claims of Bohemund, the offspring of a former marriage, who, finding himself unequal to a contest with his brother, supported by his uncle Roger earl of Sicily, accepted of the terms they offered. It was not long before an accident furnished him with an opportunity of being revenged of them both.

The city of Amalfi having taken advantage of the dissentions among the Normans, and attempted to recover its ancient independence, was invested by the joint forces of the three princes. To this siege came Peter the Hermit, to preach the first crusado, armed with papal benedictions, fired with zeal, and endowed with that ecclesiastical unction, and all-persuasive eloquence, which men, even in the most enlightened ages, are seldom able to withstand. At that barbarous æra, such a preacher was irresistible; his call was listened to, his predictions believed, his crosses

4          seized

feized with eagernefs. Bohemund, whether hurried away by the phrenzy of devotion and enterprize, or feduced by the defire of revenge, feconded the endeavours of the en-thufiaft, and, at the head of the flower of the army, marched off for Paleftine, leaving his two relations before the walls, with fcarce a fufficient fo ce to fecure their retreat.

Roger was fucceeded by his fon William, on whofe demife without iffue, all the Norman poffeffions in the two Sicilies devolved upon his coufin Roger, fon of the firft earl of Sicily aforementioned.

*William.*

*1127.*

## VIII.

This prince, difdaining the ftyle of Duke, which he thought inadequate to the prefent fortunes of his houfe, affumed the title of King. The Pope, alarmed at the rapid progrefs of the Normans, and apprehenfive of their proving an obftacle to his own private views of aggrandife-ment, called in the affiftance of the emperor Lotharius, in order to check a power, which, if timely oppofition were not made, might endanger the liberties of Italy. Lotharius marched a formidable army into the new erected kingdom, and carried all before him; while Roger wifely retired from the ftorm, to collect his ftrength. The fury of the invaders was foon fpent, and they wafted away with inaction and malady. The King haraffed them in their retreat, reco-vered every poft, drove the Germans out of the kingdom,

*Roger, firft king*

C 2

and

and having taken Pope Innocent II. prifoner, forced him to recognize his title, and grant him inveftiture.

Roger then deftroyed the fhadow of independence which ftill exifted in fome maritime cities, invaded Africa, conquered Tunis, and afterwards made a fuccefsful invafion into Greece. He did not, however, confine his ambition to military renown, but was alfo attentive to the internal adminiftration of affairs; and at his death left every department of government in fo flourifhing a ftate, that, as far as the feeble wifdom of man could forefee, he had juft caufe to hope that his throne was fixed upon a moft immoveable bafis. The confequence of fupine negligence in his fucceffor fhewed how fallacious are all human projects, and how eafy it is for mifmanagement to overfet the beft concerted plans.

*1154*

The fecond King was Roger's fon William, an unhappy prince, though little molefted by foreign enemies. Indolence gave him up a willing prey to wicked minifters; but whenever he was roufed to action by attacks from abroad, the fpirit of his anceftors rofe within him, and he repelled every hoftile affault with the courage of a Guifcard. The Pope and the Emperor preffed at one time very hard upon him, but he baffled all their attempts: had he been as fuccefsful at home, his reign would make a very different figure in the Sicilian chronicles from what it now does. Majone, his favourite, governed the nation in fo oppreffive a manner, that he provoked the barons to confpire againft him.

*William I.*

him. They murdered the minister, imprisoned the monarch, and placed the crown on the head of his infant son. This unfortunate child being killed by a random arrow, the courage of the rebels sunk, William regained the sceptre, glutted his revenge with the blood of the conspirators, and passed the remainder of his days in melancholy peace. Deprest with misfortunes, sick of ambition, destitute of friends, and incapable of any laudable occupation, he arrived at length at such a pitch of apathy, as to forbid his attendants to inform him of any circumstance that might disturb his quiet. The consequences were, that, under the sanction of his authority, his officers exercised the most brutal tyranny with impunity; and William descended to the grave, detested by all good men, and branded for ever with the odious appellation of the Bad.

The factions among the great vassals disturbed the first years of his son William's reign, but when he grew up to manhood, all these turbulencies subsided. A mild, prudent, and equitable administration, added to the merit of boundless munificence to the church, and unshaken attachment to the See of Rome, procured for him the inestimable name of the Good. The greatest proof that can be given how well he deserved this honourable epithet, is the desire which the Sicilians expressed, in all subsequent quarrels with their sovereigns, of having things put upon the same footing, and the laws exercised with the same impartiality, as they were in the days of Good King William. Not having

Not/

any heirs of his body, and being defirous of preventing a civil war, he gave his aunt Conftance, a pofthumous child of King Roger, in marriage to Henry of Swabia, king of the Romans; and foon after died, having reigned twenty-three years in fuch profound peace and tranquillity, that hiftorians, who delight more in tumultuous and bloody fcenes, have neglected to tranfmit to us any particulars of

1189          the laft ten years of his reign*.

Tancred.          When this good king died, his appointed fucceffors were abfent, and the Sicilians, in defiance of the allegiance they had fworn to them, called to the throne Tancred earl of Lecce, natural fon of Roger, elder brother of William I. This reign was fhort and turbulent; but the Germans would in all probability have been completely excluded, had Tancred, who was an excellent and valiant prince, lived long enough to fettle himfelf on the flippery feat  Exceffive grief for the lofs of an accomplifhed and favourite fon, on whom he had refted every fond hope of future joy and

1192          greatnefs, brought this affectionate parent to an un-timely grave, and blafted at once all the budding fortunes of his family.

William III.          William, his furviving fon, was too young and weak to refift the power of Henry, now become emperor, and affifted by the fickle barons.  The unhappy youth was

* Montagne fays, ‘ Les bons hiftoriens fuyent comme une eau dormante
‘ et mer morte des narrations calmes pour regagner les feditions, les
‘ guerres, où ils fçavent que nous les appellons ’

obliged

obliged to furrender himfelf to his rival, who, contrary to his plighted faith, deprived him of liberty, fight, and manhood.

1194

## IX.

Henry, who was a monfter of cruelty, put to death every adherent of Tancred's, not even fparing the traitors, who had deferted William to join the Imperial ftandard. His mean brutality led him to dig up the body of Tancred, and expofe it to the birds of prey. Sicily was laid wafte, her churches plundered, her wealth tranfported into foreign countries, and her ftreets ftained with the blood of her moft diftinguifhed citizens. But now the Sicilians perceiving that the Emperor was bent upon exterminating the whole Norman race, rufhed to arms An univerfal rebellion broke out, at the head of which appeared Conftantia herfelf, unable any longer to bear with the inhumanity of her hufband. Henry was driven out of the ifland, and forced to fubfcribe to the moft humiliating terms of pacification. He did not long furvive his difgrace; and the Imprefs died foon after, leaving the crown to Frederick, then only fon, an infant.

Swabians.

Henry and
Conftantia

1198

A moft diforderly minority enfued, but by the good management of Pope Innocent III., who ruled as regent and guardian to the young king, his dominions were pre-ferved entire . and, as foon as he came of age, Frederick obtained the Imperial diadem by the influence of his lead tutor.

tutor. This cordiality between the two powers was but of short duration; and their subsequent animosity was violent in proportion to the warmth of their former attachment. During a long course of years, they persecuted each other with unremitting malevolence: these dissentions embittered the best part of the Emperor's life, and laid a foundation for troubles and intestine commotions, which at length brought the house of Swabia to utter destruction. In hopes of pacifying the pontiff, Frederick embarked for the Holy Wars; but scarce had he set foot in Palestine, when news was brought him that Gregory IX. had debauched many of the barons from their allegiance, and invaded the kingdom of Naples The Emperor immediately patched up a peace with the Infidels, and returned to Italy. Surrounded by domestic enemies, pestered with papal anathemas, and worn out in counteracting their machinations, Frederick expired, not without some suspicion of poison, said to have been administered by his natural son Manfred; but no satisfactory reasons have been given for suspecting him of this parricide.

1250

As soon as the Emperor's death was known, the Pope renewed his attack, expecting to find the kingdom a defenceless prey, but the sudden appearance of Conrad, son and heir of Frederick, overturned his projects. This young Emperor crushed the insurgents, stormed Naples, and exercised great cruelty upon his opponent He reigned only four years; and his death is also ascribed,

Conrad

1254

by

by the ecclefiaftical writers, to their capital enemy Manfred.

Conradine, the only fon of Conrad, being abfent in Germany at the time of his father's death, the pope feized upon the kingdom; but Manfred, as regent, difpoffeffed him, and, a report being fpread of Conradine's death, affumed the reins of government in his own name. The Roman pontiffs, finding themfelves foiled in their military attacks by the fuperior fkill of their adverfary, and their fpiritual thunderbolts of little avail againft an enemy that fcreened himfelf behind the fhield of incredulity, took another method, and offered the crown of Sicily to any prince that would drive out the prefent excommunicated poffeffor. The firft that was found able to put this plan in execution was Charles of Anjou, brother to Lewis the Ninth king of France. He accepted the offer, whether folely urged by his own ambition, or pufhed on by the vanity of his wife, who longed to be a queen as well as her fifters [*]. He penetrated into the kingdom, and gained a decifive victory, at Benevento, over Manfred, who fell in the field of battle. Conftance, daughter of this unfortunate prince, married Peter king of Aragon [†].

---

[*] The daughters of Raymund, Earl of Provence, were Margaret married to Lewis IX King of France, Eleanor, to Henry III king of England, Sancha, to Richard Earl of Cornwall, and King of the Romans, and Beatrix, to Charles Earl of Anjou

[†] It is remarkable, that their prefent Sicilian Majefties are both defcended by Conftantia from the heroic houfe of Swabia

## X.

A 1g r1 es.
C  rl s the
J  t.

Charles no sooner thought himself firmly seated on his new throne, than he gave a loose to his natural temper, and ruled his subjects with a rod of iron. This usage provoked them to invite Conradine to the inheritance of his ancestors, but their good intentions served only to complete the ruin of the Swabian family. The unfortunate youth was defeated, betrayed, taken prisoner, and beheaded. His death did not, however, remain long unrevenged: Charles and his Frenchmen rendered their yoke so galling to the Sicilians, whose honour, property, and lives were become the sport of the licentious conquerors, that on Easter Tuesday, in the year 1282, the people of Palermo raised the standard of revolt. The whole island followed the example of the capital, and a general massacre ensued, in which every Frenchman but one * was put to the sword without mercy: an event known in history by the name of the Sicilian Vespers. The insurgents offered the crown to Peter of Aragon; a long war ensued, in the course of which Charles met with nothing but misfortunes, and died of a broken heart.

1285

Charles II

Charles, his eldest son, was actually a prisoner at the time of his father's death: having recovered his liberty, and made many ineffectual attempts to drive the Aragonese out of Sicily, he concluded a peace with them, and, being

* William Porcelet, whose life was spared in consideration of his virtue and justice

a good

a good and moderate man, turned his whole attention towards the welfare and improvement of his kingdom of
Naples

1309.

He was succeeded by his second son Robert, though
Charles Martel, king of Hungary, who was the eldest, and
died before his father, had left children. Charibert, king of
Hungary, put in his claim, upon which it was agreed by
both parties, to submit to the umpirage of the Pope. The
papal decree confirmed Robert in the possession. He has
been accused of having poisoned his brother, in order to
pave his way to the throne.

Being little molested by external enemies, his long reign
was glorious and fortunate, as far as foreign affairs were
concerned; but, in the circle of his own family, he was
completely wretched. He had outlived his only son, and,
with a view of preventing disputes about the succession, had
given his grand daughter and heiress Joan in marriage to
Andrew of Hungary, a worthless prince, with whom she
was likely to be very miserable. The foresight of approaching disasters oppressed his aged spirit, and hastened his dif-
solution.

Andrew soon became so hateful to his queen and her
subjects, that a conspiracy was formed to take away his
life: the murder was committed at Averfa. Modern authors pretend, that his wife was not privy to it, but I do
not think their proofs sufficient to refute the arguments of
those cotemporaries that lay it to her charge. Her widow-

hood

hood was fhort: Lewis of Taranto, of the blood royal, a prince endowed with many good qualities, was her fecond hufband. He and Joan were obliged foon after to fly before the king of Hungary, who invaded Naples, to revenge his brother's murder, and put feveral nobles to death on that account. The Hungarian being recalled by domeftic tumults to his own dominions, Joan returned to Italy. Her third hufband was James of Aragon ; and her fourth, Otho of Brunfwick. Being now far advanced in years, and paft all hopes of having children, fhe inftituted her relation, Charles of Durazzo, her heir. This prince, jealous of the defigns of Otho, doubtful of the queen's fteadinefs, and impatient to be in poffeffion of the crown, affembled an army, attacked Naples, took the queen prifoner, and is fuppofed to have put an end to her exiftence.

1382

## XI.

Durazzo
Charles III

When Charles invaded her dominions, Joan had no commander of eminence to oppofe to him : fhe therefore called to her aid, and adopted, Lewis of Anjou, fon to John, king of France; but he came too late to prove of any fervice to his ill-fated benefactrefs. However, he fecured to himfelf the quiet poffeffion of her French territories, and was in a fair way of conquering the Neapolitan ones, when he fell fick and died

Charles, though peaceable poffeffor of Naples, could not reft fatisfied with his good fortune, but liftened to the

invitation

invitation of the Hungarian malcontents, who wished to depose Mary, the only child of his old friend and protector, King Lewis. He agreed to their proposals, went to Hungary, and was proclaimed king; but, not long after, the young queen's party recovered from their consternation, and assassinated him in the palace.

The kingdom of Naples alone descended to his infant son Ladislaus, during whose non-age every thing was in perpetual ferment. On coming of age, he found the Angevines masters of three-fourths of the realm; and to recover them out of their hands, required all his courage and good fortune. He afterwards took a leading part in the troubles of Italy, tyrannized over Rome, dictated to most of the petty potentates, and attempted to conquer Hungary. The pope, alarmed at his prosperity, called in Lewis the Second, of Anjou, who defeated the Durazzians at Ceparano, and, had he known how to make use of his victory, would have ruined their party beyond redemption; but, having loitered away his time, instead of pursuing his advantage, he gave his adversary an opportunity of collecting fresh forces, and gaining such a superiority as was no longer to be resisted. Ladislaus, delivered from enemies at home, and an over-match for those abroad, gave himself up to pleasure, and shortened his days by excess of debauchery.

His only sister, Joan, succeeded him: a woman more noted for her lasciviousness than any princess since Messalina,

lina, without one virtue to balance her vices; a flave to
luft and vile favourites, her life was a continual round of
riot, diftrefs, and civil turmoils. At the age of forty-
feven, and much againft her will, the clamours of the
people forced her to contract a fecond marriage, and take
to her bed the Count of La Marche, who aimed at abfolute dominion, and ufed her with great feverity. She
plotted with Sforza, an adventurer, recovered the reins of
government, and fent her hufband back to France. Joan
was fcarce rid of this incumbrance, when another opponent ftarted up. This was a third Lewis of Anjou, who
carried on his attack with fuch vigour, that the queen was
under the neceffity of applying for fuccour to Alphonfus,
king of Aragon and Sicily, whom fhe adopted. No fooner
had the Spaniard deprived the Angevines of the power of
giving her uneafinefs, than the fickle old woman grew tired
of her adopted fon, revoked the deed of gift, and beftowed
the reverfion upon Lewis, her former antagonift. Alphonfus was driven out of the kingdom, and feemed to
have laid afide all thoughts of adding Naples to his hereditary dominions, when the death of Joan and Lewis left
the kingdom once more open to his attack; but it was
not without a long ftruggle, and much bloodfhed, that
he achieved the conqueft.

## XII.

The crowns of the two Sicilies being thus re-united upon
one brow, thefe defolated provinces were by degrees reftored

ftored to peace and opulence: bleffings to which they had been long ftrangers. This great prince died without legitimate iffue, having furvived Joan twenty three years. Sicily and Aragon devolved to his brother John, king of Navarre; and Naples, by virtue of a previous agreement, fell to his natural fon Ferdinand.

The reign of Ferdinand the Firft was long, but not happy, being difturbed by two dangerous rebellions, which fhook his throne to the centre, though he triumphed over them both. By every method, which victory and breach of faith could enable him to purfue, he exterminated the principal families engaged in thofe revolts; but their fpirit furvived, prepared, and enforced the blow that fo fuddenly and irrefiftibly overwhelmed his fucceffor. Ferdinand, however, died in peace, and was fucceeded by his fon,

Alphonfus the Second, a man of great military fame, but of a moft fanguinary temper, the inftigator and actor of all the treacheries and cruelties that fullied his father's annals. Chaftifement was not tardy in overtaking him; for he had fcarce held the fceptre a few months, before Charles the Eighth, king of France, as heir to the houfe of Anjou, marched to Naples at the head of a formidable army. On his approach, Alphonfus was ftruck with fuch a panic, that, forgetful of honour and intereft, he abdicated his crown, left his fon to make the beft defence he could,

1458
Ferdinand I.

1494

Alphonfus
the Second.

I
could,

could, and fled to Sicily, where he foon died of fhame and defpair.

Ferdinard the Second retired before the enemy, while Charles made his triumphal entry into the capital. This blaze of French glory was, like a wintry fun, glaring and tranfitory. Charles returned to France, and Gonfalvo, the great Spanifh captain, reinftated Ferdinand in all his pof-feffions. Unfortunately he did not live long enough to reftore any degree of firmnefs to the tottering fortunes of his family.

Upon his deceafe, his uncle Frederick fucceeded: a learned good prince, and worthy of a better fate. He was overpowered by a confederacy entered into by Ferdinand the Catholic, king of Spain, and Lewis the Twelfth, king of France, to feize upon and divide the kingdom of Naples between them. The execution of the project was eafy for two fuch powerful monarchs, and Frederick, bereft of friends and hopes, furrendered up his perfon to Lewis, expecting better treatment at his hands, than at thofe of his perfidious coufin of Aragon. But he had little reafon to rejoice at the truft he had repofed in French generofity; for he was confined the few remaining years of his life at Tours, while his wretched family was left to wander about the world hopelefs and unbefriended.

XIII. The

## XIII.

The unnatural compact between these kings could not long hold together, as fraud and violence were its foundation. Matters were soon embroiled, and war ensued, the French were expelled, and both shares irrecoverably reunited to Ferdinand. At his death, Naples, with all his other dominions, passed to his grandson

## XIV

Charles of Austria, afterwards emperor of the Romans, the fifth of the name.

During this, and every succeeding reign of the Austrian family, these kingdoms were governed by viceroys, and seldom honoured with the presence of their sovereign. The oppressions of the governors, the complaints of the people, and outrages of the barons, the depredations of the Turks, French, or banditti, were the only interruptions to the public peace, till the year 1647, when a famous insurrection broke out. Masaniello, the leader of the sedition, stirred up the mob of Naples, on account of some duties laid upon fruit, drove the viceroy into the castle, and, for a few days, strutted the dictator of the Neapolitan republic. On his being murdered, things returned quietly to their wonted channel. About this time, the duke of Guise came to Naples, and endeavoured to make himself

king;

king; but his enterprize failed for want of support from France.

Thus fatigued with every disquiet and inconvenience incident to a delegated administration, Naples continued to obey the Spaniards with a heavy heart, until the extinction of the Austrian line in 1700 opened a new field for litigation.

## XV.

The great contest for the inheritance of Charles the Second changed the whole political system of Italy. Naples, at first, was occupied by Philip of Bourbon; but, in 1706, was conquered by the Austrians, and at the peace of Utrecht, in 1713, confirmed to the emperor Charles the Sixth.

## XVI.

In 1734, Elizabeth, second wife of Philip the Fifth, king of Spain, being ambitious of procuring a settlement for her son Don Carlos, caused Spain to engage in a war with the emperor; the event of which was, that the Infant conquered Naples, and, by the treaty of peace, was left in full possession, with the title of King of the Two Sicilies.

In 1759, on the death of Ferdinand the Sixth of Spain, Charles succeeded to the Spanish crown, and resigned his Sicilian dominions to his third son, Ferdinand the Fourth, now reigning. Philip, the eldest, was set aside for idiot-
ism;

ifm ; and Charles, the fecond, taken by his father to Madrid as prince of Afturias, and heir apparent to the Spanifh monarchy.

N. B. As any difcuffion of chronological doubts would have been abfurd in an abridgment of hiftory, I have fixed all epochas at the moft probable dates.

A

# V O Y A G E

FROM

# M A R S E I L L E S

TO

# N A P L E S,

1776

----

## S E C T I O N  I.

THE season of the year being far advanced, and the
Alps covered with snow, I thought it unadviseable
with a family to undertake a journey into Italy by land;
and therefore, in company with S. T. G., hired a French
polacre at Marseilles, and embarked for Naples on the
17th of December 1776.

The getting under sail was tedious, as the currents obliged us to tow it from buoy to buoy, but when once
clear of the land, we went at a prodigious rate, before a
brisk

brisk north-west wind, which in the evening increased to a storm.

All that night, and the ensuing day, the gale continued, and drove us on very fast. As the sea was rough, and the waves short, the irregular jerks and tossings of our ship kept us in perpetual alarms; but fortunately it was tight and well built. The Alps, immersed in snow, appeared on the left hand, about four leagues off, rising out of the waters to a wonderful height: the sea ran so high, that we could discern nothing near their base. About sun-set, we got under the shelter of Cape Corso, the N. E. point of Corsica, and lay-to all night in still water. By this delay, we lost the opportunity of passing through the straits of Piombino; for, before morning, the boisterous MAESTRAL sank into a very dull zephyr, which faintly brought us to the island of Elba, and there left us in a dead calm. We were towed into the harbour of Porto-Ferraio, where Monf de Langres, the governor, a native of Lorraine, received us with great politeness, and contributed every thing in his power to make our involuntary visit to his port less irksome.

The island of Elba, known to the Greeks by the name of Aithalia, and to the Romans by that of Ilva, has been renowned for its mines from a period beyond the reach of history. Aristotle speaks of them as opened from time immemorial, and Virgil brings a succour to Æneas of three hundred men from

PORTO FERRAIO

——————————————Ilva,

Insula inexhaustis chalybum generosa metallis[*]

It lies about ten miles S. W. from Tuscany, in latitude 42° 50'. Its figure is that of an equilateral triangle. Pliny gives it a circuit of an hundred miles. Late geographers allow only sixty to its circumference, but, as no map has yet been made upon exact obfervations, and as the circuit would be much more confiderable, if every creek and inlet were meafured, perhaps the Roman menfuration may come nearer the truth than the modern one. The difference might even be accounted for by the encroachments of the fea, and by the tumbling in of the rocks, which are, in many places, of a mouldering contexture.

Being extremely mountainous, Elba affords but fcanty room for cultivation, and produces little more than fix months provifion of corn for its feven thoufand inhabitants. It is faid to have been peopled from Volterra, in very ancient times, the capital of Tufcany, and perhaps of all Italy.

The property is at prefent divided between the Prince of Piombino, who poffeffes the largeft fhare; the King of Naples, to whom Porto-Longone belongs; and the Great Duke of Tufcany, who is mafter of Porto Ferro

The climate is much milder than that of the adjacent continent; for Elba produces many plants and fruits that cannot ftand the Tufcan winters

[*] " Elba, an ifland rich in inexhauftible mines of fteel "

The

The south-west part of the island is the most elevated, and consists of lofty unfruitful mountains, composed of black and white granite susceptible of a fine polish. In an old quarry, on the south shore, may be seen several pillars and basons roughly hewn, and left unfinished. The columns of the cathedral of Pisa are said to have been cut out of these rocks. Under this granite is a stratum of slate.

The N. E. and S. E. parts are chiefly argillaceous slate and iron-stone, with a quarry of grey marble, and some veins of serpentine. Amianthus is frequent among the shivery rocks. Near the N. E. point is the hill, or mine of iron ore, belonging to Rio, which supplies most of the forges of Italy. At the S. E. cape is the Monte della Calamita, so called from the loadstone with which it abounds. This is the *magnes colore ferreo rubente* of the mineralogists, and appears to be a ferruginous substance that has passed through a very violent fire without vitrification. The efficient of magnetism still remains in the unfathomed depths of nature's first causes. Monf. de Buffon defines it, a constant effect of electricity produced by the interior heat, and the rotation of the globe; but if it depended on no other cause, we should not experience such variation in the compass. The best magnets in Elba are found near the sea; but to come at strong ones, the ground must be dug into: because the air, or the rays of the sun, eat out the force of those that lie long exposed to them on the surface. The earth, mixed with these stones, is full of

martial

martial particles, which stick to the pick-axe in the shape of little tufts of bristles. The layer that supports the magnetic heaps is a blue whetstone stone, with a small mixture of calcareous stones. At the bottom of the mountain is found a bole, very highly esteemed ......., not from any its attractive virtue, but from a dryness that causes the tongue to adhere to it. It was formerly much worn as a charm by lovers, and supposed to draw, with great force, the affections of the beloved object towards the wearer.

The soil of Elba is very shallow, with few places level enough for corn. The wine is good, if made with care, and properly kept, the fruit of its standard trees is said to be exquisite; orange and lemon trees seem to thrive very well in the sheltered vales and narrow plains near the sea.

About four thousand tons of salt are made near Porto-Ferraio, which has likewise a tunny fishery, worth annually to the Grand Duke one thousand three hundred pounds Sterling. The Prince of Piombino has another at Marciana, that clears one thousand pounds per annum.

Porto-Ferraio* is a very pretty town, built on a stretching rock that closes in a large circular bay, .... ...

---

* It was called Porto-Argous from Argo the ship in which Jason ...... country in ancient story legend of the ancients brought it into honour. Mr. Par-rinuan, that Medea might have an opportunity of consulting .... siller .... Circe. Homer, in his Odyssey, informs us, that, by the particular favour of Jove, this celebrated ship passed unscathed through the Straits of Scylla and Charybdis.

F                                                    around

around is high and woody; the entrance of the bay wide, and eafy to hit; but fo open to the N. E. winds, that, when they blow with violence, there are few anchoring-places where a fhip can ride in fecurity. The ftreets and fortifications rife one above another, like rows of feats in an ancient amphitheatre, and prefent a moft beautiful fpectacle to thofe that approach by water. To the fea, nothing appears but the two citadels, Stella and Falcone. All the upper range of works is cut out of the rock into vaults and intricate communications. In the centre of the femicircle, is a fmaller port or darfena for boats and gallies, defended by a couple of baftions, and fhut up every evening with a boom. A commodious quay communicates with all the ftreets, by means of large flights of fteps

Elba was held with Piombino by the Appiani as a fief of the empire, till Charles the Fifth thought proper to transfer it to Cofmo the firft duke of Florence, that he might fecure it and the adjacent coaft from the infults of the Turks and French, which the preceding feudatory was not in a condition to repel. The duke built Ferraio in 1548; but it was not brought to the prefent ftate of perfection before the reign of Cofmo the Second, who completed thefe fortifications in 1628, with a magnificence equal to that difplayed by the old Romans in their public undertakings. The gates are decorated with fculpture, and the rings for faftening cables to are of carved bronze. The garrifon is fmall, and the artillery trifling, for fo

large

large a fortrefs; but the neutrality of its mafter is its prefent fecurity, and renders a ftronger force unneceffary.

## SECTION II.

THERE being no appearance of a favourable change in the wind, we made an excurfion to the iron mines.

We croffed the bay, and afcended the mountain by a very rugged path. The gullies that feam its fides are full of orchards, with fome few orange-trees, cut to pieces and ftunted by the N. W. wind. The wafte is covered with myrtle, lauruftinus, lentifcus, arbutus, and many other flowering fhrubs. The fummit of thefe mountains is bare of wood, but not of verdure.

On a flaggy rock ftands the Tower of Voltoraio, where fix foldiers defend the frontiers of the Tufcan ftate, marked out by ftones placed in angular directions along the top of the ridge that encompaffes the bay of Porto-Ferraio. The view from this Tower is wonderfully fine every way, as the eye overlooks the whole ifland, that of Corfica, many fcattered iflets, the channel of Piombino, and a great range of continent.

We defcended on the eaft fide of the mountain to Rio, a poor village inhabited by miners. Under it breaks out the only rivulet in Elba, which does not run above a mile

F 2 before

before it falls into the sea; but the water gushes out of the rock in such abundance, that it turns seventeen mills in that short course. We followed this pretty stream down a narrow vale, cultivated with great nicety, and planted with orange and other fruit trees, till it brought us to the celebrated iron mine.

This mine is not, like most others, composed of ferruginous strata, or of pieces of ore dispersed among heterogeneous substances, in horizontal streaks or accidental lumps, which are come at with difficulty, by means of galleries, engines, and deep pits; on the contrary, it forms one large hill of solid ore, worked in three terraces, after the manner of a fine quarry of stone, by clearing away the top, and hewing or blasting the rock, till it drops in shivers into the area, from whence it is wheeled to the place of sale. The circumference of this iron hill is near three miles, and the depth of the ore to the slaty foundation about three hundred feet. Where it has not yet been touched, or has lain undisturbed many years, vines and other plants grow tolerably well on the surface, and are said by Koestlin * to contain particles of iron in their leaves and stems, as may be discovered by calcination. If this were really the case, which I very much doubt, it would give a greater degree of credibility to the stories told in Hungary, where bits of gold are shewn adhering to the

* A German physician, who published an account of Elba in 1780.

stalks

ſtalks and grapes of the Tokay vines, ſuppoſed to have been drawn out of the ground by the plant in the courſe of vegetation.

The place where the preſent works are carried on reſembles a funnel with one ſide broken down. About ſeven hundred pounds weight of gunpowder are conſumed annually in blaſting, and one hundred and ſix men conſtantly employed with the pickaxe or barro. From a ſcarcity of wood, none of the ore is ſmelted on the iſland, but is ſold to the agents of the Tuſcan, Roman, Corſican, and Neapolitan furnaces, at the rate of fifty-one crowns *per cento*, a weight conſiſting of thirty-three thouſand three hundred and thirty three pounds and a half each. The Corſicans and Tuſcans have a right to pick the ore, for which they pay an additional price. All others take it unſorted, and, with every parcel of huge ore, are obliged to take a tenth part of the reſiduc: the two privileged traders have a fifth.

This ore is beautiful, abounding in rainbow ſhoots and chriſtallations, but although it appears to the eye and the feel to be almoſt one third of pure iron, it is by no means ſo rich as many iron ores in the ſouth of Europe, and hardly yields half its weight in pure iron.

It is a doubt, whether this mine of iron be the ſame mentioned by Ariſtotle, and other ancient authors, to have been open in their time, but it is generally believed to be ſo. Pini, who in 1777 gave a diſſertation on Elba, makes a cal-

a calculation to prove, that it is possible these mines may
have been continually wrought since that very distant period,
without being more exhausted than we see them. He sup-
poses the present area, where the ore is dug, to be a
cylinder of five thousand feet in circumference, upon a depth
of two hundred feet, capable of containing three hundred
and ninety-seven millions seven hundred and twenty-seven
thousand cubic feet of earth or ore, of which only one
third part, or one hundred and thirty-two millions five
hundred and seventy-five thousand six hundred and sixty-
six two thirds is to be assigned to the solid mineral; that
each cubic foot of ore weighs four hundred and eight
pounds, and therefore, that the whole weight of the ore
likely to dug out amounts to fifty-four thousand and ninety
millions eight hundred and seventy-two thousand pounds.
Now, so many years back, the annual exportation has not
exceeded forty-one millions six hundred and sixty six thousand two hundred and fifty pounds weight, by which com-
putation it appears, that it would require one thousand two
hundred and ninety-eight years to work out a quantity
equal to what may be contained in the above mentioned
area. But as the Steward assured me, he did not sell, upon
an average, more than thirty-five millions of pounds weight
a year, the allowance made by Pini is too great by near a
seventh. Besides, much more copper was used anciently
in arms and utensils than at present; gunpowder was un-

4                          known,

known, and consequently greater difficulties attended the
miner's art. The ore of Elba was probably smelted at no
other place than that from which it derived its name,
*Populonium*, and therefore we may believe, that a much
smaller quantity than thirty-five millions was annually extracted; consequently the mine could not be worked down
to its actual state in so short a term as one thousand two
hundred and ninety-eight years. The extent of the part
yet untouched will afford employment for many ages to
come, notwithstanding the greater expedition used in modern metallurgy. The Prince of Piombino, to whom these
treasures belong, receives from the sale, *communibus annis*,
about forty thousand Roman crowns (nine thousand five
hundred and twenty-three pounds Sterling), clear of all
expences.

The ancients were of opinion, that the ore was re-
produced in a course of years by a species of vegetation,
and such has been the sentiment of some modern, who
allege, that many pickaxes, and other implements, have
been found in old workings, covered with an incrust tion
of iron. As none of these tools have been met with in
the heart of the virgin rock, but always in the trenches,
where the shiver of old grooves has been thrown, the crust
gathered round them is no proof of the regeneration of iron,
It is plain, that this coat is not produced by the same causes
that create an increase of bulk in plants, viz. the accession
of proper food and juices assimilating themselves to the
plant,

plant, and becoming part of it. This incruftation is no
more than the junction of innumerable minute particles
of iron difperfed in the rubbifh of the works, which run
together, and by length of time confolidate into a mineral
mafs.

## S E C T I O N   III.

ON the twenty-fecond, a faint breeze carried us out
of the harbour of Porto-Ferraio, into the channel that
divides Elba from the Tufcan coaft.

The captain affured me, that the compafs was of no ufe
in fteering a fhip within four leagues of Elba, as the
needle veered about continually with great irregularity.
Some authors deny the exiftence of any fuch attraction in
the ifland, or even its poffibility, others are of opinion,
that if this attractive power exift, it can be perceptible only
on the fide where the mines lie, and that a veffel muft be
very near the ifland to be within the reach of its magnetic
action. Without attempting to argue the point, I fhall
content myfelf with mentioning, that I perceived the utmoft confufion and variation in the needle moft part of
the day, though we conftantly kept at the diftance of a
league from Elba.

The wind was low and unfettled, and twenty-four hours
paffed in tacks. This delay, and the finenefs of the wea-

ther,

ther, afforded leisure to examine the coast of Tuscany, which is flat and woody, backed at a great distance by the mountains of Sienna; those of Montenero, near Leghorn, bound the horizon to the north; and on the south quarter, the ridge behind Orbitello, with the insulated promontory of Monte Argentato, closes the prospect. The channel is about ten miles wide; but, from the clearness of the atmosphere, does not appear to be more than five. Some small islands dispersed in the passage, the high lands of Elba, the city of Piombino, and a great variety of vessels sailing in all directions, composed a most delightful marine piece, worthy of the pencil of a Claude or a Vernet.

Piombino, built on the point of a little bay, is the capital of a principality formerly belonging to the republic of Pisa, and on the destruction of that commonwealth, occupied by private usurpers. From the fifteenth century, it was possessed by the Appiani family, which became extinct in the reign of the Emperor Ferdinand the Second. He seized upon it as an imperial escheat; and in 1634, sold it to Nicholas Ludovisi, nephew to Pope Gregory the Fifteenth. A grand daughter of Nicholas carried the estate and honours into the house of Buoncompagno, Duke of Sora.

Not far from hence stood the ancient city of Populonia, a colony of the Volterrans, and one of the first cities built in Italy near the sea-coast. After the fall of the Roman empire, this place became a prey to the Goths and Lom-

G                                      birds:

bards; and at laſt, Charlemagne made the Pope a preſent of it, who did not long enjoy the advantages of the donation; for in 809, ſome lawleſs tribes of mountaineers levelled Populonia with the ground.

In the morning of the twenty-third, ſo ſtrong a gale ſprang up in the S. E. that we were glad to run into Porto Longone, to avoid being blown through the channel back to the coaſt of France.

Porto Longone is a conſiderable fortreſs, begun in 1606, and completed in thirty years. Cardinal Mazarin, with a view of diſturbing the Spaniards in their communication with Italy, and of mortifying the Pope, whom he knew to be a zealous partiſan of Spain, ſent the Marechal de la Meilleraie, in 1646, with a fleet and army, to attack Piombino and Porto Longone. The former was carried in a few days, and the latter obliged to capitulate after a fortnight's ſiege. Both places were retaken, in 1650, by Don John of Auſtria.

It is now garriſoned by Neapolitan troops, as being annexed to the crown of the Two Sicilies, with the reſt of the Tuſcan Preſidii, ſince Philip the Fifth ceded to his ſon Don Carlos all his claims upon that kingdom. It ſtands upon the north-eaſt promontory of a large bay. At the bottom of this bay, a projecting rock, with a ſmall caſtle upon it, defends and hides the entrance of the harbour, a pleaſant and well-ſheltered cove. At the foot of the hills are ſmall vallies full of cottages and vineyards, interſected

by

by gravel paths, and inclofed with hedges of arbutus, which, at this feafon of the year, are rendered particularly beautiful by the fcarlet berries that almoft cover the bufhes. On the fouth fide is a fine well under the rock, where fhips fend their boats to take in water.

## SECTION IV.

ON the twenty-fourth, the wind coming about to the northward, and the weather fetting-in fine, we hoifted anchor and failed, much againft the will of our crew, who had promifed themfelves a pleafant trip on fhore, to hear midnight mafs, and make a Chriftmas fupper. There does not exift a more dilatory race of mariners than the Provençals. If they were not prevented by fupercargoes and paffengers from indulging their loitering difpofition, they would call at every port in their track, and wafte time in each of them. The captains of thefe veffels eat out all their profits in harbour, and not one in a hundred dies worth a groat.

In the afternoon, we defcried to the weft the little ifland of Pianofa, the ancient Planafia, remarkable for the exile and death of Agrippa Cæfar, the pofthumous fon of Marcus Agrippa and Julia. His indifcretion and rough behaviour furnifhed Livia with the means of ruining him in the opinion of his grandfather Auguſtus, who annulled his adoption, confiſcated his eſtates, and ſent him into this place of baniſhment. At the end of eight years, Auguſtus paid him a ſecret viſit, which being made known to Livia, rouſed her fears left Agrippa ſhould be recalled, and appointed ſucceſſor to the Imperial throne. To avert ſo fatal a blow to her hopes, ſhe haſtened the end of the ſuperannuated Emperor, and ſent a centurion to murder the exiled Prince. Agrippa, naturally intrepid and robuſt, made an obſtinate reſiſtance, though attacked unawares, and fell covered with wounds, the firſt victim of the bloody reign of Tiberius.

We ſoon after ſailed between the mainland and the iſlands of Giglio and Giannuti *, ſmall granite rocks, covered with buſhes and uninhabited.

The wind was now very fair, and we might have made much way, had not our captain been ſo terrified with an appearance of bad weather to windward, that he inſtantly put the helm about, and ran in towards the road of Telamon ; but as ſoon as we perceived his intention, we obliged him to reſume his original courſe, having learnt from one of the ſailors, who was perfectly acquainted with the navigation of theſe ſeas, that if we reached that bay, and a ſtorm came on, we ſhould have the vexation of toſſing about at anchor, in imminent danger, for ſeveral days,

* Igilium & Dianium.

without

without a poffibility of landing. All thefe manœuvres took up a great deal of time, and made us lofe the benefit of the breeze. During the next thirty hours, we were under the neceffity of ftanding out to fea in a heavy fwell, in order to keep clear of the Spiaggie Romane, a lee-fhore, extending thirty-fix leagues to the fouth, and extremely dangerous with a wefterly or S. W. wind, as it is not dif-cernible at a diftance, and the fands are faid to reach out near feven leagues from the land.

We fteered a S. W. coaft from Giglio, with a very hard gale and a terrible fea, for at leaft twenty-four leagues, a very unneceffary elbow. The night was fqually, the waves fhort and furious; our polacre rolled like a barrel, with fuch violent, uneven, and fudden fhocks, that it was impoffible to be prepared againft them. The confidence we had in the foundnefs of her timbers fupported our fpirits in fuch a tremendous fituation; but two alarming cir-cumftances happened in the night, that would have ftartled older and bolder feamen than we were. Our horfes, that ftood in ftalls upon deck, broke loofe, and were with diffi-culty fecured; our kitchen took fire, but we luckily ex-tinguifhed the flames before they got a-head. The return of day-light afford-d but a dreary profpect: a raging tumbling fea, a rolling fhip, fcarce able to carry any fail, and no land in fight. We paffed twelve hours very unplea-fantly, beating back in a S. E. direction for the coaft of Italy; and I think I never heard a found more grateful

to

to my ears, and relieving to my fpirits, than the voice of the boy, who about funfet called out from the maft-head, that he faw Cape Circelli*. We were now paft all danger from the Roman coaft; the wind was fallen, and though it was extremely cold, and fnowed all night, the fight of land made us quite happy and reconciled to every inconvenience.

Before day-break, we were called up to behold the flames iffuing out of Mount Vefuvius, a new and ftriking fcene to us all. This welcome to Naples was doubly agreeable, as being unexpected; for at this time of the year, we did not imagine there would be an eruption. Snow and hazinefs foon deprived us of the view. It fell a dead calm off a clufter of iflands, called, from the largeft among them, the Ponza Ifles. There is tolerable anchorage and a town at Ponza, which was a Roman colony, where Tiberius caufed Nero, fon of Germanicus, to be ftarved to death. The afhes of this unfortunate Prince were removed to Rome by his brother Caligula, who, not long after, banifhed his fifters Julia and Agrippina to the fame fpot. Among the writers of martyrology, Ponza is famous for the exile and death of Flavia Domitilla, a re-

---

* This is a high infulated mountain, at the fouthern extremity of the Pomptine Marfhes, in the Ecclefiaftical State, renowned in fable for having been the refidence of the Enchantrefs Circé, who transformed men into brutes, and whofe connections with Ulyffes are defcribed by Homer in the tenth and twelfth books of his Odyffey.

*

lation of Domitian, and one of the moſt diſtinguiſhed proſelites of the infant church of Chriſt.

Moſt part of the day was ſpent in weathering Vento-tiene, a ſmall iſland at ſome diſtance E. of Ponza. It is a rock formed of vulcanical matter thrown up by fire, as the obſervations of Sir William Hamilton ſufficiently demonſtrate. The layers of its cliffs are tinged with very remarkable red and yellow ſtreaks. The ancients called it Pandataria, and made uſe of it as a receptable for criminals of an exalted rank. Julia, the daughter of Auguſtus, was confined here with her repudiated mother Scribonia, who, from mere maternal tenderneſs, followed her daughter to this deſert, a voluntary exile. After ten years miſerable exiſtence on this rock of deſolation, the unhappy Julia was removed to the coaſt of Rhegium, where ſhe died of hunger.

Pandataria, which had been the priſon of the wanton Julia, became, not many years after, the place of con-finement allotted to her virtuous daughter Agrippina. The ſpotleſs reputation of this matron, joined to the memory of her injured huſband Germanicus, had rendered her and her children objects of love and hope to the Roman people, and conſequently of jealouſy and hatred to Tiberius. To quiet his apprehenſions, and cruſh at once all the expecta-tions Rome might cheriſh of ſeeing better days, the tyrant cauſed the young Princes to be murdered, and their mother to periſh in Pandataria, through ill uſage, and the want of every neceſſary of life. Caligula, her only ſurviving ſon,

brought

brought her afhes from the ifland, and depofited them with great folemnity in the Auguftan Maufoleum.

At the inftigation of Poppæa, Nero fent hither his wife Octavia, daughter of Claudius, and ordered her to be put to death, by opening her veins in a bath.

The deftination of Ventotiene is at prefent fomewhat fimilar to what it was in the time of the Cæfars; for it is now inhabited by a confiderable number of felons condemned to banifhment on this rock, where they are forced to work and improve the fcanty foil, in order to form a fettlement that may prevent the corfairs of Barbary from rendezvoufing here.

There was fo little wind, that our pilot was afraid we fhould not get under the fhelter of Procida before night, which would have been an unpleafant circumftance, as the wind might have rifen again while we were at its mercy in the open fea, and driven us down to the coafts of Sicily or Sardinia. fortunately the breeze fufficed to carry us into the channel of Procida, where we came to an anchor. The night was ftill and mild, and we paffed great part of it in contemplating Vefuvius, which we now diftinguifhed very plainly. An immenfe river of blazing lava ran down the fide, fupplied by ftreams of red hot matter vomited at intervals out of the fummit of the mountain. The whole atmofphere was illumined, and a long train of light reflected from it acrofs the gulph upon the tremulous furface

of

of the waves, was as beautiful, if not more so, than the real fiery torrent.

The twenty-eighth was a heavy damp day, and our sailors were so difputed with the rain, which seems to be as contrary to their conftitution as it is to that of the negroes, that it required the promife of an extraordinary recompence to prevail upon them to hoift their anchor. We were the whole day in failing ten miles; the celebrated views of the gulf were hidden from our eyes by impenetrable fog and drizzling rain; Vefuvius alone fometimes reared his burning head above the clouds, and, to our great aftonifhment, was covered with fnow to the very verge of the flaming tip of the cone. At ten at night we entered the port of Naples.

# NAPLES, and its ENVIRONS.

## SECTION V.

THE unavoidable hurry upon our arrival prevented me from vifiting Vefuvius while the eruption continued. As foon as I was at liberty, I hired a hackney two-wheeled chaife, called a Caleffo; which is no more than a very uneafy triangular feat, gilt and bedaubed with gaudy colours, fixed upon an axle-tree, and drawn by a fingle horfe. Some of thefe horfes fell very dear, and go at a prodigious rate, always in a high trot. The driver ftands behind, and with the whip and voice directs the horfe's motion. The hirer holds the reins, but is not refponfible for any mifchief the carriage may do, unlefs he alfo take poffeffion of the lafh. The reins are faftened to a caveffon, without a bit, and the more the animal is pulled, the fafter he goes : a hifs ftops him.

One

One of these chairs conveyed me about eight miles from
Naples, to the place where the lava ceased to run, after
filling up a road, overturning some cottages, and con-
suming a wide tract of vineyards. The poplars, to which
the vines were tied, were burnt or crushed beneath the
weight of the cooler lumps that tumbled off on each side
from the fiery mass. The surface of this black and now
stagnant river is very uneven, full of points and protuberances, and broken into chasms. It answers the idea I
have of a rocky mountain overturned into a valley, and
shattered to pieces by an earthquake. In colour, the lava
resembles flag, or the first clearings of an iron mine. The
intense heat that still issued from it, though the flames
were not visible by day-light, kept me at a distance. By
night, fire may be seen through the crevices of the dusky
crust. It had run close to a lava of seventeen years date,
which is not yet sufficiently triturated by the action of
air, to afford hold to the seeds of any plant, except a long
hoary moss, commonly the first settler on these cinders,
which are infinitely softer, and sooner crumbled to dust,
than the *Sciarras* of *Ætna*.

After satisfying my curiosity with an attentive examina-
tion of these objects, I returned to Portici, hired a guide
and mule, and rode up through the vineyards to the foot
of the mountain, where vegetation terminates in a long
coarse grass, the only plant that can bear the vicinity of
the hot ashes and sulphureous exhalations. I ascended

the steep cone of cinders in a direct line, up to the ancles at every step in purple lukewarm ashes. The heat was not very powerful till we came within a few yards of the summit, and there smoke breaks out through many crannies. On the Portici side there is very little lava, except a few scattered stones that serve to rest upon. It is impossible to give a just idea of the fatigue of this climbing. Before that day I had mounted some very exalted points of the Alps, and clambered up the highest peak of the Pyrenees, without feeling such oppressive weariness and exhaustion of spirits and strength as I experienced on Vesuvius. Perhaps, the mephitic effluvium, which attacked my respiration, may also have had a debilitating effect upon my nerves and muscles. I should hardly have been able to proceed, had I not held by my guide, who went before with a handkerchief tied round his waist.

I confess I was a good deal disappointed on reaching the summit; for the descriptions I had read had raised in my imagination an expectation of every thing that could be glaring and striking in colours, pompous and tremendous in a scene of igneous phenomena, but the late eruption had, for a time, laid all the mountain's fury asleep, and every thing was dull and dark. The vent, by which the lava ran out, is much below the top of the mountain, and on that side the sulphureous steams are very pungent. I was on the point of returning rather frustrated of my hopes, when a curling column of smoke and flame rose

slowly

flowly out of the gloomy abyfs, and brought up with it
a thick white cloud, that had hitherto rendered the crater
impervious to my fight. The wind quickly caught hold
of this column, and whirled it round the immenfe caldron
feveral times with inconceivable noife and velocity, till
it forced part of the fmoke to fly off horizontally from the
mountain, and dafhed the remainder back into its original
cavern. During this conflict, on the oppofite fide to that
where we ftood, I had a peep very far into the crater. The
fides feemed all lava and fcoria, with very little variety in
the tints, clofed at bottom by an impenetrable fcreen of
fmoke. I have feen old ruined coalpits, that afford a
tolerable idea of this volcanic kettle. As foon as the
fmoke was driven away, the roaring below grew loud,
and frequent explofions were heard with a hollow found;
and at every throe, which caufed a very confiderable
commotion in the thin arch on which we ftood, a fhower
of red-hot ftones was fhot up; but not rifing many feet
above the mountain, they did not come within the fweep
of the wind, and fo fell back perpendicularly into the
rumbling gulf.

I fhall not prefume to inveftigate minutely the origin,
compofition, or operations of the mountain, as we have
ample information on this fubject in the works of Sir
William Hamilton. His knowledge of the volcano is fo
complete, and reputation on that head fo firmly eftablifhed
at Naples, that more than once the court has waited to

regulate

regulate its ſtay at Portici, or removal from thence, till he had declared, when he thought the eruption would begin, and what direction the lava was likely to follow. Many writers of diſſertations on ignivomous mountains have been led into a labyrinth of miſtakes, falſe poſitions, and falſe conſequences, by truſting ſolely to the relations of others, and not being at the pains of examining the phænomena with their own eyes. Whoever has not had the advantage of inſpecting an active volcano, ſhould not preſume to write upon that ſubject, as he muſt unavoidably fall into error, in ſpite of all the learning, combinations, and ſagacity the wit of man is ſuſceptible of. Indeed, ſome authors, who have had Veſuvius before their eyes for forty years, have likewiſe fallen into ſtrange indefenſible opinions concerning its component parts, original formation, and modes of operating. Attachment to ſyſtem miſleads us all, and frequently cauſes us to ſee things, not as they are, but as we wiſh to find them. Nothing but the deſire of proving Veſuvius to be a primordial mountain, and not the produce of eruptions, could have brought Padre della Torre to believe, that he ſaw regular, original, calcareous, and granite ſtrata, far down in the bowels of the mountain; where, if he ſaw any thing, it was probably ſtreaks of ſulphureous and mineral effloreſcences adhering to the coats of the funnel. Nothing but ſyſtem could have ſo blinded Richard, as to prevent his finding a ſingle pumice ſtone, or other mark of fire, in the rocks of Poſilipo, where any

trivial

trivial obferver may meet with innumerable black calcined ftones, though he may not be fufficiently converfant in the fubject to difcover, that the whole rock owes its birth to workings of volcanic fires. Without prejudices of this kind, could other authors have feen nothing in Monte Somma, and the hills of Naples, but primitive fubftances, unaltered fince the deluge; when, in reality, every ftone befpeaks a fiery origin?

To be convinced that Vefuvius has been raifed from the level of the plains, or, more properly fpeaking, of the fea, by the fole action of fire contained in its bowels, requires, methinks, nothing but an eye accuftomed to obferve, and a found judgment unbiaffed by party. I own I cannot entertain a doubt of it, after having confidered the infulated pofition, and apparent compofition of the mount in, together with the foil of all the adjacent country, after having reflected upon the birth of Monte Nuovo thrown up to the perpendicular height of two hundred feet, in the fhort fpace of forty eight hours, and upon the apparition of many iflands raifed out of the bofom of the waters by fubmarine fires, of which both ancient and modern hiftory afford examples. The ifland of Afcenfion, and many in the Archipelago, one of which rofe out of the fea in 1707, completely prove this affertion. The origin of the ifle of Rhodes, as related in Pindar's feventh Olympic, feems to be of the fame clafs. This poet calls Rhodes a native of the floods, and tells us, " that ancient tales of men relate,

I " that

" that when Jupiter and the gods divided the earth,
" Rhodes was not vifible amidft the marine waves, but
" lay hid in the briny deep*." Apollo, being abfent, was
left out of this partition-treaty, and, on his appearance,
Jupiter would have proceeded to a frefh divifion ; but the
God of Day declined the offer, contenting himfelf with
dominions that did not interfere with any god's fhare : " for
" (fays he) I behold in the frothy fea a fruitful land rifing
" from the bottom." And accordingly, as he fpoke,
" Lo! the ifland fhot up out of the waters." It is eafy
to trace this fable to its fource, the heaving up of the foil
at the bottom of the fea by the vehemence of fire.

Whatever may have been the origin of Vefuvius, whether
as a mountain it be coeval with the firft-created protuberances of this globe, or whether it be an irregular production of ages fubfequent to the creation, this we may fafely
affirm, that it has been a volcano beyond the reach of

Φα`ὶ ἰανθρώπων παλαιαὶ
Ῥήσιες ἔπω ὅ]ε
Χθόνα δαῄεοντο Ζεύς τε καὶ αθάναῖοι
Φα. εραν εν πελάγει
Ῥ.δον εμμεν ποντίω
Ἁλμιρο῀ς δ εν βένθεσιν νᾶσον κεκρύφθαι

—————————επεὶ πολιᾶς
Ειτε τὶν ο῀ρος ὁρᾶν ἔιδον θαλάσσας
Λυξομέναν πεδόθεν
Πολυβοσκει, γαῖαν ἀνθρώ
τοισι κ᾽ ευτροκα μαλοις

Βλάστε μὲν εξ αλὸ, ὑγρᾶς,
Νᾶσος———

hiftory

hiftory or tradition. Long before it laid Herculaneum wafte, it was defcribed by authors as bearing the marks of fire on its fummit. Some even fay, the report of its having vomited flames went fo far back into 〰 〰 ty as to border upon fable. A moft animated defcr〰 its ravages in 79 is left us by the younger Pliny, who was a woeful witnefs to all he relates. From that time, it now and then burft out, and alarmed the neighbouring country; but feemed by degrees to lofe its vigour, till, in the lower ages, it fcarce gave fufficient alarm to merit a place in the chronicles of the times. In 1631, it broke out again with accumulated fury, and fpread fuch devaftation around, as almoft equalled the horrors of the firft year of Titus. Since that epocha, it has had its periods of turbulence and repofe; and of late years it has fo redoubled its violence, as to emit fmoke continually, and every year, at leaft, a torrent of lava. Whence it draws its immenfe fupplies of combuftibles, and how long its prefent cone will be able to bear thefe unremitting efforts, exceeds the power of all human calculation. I believe, however, that with all its terrors, Vefuvius, open and active, is lefs hoftile to Naples, than it would be, if its eruptions were to ceafe, and its ftruggles were to be confined to its bowels: then undoubtedly would enfue moft fatal fhocks to the unftable foundation of the Terra di Lavoro.

The day being clear, I made fome ftay on the top, to obtain a juft idea of the topography of this curious country. There cannot be a more advantageous ſtation for examining Naples and its environs, as Veſuvius ſtands ſingle, at a diſtance from all other mountains, and commands the plains of Nola, Capua, and Sarno, the chain of the Apennines, the promontory of Sorrento, the hills and gulf of Naples, with all its iſlands. I obſerved, that the ridge extending weſtward from Poggio Reale to Monte Gauro, is entirely ſeparated by the plains from every other eminence, and conſtitutes a vaſt detached promontory, full of lakes and hollows, the craters of extinct vulcanos. On ſurveying thoſe regions from this elevated pinacle, it appeared to me, that, in times of the remoteſt antiquity, there may have exiſted an enormous flaming mountain, with its centrical point between Iſchia and the Camaldoli, and that Solfatara, Aſtruni, Barbaro, &c. may be but the excreſcences and *montagnuole* of one gigantic maſs, which, after exhauſting its force, and wearing out the ſurface, till it grew unable to ſupport its own weight, may have ſunk, and been overwhelmed by the wave. The gulf of Baia, and the channels of Iſchia and Procida, may have been formed by this cataclyſm. The ſize of Ætna renders ſuch an extent no objection to my hypotheſis, and ſhews to what a monſtrous bulk a mountain can ſwell itſelf. Monte Epomeo in Iſchia, and the Camaldoli, are both abruptly broken down facing each other, and both ſlope off very gradually different ways, till one is loſt in the Campi Leborini, and the other ſinks into the ſea.

SEC-

## SECTION VI.

IN Chriſtmas time, all quarters of Naples reſound with *Paſtorali* or *Siciliane*, a kind of ſimple rural muſic, executed by Abruzzeſe or Calabrian ſhepherds, upon a ſpecies of big pipes, called in Abruzzo, Zampogna, and Ciaramelli in Calabria. The tunes vary according to the provinces. in the ſouth, they have three different airs; the northern ſhepherds know only two, to which they add what variations the boldneſs of their own genius inſpires. The boys learn of their fathers to play upon this inſtrument as the means of ſubſiſtence\*. At other ſeaſons, it is rare to hear any agreeable ſounds in the ſtreets of Naples, though it is the nurſery of muſical profeſſors: a ſchool, where the greateſt maſters have imbibed their principles, and acquired that knowledge of compoſition, which has enchanted the ears of all Europe. There is no ſuch thing as a national muſic, unleſs we give that name to a monotonous drawling ſeguidilla, that ſerves the nurſes † as a lullaby to put their children to reſt, and

* The waits ſtill kept in the pay of ſome corporations in England, are counterparts of theſe ſhepherds

† To ſecond its narcotic influence, they adminiſter to them copious doſes of Venice treacle, of which ſuch quantities are uſed, as render it a material article of importation The Neapolitans have tears at command, and are very eaſily moved to ſhed them Neither blows nor careſſes can ſtop their children when once they begin to cry they muſt roar till they are tired

3

feems borrowed from the Spaniards, who, I believe, learnt it of the Moors. I never refided in any Italian town where there was a lefs mufical turn in the populace: few fongs, guittars, vielles, or organs, enliven the evenings, as in the northern ftates of Italy, unlefs they be fent for to entertain the parties that in fummer fup on the fhore of Pofilipo*.

They do not even dance to mufic, but perform the Tarantella to the beating of a kind of tambourine, which was in ufe among their anceftors, as appears by the pictures of Herculaneum. The Tarantella is a low dance, confifting of turns on the heel, much footing and fnapping of the fingers†. It feems the delight of their foul, and a conftant holiday diverfion of the young women, who are, in general, far from handfome, although they have fine eyes and ftriking features. Their hands and feet are clumfy, their fhapes neglected, their necks flabby, and their fkins difcoloured by living fo much in the fun without bonnets. Amongft them we may find almoft every mode of hair-dreffing feen on the Greek and Roman coins‡.

---

* I have been told, that before the famine and calamities of 1764, the populace of Naples was more cheerful and mufically inclined than at prefent

† Perfons of all ranks here dance very low, but mark the time as perfectly with their fteps, as other nations do by fpringing from the ground.

‡ The coiffure of the younger Fauftina, with the coil of plaited hair upon the crown of the head, occurs frequently in the old town  that with the coil lower down, which may more properly be ftiled Lucilla's head-drefs, is common among the younger part of the fex in the fuburbs of Chiaia, and Plotina's among the women more advanced in years  I do not recollect to have feen any with the roll of treffes fo high up as it appears on the head of Fauftina the elder.

The

The women are always fighting and scolding, but never resist their husband's authority, when he comes to separate the combatants, and carry home his dishevelled spouse, who seems to stand as much in awe of her consort, as the Russian wives do of theirs, and suffers herself to be beaten by him with as little murmuring  I was shewn a woman here, who, during the life of her first husband, was a pattern of modesty and evenness of temper to the whole parish; but upon contracting a second marriage, surprized and scandalized the neighbourhood with her perpetual riots and obstreperousness.  On being reprimanded for her behaviour by the curate, she very frankly acknowledged that her former husband understood the management of a wife, and used to check her intemperate bursts of passion by timely correction; but that her present helpmate was too mild, to apply the proper chastisement which every wife requires more or less.  Men seldom interfere in feminine brawls; and if they do, generally content themselves with abusing, threatening, or shaking a cudgel or pitchfork at their antagonist, till the crowd comes in to part them. Sometimes a man is stabbed, but this is a rare event among the fishermen, the class of inhabitants I have had most constantly under my eye.  Manners vary with the districts, in some they engage with bludgeons, and those are the true lazaroni of Massaniello; in others the attack is made with knives and other deadly weapons; but the Neapolitans are by no means so bloody and revengeful a people as they are repre-

sented

sented by many travellers. It requires more than a slight provocation to lead them to extremities. During the prodigious hurry and confusion of the races in carnival, not the least tumult or quarrel was heard of; and even in the cruel famine of 1764, the only act of violence committed by a hungry populace, increased to double its number by the concourse of peasants from the provinces, where all crops had failed, was to break open and pillage a single baker's shop. Can as much be said for the temper of the mobs at London and Edinburgh? Drunkenness is not a common vice at Naples, and therefore quarrels, its usual consequences, are rare; besides, the Neapolitan rabble allow each other a great latitude of abuse and scolding before they are wound up to a fighting pitch. It is also uncommon to see any thing in public like gallantry among the people; no soldiers are met leading their doxies, or girls going about in quest of lovers, all which are, in other countries, sources of riot and bloodshed. At Naples there is nothing but a mere nominal police, yet burglaries are unknown, riots still more so, and the number of assassinations inconsiderable: it bears no proportion to that of the murders committed in the distant provinces, where, I am credibly informed, no less than four thousand persons are killed annually. Most of these crimes are perpetrated with guns in the mountainous countries, where a great ferocity of character, and wildness of manners prevail, and where the inhabitants are more wandering, and less exposed to the pursuits of the law, which is

indeed

indeed far from formidable in any part of the realm. It would require a prudent, inflexible, and long exertion of impartial criminal juftice, to reduce to order the fierce untractable affaffin of the mountainous regions of Calabria, who being driven by the oppreffion of the barons and officers of the revenue to penury and defpair, fets little value upon his life, and braves danger to the laft drop of his blood. The execution, however cruel, of a few banditti, would ftrike but little terror into their affociates, and produce no effect but that of ridding fociety of one or two bad members; nor will any meafures of police ever prove effectual, unlefs government adopt and purfue, with fteadinefs, a fyftem that may leffen the grievances of the poor, reftrain the defpotifm of the petty tyrants, and, by providing the peafant with more means of fupporting himfelf and family by honeft labour, guard him againft the temptation of taking up a lawlefs line of life. The cafe is different in the foft and fertile plains of the happy Campagna; there the welltimed prompt execution of a criminal, without allowing him any unneceffary refpite to prepare for death, and without fuffering priefts to affemble round him, to excite the devotion, compaffion, and almoft admiration of the crowd, would operate with great energy on the daftardly minds of the docile race that inhabits this charming climate; the terror of active juftice would prove a powerful check to murder, and violent outrages.

At

At prefent, the forms of criminal jurifprudence are here fo ill ordained, fo' multiplied and fo complex, that if the king were to infift upon a villain, who was taken in the fact, being tried, and if found guilty, hanged before the end of three days, the difpatch would almoft kill the judges with fatigue ; for the trial and procedures would employ them eighteen hours out of each twenty-four : Firft, the ac-cufation muft be laid according to rule, and witneffes exa-mined ; next the council for the prifoner pleads a couple of hours ; then the advocate for the *fifco* replies during one hour, and after him the advocate of the poor makes a re-joinder, which he has a right to fpin out for two hours : this done, every one of the four judges harangues ; then all the notifications are made, examinations canvaffed, proofs debated, and a thoufand trifling formalities obferved, which occafion fuch fhameful, infurmountable delays, as eternize a criminal procefs. It happened lately, that upon the final de-termination of the trial, and condemnation of a malefactor, a meffage was fent to the jailor to bring the culprit into court in order to receive fentence ; when, behold ! the turn-key appeared, and made affidavit that the prifoner had died of a long fit of ficknefs the Chriftmas twelvemonth before. As the falary of a judge in Naples is only fifty ducats a month ($£$ 9 : 7 : 6), he cannot afford to be honeft or ex--"peditious : but the cafe is ftill worfe in the provinces, where the judges have but twenty-five ducats, and with that muft keep a coach and proper houfehold eftablifhment. The fcri-

vani,

vani, or commiffaries, who have the department of warrants, arrefts, and police, are allowed no pay, though they muft keep thirty bailiffs a-piece under them ; fo that they are naturally very active in taking up an offender, where there is a probability of extorting any money out of him : when once in durance, the prifoner ceafes to be an object of confideration to them, and therefore they take no pains to forward his trial, or bring him to juftice : there are at this day above twelve thoufand criminals rotting in the different prifons of the kingdom, whofe maintenance cofts the ftate above two hundred thoufand ducats a year (thirty-feven thoufand five hundred pounds).

The fifhermen of Santa Lucia are the handfomeft men in Naples ; they have the true old Grecian features, and fuch well-proportioned limbs, that they might ferve for models in any academy of defign : they are the moft fubftantial and beft lodged portion of the Neapolitan populace. It is true, as moft writers affert, that the houferoom of this metropolis is very inadequate to the population, which, according to authentic accounts, amounted, at the clofe of the year 1776, to three hundred and fifty thoufand fixty-one fouls ; and that numbers of thefe are deftitute of houfe and property. But it is not equally a fact, as they affert, that winter and fummer thefe houfelefs inhabitants pafs their lives in the open air, and fleep in all weathers in the ftreets. In fummer it is very pleafant fo to do, but in winter not even a dog could bear the inclemency of the weather, not fo much on account of

cold

cold, as of wet.  When the rainy feafon fets in, it commonly lafts feveral fucceffive weeks, falling, not in fuch showers as we are acquainted with in England, where we have rain more or lefs every month in the year, but by pailfuls, an abfolute water-fpout, that carries all before it, and almoft drowns the unfortunate paffenger who is caught out of doors by the ftorm.  The quantity of rain at Naples is much more confiderable than that which falls on the fame fpace of ground in England.  Whole months of drought are compenfated by the deluge of a day : and befides, the fouth winds are frequently fo boifterous in winter, as to burft open the bolts of both doors and windows.  At that rainy time of the year, few are fo wretched and helplefs as to lie in the ftreet, but moft of the vagrants refort to the caves under Capodi Monte, where they fleep in crowds like fheep in a pinfold.  As they are thus provided with a dwelling, for which no rent is exacted, they alfo procure food without the trouble of cooking or keeping houfe : the markets and principal ftreets are lined with fellers of macaroni, fried and boiled fifh, puddings, cakes, and vegetables of all forts ; where, for a very fmall fum, which he may earn by a little labour, running of errands, or picking of pockets, the lazaro finds a ready meal at all hours : the flaggon hanging out at every corner invites him to quench his thirft with wine ; or if he prefers water, as moft of them do, there are ftalls in all the thoroughfares, where lemonade and iced water are fold.  The paffion for iced water is fo great and fo

general

general at Naples, that none but mere beggars will drink it
in its natural ftate; and, I believe, a fcarcity of bread would
not be more feverely felt than a failure of fnow. It is brought
in boats every morning from the mountains behind Caftelamare, and is farmed out at a great rent: the Jefuits, who
poffeffed a large capital, as well as the true fpirit of enterprize, had purchafed the exclufive privilege of fupplying the
city with it.

Very little fuffices to clothe the lazaro, except on holi-
days; and then he is indeed tawdrily decked out, with
laced jacket and flame-coloured ftockings: his buckles are
of enormous magnitude, and feem to be the prototype of
thofe with which our prefent men of mode load their in-
fteps. The women are alfo very fplendid on thofe days of
fhew; but their hair is then bound up in tiffue caps and
fcarlet nets, a fafhion much lefs becoming than their every
day fimple method. Citizens and lawyers are plain enough
in their apparel, but the female part of their family vies
with the firft court ladies in expenfive drefs, and all the va-
nities of modifh fopperies. Luxury has of late advanced
with gigantic ftrides in Naples. Forty years ago, the Neapolitan ladies wore nets and ribbons on their heads, as the
Spanifh women do to this day, and not twenty of them
were poffeffed of a cap: but hair plainly dreft is a mode
now confined to the loweft order of inhabitants, and all diftinction of drefs between the wife of a nobleman and that of
a citizen is entirely laid afide. Expence and extravagance

are

are here in the extreme. The great families are opprest with
a load of debt; the working part of the community always
spend the price of their labour before they receive it; and
the citizen is reduced to great parsimony, and almost penury, in his housekeeping, in order to answer these demands
of external shew: short commons at home whet his appe-
tite when invited out to dinner; and it is scarce credible
what quantities of victuals he will devour. The nobility in
general are well served, and live comfortably, but it is not
their custom to admit strangers to their table; the number of poor dependants who dine with them, and cannot
properly be introduced into company, prevents the great families from inviting foreigners: another reason may be, their
sleeping after dinner in so regular a manner as to undress
and go to bed: no ladies or gentlemen finish their toilet
till the afternoon, on which account they dine at twelve or
one o'clock. The great officers of state, and ministers, live
in a different manner, and keep sumptuous tables, to which
strangers and others have frequent invitations.

The establishment of a Neapolitan grandee's household is
upon a very expensive plan; the number of servants, carriages, and horses, would suffice for a sovereign prince; and
the wardrobe of their wives is formed upon the same magnificent scale; yet it is a fixed rule, that all ladies whatever,
be the circumstance of their husbands affluent or circum-
scribed, have an hundred ducats a month, and no more,
allowed them for pin-money. At the birth of every child,

the

the hufband makes his wife a prefent of an hundred ounces, and fome valuable trinkets, according to his fortune. Marriage portions are not very great in general; it does not coft a nobleman more to marry a daughter than it does to make her a nun; for a thoufand pounds will not defray the expence of the ceremonies at her reception and profeffion: fhe muft have a penfion fettled upon her, and referves, befides, a power over her inheritance, in cafe fhe fhall arrive at any dignity in the convent, and wifh to enrich it with buildings, plate, or veftments.

Servants and artificers of the city give from fifty to an hundred ducats with their daughters; peafants and country workmen go as far as three hundred. Females at and near Naples are efteemed helplefs and indolent, and therefore have always twice or thrice as much fortune as their brothers, who have greater refources in their ftrength and activity. A girl would fcarce get a hufband, if her lover did not expect to be reimburfed by her portion the fum he had paid away with his own fifters. In the plains, it is cuftomary for a peafant, on the birth of a daughter, to plant a row of poplar trees, which are cut down and fold at the end of feventeen years, to make up a fortune for her. The proverbial benediction of *Figly mafchi*, Male children, which a Neapolitan gives a woman when fhe fneezes, is founded on the great facility with which the common people provide for their fons: as foon as they can run about they are able to earn their bread, while their fifters remain

idle

idle at home, or beg till they are old enough to attract the notice of the men.

## SECTION VII.

THIS kingdom confifts of twelve provinces, of which the fuperficies meafures fourteen millions five hundred and eight thoufand nine hundred and feventy-three moggie. In two thoufand and fixty-feven cities, towns, villages, or hamlets, it contains about four millions five hundred thoufand inhabitants, which is not more than half the population that fo fertile a country might fupport. A duty is levied upon landed property, partly by a land tax, and partly by impofitions on confumption, taxes for roads, bridges, repairs, and other public exigencies, in the perception of which infinite abufes are committed *.

Upon a calculation of ten years, the average quantity of wheat fown in the kingdom amounts to little more than two million five hundred thoufand tomoli ; a tomolo is a fufficient quantity for a moggia. Six hundred and twenty-

---

* In fome parts of the kingdom an affeffment is made by the king's officers, and thofe parts are governed by gabella. Others are upon a freer footing, and regulated by a cataflo, this is a regifter kept in each diftrict, or univerfità, wherein are marked the incomes of all the inhabitants, who are taxed in proportion to the number of ounces they poffefs, towards completing the fum demanded of the diftrict by the king. This ounce contains three carlini. A fuoco implies a family, or five perfons.

five

five thousand moggie are sown with barley and lent grain,
and two hundred and fifty thousand with Indian corn and
pulse; but it is supposed by good judges, that one million
seven hundred and sixty four thousand, five hundred and
eighteen moggie more might be sown with wheat, five
hundred and eighty-four thousand and eighty-one moggie
with barley, oats, and other lenten corn, and with pulse
and Indian corn, one hundred and twelve thousand, seven
hundred and twenty-four moggie, or thereabouts.

The usual produce of wheat, on an average, of the last
ten years, comes to about twenty-two millions tomoli, reck-
oning it about eight tomoli per moggia per annum between
the more and less fertile lands.

|  | Tomoli. |
|---|---|
| For feed there go      -      - | 2,500,000 |
| For the consumption of the inhabitants, in num- | |
| ber 4,487,628, at five tomoli a head,   - | 22,438,140 |
|  | 24,938,140 |

But four tomoli a head being a juster calculation, because in several provinces the common people live upon
bread made of Turkey wheat, barley, chestnuts, &c.
the necessary consumption in wheat ought to be stated
only at      -      - | 17,950,512

| Add for feed      -      - | 2,500,000 |
|---|---|
|  | 20,450,512 |

Confequently there remain for exportation, one year with another, about one million and a half of tomoli.

In fome grounds, where beans and Indian corn have been gathered, it is ufual to fow wheat the fame year, and thofe lands are called Maggifi. It is thought that four millions of Moggi are fit for the reception of wheat, but two thirds of them are not fown, through the bad œconomy of government, impofitions, vexations, &c. In the territory of Foggia, part of Puglia, there is reckoned to be an extent of one hundred and fifty thoufand verfure proper for corn; each verfura will take three and a half tomoli of wheat to fow, or four and a half tomoli of barley. However, till the year 1767, no more was ever fown than fifty-three thoufand verfure, not even in 1764, at the time of the famine, though, in order to fecure an ample fupply for the next year, the tenants threw upon the lands more feed-corn than ufual, and exerted themfelves to the utmoft of their abilities. Abufes in adminiftration, and rapacity in the tax-gatherers, defeat all fchemes of improvement in hufbandry. In 1767, one hundred and eleven thoufand verfure were fown in the territory of Foggia. If the three million moggie of land fit for the plough, more than the quantity actually in tillage, were fown with corn, the kingdom might probably produce thirty-two millions tomoli of wheat, inftead of twenty-two millions, and the exportation of grain might then be always kept open without danger, and to the great advantage of the cultivators.

It

It is calculated that the culture of corn employs ten perfons, that of the vine at leaft twenty.

The chief exportation of corn is made from the provinces of Capitanata, Bari, Otranto, Abruzzo, Molife, Calabria, and Bafilicata: they fupply the internal confumption of the kingdom and foreign markets. The product of the Terra di Lavoro, and Salerno, is referved for the ufe of the capital.

The exports of the kingdom of Naples are, wheat, barley, legumes, Indian corn, hemp, line, cummin, fennel, and anifeeds; wool, oil, wine, cheefe, fifh, falt flefh, honey, wax, frefh and dry fruit, manna, faffron, liquorice, feccia brucciata, gums, locuft beans, capers, lupins, *pifta*, macaroni of various forts, falt, potafh, brimftone, nitre, argal, pitch, tar, fumach, fkins, cattle, oranges, lemons, brandy, vinegar, metals, minerals, marble, filk, hemp, flax, cottons, and divers forts of manufactures. All thefe products might be fent out in very great quantities, if proper encouragement were given; and both horfes and cattle might become valuable articles of exportation, if the breed were attended to.

The provinces moft abundant in oil are, Bari, Otranto, Calabria, and Abruzzo. The product, upon ten years average, has been efteemed at fix hundred thoufand falme. The confumption of the whole kingdom, including the capital, rarely exceeds three hundred thoufand falme, yet the exportation of late years has feldom amounted to forty thou-

fand

sand salme, except in the year 1767, when it was greater, on account of the general failure of olives throughout Spain.

The city of Naples consumes annually thirty-seven thousand five hundred salme of clear oils, and about three thousand of dirty oils.

The duties upon a salm of oil exported from Gallipoli or Taranto are,

|  | Duc. | Gr. |
|---|---|---|
| For the treasury, - = | 1 | 0 |
| Farm of oil and soap, called Arrendamento, - | 3 | 30 |
| Customhouses of Puglia, for extraction, - | 0 | 75 |
| The customhouse's valuation of said oil in the ports should be D. 12 per salm, on which should be paid at the rate of 67 G. per ounce of D. 6, which comes to - - | 1 | 34 |
| D. | 6 | 39 |

But this varies, and is now got up to near D. 8 per salm. Oil imported into Naples bears a Duty of D. 1 32½ per salm.

The high excise and farm upon brandies prevents the distillation of that commodity from the immense quantity of wines that are produced. Most of these wines would bear long sea voyages, if the proprietors could afford the expence of good brandy to mix with them. From the high duties a small exportation only takes place of coarse wines for Holland, and of the Greek wine of Vesuvius for other places.

The

The produce of silk in the kingdom is computed at about eight hundred thousand pounds weight annually, of which half is supposed to be worked at home, and the other half exported raw. Double the quantity might be sold unwrought, and double might be manufactured, were it not prevented by the high duties on exportation, and on importation into the capital, together with the tyranny and exactions of the excise officers of the provinces.

The exportation of thrown silk, upon an average of many years, amounts to one hundred and forty-eight thousand two hundred and seventeen pounds.

The exportation of raw silk from the Calabrias, through the custom-house, is about fifty-three thousand pounds; but perhaps double that quantity is smuggled to Leghorn and other parts.

Among the many vexations and impositions on raw silk produced in the kingdom, may be reckoned the unjust proceedings of the deputies of the royal farms, and administrators of the excise, who, as soon as the silk is drawn off by the poor people from the pods, out of the caldron, weigh it, and note down the weight in a book. When the silk is sold, they oblige the vender to pay the duty upon the said weight, though the silk was heavy with water, on a cruel supposition that they have smuggled the difference; so that the poor creatures actually pay duty for a portion of water.

A gabel of a gran a pound is even laid upon the refuse pods, which formerly were untaxed. The duties upon filk in Calabria come to forty-two and a half grains per pound, including feven grains per pound for a duty called di Bifignano. That of the Terra di Lavoro, Bafilicata, Salerno, and Abruzzo, is forty one grains per pound: but then there is another duty of twelve grains and feven tenths per pound on the exportation of raw filk lefs ten per cent. for package, and about ten grains for thrown filk lefs twenty per cent. for package, and five per cent. for wet.

No fmall quantity of cotton is gathered in the Terra di Bari, and the diftricts of the cities of Turfi and Gravina; but the beft is in the province of Lecce. Venice takes off a good deal annually, as alfo of the wool.

Almonds abound in the territories of Bari, Lecce, and the Abruzzi; but the beft come from Bari, where they are exported to Venice and Triefte. A duty of three ducats ninety four grains per canto ruins this trade.

In Calabria there are natural mountains of falt, ftronger and more active than fea falt; but the mines are fhut up, not to hurt the revenue, which reaps great benefit by the high duties upon that article. At Naples the gabel is almoft five times more than the firft coft of the commodity in Sicily.

All manufactures fent from the capital into the provinces, and all that are exported out of the kingdom (though the firft fpecies with which they were fabricated had already paid the cuftomhoufe duties) are neverthelefs liable to a charge of fixteen to twenty per cent. called Miglioria. Nothing is excepted but fweetmeats and chocolate.

The

The duties levied upon the Miglioria or Minutillo, amount annually to seventy-four thousand nine hundred and nine ducats, of which fourteen thousand belong to the city of Naples, upon the imposition of twenty-three grains per ounce, and the rest goes into the customhouse, paid upon manufactures.

Consumption of corn in the city of Naples.

|  | Tomoli. |
|---|---|
| In bread for the public, - - | 400,000 |
| Maccaroni, - - | 160,000 |
| Tarali, or little biscuits, - - | 50,000 |
| Meal at the great market, - - | 300,000 |
| Meal at twelve other stalls in the city, - | 500,000 |
| Fine flour, 95,000 cantara, - - | 300,000 |
| For the land and sea troops, - - | 120,000 |
| Charity schools and convents, - | 1,200,000 |
| Per annum, | 2,530,000 |
| Horned cattle, - - | 25,000 |
| Sorrento calves, - - | 3,000 |
| Hogs, between the market and other places, | 45,000 |

Eggs from the neighbourhood, besides what are produced in the city, 60,000 per diem.

| Oil, stars of ten and one third rotoli each, - | 600,000 |

There is in the kingdom of Naples a fund of more than fifty millions of ducats belonging to the exchequer, duties, and other public effects. It ought be converted into a

public

public bank, bearing proper intereſt ; but, inſtead thereof, the produce is in a great meaſure abſorbed by the ſalaries and peculation of the ſubaltern financiers, to the great diſadvantage of the public.

According to the beſt authenticated accounts, the current coin of the kingdom of Naples, in gold, ſilver, and braſs, is between eight and nine millions of ducats, which is not ſufficient for the circulation of a very extenſive commerce : for although the notes of ſeven public banks, eſtabliſhed in the city of Naples, circulate even down to the value of the ſmalleſt ſums, yet the equivalent is paid into theſe banks by the proprietors, or by creditors, in money, as into bankers hands in London, without any allowance of intereſt : and therefore this mode of payment only ſerves for the readier diſpatch of buſineſs, and ſaving of ſome trouble, but does not increaſe the circulation, nor is there any paper iſſued out that bears a premium.

All bills of exchange, court tranſactions, civil, military, eccleſiaſtical and mercantile payments, are made either by bank-bills, called fedi di credito, or by drafts on the ſaid banks, explaining the cauſes at length of ſaid payments, for which reaſon no receipts are taken. The perſon who is in poſſeſſion of a bank-bill or draft, is in rigour obliged to paſs it as his own in the ſpace of twenty four hours; otherwiſe ſhould the bank fail, the holder of the bank-bill has no redreſs againſt the perſon who paid it him. In this century there has been an inſtance of the failure of a bank, viz.

that

that of L'Annunziata. There is a law ftill exifting, though not enforced, which declares, that no payment above fix ducats fhall be valid, unlefs made by one of the banks. Thefe banks are at prefent feven in number, viz. S. Giacomo, S. Eligio, S. Salvatore, Poveri, Pieta, Spirito Santo, and Popolo. They ferve as public depofitories of money; more or lefs they all take in pawns to an immenfe value, at ftated interefts, and lend money alfo upon proper fecurity of lands, houfes, &c.

There is a company of affurance, with a jus privativum, which is contrary to the intereft of commerce. The profits of this affociation, in the firft ten years after its inftitution, were upwards of ten per cent and at the end of the next five years, in 1766, rofe to twenty per cent. It would therefore be an advantage for the ftate, if the number of infurance offices were increafed, as the gains on the whole, though divided, would increafe alfo. The rifk begins from the moment the goods are put on board, and continues till the arrival of the fhip, and her total difcharge of the goods, which is a good cuftom for the infured.

### Merchandise imported into Naples.

From England—Woollen goods of all forts, filk and worfted ftockings, hats, tanned hides, lead, tin, pepper, hardware, linens, handkerchiefs, fans, canes, gums, dying-woods, drugs, watches, clocks, mathematical inftruments,

M                                                houfehold

household furniture, falt cod, pilchards, herrings, coffee, tea, cocoa, fugar, and occafionally calicoes and Eaft India goods.

Holland——Cinnamon, cloves, nutmeg, pepper, medicinal drugs from the Eaft and Weft Indies, fine cloths, particularly the black, called Segovia, linen for fhirts and other ufes, muflins, chintz, callicoes, feveral forts of cocoa, whalebone, tobacco, filk ftuffs and velvet.

France——An immenfe quantity of fugar, indigo, coffee, dying-woods, verdigreafe, Levant drugs, cocoa, hardware, filk ftuffs, gold and filver, fays of Le Mans, du roy, cloths of Elbeuf, and all forts of women's apparel.

Spain——Sugar, cochineal, dying-woods, cocoa, hides falted and in the hair, medicinal American drugs, Jefuits bark, falfaparighia, jalap, balfam of Peru, hippecacuana, cloths of divers forts, wine, tobacco, fnuff of Seville and Havanna, lead, gun-barrels, honey, &c.

Portugal——Brazil fugars, tobacco, cocoa of Maringan, drugs, hides, &c.

Venice——Books, cordavans, looking glaffes, chryftals and glaffes of all forts, luftres, coach and window glaffes, Padua cloths, called Venetian fays, for the confumption of the provinces, fine Verona cloths, equal to Englifh fcarlet, ftockings, caps made of wool, fine hats ufed in the provinces, wax candles, white loaf fugar, fine linen, medicinal and Levant drugs, all forts of paints, fublimate, cinnabar, quickfilver, turpentine, dragon's blood, copper, iron of

divers

divers forts of the manufactures of Germany and Brescia, excellent paper, much ufed in the provinces.

Genoa—American goods from the Spanish main and the Portuguese East Indies, velvets, iron in great quantity, nails, ordinary hats, wax from Tunis and the African coaft.

Leghorn—All forts of goods, at fecond hand, from the Levant, Barbary wools, linens of Egypt, wax, and many filk manufactures.

Peterfburg—Hides, wax, iron, furs, &c.

Sardinia—An immenfe quantity of tunny fifh, and white cheefe.

Germany—Silefia linens of all forts, white and painted, iron of divers manufactures, vitriol of Hungary, chryftals of Bohemia, large glaffes for coaches and windows, hats and goods of the new Vienna fabrick, turpentine, quickfilver, hardware, manufactures of Ofnaburg and Nuremberg, copper, tin plates, boards, cloth, &c.

The duties in general upon goods imported into the city of Naples amount to about twenty-five per cent. upon the cuftomhoufe eftimation, paying fo much per ounce ad valorem, which ounce is regulated at fix ducats value. Sugars and wax, by the new impofitions, pay forty or fifty per cent. upon the market price. The duty upon fugar produces about eighty thoufand ducats annually.

SECTION

# SECTION VIII.

*March* 26th. } HAVING received an invitation to be present at the opening of some lately discovered rooms at Stabia, I went thither with a party. On our way we visited Herculaneum and Pompeii *. We then traversed the rich plain that lies between Vesuvius and the Sorrentine branch of the Apennines, and came by a gentle ascent to the excavations. Stabia was a long string of country houses, rather than a town; for it had been destroyed by Sylla, and before the reign of Titus, all its rebuilt edifices were overturned by an earthquake. In the catastrophe of seventy-nine, the wind blowing furiously from the north, brought the ashes of Vesuvius upon it; all the country was covered with cinders and rapilli, or small pumice-stones, many yards deep. Towns, houses, and trees, were buried, and their situations remained marked in the plain by hillocks like barrows. Stabia, though six miles from the mountain, was overwhelmed and lost, till it was casually discovered about twenty-eight years ago. The earthquake had so damaged the buildings, that none of them can be preserved, and therefore as soon as every thing curious is taken out,

---

* I shall reserve for the second volume what I have to say concerning them.

the

the pits are filled up again. The afhes penetrated into all parts, and confumed every thing that was combuftible.

On our arrival, the workmen began to break into the fubterraneous rooms, and, as the foil is all a crumbling cinder, very little labour was requifite to clear them When opened, the apartments prefented us with the fhattered walls, daubed rather than painted with gaudy colours in compartments, and fome birds and animals in the cornices, but in a coarfe ftyle, as indeed are all the paintings of Stabia. In a corner, we found the brafs hinges and lock of a trunk; near them, part of the contents, viz ivory flutes in pieces, fome coins, brafs rings, fcales, fteel-yards, and a very elegant filver ftatue of Bacchus, about two inches high, reprefented with a crown of vine leaves, bufkins, and the horn of plenty.

The brow of this hill affords a rich and varied profpect towards Vefuvius and the gulf.

The company returned to Naples; but I remained all night at Torre della Nunziata, a large village belonging to the princes of Valle and Dentici, and a hofpital. It was of little note while the high road from Naples paffed between Vefuvius and Nola, the communication by land along the fhore being impeded by repeated eruptions. All that tract was for many ages one dark foreft, fucceffively confumed by fiery torrents, and fpringing up again upon the old cooled lavas. As foon as a road was opened over Herculaneum, the Torre became populous. A manufacture of

fire-arms

fire-arms was eſtabliſhed here by the preſent King of Spain, who attempted to introduce ſeveral others into the kingdom; but every branch that required nicety, patience, and fine touches, failed: that of arms ſucceeded wonderfully; and, in three years, the German artificers, he had ſent for to inſtruct his ſubjects, returned to their own country: for their pupils were become as ſkilful as themſelves.

Early next morning, I hired a ſix-oared barge, and rowed along the coaſt. We paſſed before the iſland of Revigliano, a fine object, that has been introduced into many pictures. My firſt ſtation was Caſtelamare di Stabia, a long town lying at the bottom of the bay, ſheltered to the ſouth by high mountains, that come ſo near the water edge as to leave only a very narrow ſlip for the buildings, many of which are boldly and beautifully placed on the lower points of the hills. The King has a charming villa above the city, formerly a farm of the Jeſuits The port is ſmall and entirely artificial, more frequented by Latin ſail-barks than ſhips. This place roſe by the ruin of the inland towns In 1654, the French, under the Duke of Guiſe, took it by ſtorm, and meant to puſh their conqueſts from hence into the heart of the kingdom Their hopes were ſoon blaſted by a defeat on the banks of the Sarno, which obliged them to reimbark, and abandon even Caſtelamare, but not before they had ſtripped it of every thing valuable. I continued my courſe weſtward under a

bold

bold shore : new beauties of landscape opened upon me at the doubling of every promontory. The first change of scene was to an uninhabited forest, where white cliffs rise perpendicular out of the deep blue waters : behind them, lofty mountains overgrown with wood. These rocks are calcarious, and furnish Naples with lime. The stones are burnt in the creeks, and the fire supplied with faggots cut in the hills, and flung down on ropes. Along the shore are many strong sulphureous springs.

Vico was my next stage : a little city, in a delightful position, on the brow of a hill, backed by an amphitheatre of mountains The strata of these eminences incline contrary ways to one centrical point, as if there had originally existed a similar mass in the centre, torn asunder and swallowed up by one of those shocks, which must have often overturned this unstable country. Charles the Second and Joan the First raised Vico out of obscurity, on account of the charms they found in its situation.

On doubling the next projecting rocks, we entered the spacious bay of Sorrento, three miles wide. A semicircular chain of woody mountains incloses a rich and beautiful plain, rather sloping towards the sea, full of white buildings peeping out of the groves This half moon terminates in a straight line to the sea, by a bold coast of black perpendicular rocks. It probably formed a portion of a circle, half of which broke off and sunk into the waves. This I believe to have been the case, and that the

whole

whole was once the crater of a volcano. All the soil of
the plain is cineritious, and its rocks a strong blue lava,
except near the east end, where they are of a softer piperino
kind. The encircling mountains are composed of regular
calcareous layers, that do not join or intermix in the least
with the others, but are broken off abruptly all round,
as if a place had been scooped out for the reception of the
heterogeneous mass, rising suddenly out of the bosom of
the earth or waters. Many of these limestone rocks are
twisted, as it were, into ropes, exactly in the same manner as some Vesuvian lavas: they have besides so many
peculiarities, that correspond with those of the productions
of burning mountains, that were it not directly repugnant
to the common systems of philosophy, which decide all
calcareous substances to be a sediment of the ocean, I
should be tempted to believe, that fire had a greater share
in the formation of these rocks than is generally allowed.
The materials of the lower grounds are beyond doubt
volcanical; however, I am confident that, as yet, we are
but imperfectly acquainted with the powers of fire, and
the metamorphoses it is capable of producing. As we
have discovered, that the fumes of sulphur and vitriol can
change hard black lava into soft white clay, perhaps we
may find out, that some other operation of natural chy-
mistry can convert substances into limestone.

I landed at Sorrento, a city placed on the very brink of
the steep rocks that overhang the bay, in a most enchant-

ing

ing fituation. It contains fifteen thoufand inhabitants, half the population of the whole plain. The ftreets are narrow; but this is no inconvenience in a warm climate, where carriages are not ufed, nor any communication with the metropolis practicable by land. Of all the places in the kingdom, this is bleft with the moft delightful climate. It was renowned for it in ancient times: Silius Italicus extols its foft and wholefome zephyrs*. At prefent, it enjoys fhady groves, excellent water, fruit, fifh, milk, butter, the fineft veal in the world, good wine, and almoft every neceffary of life at an eafy rate. Mountains fcreen it from the hot autumnal blafts. The temper of the inhabitants is faid to refemble the climate in mildnefs. A few infcriptions and refervoirs of water are all the remnants of antiquity it can fhew. It derives its name from the refidence or worfhip of the Syrens †. In this bay, the Prince of Salerno, fon to Charles the Firft, was, in 1283, taken prifoner by Lauria, the admiral of Peter of Aragon: a naval victory that infured the poffeffion of Sicily to the conquerors. Here Torquatus Taffo drew his firft breath in 1544: a bard undoubtedly intitled to rank in the foremoft line of modern poets, notwithftanding the farcafm of Boileau‡, who, from his ignorance of the Italian

---

* Zephyro Surrentum molle falubri

† Surrentum.

‡ Le cinquant du Taffe à tout l'or de Virgile.
  Prefers Taffo's tinfel to Virgil's gold.

N                                language,

language, and the coldness of his heart, was a very improper judge of the flights of genius. In 1558, the
Turks sacked this city, and carried off twelve thousand
captives; but, preferring money to such a quantity of
slaves, they sent to Naples to ask a ransom. Distrust, consternation, or insensibility, caused their offer to be rejected, and the infidels sailed away with their prisoners.
Soon after, by an act of generosity scarce to be paralleled
in any history, the remaining Sorrentines sold their lands
and goods, and redeemed their fellow citizens. Had such
an effort been made by Greeks or Romans, it would have
been a common-place example for school-boys, and every
dissertator, ancient and modern, would have enlarged with
enthusiasm on this trait of heroism; but at Sorrento it is
scarce remembered, and, I believe, it is entirely forgotten
in the rest of the kingdom.

On the twenty-eighth, I continued my coasting voyage
to Capo di Terra, or Puolo, the point that divides the bay
of Sorrento from that of Massa*. Here are the ruins of a
villa mentioned in Statius's Sylvæ: it belonged to Pollius
Fælix, whose name is still preserved in the modern appellation. I admired the exactness with which the poet
has described the spot; for however altered and disfigured
the minuter features may be, the great outlines of the

* Est inter natos Syrenum nomine nico,
Saxaque Tyrrhene templis onusta Minervæ

place

Ruins of the Surrounding of Villa of Pollius at Capo di Paolo

place are ftill difcernible. On the very extremity of the
Cape, impending over the fea, ftands a row of vaulted
chambers, before which appear the veftiges of a portico *,
or hall. Its form is that of an obtufe angle. Thefe rooms
commanded a double view : one of Sorrento and Vefuvius ;
the † other, of Naples ‡, Puzzoli, and Ifchia §. Part of
the painting remains upon the walls. Behind thefe buildings, the promontory narrows into an ifthmus, pierced in
the middle with a deep round bafon, into which the fea
has accefs by a paffage under the rocks. As the waves
have no force left when they enter it, and its opening is
furrounded by ruins, this was no doubt the fituation of
the baths. Three arched conduits brought frefh water
to them from a large refervoir at the foot of the mountain; high rocks, covered with olive-trees, defend † † this
place from the boifterous fcirocco, and boats find a fafe

* Per obliquas erepit porticus arces
   Ubis opus, longoque domat faxa afpera dorfo
   Una Dicis
   Parthenopen directo lumite ponti
‡ In out
   Cella Domeher fj coulit is villa profundi
§ Hic vilct Inarimen, illi Prochyta afpera paret
‖ Gemini teftudine fumant
   Balnea
** Terras occupat dulcis vado
   Nympharum
†† Montis intervene area
   Littus et in terras fcopuli pendentis ext.

retreat in a circular creek, which divides the Cape into two peninſulas*. From hence I ſailed along the woody coaſt of Maſſa, a dioceſe without a town; for all the dwelling-houſes are diſperſed in ſmall cluſters along the verdant declivity. We lay upon our oars a few hours to take ſome refreſhment, and then ſailed to Naples, where we arrived by moonlight. The evening was warm and mild, and the ſea ſmooth as glaſs; the lights of the fiſh-markets reflected on its ſurface, formed a moſt ſplendid illumination.

* Placido lunata receſſu,
　Hinc atque hinc curvas prorumpunt æquora rupes—
　Ponunt hic laſſa furorem
　Æquori
　Nulloque tumultu
　Stagna modeſta jacent.

JOURNEY

# J O U R N E Y

### F R O M

## N A P L E S TO T A R A N T O.

---

### S E C T I O N   IX.

ON the twelfth of April 1777, I set out with
S. T. G. from Naples by the Porta Capuana. We
rode our own horses, but had a chaise to carry our baggage and ourselves occasionally. A broad avenue of
poplars renders this outlet more regular than any other.
On the left hand are the aqueducts that convey water to
the city, and supply several fountains erected by the
Viceroys, in the last century, for ornament and the relief
of travellers. Above is a beautiful ridge of woody hills,
called Il Campo di Lautrec, from Odet de Foix, Maréchal

7                                                                                          de

de Lautrec, who, in 1528, at the head of the French
army, invaded the kingdom of Naples, subdued the northern provinces, and drove the Imperialists into the capital.
On the twenty-ninth of April, he pitched his camp on this
eminence, and by his approach threw the Neapolitans into
the utmost consternation. Their terrors redoubled on the
failure of their usual miracle, the liquefaction of the blood
of St. Januarius: a disappointment, in their opinion, the
certain forerunner of some weighty calamity. The horrors
of famine soon began to be severely felt in so populous a
town, and the distress was enhanced by the enemy's break-
ing down the aqueducts; but what was intended for its
ruin proved its salvation, and the contrivance turned
against the besiegers: for the waters, thus diverted from
their channel, and obstructed in their passage, ran waste
over the low grounds, stagnated in pools, and, through
the excessive heat of the season, corrupted. The putre-
faction was accelerated by the fermentation of a great
quantity of corn, which Virticillo, a famous outlaw,
purposely threw into the ditches as he passed along with
a supply of provisions for the city. From the malignant
vapours exhaled by these putrid swamps, a pestilential
disease arose, which, in a short time, destroyed the greatest
part of the French army, and, on the fifteenth of August,
died their brave commander. His remains were interred
under his own tent, the siege was raised, most of the
French that survived the contagion were taken or put to

the

the fword, and few efcaped to carry an account of the cataftrophe to their own country.

Were it becoming a reafonable man to adopt the Neapolitan idea of St. Januarius's blood being endowed with the gift of prophecy, one might fuppofe, that its obftinate induration had not in view the mere event of the fiege, but rather pointed to a cruel difeafe, which made its firft appearance in our hemifphere at that period, and in that camp. It is faid, that this tremendous fcourge of debauchery was firft imported by the companions of Chriftopher Columbus from the Charibbee iflands, where it was an aboriginal malady, and that women infected by them were defignedly fent out of Naples to fpread contagion among the French, by whom the infernal poifon was communicated to the reft of Europe. But authors differ in their opinions concerning the introduction of this diforder: fome incline to give it an eaftern or Egyptian, not an American origin, and ground their notion upon the infcription of a tomb in the church of S. Maria del Popolo at Rome*. This monument is erected to the memory of a noble Roman, who died *pefte inguinaria* in 1485, which is fix years before Columbus's return from the New World. The difficulty lies in proving this peftis inguinaria to be really the difeafe in queftion, and not a

* Marco Antonio equiti Bonini filio ex nobili Albertonum familia corpore animoque infignis, qui annum circis xxx peft inguinaria interiit an. falutis Chrifti mcccclxxxv. die xxii Julii heredes B M P

plague that had its ulcer in the groin, as others have theirs
under the arm, in the side, or elsewhere; for it is an observation made by many medical practitioners in the Levant,
that each plague throws out its mortal tumour in one particular part of the body upon all patients. If this sentiment of the lues coming from the East were incontrovertible, it would follow, that to all the accumulated horrors
of tyranny, rapine, and murder, exercised by the Europe-
ans upon the innocent Americans, we might add the introduction of a fatal and loathsome disease, which completed the desolation of that continent, by destroying the
few wretches their sword had spared.

On the declivity stands the church of Santa Maria del
Pianto, or of Tears, erected over the mouth of some deep
excavations, where the bodies of many thousand persons,
carried off by a plague in 1656, were brought in carts
from Naples, and walled up. This pestilence far exceeded in devastation that of 1528; for, in the space of
six months, it dispatched 400,000 people in the kingdom of Naples, although the provinces of farther Calabria and Otranto escaped the infection.

An avenue of cypresses, sloping up the hill, gloomily
points out the Campo Santo, or Cemetery of the Hospital
for Incurables. It stands loftily, and remote from all habitations of the living, and is most admirably contrived
for its melancholy purposes. Divine service is performed
under a spacious portico at the entrance, and a high wall

incloses

inclofes a flagged court, about two hundred and fixty feet fquare. Under it are three hundred and fixty-five very deep vaults hewn in the rock, one of which is in its turn opened each day of the year, to receive the bodies of fuch as died the preceding evening in the hofpital. The firft tenants of this repofitory were the wretches who perifhed in the great famine in 1764. The tufa, of which the rocks of all thefe hills are compofed, has a moft powerful drying quality, and foon parches up the corpfes that are configned to its bofom.

At the diftance of one mile from Naples, we paffed by the ruins of Poggio Reale, a villa built by Alphonfus the Second, while Duke of Calabria. He caufed to be painted in the apartments the principal occurrences of his father's reign, and took great delight in embellifhing this palace, which, neverthelefs, does not appear to have been pof-feffed of any natural beauties worth cherifhing. It was rilely fituated at the foot of the hills, on the very edge of the marfhes that lie between Naples and Vefuvius. The waters of the Sebeto, an infignificant brook, dignified with the title of river, make thefe lands extremely fruitful, and proper for kitchen-ftuff; but, in fummer, aguifh and dangerous to inhabit. In ancient times it may have been more confiderable, and received many fupplies, which the eruptions of Vefuvius have dried up or turned off; but its

fize

ſize has long been very trifling.   Boccaccio, who ſaw it in
the days of King Robert, pleaſantly ſtiles it a river,

*Quanto ricco d'onor, tanto povero d'acque.*

As rich as it is in fame, ſo poor is it in water.

We ſoon after left the hilly grounds to deſcend into the
immenſe plains of Nola, one entire grove of tall elms and
poplars, planted in rows to ſupport the vines growing at
their feet, and ſtretching their branches from tree to tree
in beautiful garlands.   Between the lines, the huſbandman
ſows corn and pulſe without any fallow; and, to prevent
the land from being exhauſted, raiſes early crops of lupins
and beans, which he hoes up before they fructify, and
buries for manure.   The harrowing and rolling is performed by oxen.   This ſcene for a while aſtoniſhes and
fills the eye; but, from the extent of the plantation, the
ſameneſs of objects, and the total excluſion of all proſpect,
it ſoon becomes unpleaſant and fatiguing.   The ſoil is a
ſandy volcanic loam, in a high degree rich and vegetative.
The cloſe ſhade of ſo much wood preſerves it in a due
ſtate of moiſture, without which its fertility would be
greatly diminiſhed by the heat of the climate; but this
ſhade gives the whole country a diſagreeable damp ſmell.

Near a village called Ciſterna, we found maſons at
work in a quarry of dark-blue lava, ſimilar to the pavement of Naples.   This place is exactly ſituated ſo as to
have

have Monte Somma in a line between it and the cone of Vesuvius, of which nothing appears but the column of smoke: a clear proof, that these layers of lava cannot have run out of the present crater, as the height of the ridge of Somma would prevent any matter from being poured over it, unless the actual volcano first filled up and levelled to the brim the intermediate valley, called Atrio del Cavallo. Every naturalist, that is not blinded by the prejudices of some system formed in his closet, and implicitly adhered to in all his researches, must allow, that it is impossible to account for these quarries, without supposing Somma to have been, in former ages, one of the sides of a much larger volcano than the present ignivomous mountain; and that, upon the falling in of that enormous mass, subsequent eruptions must, out of one of the sides, have heaved up Vesuvius as we now behold it.

## SECTION X.

WE turned off to the left to see Nola, a city that affords little scope for observation, as the ruins of its ancient edifices are almost obliterated. Nothing remains of the two amphitheatres but some brick walls, the marble casing having been taken away by an Earl of Nola to build his palace.

Some anecdotes render its history interesting. Augustus died here at the age of seventy-five years, said to have

O 2

been poifoned in a difh of figs by Livia, upon his betraying a return of tendernefs towards his own family; but,
methinks, old age and infirmities were fufficient caufes
for the death of a man worn out with the fatigue of a long
reign over a nation of conquerors, whom his cruelty and
policy had reduced, from the haughtieft of republicans,
to the moft abject flaves that ever crouched beneath the
iron rod of defpotifm. His faithful friend and fortunate
general, Marcus Agrippa, was furprifed by death a few
years before him in the fame place.

Saint Paulinus, a native of Bourdeaux, died Bifhop of
Nola in 431 He was an ingenious poet, and had been
Conful. He is faid to have been the inventor of bells by
the Nolans, who arrogate to themfelves the merit of
having furnifhed fociety with this ufeful inftrument; but I
rather fuppofe him to have been the firft who introduced
them into churches, and hung them up in fteeples, for
the purpofe of fummoning the faithful to prayers. Before
his time, Chriftians made ufe of wooden rattles, *facra
ligna*, to call the congregation together, no bells being
allowed by government to a profcribed fect. The ancients
had bells both for prophane and facred fervice. Polybius
mentions them, and we learn by a tale in Strabo, that
market-time was announced by them *.

Pliny

---

* He relates, that at Jaficum, a mufician, who had drawn a great crowd
of auditors about him, was fuddenly deferted by them all, except one man,
who

Pliny assures us, that the tomb of Porsena, King of Tuscany, was hung round with bells, and the *Lebetes* of the temple of Dodona were certainly a species of them. The hour of bathing was made known at Rome by the sound of a bell; the night watchman carried one, and it served to call up the servants in great houses. Sheep had them tied about their necks to frighten away wolve, or rather by way of amulet. In our days, this custom, like many other ethnic ones, serves as a wild stock to graft a devout ceremony upon. Bells are now placed under the protection of St. Anthony and others, blessed and slung round the necks of cattle and sheep, to preserve them from epidemical disorders. Shepherds also think the sound pleases the beast, and makes it eat its meat with more cheerfulness and benefit; at least, this facilitates the finding of those who have strayed from their pasture.

We are told by Lucian, that the priests of the Syrian goddess had bells, which they tinkled by way of awaking the charity of bigots. I have seen many counterparts of these beggars in Italy, hermits and mendicant friars, who warn you with a bell, that they are about to make a demand upon your purse.

who was rather hard of hearing. The performer paid him a compliment upon his taste for harmony, which detained him after the sound of the bells had caused all the rest of the auditory to quit the place. "What (says the "deaf man) has the bell rung? then the fish market is open, and I must "run away too"

Zonaras

Zonaras writes, that criminals going to execution had a bell tied to them, to give notice to all paffengers, that no one might unawares crofs their way, and by the accidental touching of them become unclean. This fuperftition may be the real origin of the cuftom in England of parifh bells ringing while a malefactor is on his way to the gallows; though it is generally fuppofed to be meant as a fignal to all hearers, admonifhing them to pray for the paffing foul. Moft of our religious practices date higher than we are willing to allow; and, at all events, I cannot be blamed for hazarding an opinion, which, by fhewing the cuftom to be of heathenifh extraction, tends in fome degree to relieve many tender confciences, who daily lament, that fo many relicks of popery are fuffered to fubfift in this proteftant country.

According to Suetonius, Auguftus having built, on the edge of the Capitoline hill, a temple to Jupiter the *Thunderer*, where he was remarkably conftant in his devotions, dreamt that the *Capitoline* Jupiter appeared to him, and chid him for debauching all his votaries from him; and that he had anfwered the god by declaring, He had placed the *Thunderer* fo near only by way of porter. In order to make good the affertion, the fuperftitious Emperor fixed bells under the roof of the new temple, within reach of the door. We may infer from hence, that ftrangers rang

for

for admittance at the gates of grandees in those days, just as they do in ours*.

Giordano Bruni, born at Nola in the sixteenth century, made a great noise in the theological world, by means of a small book, mentioned with contempt by the Spectator, who, in his 389th number, gives an account of it. This pamphlet, under the title of *Spaccio della bestia trionfate*, treats all religions equally as human inventions, laughs at miracles and revelations as so many impostures rendered mischievous by the arts of an interested priesthood: it declares the plain law of nature to be the only rule of life worthy to be followed by a being endued with reason; besides many other opinions, which the whole church of Christ holds in utter abhorrence, and unanimously anathematizes. Bruni resided long at the court of Queen Elizabeth, under the protection of several great men; but venturing back to Italy in 1600, was seized by the inquisition, and burnt at Venice.

It is impossible to ascertain who were the first people that settled at Nola, but its coins prove it to have been at

* Bells appear to have derived their Latin appellations of *Nola* and *Campana* from this city and its province, either on account of its mines of copper (if any such there were), the celebrity of its founders, or the expertness of its bell casters. Quintilian is the first author that makes use of the term *Nola*, before him, *Tintinnabulum* was the common name; and in St Jerome's time was the first appearance of the word *Campana*.

The modern Nolans can boast of little skill in the founding art, and, indeed, a good ring of bells is a thing ill thought of in the kingdom. It does not enter the head of a Neapolitan, that any skill can be required in a bell-ringer.

one time inhabited by Greeks.    They differ in nothing but the legend from thofe of ancient Naples *.

Nola feems to have been a city of confequence under the firft Emperors, and to have had a navigable cut that communicated with the Sarno, or the fea.    What makes this idea lefs paradoxical is, that anchors, rings, and other appurtenances of navigation have been dug up near the town.    Vefuvius has overwhelmed fo many more confiderable objects, that it ought not to excite much wonder, if, at this day, all traces are loft of any fuch canal; but, perhaps, thefe fragments of fhipping ought to be afcribed to thofe very remote ages, in which the fea flowed up to the foot of the Apennine, and fpread itfelf over the whole intermediate plain.

This lordfhip was included in the grants made by Charles of Anjou to Guy † de Montfort, the companion of his victories, and one of the fons of our famous Earl of Leicefter.    His only daughter married Raymond Orfino, the firft of that illuftrious Roman family that fettled in

---

* Numm. Nol —1. Caput Dianæ —Minotaurus gradiens victorii fupervolitante ΝΩΛΛΙΩΝ    Arg    L x Cimel    meo.

2 Caput Palladis galeatum cum lauro et noctua —Minotaurus fub Æ.—ΝΩΛΛΙΩΝ—Æi

† This Guy was the man, who, in revenge of his father's death, murdered Henry, fon of the King of the Romans, in the church of Viterbo After a fhort retreat from court, and a mock penance, he was reftored to favour by Charles, whofe character fuffered much in the opinion of all good men for this partiality to an affaffin.    Guy was at laft taken prifoner in a fea-fight by the Aragonefe, and caft into a dungeon, where he died

the

the kingdom of Naples, where his posterity afterwards became Princes of Taranto and Salerno, and still remain Dukes of Gravina. Orso Orsini, Earl of **Nola**, made a great figure in the wars between the Kings of the Aragonian line and their Barons. His branch failed in **1533**; and since that time this honour has remained vested in the crown.

## SECTION XI.

WE joined the road again at a village belonging to the Albertini. It is called Cimitile, by corruption from Cœmeterium, the real name, which it received from a great number of martyrs buried here in the suffering ages of Christianity. Here begins the road through the mountains into Puglia, opened in **1593**, and repaired by the present King of Spain. The late learned Canon Mazzocchi composed elaborate Latin epigraphes in honour of the undertaking, which are placed upon screens or pieces of wall ornamented in a very bad taste.

We now entered a pleasant valley that winds up between hills into the very bosom of the Apennines. These hills advance into the plain like bold promontories, and seem to indicate that, in some remote century, they were washed by the waves of the sea, till the soil at their foot was so raised by the increase of marine subsidences, the workings

P

of

of underground fires, or the accumulation of cinders vomited out of Vesuvius, as at length to confine the waters to the bounds of the present gulf. Cinerated substances compose the interior strata of these eminences; but it is a debateable point, whether they were cast hither in showers by the neighbouring volcano, or thrown up by particular eruptions of their own. The surface is covered with thick woods of chestnut-trees, a plant I have observed to delight in this sort of soil: it grows luxuriantly on Monte Somma, the heights of the Camaldoli near Naples, the Pyrenees near medicinal springs, and, in general, in the neighbourhood of subterraneous fires; not to mention the gigantic trees that for ages have darkened the sides of Etna.

On the skirts of the plain appear the castle and town of Avella, in a delightful situation, commanding a view as far as Naples. They gave name to a family descended from the ancient Dukes of Austria. Rinaldo Avella commanded the army of Charles the Second in Sicily, and gained great honour by his gallant defence of Augusta. In the reign of Joan the First, the heiress of the Avelli married into the house of Baux, or Del Balzo *. By a grant of Ferdinand the First, Avella went to Orso Orsini, then

---

* It passed for being a branch of the Visigothic Balti, a family that boasted of having given a long line of monarchs to the Western Goths, with the formidable name of Alaric at the head of the list. The De Baux accompanied Charles the First from Provence, where they had once possessed an independent sovereignty. From his liberal hand they received ample infeudations

**of**

then paſſed through the Spinelli and Cataneo lines, and now gives the title of Prince to Doria of Genoa.

Not far from hence are the ruins of Abella, a place, as Virgil informs us, celebrated for the quality of its apples :

Et quos malifera deſpectant mœnia Abellæ *.

Some editions read *mellifera*. Either reading is characteriſtical ; for the environs are ſtill as remarkable for the abundance and perfection of their fruit, as for the flavour of their honey. The ancient walls remain in many places, and incloſe a circuit of near three miles. In the middle are the fragments of an amphitheatre, with ſome dens and ſubſtructions.

At a large village, called Cardinale, we came to the head of the valley, and began to climb up a very lofty ridge, the aſcent eaſy, and the road good, overhung with fine woods that ſtretch from the top of the mountain to the bottom, now and then leaving openings for bold rugged cliffs to riſe up in ſhaggy horror along the ſummit These mountains are rendered famous in Neapolitan hiſtory by the adventurous journey of Manfred, who, after making his eſcape from the Pope, wandered over theſe rocky

of the conquered country, but marriage proved a ſource of much greater riches, and enabled them to vie in wealth, rank, and power, with the Sanſeverini, Marſans, and Orſini Their race ended with the Earl of Caſtro in Charles the Fifth's reign

* " And thoſe whom the walls of apple-bearing Abella look down upon."

wilderneſſes,

wildernesses, in order to penetrate into Puglia, where he expected to meet with partisans; and by the still more hazardous passage of René of Anjou, who, in the middle of winter, in the darkest night, travelled through deep snows and pathless forests, to avoid being stopped in his way to Abruzzo, where he was obliged to make his appearance in person, to rouse Anthony Caldora, his most powerful adherent, from a fatal political lethargy. René was the father of Margaret, wife of our Henry the Sixth. He was one of the most amiable of men ; he not only patronized learning in others, but cultivated letters him-self, with no contemptible success for the times he lived in, when ignorance and barbarism still reigned in France, though Petrarch and Boccaccio had already carried Italian literature to a wonderful degree of perfection. René strug-gled long with Alphonsus of Aragon before he gave up the contest ; and, when deprived of every means of sup-porting the war, still kept a large party together by no other tye than the veneration and love with which his affability, courage, and noble spirit, had inspired all that approached his person.

Montforte, a village with a ruinous tower, wildly situ-ated on the point of a rock, commands the pass, and an extensive view into the heart of the Principato Ultra. This insignificant place, from the singular advantages of its position, has more than once stopped whole armies. Charles the First bestowed it on the Montforts, more

on

on account of a fimilarity of name, than the value of the fief.

The defcent on the eaftern fide is fhorter than that into Terra di Lavoro, as the plains of the latter lie much below the level of the valley we were entering. The landfcape before us was extremely beautiful, being embellifhed with great variety of culture, enlivened by the whitenefs of the houfes, and the waters of the Sabato, a clear ftream, that winds its way through woods and orchards; dark folemn mountains overfhadow it on every fide, except where a large opening lets in a view of the diftant hills, and of the paffage to the Adriatic.

The Sabato takes its rife, at no great diftance up the vale, from numberlefs fprings bubbling up through a bed of pebbles, and running together into a pool full of trout. The fcenery round the pond, and down the courfe of this pleafant rivulet, is exceedingly romantic, as the wild beauties of nature melt gradually into the more regular features of art and cultivation.

An avenue, near a mile in length, conducted us to the gates of Avellino. The trees are poplars, remarkable for their height, bulk, and clofenefs of foliage.

SECTION.

## S E C T I O N   XII.

THE prefent city of Avellino moſt probably owes its
foundation to the Lombards.   The firſt of its lords
that I find mentioned in hiſtory is Ranulph, who flou-
riſhed in the twelfth century, was a baron of mighty
power, and brother-in-law to King Roger.   This alliance
did not prevent his heading a party againſt that monarch,
whofe forces he defeated in feveral encounters : had not
death put a ſtop to his progreſs, he would undoubtedly
have ſtripped the King of many rich provinces, and formed
to himfelf an independent ſtate, as the Pope and the Emperor had already granted him inveſtiture of the Dutchy
of Puglia.   Roger dell' Aquila was Earl of Avellino in
1160.   It was granted by Charles the Firſt to Simon de
Montfort ; but he being killed in a duel by Fulk Ruffo,
the honour returned to the crown.

The family of Baux was afterwards poſſeſſed of it.
The Filangeri had it next by a donation from Charles the
Third ; and their heirefs having married Sergianni Caracciolo, the famous favourite of Joan the Second, the eſtate
came into the family of Caracciolo, in which it remains to
this day with the title of Prince   However, it appears to
have been forfeited, as Marino Caracciolo purchaſed it

long

long after. It is not clear whence the Caraccioli came, nor can much confidence be placed in the stories promulgated by some authors, who make them out to be descendants of the ancient Greeks, Romans, or Goths. A learned friend of mine is of opinion, that they came first out of Germany with Frederick or Henry, and these are his reasons: They are never mentioned in any public transaction before the time of the Swabian princes. An ancient chronicle says expressly, that the Emperor Frederick the Second never entrusted the command of his armies or fortresses to any but Germans or Saracens; and in the next page speaks of a *Caracsols* as leader of a division of the Imperial forces. Matthew Spinelli of Giovenazzo, a cotemporary writer, furnishes a still stronger proof, by assuring us, that Peter Pignatelli rendered himself very odious to many families, particularly to the Caraccioli, by advising Charles of Anjou, on the approach of Conradine, to banish all the nobles of German extraction, as being men of doubtful loyalty. The foundation of their grandeur was laid by the unshaken fidelity of John Caracciolo, who, being besieged by rebels in the castle of Ischia, of which he had been appointed governor by the Emperor Frederick, chose rather to perish in the flames that consumed the fortress, than surrender his trust. His master was not insensible to such a proof of attachment, but expressed the warmest sentiments of gratitude for his memory; and conferred such honours and riches on his sons, as raised them

2

to great confequence in the ftate. The family has ever
fince been much confidered by its fovereigns ; and the
branches fent off from the main ftock have become as
wealthy and powerful as itfelf, and are at this day upon a
par with the nobleft and richeft houfes in the kingdom.
Five of thefe branches are proprietors of a very fingular
Bank, called *Il Monte Ciarletto,* which fecures a noble
portion to their daughters, and of late to their younger
fons. The ftory of its foundation is as follows :——Charles
Caracciolo had an only daughter, whom he was determined
to marry to one of his kinfmen, that his rich inheritance
might remain in the family. This match was contrary
to the inclinations of the young lady, who pofitively refufed to acquiefce in it. Her enraged father fhut her up
in a convent, where fhe took the veil by compulfion ; but
foon after, in a fit of defpair, put an end to her exiftence.
Charles, diftracted with remorfe and grief, did not long
furvive the child he had ufed fo cruelly ; and by way of
atonement determined, if poffible, to prevent any Carac-
ciola from becoming a nun, at leaft from a want of fortune : he therefore eftablifhed a fund to accumulate for
them. When any daughter of the family marries, fhe receives the interefts and favings accruing from the bank
fince the laft perfon was endowed. It never has been
more than an hundred thoufand ducats (£18,750). A
change has lately taken place, through the addrefs and
management of a lady married to one of thefe Caraccioli.

The

The marriage portion of the women is limited to 70,000 ducats, and the remainder of the produce is to be appropriated to the education and maintenance of the younger fons. The director of this Bank has a houfe, table, and equipage, provided for him. Several fimilar funds have been eftablifhed by affociated families, in imitation of the bank of the Giraletto.

Avellino is a confiderable city, extending a mile in length down the declivity of a hill, with ugly ftreets, but tolerable houfes. The churches have nothing to recommend them, being crowded with monftrous ornaments in a barbarous ftyle, which the Neapolitans feem to have borrowed from the Spaniards. The cathedral is a poor building, in a wretched fituation, with little to attract the eye, except fome uncouth Latin diftichs, and fhapelefs Gothic fculpture. The good people of this town need not run to Naples to fee the blood of St Januarius; for they have a ftatue of St. Laurence, with a phial of his blood, which for eight days, in Auguft, entertains them with a fimilar miraculous liquefaction. Their only edifice of note is a public granary, of the Compofite order, adorned with antique ftatues, and a very elegant bronze one of Charles the Second, King of Spain, while a boy, caft by Cavalier Cofimo.

The number of inhabitants amounts to eight thoufand, fome fay ten thoufand. The Bifhop's revenue is about fix thoufand ducats ($£1,125$) a year. The magiftracy

Q

confifts

confifts of a Syndic and four Electi, all annual; which offices are engroffed by a certain number of families of fome diftinction, that neither intermarry nor affociate with the reft of the burghers.

The Prince has eftates here to the yearly value of twenty thoufand ducats (£ 3,750), of which two thoufand arife from duties on the dye of cloth, which is made of various qualities and colours, but chiefly blue. The fineft fells for thirty carlini a canna, and pays twenty fix grana duty of entrance into Naples. This tax is a piece of blundering management, but too common in the kingdom; the off-fpring of fhort-fighted rapacity, foftered by government at the expence of all home-trade, and to the difcouragement of every fpecies of induftry. Many wealthy merchants have a concern in this cloth bufinefs, fome with a capital of eighty thoufand ducats (£ 15,000). The poor women, who fpin the wool, muft work very hard to earn above four grana a day.

The fecond article of trade is *maccaroni* and *pafte* of many kinds, which, being of an excellent quality, are in high repute all over the country. Wooden chairs are alfo made and fold here in great quantities

Avellino abounds with provifions of every fort, each ftreet is fupplied with wholefome water; the wine is but indifferent. The foil of this diftrict, which confifts chiefly of volcanic fubftances, produces little corn, but fruit in abundance, of which the apple is defervedly held in great

esteem.

esteem. The most profitable, however, of all its fruit-trees is the hazel. Nut bushes cover the face of the valley, and in good years bring in a profit of sixty thousand ducats (£11,250). I enquired into many particulars concerning the nuts, and believe they are mostly of the large round species of filbert, which we call Spanish. These bushes were originally imported into Italy from Pontus, and known among the Romans by the appellation of *Nux Pontica*, which, in process of time, was changed into that of *Nux Avellana*, from the place where they had been propagated with the greatest success. The proprietors plant them in rows, and by dressing, form them into large bushes of many stems. Every year they refresh the roots with new earth, and prune off the straggling shoots with great attention.

## SECTION XIII.

THE women of this neighbourhood are handsome, and take great pains to deck out their persons to advantage. Once a week they wash their hair with a lye of wood ashes, that changes it from a dark brown colour to a flaxen yellow of many different tints in the same head of hair. This I take to be the true *flava caesaries* of the Latin poets. Experience has taught me to discover many traces of ancient customs in the modes and habits of the modern

Italians.

Italians. Attentive obfervation will make a perfon, to whom the claffic writings are familiar, fenfible of this re-femblance every day he paffes in the fouthern parts of Italy, efpecially if he has opportunities of ftudying the manners of the lower clafs of inhabitants, whofe character has as yet received but a flight tinge from a mixture with foreigners. He will recognize the *Præficæ* of the ancients, in the appearance and actions of old women that are hired in Calabria to howl at burials. The funeral behaviour and meafure of grief in the Calabrefe are regulated by the ftricteft etiquette. The virtues as well as vices of a deceafed father of a family are recapitulated by the oldeft perfon in company. The widow repeats his words, adds comments of her own, then roars out loudly, and plucks off hand-fuls of her hair, which fhe ftrews over the bier. Daughters tear their locks, and beat their breafts, but remain filent. More diftant relations repeat the oration coolly, and com-mit no outrage upon their perfons. When the kinfman of a baron or rich citizen dies, a number of old women are hired to perform all thefe ceremonies for the family.

At Naples, the forms are rather different. I was one day witnefs of the funeral of an old fiherman. The actions of his widow were fo overftrained as to be truly ridiculous: fhe tore off her hair and clothes, and yelled in the moft hideous manner, till her ftep-fons appeared to take pof-feffion of the goods: fhe then turned her fury upon them, and beat them out of the houfe. The priefts now came for

the

the body, and she opposed their entry for a decent length of time ; but at last, suffering herself to be overpowered by numbers, flew to the window with her daughters and her mother (who, from having outlived many relations, had scarce a hair left on her head , and there beat her breast, scratched her cheeks, and threw whole handfuls of hair towards the bier with the frantic gestures of a demoniac. The procession was no sooner out of sight, than all was quiet ; and in five minutes I heard them laughing and dancing about the room, as if rejoicing to be rid of the old churl.

In some parts of the country, it is a rule to fast the whole day of the interment. Two women, in a village near Salerno, mother and daughter of a farmer, at whose removal from the house they had acted their parts with great applause, locked themselves up, and, in order to re-cover strength after the fatigue they had undergone, began, in defiance of custom, to fry some pieces of tripe for their dinner. As ill luck would have it, a couple of relations, who, living at a great distance, had come too late for the ceremony, knocked at the door to pay their respects to the disconsolate widow. Great was the difficulty they found in gaining admittance : all the parade of grief was again displayed, the dinner slipped into a napkin, and hid under the bed, and nothing heard in the room but groans and lamentations. The strangers entered with composed mien, and

and were endeavouring, with little fuccefs, to adminifter comfort to their unhappy kinfwomen, when, behold! a dog they had brought with them winded the fry, and dragged it out into the middle of the floor, to the great fcandal of the vifitors, and the utter confufion of the mourners, whofe reputation was irretrievably ruined in the efteem of the whole parifh.

The verfe in Virgil,

* Hinc altà fub rupe canet frondator ad auras,     ECL 1.

naturally occurs, when, in our walks under the rocky cliffs of Pofilipo, we fee the peafant fwinging from the top of a tree on a rope of twifted willows, trimming the poplar, and the luxuriant tendrils of the vine, and hear him make the whole vale ring with his ruftic ditty

A claffic fcholar cannot ftroll under the groves of the plain, without calling to mind Horace's

† Durus
Vindemitor et invictus, cui fæpe viator
Ceffilet, magnà compellans voce cucullum.     SAT 7.

if he attend to the vine dreffer fitting among the boughs, lafhing raw lads and bafhful maidens, as they return from market, with the fame grofs wit and rough jokes that gave fuch zeft of old to the farces of Atella.

* " The lopper fhall fing to the winds under the lofty rock "
† A rough and invincible vine dreffer, before whom the traveller often retired, calling him with a loud voice Cuckow."

The

The Neapolitan girls dance to the snapping of their fingers and the beat of a tambourine, and whirl their petticoats about them. With greater elegance in the position, and more airiness in the flow of the drapery, striking likenesses of them may be found among the paintings of Herculaneum.

A young fisherman of Naples naturally throws his limbs into most graceful attitudes, and it was, no doubt, from the study of similar figures, that the Grecian statuaries drew their nice ideas of beauty and perfection of forms.

If an antiquary longs for a Roman dish, Sorrento will supply him with the paps of a sow, drest in the antique taste, by the name of Verrina; and I believe Peregrine Pickle's learned friend might, with a little attention, discover sufficient remnants of ancient cookery in the environs of Naples, to make out a tolerable bill of fare.

To this day, the rigging of small vessels on the Neapolitan coast answers the descriptions left us of ancient sailing. I doubt whether it be an easy matter to comprehend the manœuvres of Ulysses or Æneas in their various navigations, without having examined the trim of one of these boats, nay, I believe it scarce possible to enter into the spirit of the classic authors, without a previous visit to Italy or Greece. I am certain at least, that my travels on classic ground have rendered me infinitely more sensible of their beauties, than I ever should have been had I remained at home.

## SECTION XIV.

WE made an excursion, two miles to the right, to
Atripalda, a small town built upon the ruins of
Abellinum Marsicum, as a great number of mutilated basso-
relievos, altars, and inscriptions attest. The inhabitants
are supposed to have retired from it in the middle ages, and
to have founded the present city of Avellino, a situation
more convenient for traffic. Atripalda, which drives on
some trade in paper, cloth, and hardware, stands upon an
eminence composed of strata of a soft-coloured tufo. This
kind of petrifaction has been produced by the cementation
of ashes, earthy particles, and water, thrown out of burning mountains; is generally of a yellow cast, with fissures,
and marked with horizontal wavy streaks. I saw here a
very delicate species of knot-grass, called Finello, which
grows in the woods, is silky, and used in stuffing pack-
saddles and chair-bottoms.

In 1501, when the French and Spaniards divided the
kingdom between them, the former held their courts of
justice for the principality of Benevento at Avellino; and,
upon a dispute arising between the two nations concerning
their claims to the possession of the province, the Spaniards
sent their law-officers to hold an assize at Atripalda. The
French immediately attacked them there, and by this act
of

of hoftility provoked a war that ended in their own expulfion out of the realm.

This town was firft held in fee by the Montforts; it was
afterwards granted by Ferdinand the Firft to George Caf-
triot, known by the name of Scanderbeg, Prince of Epirus,
as a reward for his timely affiftance in 1460, when he
came from Greece with a ftrong force, raifed the fiege of
Barletta, and difcomfited the army of John of Anjou: it
now gives title of Duke to the Prince of Avellino's eldeft
fon.

The road was thronged with mules, pigs, fheep, and
cattle of a large grey breed, going to the fair of Atripalda.
The current price of a good mule is fixty ducats
(11 l. 5 s.); of a pair of bullocks, a hundred ducats
(18 l. 5 s.).

As we returned very early, it was agreed to fpend the
afternoon in a vifit to the Convent of Monte Vergine,
which our guide pointed out to us on a wild mountain,
hanging over Avellino, every now and then hidden from
our fight by white clouds that drove along its fide. The
journey to it was rather fatiguing; but the incomparable view it afforded made us pay little regard to the
trouble of climbing. We unluckily arrived at an undue
hour, which deprived us of the pleafure of converfing
with any of the monks, except an ignorant lay-brother,
who fhewed us the church. Not having had an opportunity of procuring information on the fpot, I fhall give a

R                                    fummary

summary of what I have since learnt concerning this monastery.

In Pagan times, this mountain was sacred to the Mother of the Gods, who had here a sumptuous temple, of which four columns of Portasanta marble * are employed in the present fabric. In the musæum of the convent is preserved a basso-relievo, representing a boy with a cornucopiæ, a serpent twined round a fig-tree, and a tripod, emblems of the worship of Cybele; she was supposed to wander through the woods, in search of medicinal herbs for the cure of disorders incident to little children, and was therefore looked upon as the universal mother; Atys, her high-priest, pronounced oracles, or gave out prescriptions, from a three-legged stool. Tradition says, the mountain took its name from one Virginius, or Virgilius, a great necromancer, who had a garden full of medicinal herbs, with which he composed his magical drugs; there is still a level spot of ground called l'Orto di Virgilio, and the mountain abounds with vulnerary plants.

Long after Christianity had seated itself on the throne of the Cæsars, long after the inhabitants of most cities had conformed to the sovereign's mode of worship, the wild mountainous parts of Italy remained obscured by the clouds of idolatry. The Apennine was full of heathens, and from their residing in pagi, or villages, the name of Pagani came

---

* A species of marble, so named from the Jubilee-door of St. Peter's at Rome, which is composed of it.

to be synonimous to that of Believer in the ancient deities of the empire*. The missionaries sent among them to preach the faith of Christ, found no means of conversion so easy and efficacious as those of admitting some of the names and ceremonies of the old church into the ritual of the new one. By thus adopting many tenets and forms of Paganism, they reconciled their proselytes to the idea of exchanging Jupiter for Jehovah, and their lares and penates for saints and guardian angels. To this expedient of priestcraft must be ascribed many strange devotions and local superstitions, still prevalent in Roman Catholic countries, which ought not to be confounded by the adversaries of that church with its real doctrines. All the truly learned and sensible persons of that communion reject, abhor, and lament such depravation; and, were it possible to reason rude minds out of hereditary prejudices, would long since have abolished them.

It was no doubt in compliance with the above conciliatory method, that in 1119 the mountain was rescued from the patronage of the mother of the false gods, and dedicated to the Mother of Christ, by William of Vercelli. He retired into these solitudes to exercise upon his youthful flesh all manner of holy barbarities, and when zeal and

* From an inscription found at Atripalda, in 1712, we learn that the pagan religion flourished in the Neapolitan provinces after the death of Constantine the Great. It tells us that the senate and people of Abellinum erected a statue to C. J. Latinius, Consular of Campania, Priest of Vesta and Hercules. He was in office during the reigns of Constantine's children

lasting

fafting had well heated his imagination, was favoured with an apparition, that enjoined him to erect a convent on the fpot. In obedience to the command, he founded this abbey, the mother church of a reform of the Benedictine order. The monks are dreft in white, and had once fpread themfelves over feveral countries; but are at prefent confined to one houfe in the Roman ftate, and twenty-feven in the kingdom of Naples. Frederic of Swabia was very partial to the Verginians, and inftituted a confraternity of knights aggregated to their fociety. Charles of Valois introduced the order into France; but all traces of it have long been loft there; and we fhall probably foon hear of its abolition in Naples, fuch a project having been in contemplation.

In 1124, William finifhed his monaftery, which was foon enriched with relics fit to attract the notice of pious believers; but it loft a moft capital jewel of its treafure in 1467, when Ferdinand the Firft, under pretence of oppofing it to the fury of the plague, obtained leave to tranfport the body of St. Januarius to Naples. The roguifh Neapolitans, having once got poffeffion, refufed to return it to the right owners, who are obliged to comfort themfelves under this misfortune with the coloffal portrait of the Virgin Mary. It was formerly venerated in Antioch, and prefented to this fanctuary by Catherine, wife of Philip of Anjou, titular emperor of Conftantinople. The head of this picture is very old, but the buft was added by Montano d'Arezzo,

a celea celebrated artiſt, to whom Philip gave land near Nola, as a recompence. This image is of gigantic or heroic proportion, and paſſes for the work of St Luke the Evangeliſt, though the very ſize is an argument againſt its being a portrait from the life, had we even the ſlighteſt reaſon to believe that he had ever handled the pencil. There are in Italy and elſewhere ſome dozens of black, ugly Madonnas, which all paſs for the work of his hands, and as ſuch are revered *.

The concourſe of votaries is prodigious on the eighth of September, the feaſt of the nativity of the Patroneſs. The rule of the Order allows neither freſh nor ſalt meat, eggs, milk, butter, nor cheeſe; and ſurely nobody will venture to bring up any of theſe prohibited viands, if he be acquainted with an inſcription in the court, relating the cataſtrophe of four hundred pilgrims, burnt in their beds in 1611, becauſe one of them had brought up a luncheon of cheeſe in

* The origin of this fable, or rather miſtake, appears to be, that, about the time that paintings of holy ſubjects came into faſhion, there lived at Conſtantinople a painter called Luke, who, by many repreſentations of the Virgin, acquired a very tranſcendent reputation. He was a man of exemplary life, and on account of his piety, and the edifying uſe he made of his talents, was generally known by the name of Holy Luke. In proceſs of time, when the epocha and circumſtances of his life were forgotten by the vulgar, and his performances had acquired by age a ſmoky, duſky caſt, ſufficient to perplex the ſhort ſighted connoiſſeurs of thoſe days, devotees aſcribed his pictures to the Evangeliſt, who was pronounced a painter, becauſe they knew of no other ſaint of the name, and becauſe, if he had been a painter, no one could have had ſuch opportunities of examining and delineating the features of the holy model.

his

his pocket. Our guide hinted to us, that if any one were to eat meat here, or even have a little greafe about his perfon, it would caufe a moft tremendous hurricane, and overwhelm the whole mountain with a deluge of rain. Charles, King of Hungary, Prince of Salerno, fon of Charles the Second, granted to thefe fathers a patent, by which he forbade all falt fifh to be expofed to fale in the fair of Salerno, till the agents of Monte Vergine had made their provifion; a privilege they enjoy to this day.

The moft ancient monument in the church is a large farcophagus, which was made to contain the afhes of Minius Proculus: King Manfred intended it fhould be the repofitory of his own, and placed it in a chapel he had founded in this religious houfe; but his bones are left to blanch in the fields unknown, while the urn remains without a tenant. John di Lioneffa, marfhal of the Angevine army, obtained a grant of the chapel, which became the fepulture of his family. Here alfo lie the bodies of the Emprefs Catherine, Mary her daughter, and Lewis her fon, married to Queen Joan the Firft.

On the fecond of Auguft, 1629, the nave of the church was thrown in by an earthquake, and moft of the monuments beaten to duft. The Verginians rebuilt it in nine years, and over an arch of the court placed a pompous infcription, which contains an epitome of their hiftory, and may ferve as an epitaph to their expiring Order.

## SECTION XV.

THE traces of fire are still very strong for several miles beyond Avellino, though here and there the burnt matter is intermingled with blocks of breccia, or coarse pudding-stone, which is a conglutination of pebbles. Perhaps, even these have undergone the trial of fire, as it is not uncommon for volcanos to cast up small stones in their natural state, with a quantity of water full of gross vitious particles, all which together may consolidate into masses of breccia. This sort of soil extends as far as La Scala, a straggling hamlet pleasantly situated near Monte Fuscolo.

Benevento being in the possession of the Roman see, the residence of the president and civil officers belonging to the Principato Ultra is fixed at Monte Fuscolo, as being the most central place among the demenial towns. Its prisons are noted for being constantly full of malefactors, which gives but a poor idea of the moral character of the neighbouring inhabitants. They are indeed in very bad repute for robbery and assassination, but a considerable portion of the delinquents are confined for smuggling, to which the vicinity of the papal territories is a great encouragement. The situation of Monte Fuscolo is exceedingly bleak, and the prospect grand over an immense tract of

mountainous

mountainous country.   Charles of Anjou gave it to Henry
de Vaudemont, of the houfe of Lorraine.   It has long been
reunited to the crown.

The hills are fteep, but the road broad and well made.
Upon a rifing ground, near the inn of Mirabella, it paffes
through the ruins of Eclanum, an ancient city, now
called by the peafants La Colonia*.   In the early ages of
Chriftianity, here was a bifhop's fee, fince removed to
Frigento, and from thence to Avellino.   Julian, chief of
the Semipelagian heretics, was one of its prelates.   It is
not known by whom, and at what period, this city was
deftroyed ; at prefent, the only remains are fome mounds,
brick walls, fragments of marble columns and entablements
of the Doric and Corinthian orders.   A little folitary farm-
houfe has been added to an antique brick front, ornamented with brick pilafters, that have capitals with one
row of leaves.   As it ftands at a diftance from the other
ruins, and much refembles fome monuments near Rome, I
take it to be a maufoleum.   We purchafed here a few
cornelians and medals of the lower empire, dug up by the
hufbandmen.

In the afternoon, we rode fix miles fouth to Frigento,
by a deep valley, where our horfes were almoft up to the

* From Benevento the Appian way paffed through Eclanum (where the
Via Trajana branched off to the left), and from thence through Frigento,
Venufia, and Tarentum, to Brundufium

girths

girths in clay, though the weather had been long dry. The country for the moſt part arable, and poorly cultivated  Frigento is a ruinous place on a hill, moſt wretchedly built, and ſcantily provided with the neceſſaries of life. Its inhabitants, in number two thouſand, ſubſiſt by the ſale of ſheep, hogs, and corn. In the whole town there was not a tolerable inn, where we could venture to paſs the night; and ſhould have fared very ill, if we had not accidentally met with an old prieſt, who carried us to his houſe in the neighbourhood, where he gave us board and lodging, and entertained us after ſupper with a relation of his own adventures.

He was born in this province, and educated at Rome. He there attached himſelf to a prelate likely to riſe in the church, and accompanied this clergyman to ſeveral courts in quality of ſecretary to the nunciature ; but, on his return to Italy, was ſupplanted by the artifices of a colleague, turned out of doors, and reduced for a maintenance to copy writings in a public office. His enemies, not ſatisfied with having ruined his fortunes, cauſed him to be ſuſpected of being the author of a libel againſt a cardinal ; for which offence he was ſhut up in the caſtle of St. Angelo, and, after ſix months confinement, baniſhed the Roman ſtate. At Naples he entered into a nobleman's family as ſecretary, and unfortunately becoming the confidant of the eldeſt ſon, a mean profligate youth, was engaged in a nocturnal riot, where he ſaved his patron's life at the expence of two dangerous wounds. The un-

S

gratuful

grateful nobleman took no further notice of him, but left him to languish for many months in a hospital. As soon as he was cured, he set out on foot, penniless and in rags, for the place of his nativity; where, after many years humble attendance on an old relation, he inherited an estate, and obtained a benefice, sufficient to supply him with all the necessaries and comforts of life that so retired a part of the world admits of. This good old philosopher, who saw but little of the people of the neighbourhood, was delighted to spend an evening with company that could converse of Paris, Rome, and other places which he had seen in his juvenile days, a pleasure he seldom tasted; but he could not help expressing, with a sigh, his apprehensions that our visit would cost him a few bitter reflections, as it revived sensations that had been long lulled to rest in the bottom of his soul.

Next morning he accompanied us four miles to the Moffetta, supposed to be the same as the Amsancti Valles, through which Virgil makes the fury Alecto descend to hell. His dark hanging wood, rumbling noise, and curling vortex, agree perfectly well with the present appearances *.

We were led into a narrow valley, extending a considerable way to the south-west, and prest in on both sides by high ridges thickly covered with copses of oak. The

bottom

* Est locus Italiæ medio sub montibus altis
  Amsancti valles   densis hunc frondibus atrum
  Urget utrimque latus nemoris, medioque fragosus
  Dat sonitum saxis et torto vortice torrens        ÆNEID. lib 7.

  " There

bottom of the dell is bare and arid: in the lowest part, and close under one of the hills, is an oval pond of muddy ash-coloured water, not above fifty feet in diameter: it boils up in several places with great force in irregular fits, which are always preceded by a hissing sound. The water was several times spouted up as high as our heads in a diagonal direction, a whirlpool being formed round the tube, like a bason, to receive it as it fell. A large body of vapour is continually thrown out with a loud rumbling noise. The stones on the rising ground that hangs over the pool are quite yellow, being stained with the fumes

"There is a place in the centre of Italy under lofty mountains, called the
"Valley of Amsanctus  On each side a bank of wood, black with thick
"foliage, presses upon it, and in the middle a thundering torrent whirls
"about the stones, and curls up its waves"

The Abbe Chaupy, author of an ingenious eccentrical dissertation on Horace's country-house, is of opinion, that Virgil meant the sulphureous ponds of Cutiliæ near Rieti, because they are more truly in the center of Italy, and surrounded by higher mountains, and because, when Alecto blows her horn to call the shepherds to arms, he says, it shook the river Nar, and the sources of the Velinus, both which are in the neighbourhood of Cutiliæ, nevertheless, as Chaupy exhibits no proof that Cutiliæ ever bore the name of Amsanctus, and as the mountains of the Principato are certainly lofty enough to justify the expression of " sub montibus altis," I rather incline to leave the Hirpini in quiet possession of this passage into the infernal regions

Venuti, in Monaldini's folio edition of Virgil, gives a dissertation and print to prove, that the fury went down in a hole at Monte Catino, though he acknowledges there is no pestilential vapour, nor much wood, in that place  The boundaries of Italy have so often varied, that the middle of it cannot be fixed in any precise spot, and I see no reason why a place, equidistant from both seas, may not be said to be in the middle of the country.

of

of fulphur and fal ammoniac.     A moft naufeous fmell
rifing with the fteam obliged us to watch the wind, and
keep clear of it, to avoid fuffocation.     The water is quite
infipid both as to tafte and fmell ; the clay at the edges is
white, and carried into Puglia to rub upon fcabby fheep,
on which account the lake is farmed out at one hundred
ducats a year.

On a hill above this lake ftood formerly a temple dedicated to the Goddefs Mephitis; but I perceived no remains of it.

Having taken leave of our kind conductor, we returned to the great road, and travelled eight miles farther
to Ariano, over very high naked hills, not unlike thofe of
Upper Andalufia.     Near Grotta Minarda, the Roman
road, which Horace followed, ftrikes off to the right
hand to Trevico *, a baronial town on an eminence,
which recommended itfelf to our notice, by holding a
place in that poet's journal ; for, fince that of the journey
from Rome to Reggio, faid to have been written by the
fatirift Lucilius, has not reached us, we may confider
Horace's fifth fatire as the prototype of all tours and
travels ; and therefore every ftage of it is an object of
curiofity and veneration.

* Trevico is a marquifate of the Loffredi, a family of Lombard or Norman origin   Of this houfe was Francis, who harangued Charles of Anjou
on his triumphal entry into Naples, and was employed by that prince in
many embaffies and negociations

## SECTION XVI.

ARIANO is an ugly city, built upon the uneven summit of a mountain, with an extensive look out on all sides, but exposed to every blast that blows. We found the season very backward here, when compared with the spring we had left in the Terra di Lavoro It does not appear to be so old as the time of the Romans, therefore may be supposed to owe its rise to the demolition of some neighbouring town, and to the advantages its situation afforded for discovery and defence *.

The first Earl of Ariano I find recorded in history, was Roger, a person, no doubt, of Norman extraction : he rebelled against King Roger, was taken, stripped of his possessions, and sent prisoner to Sicily. Charles the First gave it to Henry de Vaudemont ; the Sabrans were afterwards its lords ; and then the Caraffas, the Gonzagas, and, under Alphonsus the First, the Guevaras. In 1466 it became part of the demesne of the Crown.

It is but a poor place, without trade or manufactures, having declined ever since the desolation caused by an earthquake in 1456. It reckons about fourteen thousand inhabitants, and no less than twenty parishes and convents, besides an ill-endowed cathedral.

* Cluver places Æquotuticæ here, without proof or probability.

The

The wine of Ariano is pale, like red champagne, which it also resembles in a certain tartness, exceedingly refreshing in hot weather.

The soil here lies upon a soft argillaceous stone. At a small distance to the east, is a bank consisting of layers of volcanical earths, interspersed with thick strata of oyster-shells. The partizans of a watry system will account for these ostracites by the subsiding and gradual depositions of the sea. Theologists will seize upon them as proofs and memorials of a general deluge. Others again, inclining to attribute more to the agency of fire, will insist upon these shells having been pumped out of the sea by the force of an eruption, in some very distant age, when the salt waters came much nearer the heart of Italy than they do at present. It is the opinion of many learned observers of the operations and progress of Nature, that most parts of Italy owe their origin to fire, and that at first, only the chain of calcareous mountains called the Apennine, towered above the level of the waters, which then covered all the lowlands. Others carry it still farther, and assert, that nothing south of the Alps existed ab origine above the surface of the waves, but that the first eruptions began between the gulphs of S. Eufemia and Squillace, from whence they spread gradually, till they had completed the production of all Italy According to them, after the first dry point was fixed, hills rose upon hills, volcanoes shot up in clusters, and formed an invincible barrier, which for ever shut out all return of

2                                                    the

the fea. Man defcended from the Alps to cultivate the new exuberant foil; and the mountains being now far removed from the warm fteams of the wateis, to which they were indebted for their fertility, were abandoned to the wild beafts of the foreft. The very name of Italy is by fome faid to imply a fiery origin, or an elevation above the ocean.

One paradoxical writer affirms, that the coins of Magna Græcia allude to thefe revolutions. In the bull of Sybaris he fees a fmoking mountain, or a river choaked up by an eruption. The Hercules of Heraclea fignifies a volcano; his arrows lightning: the aquatic plant, the ftagnated watry ftate of the country before the efforts of fire divided and dried it; the fhell reprefents the crater; the upright vafe, a lake; the failing jug, an overturned country; and a veffel with the bottom upwards, the draining of it.

We procured a lodging at the Dominican convent below the town. Within thefe laft hundred years, their houfe has been thrice rebuilt, having been as often thrown to the ground by earthquakes. The laft and moft deftructive happened in 173², fatal to all the country that lies along the eaftern verge of the Apennine. In order to fecure a retreat, in cafe of future accidents, which from their fituation they have every reafon to expect, thefe fathers have conftructed a fmall building of wood, the parts of which being joined together with ftrong iron chains, are contrived fo as to have a proper play, and by yielding to the ofcilla-
tory

tory motion of the earth, return eafily to their equili-
brium.

It is remarkable that Abruzzo, Puglia, and Calabria are
repeatedly laid wafte by earthquakes, while the fhores of
Tara di Lavoro, though expofed to the fury of Vefuvius,
are feldom damaged by fimilar concuffions. The iffue that
is given by that mountain to the fubterraneous fires and
vapours, no doubt preferves the neighbourhood from all
violent fhocks, and the want of fuch a vent-hole on the
eaftern coaft, is the probable caufe of the convulfions that
fo often overturn its cities. A paffage in Strabo corrobo-
rates this opinion, by informing us that in his time Campania was fubject to frequent and deftructive earthquakes,
and we know that, fixteen years before the firft recorded
explofion of Vefuvius, Pompeii, Stabia, and many neighbouring towns, were thrown down, and only in part rebuilt,
when the great cataftrophe of 79 buried them in lava and
afhes. From the fcanty chronicles of the lower ages,
during which few eruptions are mentioned, we may gather
that Naples and its diftrict were continually torn to pieces
by earthquakes; except in the firft efforts of an eruption,
they are now feldom felt there, fince the mountain has
enjoyed free and conftant exhalation. Buffon thinks the
vicinity of the fea fo effential to the operations of a volcano,
that without the convenience of water, a fufficient effervef-
cence cannot be obtained in its bowels, and all its efforts to
burft the earth, in order to give paffage to the fiery con-

tents,

tents, become of courfe feeble and ineffectual. According to this hypothefis, the retreat of the fea from the Apennine diminifhed by degrees the force of the volcanoes which once abounded in that chain of mountains; but, by their impotent ftruggles, they ftill are able to fhake the foundations of the whole country, and extend their ravages to a much greater diftance than Vefuvius ever does in the moft terrible paroxyfms of its rage.

From Ariano we defcended very rapidly towards the Adriatic, having hitherto been continually mounting from the level of the Mediterranean fea; and being affured that many robbers were lurking in the forefts, we took an efcort of cavalry, not to appear obftinate and foolhardy, though we gave very little credit to the report. Thefe detachments of troopers are ftationed by order of government at proper diftances, to take travellers and merchants under their fafe-guard.

After paffing over a very high champaign country, the road falls into a deep valley of confiderable length; at the end of which the Puglian plains and the Adriatic fea appear like horizontal ftripes of different fhades.

Two fmall towns, Savignano and Gicci, ftand loftily on each fide of the defile. The latter is a colony of about one thoufand four hundred Albanefe, who ftill fpeak a mixed jargon between Italian and the Epirote language. Till 1731 they followed the Greek rite; but then, by royal mandate, exchanged it for the Latin liturgy.

Our

Our ride now became more agreeable, as we travelled down the pleafant banks of the Cervaro. Handfome woods clothe the mountains on each fide from the fummit to the water edge. Our fmell was refrefhed by the fragrance rifing from thickets of flowering fhrubs ; and our fight delighted with the gay bloom of the arbor fuda, which grows abundantly in this wildernefs. There is but little timber of any value, moft of the oaks having been lopped for fuel. The inn at the bridge of Bovino is placed in a cheerful fituation ; but from the lownefs of its pofition, and the proximity of the woods and water, in the fummer feafon is fubject to malignant fevers.

The city of Bovino ftands very high on the fouth fide of the river. This is a dutchy belonging to the Guevaras, one of the Spanifh families that followed the fortunes of Alphonfus the Magnanimous *.

We continued our journey on the north fide of the river, through an immenfe woody plain covered with low ftunted oaks and very coarfe benty grafs. On the edge of this foreft the King has a hunting feat, to which the public is indebted for the noble road his father made from Naples hither. It is a pity the prefent fovereign does not honour Bovino now and then with a vifit, as repairs begin to be very neceffary for the roads. Their covering is quite worn

---

* There are ftill three other Aragonian houfes in Naples, viz. Cavaniglia, Cardines, and Avalos, which, with Guevara, walk in folemn proceffion through Naples, on the octave day of Corpus Domini, and vifit four altars magnificently decked out at their joint expence.

out,

out, and cut through to the very foundations. Their deftruction is haftened by the wafte waters of the fountains erected by King Charles. The conduits are broken or choaked up, and the water runs down the highway, where it forms quickfands and dangerous floughs.

We croffed an ancient Roman road, ftill difcernible among the bufhes *.

A few miles to the left, is Troja, built on an eminence out of the ruins of Æcas, a city deftroyed by Conftans the Second. Bagianus, Catapan or Viceroy of the province, is faid to have founded Troja in the eleventh century, by order of the emperors Bafil and Conftantine, to ferve as a bulwark againft the inroads of the Norman adventurers, and to have given it that name in commemoration of the famous city which by its fall has immortalized the heroes of Greece. It was long accounted a key to the Apennines, and as fuch was expofed to many affaults and fieges. The very year of its foundation it was ftormed by the Germans, and King Roger alfo took it very foon after. Scarce a rebellion happened under the Normans, but this place was a principal fufferer. It is memorable for the overthrow of John of Anjou by Ferdinand the Firft. Under Robert and Joan the

* It was the Æquotutican, which came through Trajan's arch at Benevento, where it branched off from the Via Appia, paffed by the Ponte Valentino, under Ferum Novum now La Pidula, by Æquuftunicus now Buen Albergo, Æcas now Troja, and croffing the prefent road from Foggia, ran to Herdonia now Ordona, and at Canofa joined the way that came from Grotta Minarda and Afcoli.

Firft,

Fiift, I find Troja was a fief of the Capuas; in the reign of Charles the Third, Perotto of Ivrea had it; Cavanilla poffeffed it after the acceffion of the line of Aragon; and now it is in the houfe of Avalos.

## S E C T I O N   XVII.

WE foon after left the woods, climbed up the laft ridge, and then, through a wafte covered with wild pear-trees, defcended into the extenfive plains of Puglia, which afford a profpect curious from its novelty, but difagreeable after the furvey of a few minutes.

In the centre ftands Foggia, without walls, citadel, or gates, though a principal town of the province of Capitanata. It is neatly built of white ftone, and has two or three good ftreets. The cuftom-houfe is a handfome edifice.

This town, with many others on the coaft, was ruined in 1732 by an earthquake, which has occafioned its being rebuilt with greater neatnefs and regularity. In fummer the air is unwholefome, and all perfons, that can afford to remove, defert it during the hot months. In winter it is computed to contain about twenty thoufand inhabitants, including ftrangers. All the large ftreets and open fquares are undermined with vaults, where corn is buried, and pre-ferved found from year to year. The orifices are clofed

up

up with boards and earth ; the fides within faced with ftone *.

I find little mention made of this place before the coming in of the Swabians. Frederick built a fortrefs here, to overawe the Puglians, and took great delight in this refidence. His fixth wife, Ifabella, daughter of John, King of England, died here in 1241. Here, according to moft Liftorians, was murdered, by order of his brother Conrad, Henry, fon of Frederick and Ifabella, to whom that emperor had bequeathed the kingdom of Jerufalem, with large poffeffions in Europe, reannexed in 1253, by this abominable fratricide, to the crown of Sicily. In 1254, Foggia was facked by the foldiers of the regent Manfred, and hither fled the Pope's legate and army before the victorious troops of that prince. The papal general demolifhed the imperial palace, and employed the materials to ftrengthen his entrenchments, but was neverthelefs foon obliged to capitulate. In 1268, the Angevines pillaged this town, with every circumftance of cruelty and licentioufnefs. Here Philip, the fecond fon of Charles the Firft, was married with great folemnity to the Princefs of Morea, and here alfo he foon after died. A general of the King of Hungary abandoned it in 1350 to his foldiers, who found in it immenfe booty, as Foggia was at that time the moft opulent place in Puglia. Its confequence, both in ancient and modern times, has been, and ftill is, owing to its being a

* From thefe holes, or *foffe*, comes the word Foggia.

ftaple

ftaple for corn and wool, and to a tax or regifter office, known by the name of the *Tribunale della dogana della mena delle pecore di Puglia*; i. e. " The cuftom-houfe for the toll of the fheep that pafs to and from Puglia." It is managed by a governor, auditor, and two advocates, and has the diftribution of a fixed affeffment upon all fheep that defcend in autumn from the mountains of Abruzzo, into the warm plains of Puglia, where they yean, and in May return to the high country.

We have the authority of Varro and others for afcribing the invention of this duty to the ancient Romans; who, on fubduing the Italian ftates, were wont to allot the improved lands to colonies of their own citizens, while they left the original poffeffors the ufe of the waftes and lefs cultivated tracts, under the obligation of paying a tenth of the produce of the corn-lands, and a fifth of all other fruits. Breeders of cattle and fheep were to compound with the cenfors, who every year hung out a table of the conditions on which they propofed to leafe out the public paftures. A lift of the fheep intended to be fent to graze thereon was given in, and a proper allotment of land affigned, according to their number and the goodnefs of the pafturage: this was called Scriptuarius Ager. In later times, the Emperors appropriated all fuch common lands to themfelves, and caufed them to be confidered as their peculiar royalties. Varro fays, fheep were driven out of Apulia into Samnium before fummer, and on their paffage were obliged to be declared

(profiteri)

(profiteri) to the publican. We gather from Odofredus of Beneventum, a writer of the thirteenth century, that this duty was not loft in that age; but in the two following ones the paffage feems to have become quite free, and the paftures of Puglia open without fee to all fhepherds that chofe to bring down their flocks.

Alphonfus the Firft, forefeeing an immenfe acceffion to the royal revenue from the proper management of fuch cuftoms, but at the fame time being defirous of avoiding every fhadow of coercive legiflation and tyranny in the re-eftablifhment of them, deputed Francis de Montubler to treat with the graziers and fheep-mafters of Abruzzo, and the land-owners of Puglia. This intelligent minifter dif-pofed the minds of thofe he had to deal with fo favourably, that he brought them to terms of great advantage to the crown, and prefent profit to themfelves. The King en-gaged to fupply the breeders with a new fine race of fheep imported from Spain*; to provide winter pafturage for feven months, and a convenient road, called the Tratturo, fixty paces wide, for the paffing and repaffing of the flocks; freedom from all royal tolls, and other dues;

---

* It is affirmed by the annotator on Deliciæ Tarentinæ, that they were propagated from fome fheep fent as a prefent by Edward of England to a John of Aragon. Rapin fays, Edward the Fourth was blamed by the nation for giving away fheep, and thereby improving the Spanifh wool, to the detriment of the Englifh fale, but Edward the Fourth reigned after the death of Alphonfus, and therefore it is likely Edward the Third was the donor, as he was a cotemporary and in league with John the Firft of Aragon.

L                                                                              guards

guards and protection from all assaults and disturbances, and materials for their huts and folds at reasonable prices, and on credit. He bound himself to compel all barons and bodies corporate, on the route, to furnish herbage for the sheep during twenty-four hours, and to compound moderately for all demands at bars and bridges.

The Crown not being possessed of a sufficient range of pasture for the great flocks expected down from Abruzzo, Montubler purchased of the Puglian proprietors as much more as was deemed adequate to the purpose. The purchase, or rather perpetual lease, was only made for seven months in the year, during which time no other sheep or cattle are allowed to feed in the plains; and in case of failure of herbage, the Crown reserved a power of compelling all subjects to let a lease of such grass lands as might be wanted to make up the deficiency, and to abide by the evaluation of its officers. The ancient owners still continue absolute masters of the soil, and may dispose of the summer herbage as they think proper, and at all times turn swine into the woodlands. For all these leased grounds, the King agreed to pay for ever thirteen thousand nine hundred and twelve ducats a year, to stand all risks and losses, and to defray all expences attending the collection, which are computed at about fourteen thousand four hundred and thirty-four ducats more. These royal pastures are bounded by stones, and known by the name of *Tavoliere*. They extend sixty miles in length, and thirty in breadth, divided into twenty-three old lots, and twenty new ones, capable in all of feeding one million two hundred thousand sheep.

In return for all these attentions on the part of the King, the shepherds of Abruzzo bound themselves for ever, to descend from the mountains every year, to submit to the jurisdiction, parcelling powers, and penalties pronounced by the Dogana, and to pay, for every five score of sheep, the sum of eight Venetian crowns, equal to eight Neapolitan ducats and four taris. The Crown has since, by a stretch of prerogative, raised the duty twice: once, in 1556, to twelve crowns; and a second time, in 1709, to thirteen ducats and twenty grana. The allotment for each flock was to be declared in November, and no agreement to be for a longer term than one season. The shepherds were to provide themselves with every necessary, and not to have a power of selling any wool, lambs, cheese, or other commodity produced during their winter residence, in any fair but that of Foggia, where they were to be deposited in the royal magazines, and not touched without a permit. By way of compensation, no wools in the kingdom were to be suffered to be brought to market, till those at Foggia were vended, the duties paid, and the tribunal satisfied for all its demands.

This Dogana is one of the richest mines of wealth belonging to the crown of Naples, and with proper economy is capable of a great annual increase, provided no epidemi-

U

cal

cal diftemper attack the flocks. Its advantages were fo
well known in 1500, when Lewis and Ferdinand made a
partition of the kingdom, that it was agreed to halve the
profits between them ; and when the French attempted to
evade this contract, by ftopping the fheep and cattle at
San Severo, before they reached the ufual place of en-
regiftering, the Spaniards thought themfelves juftifiable in
attacking the French tax-gatherers, and difperfing both
collectors and flocks. Soon after its inftitution, the Dogana cleared feventy-two thoufand ducats. In 1536, one
million forty-eight thoufand three hundred and ninety-fix
fheep, and fourteen thoufand four hundred cattle, produced feventy-two thoufand two hundred and fourteen
ducats. In 1680, the profits were one hundred fifty-
five thoufand eight hundred and fixty-three. In 1700,
they amounted to two hundred feventy-two thoufand
and feventy-feven. In 1730, the tax produced two hundred thirty-five thoufand and feventy-two. At prefent,
the net profit arifing to the King from the letting of the
paftures is about forty thoufand ducats ; but, with the
duties upon wool, tallow, &c. amounts to four hundred
thoufand. The produce did not exceed two hundred and
eighty-one thoufand before the late Governor, the Marquis
Granito, was fent thither ; and all the increafe is owing to
his talents in financiering. Competent judges have affured
me, it would be no difficult matter to raife it to half a
million of ducats.

The

The commodities of Foggia are corn, cheefe, and wool. The wool is bought up by the French and other foreigners; and therefore but a fmall advantage accrues to the province in comparifon with what it might reap, were the materials employed at home. With judicious management, this country might carry on a very extenfive trade, and attain the profperity intended for it by the a'l-bounteous views of Providence, whofe partiality has been counteracted, as much as poffible, by the blunders and tyranny of man.

In the famine of 1764, inftead of encouraging the farmers of Puglia to throw a feafonable fupply of corn into Naples, by the offer of a good price and fpeedy payment, the miniftry fent foldiers into the province to take it l force, and drive the owners before them, like beaft burden, laden with their own property. Such as were willing to part with it by compulfion, and upon fuch hard terms, carried their corn up into the hills and buried it. I any were detected in thefe practices, they were hanged.

On account of the great variety of field fports to which the adjacent hills and plains are peculiarly adapted, this town was a favourite habitation of the German princes; but ftill more fo of their enemy Charles the Firft, who erected here a fumptuous palace, with gardens and orchards, in which he was fo curious, as to keep a lift of all the fruit-trees planted in them. Here he died on the feventh of January, 1285, as he was on his way to Brindifi, to haften an armament againft Sicily. Charles was long accounted,

with

with reafon, the moft fortunate of men; but the laft years
of his life were darkened with fuch a cloud of difafters, as
rank him among the moft miferable.    They broke his
proud heart, and caufed him to exclaim, in the bitternefs of
his foul, " O God! thou who haft carried me up to the
" pinnacle of glory and profperity, withdraw not thy hand!
" or if I am to be precipitated, let not my fall be fo rapid
" and headlong, but humble me by degrees!"—A fever
put an end to his anguifh, but not without fome fufpicions
of his having haftened his death by laying violent hands
upon himfelf.    This fovereign was endowed with great
qualities, overbalanced by moft crying vices.    In his perfon
he was tall and robuft; a dark complexion, and prominent
nofe, gave his countenance an air of ferocious majefty.
Undaunted courage, profound knowledge of the military
art, inviolable attachment to his word, unbounded generofity, watchfulnefs and patience under fatigue, form the
outlines of his portrait on the fair fide, and juftify the title
given him by his rival Don Pedro, King of Aragon, of the
*Mejor cabaʻlero del mundo.*    But if we turn the canvas, we
fhall behold a man four and gloomy in his difpofition, un-
bridled in his paffions, unjuft in his purfuits, devoured by
ambition, rapacious in the acquifition of wealth, vindictive,
bloody, and fteeled againft every fentiment of humanity:
in one word, a great bad prince, mean enough to treat
with indignity the mangled remains of the gallant Manfred,
and juridically to murder the innocent Conradine, whofe

tender

tender years and amiable faculties would have excited pity in almoſt any other breaſt

We were for ſome time at a loſs for lodgings, as all the inns, which are but ſorry places of accommodation, were occupied by people drawn hither by the approaching Fair. On this occaſion Foggia becomes a place of great reſort and gaiety, even for the Neapolitan nobility. They come hither to exerciſe their dexterity at play upon the purſes of the leſs expert country gentlemen, whom they commonly ſend home ſtripped of the ſavings of a whole year. This paſſion for gaming rages with wonderful violence over all the kingdom, and is a plague that never dies, though it may intermit, nor is there any lazaretto to check its progreſs.

## SECTION XVIII.

OUR next ſtage was to Manfredonia, twenty miles through a flat paſture covered with aſphodels, thiſtles, wild artichokes, and fennel giant; of the laſt are made bee-hives and chair-bottoms; the leaves are given to aſſes, by way of a ſtrengthener, and the tender buds are boiled and eaten as a delicacy by the peaſants. This plant covers half the plain, and riſes to ſuch a height, that there is an inſtance, in one of the wars between France and Spain, of the Spaniards having marched through it undiſcovered cloſe

up

up to the French entrenchments. The artichokes are given
to buffaloes.

A few miles from Foggia are some faint traces of walls
said to be those of Arpi or Argyripæ, once the capital
of a kingdom founded by Diomed after the siege of Troy.
The story of this hero was universally admitted by the
ancients, and adopted by Virgil:

> Ille urbem Argyripam, patriæ cognomine gentis,
> Victor Gargani condebat Japygis arvis *.      ÆNEID. lib. 11.

The coins † of this city, which are of Greek type, are not
very rare : they usually bear the impression of a wild boar,
perhaps an allusion to that of Calydon, the place their
founder came from.

On the left lies Aprocina ‡, a poor ruinous hamlet, that
owes its origin to a frolic of the Emperor Frederick.
He was passionately fond of the chace, and happened one
day to kill a wild boar of extraordinary magnitude upon this
very spot. He had it immediately cut up and dressed, and

---

* " Being victorious, he built, in the fields of the Japygian Garganus, a
" city, and called it Argyripa, from the name of his native country."

† Nummi Arpanorum
AUR. 1. Caput Cereris spica ΑΡΠΑΝΩΝ = Equus stella et luna, ΔΑΓΟΥ.
ARG. 1 Cap galeat = Ires spicæ ΑΡΠΑ
     2 Cap Cereris diota = Equus galea stella ΔΑΓΟΥ
ÆR. 1 Cap. Jovis. fulmen Δ ΛΕΟΥ = Aper currens. hasta ΑΡΠΑΝΩΝ.
     2 Equus ΑΡΠΑΝΟΥ = Iaurus ΠΟΥΛΑΙ
     3. Equus ΑΡΠΑΝΩΝ = Taurus ΔΑΕΟΥ.
     4. Spica.= Aper.

‡ Zannoni marks this place among the mountains of Garganus, but the
Chronicle says expressly it was in the plain.

sat

fat down with his company to fup upon the noble game. The flow of fpirits, infpired by the fuccefs of the day, and heightened by wine and good fellowfhip, made him wifh to perpetuate the remembrance of his convivial pleafures by erecting a palace here, which he called Apricena, from the two Latin words that fignify a wild boar, and fupper. Inhabitants gathered round the imperial refidence, and formed a fmall town, which flourifhed and fell with the fortunes of the houfe of Swabia.

On our approach to the fea, we came to a more barren foil, a mere heap of pebbles, except fome fmall patches, where labour and perfeverance have forced vines and corn to grow. A mile from the fhore ftood the city of Sipontum, of which, except a part of its Gothic cathedral, fcarce one ftone remains upon another.

Diomed is fuppofed by Strabo to have been the founder of this place, called by the Greeks ΣΗΠΙΟΥΝΤΟΣ, from the great quantity of cuttle fifh that are caft up on the coaft. In the early ages of Chriftian hierarchy, a bifhop was fixed in this church; but, under the Lombards, his fee was united to that of Beneventum. Being again feparated, Sipontum became an archiepifcopal diocefe in 1094, about which time it was fo ill treated by the Barbarians, that it never recovered its fplendour, but funk into fuch mifery, that in 1260, it was a mere defert, from the want of inhabitants, the decay of commerce, and the infalubrity of the air. Manfred having taken thefe circumftances into confi-

3

deration, began in 1261 to build a new city on the sea-shore, to which he removed the few remaining Sipontines. His colony was named Manfredonia, and people were encouraged to settle in it by many essential privileges and exemptions. In order to found it under the most favourable auspices, he called together all the famous professors of astrology (a science in which both he and his father placed great confidence), and caused them to calculate the happiest hour and minute for laying the first stone. He himself drew the plans, traced the walls and streets, superintended the works, and by his presence and largesses animated the workmen to finish them in a very short space of time. The port was secured from storms by a pier, the ramparts were built of the most solid materials, and in the great tower was placed a bell of so considerable a volume as to be heard over all the plain of Capitanata, in order to alarm the country in case of an invasion. Charles of Anjou afterwards removed the bell to Bari, and offered it at the shrine of Saint Nicholas, as a thanksgiving for the recovery of one of his children.

In spite of all the precautions taken by Manfred to secure a brilliant destiny to his new city, neither his pains, nor the horoscopes of his wizards, have been able to render it opulent or powerful. At present, it scarce musters six thousand inhabitants, though most of the corn exported from the province is shipped off here, and a direct trade carried on with Venice and Greece, for which reason there is a laza-

retto

retto eftablifhed; but from fome late inftances we may gather, that if the kingdom of Naples has for many years paft remained free from the plague, it is more owing to good luck, and the very trifling communication with Turkey, than to the vigilance or incorruptibility of the officers of this port.

In 1620, the Turks landed and pillaged Manfredonia.

All forts of vegetables abound here, for flavour and fucculency infinitely fuperior to thofe raifed by continual waterings in the cineritious foil of Naples; lettuce in particular is delicious; fifh plentiful and cheap; the rocky fhore covered with fhell-fifh, alga, and balls called *pila marina*, which are nothing more than a conglomeration of the finer fibres of fubmarine roots detached from their plants, and rolled up by the undulating motion of the water; of thefe fibres a delicate paper has been obtained by an experimental philofopher, whofe ftudies in natural hiftory are always directed by patriotic views, and the hope of ftrikeing out difcoveries of public utility.

April the nineteenth, we rode along the fhore to the north-eaft, for three miles, through a well cultivated tract of good land, till we arrived at the foot of Mount Garganus. This ridge of mountains, almoft entirely compofed of breccia, forms a very large promontory advancing into the Adriatic fea, and feparated from the Apennines on the weft by the plains of Lucera and San Severo. Moft geographers make it a continuation of the great chain of mountains that runs

down

down the middle of Italy, but in this point, as well as in many others concerning thefe provinces, I have had opportunities of difcovering errors in the beft maps; nor am I acquainted with one that can be implicitly relied upon with regard to the Neapolitan dominions. Few perfons travel to make obfervations on the fpot, and therefore moft of them are under the neceffity of adopting the miftakes of their predeceffors, as they have no means of coming at better information. The four-fheet map of the kingdom of Naples, drawn at Paris by Zannoni, under the direction of the eounfellor Abbate Galiani, is certainly the beft and moft ample of any yet publifhed; but as it was put together from memory, combination of different obfervations, and old maps, it is not furprifing that it fhould not be exempt from errors *. It is to be lamented, that with fuch a numerous body of engineers in times of profound peace, the Neapolitan miniftry fhould not employ a few of them in the ufeful tafk of making topographical and marine charts of their own country and coafts. The public fpirit of a Dominican friar †, who, at his own rifk and expence, has caufed the whole extent of coaft from Reggio to Naples to be drawn and engraved, fhould methinks excite the emulation, and pique the pride, of thofe that prefide over the affairs of this realm.

* Zannoni has lately been prevailed upon to come to Naples, and is actually employed in furveying the kingdom. We may, therefore, expect a better map of the Two Sicilies.

† F Antonio Minafi.

Fos

For more than an hour we climbed up a very rugged rocky path, through thickets of pine, juniper, cyſtus, lentiſcus, and other ſtrong ſcented plants; at length we reached the top of the mountain that overhangs the bay of Manfredonia, and arrived at the dirty ill built city of Sant' Angiolo, which contains about ſix thouſand ſavage-looking inhabitants. We were accommodated with lodgings at the Carmelite friars, who very politely procured us refreſhments in great abundance; we found the flavour of their mutton exquiſite, and were told that meat of all kinds was equally delicate in this diſtrict.

After dinner one of the friars conducted us to the ſanctuary, which is a cavern in the face of the rock; a grove of aged trees overſhades the approach, and on their boughs are ſlung flat ſtones drilled through, and hung up by the pilgrims, either as proofs of their having fulfilled their vow, or in conſequence of ſome whimſy of devotion, as the Pagans uſed to ſuſpend little maſks or images on the branches of trees in honour of Bacchus.

Oſcilla ex alta ſuſpendunt mollia pinu *.           Virg. Geor 2.

Through a gothic porch we were led down a flight of fifty-five ſteps of coarſe-grained marble, on which votaries have traced the outlines of their hands and feet. At the bottom, we paſſed into a damp gloomy grotto, the chapel of the Archangel Michael: his ſtatue is of the common ſoft ſtone

* " They hang waxen maſks upon the lofty pine."

X 2

of

of the country, and, with all the reſt of the decorations, below criticiſm.

The hiſtory of this church is as follows : In the days of Pope Gelaſius the Firſt, about the year 491, St. Michael is ſaid to have appeared to one Laurence in the caverns of Mount Garganus, and to have ſuggeſted to him meaſures for obtaining a complete victory over the enemies of his country, and delivering Sipontum, then beleaguered by the barbarians.   The viſion made a great noiſe in the Chriſtian world, and ſoon gained ſuch credit with the pious part of it, that altars and churches were erected in numberleſs places in honour of this Generaliſſimo of the celeſtial hoſt; but none was reſorted to with ſo much fervour, none ſo enriched with the preſents of the faithful, as the chapel conſecrated upon the identical ſpot where the ſpirit was ſaid to have ſtood.   The riches laviſhed upon it by the Greeks allured the Lombards, who took the town and ſtripped it of all its treaſures.   In 1460, Ferdinand the Firſt ſtormed this place (the inhabitants of which had joined his adverſaries), and plundered the church of an incredible ſtore of wealth belonging to the ſanctuary, or to the rebels of the neighbourhood, who had depoſited their valuable property here, as in a place of inviolable ſecurity.   The King carried it off, and coined the ſilver into crown pieces of St. Angelo, which, on one ſide, bore his image, and on the reverſe, that of St. Michael, with the legend JUSTA TUENDA. Pontanus, his ſecretary, who muſt be allowed to be good authority,

though,

though, from the known character of the Prince, the fact is rather improbable, assures us, that at the peace every thing was restored to the chapel exactly in the same form and to the same amount. Since that epocha, this sanctuary has been little talked of beyond the circuit of a few miles, and only pilgrims of a mean rank now frequent Monte St. Angelo; for great and munificent votaries have for these two last centuries flocked to Loretto.

In the first partition of the Norman conquests, Garganus and Sipontum were assigned to Ranulph of Averfa. Joan of England, wife to William the Good, had this manor settled on her as a jointure, and afterwards it formed part of Manfred's appanage.

It was bestowed upon the famous Scanderbeg by Ferdinand the first, and at present belongs to Grimaldi Prince of Gerace.

Next morning we took a pleasant ride into the heart of the mountains, through shady dells and noble woods, which brought to our minds the venerable groves that in ancient times bent with the loud winds sweeping along the rugged sides of Garganus. There is still a respectable forest of evergreen and common oak, pitch pine, horn beam, chesnut and manna-ash, still

* —————————— Aquilonibus
Querceta Gargani laborant,
Et foliis viduantur orni ——— HOR.

* The oak woods of Garganus groan beneath the northern blasts, and the ashes are stripped of their leaves by the tempest.

The

The sheltered vallies are industriously cultivated, and seem to be bleft with an excellent soil, and luxuriant vegetation; the grass is short and fine.

After a delightful wandering excursion, we sat down to dinner on the moss by the side of a clear brook that tumbles down the rocks, and loses itself among the bushes †. Our repast finished, we returned to St. Angelo, and next morning crossed the plain to Lucera, which stands on a knoll detached from the Apennine, commanding an almost boundless view of sea and land.

† Not many miles north of this place is Ischitella, a town, that in 1676, gave birth to Peter Giannone, the most celebrated writer of Neapolitan history. He was an advocate at Naples, and intended his work rather as a differtation on the laws and civil transactions of his country, than as a chronicle of its wars and revolutions, but even, according to this plan, it is imperfect in the execution, for he passes over many capital points in silence, or at best, touches upon them in a very superficial manner he too frequently transcribes the words of other authors, and, from a want of recourse to original documents, decides without warrantable authority. His reputation arose from the vigorous attack he made upon ecclesiastical power, and he is supposed to have been the first that freed the Neapolitans from the slavish terrors, with which the menaces of Rome had for so many ages impressed their minds. The success of his book rouled the Pope's partisans, who soon contrived to render him an object of execration, and an exile. He dragged on a life of poverty and misery for many years, and was at last shamefully decoyed into Savoy, and thrown into prison by the King of Sardinia, who having then in view a treaty with the court of Rome, hoped to carry his point by this unjust treatment of a man, over whom he could not possibly pretend any dominion. Giannone died in 1748, after thirteen years captivity.

## SECTION XIX.

THE origin and etymology of Lucera are equally matter of conjecture; its antiquity and former importance are proved by the testimony of many historians. It was a city of the Daunians, and an ally of the Romans, who esteemed it a place of the utmost consequence to their views of aggrandisement. In the year of Rome 433, the consuls T. Veturius Calvinus and Spurius Posthumius, were marching from Campania to its relief, when they were circumvented and made prisoners by the Samnites in the defile of Caudium. The epithet *noble* *, bestowed upon it by Horace, can allude only to its antiquity, for Strabo says it was much decayed in the Augustan age, the only remnant of Roman building is a tower in the centre of the castle. The coins of Luceria are in most cabinets †.

In 663, Lucera was sacked by Constans the Second, and lay in ruins till Frederick the Second conceived an affection

---

* Telanæ prope nobilem
    Tonsæ Luceriam.

† Nummi Lucerinorum
ÆR. 1. Cap. Herculis imb. pelle leoninâ tectum = Clava, pharetra et arcus LOVCERI.
    2. Cap. Pallad. gal = Rota octo radiorum LOVCERI.
    3. Cap. imb laur. 2 glob = Cap bov LOVCERI
    4. Cap. barb laur. 3 glob Delphin LOVCERI.
    5. Cap. mul. velat laur. 2 glob. = Concha LOVCERI.

for

for it, and erected on one of its hills a ſpacious **Gothic**
fortreſs ſtill exiſting.   He ſoon after tranſported hither the
Saracens of Sicily to remove them from the dangerous neighbourhood of Afiica, and break their pernicious connexions
with that continent.   Under the protection of the Swabian
kings, their numbers increaſed to ſixty thouſand ;   their inſo-
lence roſe in proportion to their numbers, and from Lucera,
as from a den, they ruſhed forth into the plains, where they
exerciſed all ſorts of violence upon the inhabitants ;   the
hiſtories of thoſe times abound with traits of their cruelty,
perhaps a little exaggerated on account of the inviolable
attachment which theſe Muſſulmen profeſſed and maintained
towards the houſe of Swabia, a moſt odious and unpardon-
able crime in the eyes of the ſucceeding princes and their
partiſans.   Spinelli * tells us of one Phocax, a Saracen captain, who being in love with the wife of Simon Rocca of
Trani, broke into his houſe by night, turned him out of

* Matthew Spinelli, a gentleman of Giovenazzo, wrote a journal of
events that happened, in his time, under the three laſt Swabian and the
firſt Angevine princes   We have his work both in Latin and Italian
Muratori and others try to perſuade us, that the latter is the original, but
the language is ſo widely different from the modern Puglian dialect, and
from any idiom we can ſuppoſe in uſe there five hundred years ago, that it is
quite abſurd to think Spinelli wrote it as the language now ſtands   either the
Latin is the original, or the preſent Italian is a tranſlation of the ancient
Puglian copy   There are ſome anachroniſms and interpolations in the very
curious diary, but the former ariſe from the old Puglian method of beginning the year in September, and the blame of the latter may be laid upon
the copiſts, who had a political intereſt in falſifying the text   This is a ſhort
and valuable work, relating with ſimplicity the tranſactions of the times, and
throwing great light upon the characters of many principal perſonages of that
buſy period.

his bed, and took poffeffion of his place: a complaint of this outrage was lodged before the Emperor; but he treated it lightly, and anfwered, that where there was compulfion, there could be no difhonour. If the Infidels were licentious, we learn from the fame chronicles, that the Chriftians were not behind hand in revenge.

After the battle of Benevento, where the Saracens fignalized their fidelity, and acquitted themfelves with honour of the laft duty to their benefactor Manfred, they were obliged to fubmit to the conqueror. In 1300, Charles the Second, aware of the danger of fuffering them to remain any longer in the heart of his kingdom, and zealous to re-eftablifh the worfhip of Chrift in a place, where it had been for fo many years treated with indignity, iffued an edict, by which all Mahometans, refident in his dominions, were to embrace the Chriftian religion, or be liable to be killed with impunity wherever they fhould be found. Moft of them fled beyond fea, and Charles reftored Lucera to the Chriftians, built a magnificent cathedral, caufed a bifhop and chapter, with ample revenues, to be appointed, and endeavoured to obliterate even the memory of all paft abominations by abolifhing the ancient name, in lieu of which he fubftituted that of Santa Maria; but it happened here, as at Man-fredonia, which his father had new named, the old deno-mination prevailed.

In 1590, Mark Sciarra, a captain of banditti, furprized and plundered this city. The bifhop, who had taken re-

fuge

fuge in the steeple of his cathedral, was shot at the window, as he was peeping out to watch the motions of the robbers.

The tribunal of the President of Capitanata and Molise, and an annual fair in November, are at present the chief support of the town.

From the walls, Fiorentino or Castelfiorentino was pointed out to us about six miles to the north. It is now a ruinous hamlet, but was once an episcopal city, and remarkable for being the place where the Emperor Frederick the Second breathed his last. To form a just character of this monarch, it is necessary to steer a middle course between the invectives of ecclesiastical writers, and the eulogies of the Ghibellines. It is from a comparative review of the great events of his reign that I shall sketch the outlines of his portrait. He was a warrior of consummate prudence and undoubted courage, by the help of which he weathered the storms of half a century. In prosperity he was not elated; adversity did not depress his spirit, born at an unhappy period, when the popes were straining every sinew to attain temporal as well as spiritual despotism, when the empire was exerting its last efforts to check the growing power of Rome, and preserve a footing in Italy, Frederick was early involved in disputes with the Guelph faction, which continued with very little intermission during his whole life. In the course of these disturbances, all sentiments of respect for the triple crown, which he always found on the head of his most inveterate enemy, vanished from his breast, and, when once they dis-

appeared,

appeared, it was natu I he should confound the principles of the religion with those of its chief, from hating the pontiff he came to despise the faith; sentiments enforced by Frederick's style of life and study. he was the most learned sovereign of the age, a poet, and author of some treatises on veterinarian subjects, the most fashionable a prince could employ his talents upon, he founded academies, protected men of letters, instituted good laws, and proved himself a strict observer of justice; but cruel and vindictive in the infliction of its penalties. He was a dupe to judiciary astrology, abandoned to sensual pleasures, and, notwithstanding all Giannone says in his defence, a latitudinarian in his religious opinions He is said to have observed with a sneer, as he marched through the Holy Land, that if the God of the Hebrews had ever seen the Terra di Lavoro, he would not have set such a value upon his land of promise.

From Lucera, we continued our journey southward to La Cerignuola, through an immense flat watered by the Carapelle and the Cervaro, the first of these torrents is the Daunus, from which the whole country derived its ancient name. On the north-east our horizon was bounded by the sea, on the north by Monte St. Angelo; the Apennine runs along the western side as far as the eye can discover, between it and the sea, the insulated ridge of Canosa crosses the plain, and closes the view to the south As the weather was dry, we found the road tolerably good; but in winter it must be impassable. From the warmth I felt, I conceived an idea

of

of the exceſſive power of the ſummer ſun in theſe low lands,
where neither ſhade nor ſhelter is to be found for many
miles ; there is then no breathing in them through intenſe-
neſs of heat and want of ventilation. Horace, who was
well acquainted with all the qualities of his native country,
has more than once made mention of parched-up Puglia *,
and in modern language, the following adage is not leſs ex-
preſſive of the idea the Puglieſe themſelves have of its inſuf-
ferable ſummer weather :

> Le pene ſi ſoffriſcon dell' inferno
> L'eſtate in Puglia, all' Aquila l'inverno †.

We met crowds of people returning from the feaſt or
wake of l'Incoronata : this is an image of the Madonna found
in a tree, and held in great veneration. They were all gay
and frolickſome, eſpecially the women, who ſeemed
mightily pleaſed with the day's diverſion. At the place
where this feſtival is kept, was formerly a hunting ſeat of
Manfred. In 1265, being deſirous of ſtrengthening his
doubtful title by popularity, he ſummoned a general court
of his barons at Foggia, and made a grand hunting match
in the foreſt of Incoronata, to which above one thouſand

---

* Æſtuoſæ grata Calabriæ armenta———
  Pauper aqua Daunus———
  Peruſta ſolibus uxor Appuli———
  Siticuloſæ Apuliæ———

† " The pains of hell are felt in Puglia during the ſummer, and at Aquila
" during the winter "

five

five hundred perfons of confideration were invited. After the chace, the fpoil was divided among the company, and the hunting of that day remained long memorable in Puglia for the concourfe of nobility, the great quantity of game taken, and the magnificence of the King, who fuffered none to depart without fome token of his generofity. Alphonfus the Firft inclofed eighteen miles of this country with toils, and took fo many ftags, that, befides what was carried away by the hunters, he fent four hundred head to be falted for the ufe of the garrifons of Trani and Barletta. In later times, Puglia continued to be remarkable for abundance of deer. We have the authority of Pontanus, an eye-witnefs, for a very extraordinary proof of their numbers; he informs us, that his mafter King Ferdinand having marched out of Barletta before daybreak with a view of furprizing his enemies, was ftopped by the appearance of a cloud of duft rifing in the plain from a great crowd in motion; on the report of the advanced parties, he thought it prudent to return to his camp, left his retreat fhould be cut off by that body of troops which feemed to move with prodigious rapidity. As foon as the fun rofe, this formidable hoft was difcovered to be a herd of ftags. The fame author tells us, that fome years before, Sforza, the moft experienced general of the age, had been deceived in like manner, fo as to draw up his forces to receive the charge. At prefent, game is not wanting, though kings now feldom drive it acrofs thefe plains, or by their refidence on the royal chace,

contribute

contribute to its prefervation and increafe.   It appears rather
paradoxical, that however eager, expert, and indefatigable, a
prince may be in the chace, yet wild beafts, and game of all
forts, fhall flock round him and multiply near his palace;
they feem fafcinated and hurried by an irrefiftible inftinct
towards this royal butchery.   But the concourfe is eafily
accounted for, when we confider the impunity with which
they ravage the hopes of the hufbandman, and the undifturbed fecurity they enjoy under the protection of the foreft
laws during their feafons of pairing, producing, and nurfing
their progeny.

The Puglian fportfmen run down hares with greyhounds,
and purfue the wild boar with one large lurcher, and two
or three maftiffs; the hunters ride with a lance and a pair of
piftols.

La Cerignola is a town of twelve thoufand inhabitants,
fituated on a rifing ground without tree or bufh near it.
About forty years ago an earthquake almoft deftroyed it,
and it is not yet thoroughly rebuilt, the ftreets are crooked
and dirty, the houfes all low, as the owners dare not raife
them high for fear of another fhock.   The eighty firft
Columna Milliaria, infcribed with the name of Trajan, was
the only fragment of antiquity I found here.   The commodities of the place are fheep, horfes, and corn; the bread
is thick and gritty, but well tafted.   In 1363, James Ar-
cucci, great Chamberlain of Naples, was lord of this manor:
it afterwards belonged to the Palagoni, from whom Ladif-

laus took it to give to the Caraccioli, Pignatelli, Count of Egmont †, resident in France, is the actual possessor, and farms it out at fifteen thousand ducats a year (£. 2,810). In 1503, the great captain defeated the French near this town, in an attack they made upon his camp. Their general, Lewis of Armagnac, Duke of Nemours, was killed in the engagement.

## SECTION XX.

*April* 22d. WE set out early to examine the fields of Cannæ, famous for the victory obtained over the Romans by Hannibal in the 536th year of Rome The result of our observations shall be given in as few words as the desire of being intelligible will admit of.

From Cerignola to the bridge of Canosa are reckoned six miles of open country, arable and pasture. The Olanto (anciently the Aufidus) flows under this bridge; its course is serpentine, and various in its direction, sometimes running due east, at others, rather to the south, but in general inclining to the north-east. There was but little water in it, and that whitish and muddy, but from the wideness of its

† The Pignatellis give three pots or pignate for their arms, and pretend they bear this coat in memory of one of their ancestors having entered Constantinople sword in hand, penetrated into the market place, and brought off the three pots as a trophy They reach and run Barons, Princes of Belmonte, Strongoli, and Dukes of Monteleone, &c Of this family was Pope Innocent the Twelfth, elected in 1691.

bed,

bed, the fand banks, and the buttreffes erected to break the force of the ftream, it is plain that it ftill anfwers Horace's epithets of fierce, roaring, and violent *. It flows from two fources that embrace the conical Mount Voltore, and join at the foot, being the only river †, as Polybius obferves, that rifing on the weftern fide of the Apennines, empties itfelf into the Adriatic. This double origin is expreffed by the appellation Tauriformis ‡, having two branches or horns at the head ‖.

Except a few fcattered poplars, I faw no wood near its banks; the Roman road from Benevento, through Afcoli, appears here raifed above the level of the fields, and paffes fouth in a line to Canofa. We breakfafted at an inn near the bridge, and regretted our not having followed Horace's example, in bringing a fupply of bread from fome other place §, for what we got here was as brown as mahogany,

* Aufidus acer—longè fonantem—violens obftrepit.     Hor.

† This expreffion of Polybius is not eafy to be underftood, for there are certainly many high mountains farther weft than the head of the Ofanto, it is probable, he meant that it rofe weft of the middle ridge the Sele (Silarus) rifes very near it, and difcharges itfelf into the Tirrhene fea.

‡ Sic Tauriformis volvitur Aufidus.     Hor.

‖ Perhaps Horace intended no more by this title, than an allufion to the bulls, genii with horns, minotaurs, or animals with human face and horns, by which it was ufual to reprefent rivers on coins, for, in reality, the Ofanto may be faid to flow from fifty fprings as well as two, if we take in all the brooks that fall into it.

§ Tum longè pulcherrimus, ultra
       ut foleat humeris portare viator,
          annis lapidofus.——

and

and so gritty that it set our teeth on edge to craunch it. The friable incompact contexture of the stone with which the millers grind their corn, rather than the sand of the area where it is trodden out, can alone have perpetuated this defect in the Canusian bread for nineteen centuries. I believe their millstones are of the soft concreted rock, which constitutes the greatest part of the coast. The corn is separated from the ear by the trampling of a great number of mares tied in a string by their tails, and whipped round and round. This operation is performed, in the Terra di Otranto, by a pair of oxen, who drag between them a very heavy rough stone, that breaks the sheaves, and shakes out the grain.

We were too much occupied with the evolutions of Hannibal, to think of any deviation from the direct route to Cannæ, so reserving Canosa, and its antiquities, for another opportunity, struck into the Barletta road at the corner of the inn, down the south side of the Ofanto. A ridge of low hills, bare of wood, and laid out in grass or corn land, confines the river on that side for four miles, at the end of which we came to a plain bounded by the Knolls, whereon stood the city of Cannæ *. For the next mile the Ofanto flows again close under the hills, till, upon their sinking with a gentle slope into the plains of Barletta, it winds on

---

* The Latins made the name of this city of the plural number, probably from its consisting of distinct parts, built on different eminences. The Greeks named it in the singular.

Z

some

some miles farther through a dead flat, and empties itself into the gulph of Venice. On the north side, the
rising grounds are much more remote from the sea, and all
between is an uninterrupted level.

The traces of the town of Cannæ are very faint, consisting of fragments of altars, cornices, gates, walls,
vaults, and underground granaries. It was destroyed the
year before the battle; but being rebuilt, became an
episcopal see in the infancy of Christianity. It was again
ruined in the sixth century, but seems to have subsisted in
an humble state many ages later; for we read of its contending with Barletta for the territory, which till then
had been enjoyed in common by them; and in 1284,
Charles the First issued an edict for dividing the lands, to
prevent all future litigation. The prosperity of the towns
along the coast, which increased in wealth and population by embarkations for the Crusadoes, and by traffic,
proved the annihilation of the great inland cities, and
Cannæ was probably abandoned entirely before the end of
the thirteenth century.

At the foot of the hill is a large arch over a marble
trough, which receives the waters of a copious spring.
Here we found a camp of Abruzzese shepherds on the point
of departing for the mountains. Rough in aspect, dialect,
and dress, but civil and hospitable, they offered us milk,
cheese, and cold meat. The chief of them gave us some

brass

braſs coins of Zeno and Leo, found among the ruins; and seemed aſtoniſhed at our offering to pay him for ſuch baubles.

The hill above the well being rather higher than the reſt, ſerved as a reconnoitring poſt, where I inſpected my notes, and took drawings of the country, before I entered the field of battle. My eyes now ranged at large over the vaſt expanſe of unvariegated plains. All was ſilent; not a man, not an animal, appeared to enliven the ſcene. We ſtood on ruins, and over vaults; the banks of the river were deſert and wild. My thoughts naturally aſſumed the tint of the dreary proſpect, as I reflected on the fate of Rome and Carthage. Rome recovered from the blow ſhe received in theſe fields; but her liberty, fame, and trophies have long been levelled in the duſt. Carthage lies in ruins leſs diſcernible than theſe of the paltry walls of Cumæ: the very traces of them have almoſt vaniſhed from the face of the earth. The daring projects, marches, and exploits of her hero, even the victory obtained on this ſpot, would, like thouſands of other human atchievements, have been long ago buried in oblivion, had not his very enemies confirmed him to immortality; for the annals of Carthage exiſt no more: one common ruin has ſwallowed all

The Roman Conſuls, Æmilius Paulus and Terentius Varro, being authorized by the ſenate to quit the defenſive plan, and ſtake the fortunes of the republic on the chance

of a battle, marched from Canusium, and encamped a few
miles east, in two unequal divisions, with the Aufidus
between them.   In this position they meant to wait for an
opportunity of engaging to advantage; but Hannibal,
whose critical situation in a desolated country, without
refuge or allies, could admit of no delay, found means to
inflame the vanity of Varro by some trivial advantages in
skirmishes between the light horse.   The Roman, elated
with this success, determined to bring matters to a speedy
conclusion; but, finding the ground on the south side too
confined for the operations of so large an army, crossed the
river, and resting his right wing upon the Aufidus, drew
out his forces in the plain.   Hannibal, whose head quarters
were at Cannæ, no sooner perceived the enemy in motion,
than he forded the water below, and marshalled his troops
in a line opposite to that of his adversaries.

Polybius, who had examined the place, was a military man, and may have been acquainted with persons that
were present at the battle, was the guide I followed, as he
is the original from whom subsequent historians took their
accounts, and whose authority seems incontrovertible.   He
observes, that one of the armies faced the north, and the
other the south; by which positions the rising sun incom-
moded neither.   The difficulty lies in deciding which way
each of them was turned; as the expressions of Polybius
are said by some to admit of a double meaning, though I
                                                    confess

confefs I think nothing can be more explicit *. Chaupy
taxes Livy with having mifinterpreted the paffage of the
Greek hiftorian, who, according to his opinion, did not
mean that the Romans ftood with their faces to the noon-
tide fun, but only that they were drawn up to the fouth of
the enemy †. He affirms that the topography of the plain,
and the courfe of the river, agree with this explanation, and
that if the legions had faced the fouth, the runaways could
not, after the defeat, have reached Canufium and Venufia,
without paffing through the whole victorious army. Salapia, Arpi, Luceria, would have been their places of
refuge.

However, as I cannot but think Livy well enough verfed
in the Greek tongue, not to miftake the meaning of an
author he ftudied and followed fo clofely, I am inclined to
truft to his explanation; efpecially as, according to my
ideas, the fituation of the ground is in his favour; for,
exactly in that part of the plain where we know with moral

---

* Καὶ τὰς μὲν ἐκ τῶ μείζονος χάρακος διαϐ.βάζων τὸν πόλαμον ἐυθείς
παρενέϐαλλε τὰς δ' ex ℘ατέρου συνάπλων τέλοις ἐπὶ τὴν αὐτὴν εὐθείαν ἐξέ]αντε,
λαμϐάνων πᾶσαν τὴν ἐπιφάνειαν τὴν πρὸς μετημϐρίαν Ht his q wen majo-
rum cultrorum ducens trans flumen, confeftim in acie locuvit Illos vero
minorum jungers cum prioribus rect. linea apposuit, faciens totum apparitio-
nem verfus meridiem —Βλεπϐσης de τη μὲν ⊤ ν Ῥωμαίων ταξεις πρὸς μετημϐρίαν της δε τῶν Καρχηδονίων πρὸς τὰς αρκίες, εκτ ροις αὖλα η συνεϐαινε
γίνεσθαι την καθ ἐ τὸν ἥλ α α α̃ ον ανν Spectante meridiem Romanorum acie,
Carthaginienfium vero feptentrionem, ambobus n offenfis contig r effe ab folis
ortu

† Livy's words are, " Romanis in meridiem, Pœnis in feptentrionem
" verfis" Lib. xxii. 46.

certainty that the main effort of the battle lay, the Aufidus, after running due eaft for fome time, makes a fudden turn to the fouth, and defcribes a very large femicircle. The Romans, we are to fuppofe, forded it at the angle or elbow, and placed their right wing on the banks; while the legions extended themfelves due eaft, till the whole line came to face the fouth. The Carthaginians croffed in two places within the femicircle, and were drawn out in a line, that formed the chord of which the river was the arch: the way to Canufium was therefore open for the fugitives *.

The fcene of action is marked out to pofterity, by the name of *Pezzo di Sangue*, " Field of Blood." The peafants fhewed us fome fpurs and heads of lances, lately turned up by the plough; and told us, horfe-loads of armour and weapons had been at different times carried off from thence.

Thefe plains have more than once, fince the Punic war, afforded room for men to accomplifh their mutual deftruction. Melo of Bari, after raifing the ftandard of revolt againft the Greek Emperors, and defeating their generals in feveral engagements, was at laft routed here, in 1019, by the Catapan Bolanus. Out of two hundred and fifty Norman adventurers, the flower of Melo's army, only ten

* All the maps are inaccurate in this province. D'Anville places Canufium on the northern bank of the river, and the battle feveral miles fouth of the Aufidus.

escaped

escaped the slaughter of the day. In 1201, the archbishop of Palermo and his rebellious associates, who had taken advantage of the nonage of Frederick of Swabia, were cut to pieces at Cannæ by Walter de Brienne, sent by the Pope to defend the young King's dominions.

We returned to Cerignuola across the fields.

## SECTION XXI.

NEXT day we hired a guide; or, to speak more correctly, a very talkative bustling fellow offered to conduct us across the plains to the ruins of Salapia. Our ride was pleasant for nine miles, over a fine down, with little corn or wood, but a great deal of lentiscus. We were brought at last to the edge of a long lake, separated from the sea by a narrow neck of land, cut into several ponds for making salt, which is piled up in heaps, and carried off by boats to the ships that ride at anchor in the road. We saw some lying a mile or two off, not being able to come nearer to take in their cargoes. The swamps are overgrown with sea purslain and dwarf withy, with which the shepherds and fishermen make their huts and baskets. Near the lake are the ruins we had come so far out of our way to see. They consist of a square fortification of earthen ramparts, with many divisions and fosses. I should have taken it for a camp rather than a town, as

there

there is not a ftone left near it, had not the tradition of the country, and the coins that have been found here, marked with the name of Salapia*, determined the fituation of that place. In the Punic war, Salapia was a poft of confequence, which the Romans and Carthaginians were equally defirous of poffeffing  After the death of Marcellus, Hannibal affixed that Conful's feal to fome forged letters, in hopes of gaining admittance into Salapia; but intelligence, accidentally conveyed  to the garrifon, defeated his purpofe.

Salpi was a city and bifhoprick till 1547, when the fee was united to that of Trani.  I believe it ftood at La Trinita, fome miles from the old town.

Our conductor, who during the whole journey had entertained us with wonderful ftories of apparitions and miracles, at laft difclofed the fecret caufe of his eagernefs to accompany us thus far.  This was no lefs than the hopes of difcovering, among the many cavities in thefe ancient mounds, the entrance of an enchanted grotto, which contains a column of maffive filver; and other precious things. It was, he affured us, the belief of the whole country, that whoever was pure enough from fin, and fo favoured

---

* Nummi Salapinorum
ÆR. 1 Cap Apollinis laur. ΣΑΛΑΠΙΝΩΝ – Equus. tridens ΠΥΛΛ.
2. Cap Jovis ΣΑΛΑΠΙΝΩΝ = Aper ΠΑΩΤΙΟΥ
3. Cap. Jov ΣΑΛΑΠΙΝΩΝ = Aper  tridens ΠΥΛΛΟΥ.
4. Cap Apoll = Equus. ftella ΣΑΛΑΠΙΝΩΝ.
5. Equus Λ. ΔΑΙΟΥ = Pifcis ΟΝΙΗΛ.
6. Equus ΣΑΛΑΠΙΝΩΝ = Pifcis ΓΛΑΜ ΛΙΡΓΔΑΙΓΝ.
7 Cap imb diad  Equus. ftella. ΖΑΛΑΠΙΝΩΝ.

by

by Heaven, as to penetrate into this mysterious cavern, would undoubtedly become possessed of treasure sufficient to buy up all the flocks of Puglia Piana. Our honest guide was sure of obtaining the preference, because he had been a few days before to pay his devoirs to the Madonna dell' Incoronata, and had taken every step enjoined by the church for purifying his soul from all stain; however, he could not avoid being staggered, when, upon examining the whole place, not one of us could find a hollow above a foot deep; and, with a look expressive of distress and confusion, he told us, he now recollected that many good men of his acquaintance (among the rest a capuchin friar of most exemplary life) had proved unsuccessful in their attempts to come at this bewitched cave. As he seemed to think our presence adverse to the influence of his stars, we took our leave, gave him for his trouble the only money he was likely to earn that day, and pursued our journey by the sea-shore. As long as our eyes were capable of discerning objects of that size, we could perceive him running up and down very busily, hunting after his imaginary grotto.

We rode through a rich arable country to the mouth of the Ofanto, and crossed the bridge into the Terra di Bari. There is a tide very perceptible about half a mile up the river. Three miles farther, we arrived at Barletta, through a narrow slip of an inclosed vine country, taken off the extensive corn lands of Cannæ; the soil shallow, planted with almond trees.

A a

Barletta

Barletta has, from without, a ruinous afpect; its walls tumbling down, and its ditches filled with rubbifh. But the infide of the city is magnificently built, though thinly peopled. It conveys the idea of a capital of fome mighty ftate reduced to the condition of a conquered province, or depopulated by a raging peftilence. Frequent changes of mafters, bad adminiftration, and decay of commerce, blafted the profperity of Barletta. Its ftreets are wide and well paved; the houfes large and lofty, built with hewn ftone, which, from age, has acquired a polifh little inferior to that of marble. Some of thefe venerable manfions have the ftones cut after the Tufcan manner, in angular fhapes. The ftyle of building fixes their date at the firft emergence of the arts out of the chaos of barbarifm, many of the houfes ftill retaining pointed arches, fhort twifted columns, and other remnants of Saracenic tafte; while others are decorated with pillars, entablatures, and members characteriftic of the ancient Grecian architecture This city owes its embellifhments to the policy of the Aragonian kings, who refided here to fecure the allegiance of the Puglefe.

In the cathedral, which is remarkable for its antique granite columns, Ferdinand the Firft caufed himfelf to be crowned, in hopes that the folemnity of the ceremony would infpire the people with awe and refpect for his perfon and family.

In the market-place ftands a coloffal bronze ftatue, feventeen feet three inches high, reprefenting, as is fup-

pofed,

poſed, the Emperor Heraclius, who began his reign in
610. He is ſtanding dreſt in a military habit, crowned
with a diadem, a ſhort cloak hanging from his left ſhoulder
acroſs his breaſt, and thrown over his left arm, which holds
a globe; his right is raiſed above his head and graſps a ſmall
croſs; the drawing is rude and incorrect, the attitude awk-
ward *. According to ſome hiſtorians, Heraclius was particularly attached to the worſhip of St. Michael, for whoſe
church, on Mount Garganus, he intended this maſſy repre-
ſentation of himſelf, with many other valuable preſents; the
ſhip that brought them from Conſtantinople was caſt away
on the Puglian coaſt, and the ſtatue thrown on the ſands,
where it lay many ages much damaged, and half buried.
In 1491, it was dug up, and the hands and feet being
reſtored, was placed in the great ſquare of Barletta. Pontanus thinks this coloſſus ſtood originally at the head of the
mole, which Heraclius had carried out into the ſea for the
convenience of navigators, and that the extended poſition
of the hand denotes the protection he afforded to commerce. It long paſſed for the figure of Rachis, King of

* The ſmoothneſs of the chin makes me heſitate whether to aſcribe this
ſtatue to Heraclius, who is the ſecond eaſtern Emperor that appears on the
coins with a beard, or to ſome prior monarch. Till the time of his prede-
ceſſor Phocas, ſovereigns ſhaved their chins, though their oriental ſubjects
cheriſhed a length of beard. Cedrenus, indeed, aſſures us, that Heraclius
conformed to that Imperial cuſtom, but on his medals, he is drawn with a
ſquare beard, not unlike that of our Henry the Eighth. If this image be his,
I ſuſpect it was not imported from Greece, but caſt in Italy, and conſequently dreſt after the Roman faſhion

Lombardy,

Lombardy, who, in 749, refigned his crown, and took the habit of a Benedictine monk at Monte Cafino.

The citadel is fpacious, and commands the port, which is at prefent a mere labyrinth, confifting of feveral irregular piers, where fhips are moored; but without any fhelter from the north wind, which fweeps the whole bafon. The exports here are falt, corn, almonds, and liquorice, a root that grows fpontaneoufly in the fwamps. This air is accounted unwholefome during the hot months.

Barletta is faid by Baccius, to have been at firft no more than a tower, or drinking-houfe, on the road to Cannæ, which had for its fign a barrel, barilletta; when the cities of Cannæ and Canofa fell to decay, and the advantages of trade drew people to the coaft, a numerous colony infenfibly gathered round this tower, and in 484 Pope Gelafius came down from Garganus to confecrate a church for the fettlers, which, in time, became the cathedral of the united fees of Nazareth, Cannæ, and Monteverde. The Emperor Frederick added greatly to Barletta, and is by fome called its founder. Other authors affign higher antiquity to the place, and fuppofe it to be the Barduli of the Itineraries. In 1291, the Barlettans rebelled againft the houfe of Swabia, and fet up the papal ftandard, for which they were feverely punifhed. Manfred, who had a great partiality for this part of his dominions, held a general parliament here, in which he put in practice every endearing art, likely to win the hearts, and fix the wavering affections of his vaſſals. In the fifteenth century, Barletta was eſteemed one of the four ſtrongeſt fortreſſes in Italy [*]. It was mortgaged to the Venetians by Ferdinand the Second, and re-taken from them by Gonſalvo de Cordova, who here collected his forces, and made his firſt ſtand againſt the French, in 1503.

## SECTION XXI.

ON leaving Barletta, we ſaw before us, on a peninſula, the city of Trani, at the diſtance of ſix miles; the road to it is one of the rougheſt ever trodden by man or beaſt; it runs partly along the rocks impending over the beach, and partly in narrow lanes, through vineyards, between dry ſtone walls. In every incloſure is one, and often two hovels, built in a ſpiral form, with the ſtones picked off the land after digging. Theſe conical towers ſerve as watch-houſes for the perſons that attend before vintage, to prevent the depredations of quadruped and biped pilferers; when old and overgrown with climbing weeds and fig-trees, they become very romantic objects, and appear like ſo many ancient mauſolea. The ſhape of theſe piles of rude ſtone, covered with moſs and brambles, has deceived a writer of travels into a belief of their being Roman tombs; but I am ſurpriſed the prodigious multi-

[*] The other three were, Fabriano in the Marca, Prato in Tuſcany, and Crema in Lombardy

tude

tude of them did not raise suspicion; for if they were really depositories of the dead, the ashes of the whole Roman people would scarcely have sufficed to fill the columbaria of the single province of Bari.

As soon as we arrived at Trani, we waited upon the President, with a letter from the Secretary of State, and obtained from him, an order for all convents, in his district, to receive us civilly, and afford us lodging: we were provided with similar recommendations for every province, and except letters for private families, there is no better method to be pursued in a tour through a country so ill provided with inns. Our evening was spent with the Archbishop, a worthy conversable prelate. He told us, he had taken great pains to introduce a taste for study and literature into his diocese, but hitherto without success, as the Tranians were a very merry race, gente molto allegra, but unfortunately born with an unconquerable antipathy to application. The collegians, though under his immediate inspection, were above his hand, and often, when he thought the whole seminary buried in silence, wrapped up in studious contemplation, or deep in theological lucubrations, he has been surprised, on entering the quadrangle, to find all ring again with gigs and tarantellas. We were well satisfied that he spoke without exaggeration, for never did I hear such incessant chattering, and so stunning a din, as was kept up the whole day under our windows. It is a rule established by the custom of time immemorial, that no work shall be done in

2

Trani after dinner; the whole afternoon is to be spent in dozing, chatting, or sauntering: we could not prevail upon the blacksmith to shoe one of our horses in the evening.

The exportation of corn is confiderable, but little other bufinefs is stirring, and I am afraid induftry has taken a long farewell of moft of the cities on this coaft. The great number of towns along the Adriatic, jealous of each other, shackled with honourable but baneful privileges, and averfe to all friendly intercourfe and coalition of interefts, is an almoft infurmountable bar to improvement; a province fo bleffed with articles of prime neceffity might fpeedily rife to opulence, were trade properly underftood and encouraged.

The bread of this place is white, light, and fpungy, baked after the French manner, which is contrary to that of the Capitanata, where the bakers are ignorant of the very rudiments of their trade, and knead and bake their dough in fuch an imperfect manner, that a ftranger is almoft choked in attempting to fwallow it.

Vegetables are here fo exquifitely flavoured, that, for the firft time of my life, I ate raw unfeafoned lettuces with relifh: pulfe of all kinds are huge and pulpy, the market people fell peafe and beans by weight, and make ufe of pebbles in lieu of weights; a rude mode of dealing, which muft expofe the vender to great temptation of impofing upon his chapmen, efpecially as the ftones, being of a foft kind,

kind, muſt in time loſe part of their heavineſs by frequent rubbing.

The wine of the diſtrict ſouth of the Ofanto is ſweet, ſtrong, and tawny. It is mixed with moſto cotto; that is, a certain proportion of rich wine boiled down to a jelly. This is, no doubt, a trick of the vintner's art, handed down from the ancients, who treated their moſt precious wines in a ſimilar manner, as we learn from many paſſages in the claſſics. The grapes have a fine flavour, and might produce excellent liquor, but from inveterate and rooted ignorance the proprietor brews with them a muddy unpotable mixture, that will ſcarce keep a twelvemonth without turning to vinegar.

Trani is tolerably well built of ſtone, upon uneven ground. The harbour is incircled by the town, and has ſcarcely depth of water enough to ſet a boat afloat; the corn ſhips are obliged to come to an anchor a couple of miles off, and take in their lading from lighters. The city has been at great expence in building a quay, on a peninſula that advances ſo far as to embrace the haven; but this ſlip of land, inſtead of being occupied by the warehouſes and ſtores of merchants, is entirely taken up by two or three overgrown monaſteries. We need look for no other criterion of the ſtate of commerce at Trani.

The cathedral ſtands on the oppoſite ſide of the harbour, and was erected ſix centuries ago, in a very mean taſte; the ornaments prepoſterous, and, except a few pieces of
foliage,

foliage, clumsily designed and executed; the pillars short and thick, resembling those of our oldest English churches, which were built after the Saxon manner, and before the introduction of that lighter sort of architecture, which we distinguish by the name of Gothic, and admire in the cathedrals of York, Lincoln, Westminster, &c. The columns of the nave are solid blocks of granite, the dislocated spoils of some ancient edifice. Philip, Prince of Morea, second son of Charles the First, reposes in a marble coffin, without inscription or ornament, except the cross of Jerusalem. Innocent the Third made Trani an archbishopric.

West of the cathedral is the castle, consisting of some gloomy towers, built by Frederick of Swabia, who, in revenge for the depredations committed on his coasts by the Venetians, hanged Peter Tiepolo, the *Doge's* son, on the Keep, in sight of the Venetian gallies that were then cruizing off the port.

The monastery of St. Clare is a sumptuous inclosure; its great gate is built in that stile of architecture which the Puglians learnt from the Saracens during their long residence in the country. Those Africans, however ferocious they might be in war, were certainly well skilled in the arts of peace, and excelled in many branches of science, which Christians of those dark ages despised, or despaired of attaining.

In the first division of the conquests made by the Norman adventurers, and before any chieftain had acquired such a

B b                                 superiority

superiority over the reft, as to deftroy the original equality of their ariftocratical confederacy, Trani was affigned to one Peter, from whom the family of Capece deduces its pedigree, but, I think, on queftionable grounds *.

Under the walls of Trani was fought, in 1502, a trial of fkill between eleven Spaniards and as many Frenchmen, in

* Francis Capecelatro, in his Origin of Nobility, infifts upon it, that Peter bore the name of Capece by inheritance, and was of the blood of the Gothic princes. More moderate genealogifts believe the Capeci to be Normans by extraction, and to have fettled at Sorrento, where they recommended themfelves to notice by their fkill as naval officers; they frequently are called Cicaprec in old chronicles, a name that an ingenious friend of mine thinks the original one, and allufive of their profeffion. They were raifed early to an exalted rank in the ftate, and honoured with the confidence of many fovereigns. Marino Capece fuperintended the building of Manfredonia. Conrad fignalized himfelf in the Swabian caufe, which his family had always fupported, and probably owed his fortunes to after the battle of Benevento, he cut his way through the thickeft fquadrons of the enemy, headed a party in Sicily in favour of Conradine, and maintained to the laft an unfhaken fidelity to his old mafters. This conduct rendered the Capeci extremely odious to the conqueror, who deprived many individuals of their lives, and many of their eftates; he obliged the furvivors to tack ignominious additions to their furname, fuch as Latro, Galeota, Piticelli, Zurolo, Minutolo, Tomacelli, &c. which, in time, became honourable diftinctions of the feveral branches of this numerous fept. In Naples, a family that fpreads itfelf out into many branches, acquires thereby an increafe of dignity and influence. In fome countries, fuch a divifion contributes more to the deftruction than the propagation of a houfe. That of Capece was at one period divided into fixteen branches, but half of them are now extinct. It gave to the count of St. Peter, one pope, viz. Boniface the Ninth, elected in 1389, extolled for his chaftity, and blamed for his avarice and nepotifm. Of this race was James Galeota, who, in 1488, commanded the French army, and defeated the Dukes of Bretagne and Orleans at the battle of St. Aubin du Cormier. One of its moft refpectible prefent members, is the learned and amiable archbifhop of Taranto.

support of the honour of their respective nations; the Venetians sat as umpires. The combatants fought till there remained only six Spanish and four French knights; the latter then alighted, and defended themselves behind their horses as behind a rampart, till night put an end to the contest.

## SECTION XXIII.

BISCEGLIA is four miles distant from Trani. The road is very rugged, and being worn with wheels, and the course of rain water, is cracked into figures not unlike an ancient pavement; and such it has been deemed by some writers, but I could not discover any traces of a Roman way: the great Brundusian road never came near the coast till it reached Bari.

The face of this country is delightful, and much more diversified than the neighbourhood of the Ofanto. We rode under the shade of fruit trees, of a size and vigour of growth unknown in more northern latitudes. The olives of this province are not inferior in bulk to the largest Seville ones.

Bisceglia is a pretty town, situated in the midst of orchards and villas. Its walls are of stone, and very lofty. I was unsuccessful in my researches after the antique buildings mentioned in an account of this place. I met with no

B b 2 remains

remains of baths or cellars, but hundreds of subterraneous reservoirs and cisterns, of all sizes and shapes, cut into steps in the solid rock, and arched over with stones and stucco, in order to collect and preserve the rain-water, which is the only sort they have to drink, in a district so totally destitute of springs.

This little city was granted by Charles the First to the Bruneforts; but its inhabitants seem to have had a great dislike to baronial government, by the tender they made to the Emperor Charles the Fifth, of fourteen thousand golden ducats, a large sum in those days, provided he would render them for ever a royal corporation, subject only to the jurisdiction of the King's officers. In the wars between Durazzo and Anjou, the Bisceglians, being dissatisfied with the behaviour of King Charles's garrison, sent to offer the keys of their town to his rival. The Angevines marched from Bari; but, having met with an unexpected resistance at Bisceglia, were obliged to make their entry by main force. This appearance of double dealing in the citizens exasperated the soldiers, and gave them a plea for plundering it as a place taken by assault. They would have laid it waste, had not Lewis of Anjou, their chief, curbed their fury by extraordinary activity and dint of authority. These generous exertions cost him his life, for they threw him into a fever, of which he died. He was a younger son of John, King of France, and, during the minority of Charles the Sixth, Regent of that kingdom; a trust which he did

not

not difcharge to the fatisfaction of the nation : his proceedings were arbitrary, and the extortions he committed, or
fuffered to pafs unpunifhed, brought great odium upon
him. It was the defire of accumulating funds for his
Neapolitan expedition, and not innate avarice, that put him
upon rapacious meafures, for he poffiffed a liberal and
munificent fpirit, which attached to his caufe the partizans
he had gained by his eloquence and winning behaviour.
His wit was lively, and his head clear for bufinefs, but
he was not endowed with military talents, and by no
means a match for his antagonift Charles the Third, one of
the beft generals of the age. Joan the Firft adopted Lewis,
in oppofition to Durazzo; but he came too late to fave
her.

The clergy offer to the devotion of the Bifceglians the
liquefied blood of St. Pantaleon, and two other martyrs, a
miracle performed annually at Naples, and in feveral other
places of the kingdom. This fpecies of prodigy was known
to the Greeks of the Lower Empire, who introduced many
opinions and religious practices into this part of their dominions. But miraculous liquefactions are of older ftanding
in Puglia *.

* ————Dein Gnatia————
————————dedit rifufque jocofque,
Dum flammis fine thura liquefcere limine facro
Perfuadere cupit ————                    Hor Sat 5 Lib 1
" Next, Gnatia afforded fubject for laughter, while fhe endeavoured to
" perfuade us, that incenfe would melt on the threfhold of her temple, with-
" out the help of fire."

Three

Three miles more of the fame wretched road, through olive woods and patches of vineyards, brought us to Molfetta. I did not enter the walls, but paffed on through a well-built fuburb. The outward appearance of the town is handfome; but the peep I had through the gate, fhewed me nothing but lofty old-fafhioned houfes, and narrow dirty ftreets. It is faid to contain twelve thoufand inhabitants, and to carry on fome trade in almonds and oil. The lord-fhip belongs to the Spinolas.

In or near all thefe towns are convents of a ftupendous bulk. At Giovenazzo is a moft enormous fabric, belonging to the Dominicans; an order of friars that enjoys very large poffeffions in this realm, and in almoft every city has a monaftery, generally the beft in the place. St. Thomas of Aquino, one of the great luminaries of the Latin Church, and a capital Saint of the Dominican Order, was a native of this kingdom; confequently a very natural impulfe of national pride and affection led his countrymen to revere his memory, carefs his brethren, and help them to increafe in wealth and importance.

Giovenazzo is an ugly defolate city, on a rock hanging over the fea, containing about two thoufand fouls. It is now vefted in the Crown, after having been a barony of the Ginchet.

The only fingular anecdote I meet with in hiftory concerning Giovenazzo, is the devaftation of its territory in 1437 by the Pope's general, Vitelleichi, Patriarch of Alexandria,

andria, who invaded Puglia in support of the Angevine cause. His hatred to the Aragonese was most virulent; and he seemed afraid lest his troops should be deterred from doing mischief, by motives of compassion or Christian charity. To quiet their scruples, and rouse their destructive zeal, he published an indulgence of an hundred days for every olive tree any of his soldiers should cut down. Strange perversion of the mild religion of Christ, who forbade his disciples to avenge his wrongs, and prayed for his enemies, while tormented by their malice! Our astonishment ought to be great, not that so many nations have seceded from the communion of the Pope, but rather that so many have remained faithful to him, amidst such horrid abuses committed by his ministers, in direct contradiction to the doctrine they were appointed to teach *.

Our afternoon's ride of twelve miles was cold and damp, the wind blowing fresh from the sea, and the way lying upon a bare rugged rock, high above the water, exposed to

* To efface the ill impression of this contradictory conduct, the Romans are fond of citing a tale from Boccacio.—A Jew goes from Paris to Rome, in order to acquaint himself with the Christian religion, as at the fountain head. There he beholds every intrigue, and abomination of all sorts; and, after gratifying his curiosity in every particular, returns to France, where he gives a recital of his observations to a friend, by whom he had been long instructed in the Catholic faith. From such a recital, the Christian expected nothing but obstinate perseverance in the old worship; and was struck with amazement, when the Jew acquainted him with his resolution of requesting baptism upon the following grounds of conviction. That he had seen at Rome every body, from the Pope down to the beggar, using all their endeavours to subvert the Christian faith, which nevertheless daily took deeper and firmer root, and must therefore be of divine institution.

every

every blaſt. The country flat, and divided by ſtone walls. The ſoil is naturally poor, and would ſcarcely afford nouriſh-ment for a blade of graſs, had not the huſbandmen found means to improve and fertilize it by copious manurings of rotted ſea-weed, of which there is an ample proviſion in every cove. The active diſpoſition of the cultivators has converted their ſtubborn unfavourable land into the beſt tilled diſtrict in the province, and rendered its appearance luxuriantly rich and cheerful. It yields in abundance cot-ton, wine, oil, almonds, cummin, and fruits of numberleſs kinds and delicious flavour. The moſt eſteemed are the grape, fig, pear, and pomegranate: want of ſkill in the gardeners prevents the other ſorts from attaining that per-fection they might be brought to. It has very little ſilk, and boaſts of no mines; but there are ſalt-ponds, of great profit to the crown, the ſole proprietor of all ſalt, foſſile or factitious. A valuable breed of horſes may be reckoned among its ſtaple commodities, but how inferior in numbers and renown to the ſtuds of ancient Japygia! I do not believe the whole kingdom now breeds as many horſes as were to be found in this ſingle province at the time it offered to ſupply Rome with an auxiliary force of fifty thouſand foot and ſixteen thouſand horſe.—What ſwarms of men, what droves of animals, then ſubſiſted in a tract of land, where at this day a mere handful of human creatures, and a few beaſts, find it difficult to ſubſiſt, and almoſt every year are indebted to ſupplies of corn from other countries!

Ban

View of the ...

Bari makes a great figure at a diftance. We lodged at the Dominican convent, where the good hofpitable Prior gave us his own cell, as the repairs then in hand rendered the apartment for ftrangers abfolutely uninhabitable. A plentiful fifh fupper was provided for us by our kind hoft, anxious to fupport the reputation of Bari in that article The abundance and delicacy of the fifh vouch for Horace's knowledge of the peculiar excellencies of his own country *.

## SECTION XXIV.

BARI is defended by double walls and an old caftle; it occupies a rocky peninfula of a triangular form, about a mile in circumference. The houfes, which are in general mean, and without any pretenfions to ornamental archi-tecture, are built upon a foil raifed by the ruins of former edifices near thirty feet above the level of the fea. Pieces of old pavement have been frequently difcovered by digging feveral feet below the prefent ftreets, which are uneven, narrow, crooked, and dirty. The new rampart above the harbour, is the only clean walk, and few are more pleafant; at every turn you catch a different view of the fea and coaft, ftretching from the mountains of Garganus to the hills of Oftuni. The towns that rife along this line, in various

* ———Pifcofi mænia Bari

degrees

degrees of fhade, have a beautiful effect; and nothing can be more picturefque than the fleets of fifhing-boats fteering for their refpective harbours on the approach of night. On fhore, the full bloom of Spring and lively foliage, contrafted with innumerable white cottages, form an enchanting rural fcene.

There is fome reafon to fuppofe that ancient Barium extended farther into the country than the prefent city. Ifabella of Aragon, Dutchefs dowager of Milan, began to cut a canal through the Ifthmus, about half a mile from the gates: bridges were to correfpond with the principal ftreets, and the intermediate fpace to be built upon. But this grand work, which would have redounded to her immortal honour, and the commercial profperity of Bari, was deftroyed by a fudden inundation in a rainy feafon, and never afterwards attempted to be refumed.

The Cathedral has no external beauties; its infide has lately been modernized, ftuccoed, and painted, at the expence of the Archbifhop, whofe revenues do not exceed fix thoufand ducats (£1,125). Under the choir is a chapel, fupported upon fhort columns, which give it a great refemblance to the infide of the Mofque at Cordova. It is incruftated with party-coloured marbles, after a barbarous, fantaftic defign; and contains the bones of St. Sabinus, a patron of the town. The fteeple is remarkable for being one of the higheft in the kingdom *: a fecond was begun

---

* It is about two hundred and fixty-three feet high.

*

in 1617, but the apprehension of earthquakes stopped the work. The Barian writers pretend that the Norman kings, and some of their successors, were crowned in this church with an iron diadem, which is kept among its treasures; but Giannone and others treat the matter as a mere fable.

The royal Priory of St. Nicholas is an ugly Gothic edifice, erected by Archbishop Elias and King Roger. It is a celebrated sanctuary, whither thousands of pilgrims resort to offer up their vows at the shrine of this Bishop of Myra, the patron of orphans. His relics are said to have been brought from Lycia in 1087 by some merchants; though the legend assures us they floated hither of their own accord. The lands and immunities with which it was endowed by the Norman princes, were very considerable; and one of its earliest privileges was an exemption from every jurisdiction except the papal. Charles the First held the Saint in great veneration, and gave many solid proofs of his munificent devotion. But Charles the Second put the finishing hand to its establishment; for, imagining that he owed his deliverance from imprisonment and death to the intercession of his special protector, St. Nicholas, he thought himself bound in gratitude to confer upon his church an increase of wealth and splendour. Accordingly he obtained from the Pope many honourable distinctions, augmented and settled its possessions; and instituted for himself, and the succeeding Kings of Naples, the office of Treasurer, in which he was installed with great solemnity. The church

C c 2

is

is rich in marble columns, and ornaments aukwardly arranged. Behind the high altar is a very fumptuous monument, erected by Anne Jagellon, wife of Stephen Battori, King of Poland, to the memory of her mother Bona, who was daughter and heirefs of John Galeas, Duke of Milan, by Ifabella of Aragon, widow of Sigifmund the Firft, King of Poland, and Dutchefs of Bari by inveftiture. In 1556, Queen Bona came with a fplendid retinue to refide at Bari, where fhe died the following year. Her effigy is placed on its knees, and at the corners ftand four ftatues, reprefenting Poland, Lithuania, St. Staniflaus, and St. Nicholas. Here alfo is a dirty, dark, fubterraneous chapel, the original place of worfhip, over which King Roger raifed the prefent fabric. Underneath its altar is a hole, through which devout and curious perfons thruft their heads, to behold a bone or two fwimming below in water. This liquid is drawn up by the priefts in a filver bucket, and diftributed, under the name of Manna, as an infallible cure for fore eyes and difordered ftomachs. The chaplains were fo bufied in their refpective functions, that I could not obtain a fight of this tomb, and muft therefore content myfelf with the accounts I received from others. In this lower chapel Urban the Second affembled a general council of the Latin Church, which in 1097 decided in favour of the proceffion of the Holy Ghoft, and anathematized the Greek doctrine.

The

The caftle is fpacious and gloomy, inhabited by the Governor of the town, and a fmall garrifon. Bona repaired it in 1554 for the reception of her court.

Religious Orders abound in Bari, and fome of them have rich gaudy churches, with good paintings. The beft are, a *Noli me tangere*, by Pietro da Cortona, at Santa Chiara; a Defcent of the Crofs, by Carlo Cignani; and an Invention of it, by Paul Veronefe, at the Capuchins: in the Cathedral, fome large pieces by Luca Giordano and his fcholars. The convent of the Jefuits is converted into a college for young gentlemen [*].

I faw no monuments of antiquity, except a milliary column, fome infcriptions, and a lion, of barbarous fculpture, placed in the great fquare, by the citizens of Bari, in 1002, as an offering of thanks to the republic of Venice, and its Doge, Peter Vefcolo, who came with a powerful fleet, and obliged the Saracens to raife the fiege of this city.

Not far from the town, at a place faid to have been the general cemetery of ancient Barium, chance has brought to light great quantities of funeral pots, known among the virtuofi by the name of Etrufcan vafes, though for one that was moulded in Tufcany, thoufands were baked in Campania, where the fame fort of ware was in conftant ufe. They are greatly admired for the lightnefs of the clay,

* There are twelve convents for men, five for women, and three hofpitals.

the

the elegance of their forms, and the profound learning fuppofed to lie hidden beneath the ambiguous characters and
various groups, painted upon them in tawny yellow colours,
on a dark ground. Thefe figures, and the fhape of the
urns, have been of great fervice in improving the tafte, and
multiplying the ideas, of our artifts and porcelain manufacturers; but have contributed little to the advancement of
hiftorical or antiquarian knowledge, as fcarce a fingle group
has been explained to the univerfal fatisfaction of the
learned. The great vogue thefe veffels have had among the
rich and curious collectors of the age, has fet the ingenious
Italians to work in counterfeiting them; and it is now no
unufual thing for a young dilettante to have a modern jar,
with proper cracks and dirt, palmed upon him for a real
antique. A Barian citizen, lately poffeffed of a noted
affortment of thefe curiofities, told me that the moft beautiful of them had been found in a large fepulchre, about a
yard below the furface of the earth; it contained a fkeleton
inclofed within a ftone coffin, round which thefe vafes were
placed empty. Encouraged by this difcovery, he dug in
feveral other vineyards, and met with fimilar vaults, but no
urns of a fine grain or finifhed workmanfhip.

At the fouthern corner of the peninfula, is a kind of
harbour, affording tolerable fhelter to veffels of fmall burden. As Bari had formerly gallies of its own, I prefume it
had a fafer place for them to ride in. Its traffic was once
very flourifhing, being a mart for the Dalmatians and Le-
vantines;

vantines; but the exorbitant duties, and ill-judged reftrictions with which the commerce of this kingdom is hampered, have long ago driven merchants to other markets:
however, the Barians, whofe number amounts to fixteen
thoufand feven hundred, are an active pains-taking race, and
carry on no defpicable trade in oil and almonds, befides
thefe two capital objects, they fend a confiderable quantity
of potafh, foap, anifeed, and even garlick, to the Venetian iflands.

## SECTION XXV.

I FIND little mention made in ancient authors of Barium,
its foundation or hiftory; coins ftruck by its municipal
magiftrates ftill exift †.    The Lombards, Greeks, and Saracens, difputed the poffeffion of this city in the ninth century.    In the tenth, it rofe to diftinction, on becoming the
refidence of the Greek Catapan or Viceroy, and of a metropolitan Bifhop.    In 1689, the archiepifcopal dignity was
confirmed by the court of Rome.    The book of conftitu-
tions, compiled for the juridical government of the pro-

† Nummi Barinorum.
   ARG. 1. Cap Mercuru=Gryps BA
   ÆR. 1. Cap Jovis laur = Prora nav., in qua Cupido ftans arcum
        tend fubtus delphin ΒΑΡΙΝΩΝ
      2. Cap. Palladis gal.=Navis & Cupido coronam impon.
        trophæo
      3. Cap Jovis=Prora BARI. A..

vince,

vince, and still in use, is a respectable voucher for the importance and policy of Bari, during the middle ages.

bout the year 1000, Bari became the scene of conspiracies and revolutions: here Melo formed the project of the first confederacy against the Grecian Emperors, and though he did not live to see any great success attend his schemes, yet it was owing to his sagacity in pointing out the way, that the Normans were enabled to expell the Greeks from Italy; out of respect for his memory, those conquerors raised his son Argirius to the supreme command over their league. Bari did not steadily adhere to Melo's plans, but soon returned to the obedience of the eastern Emperor, and was one of the last and firmest supports of his dominion.

In 1067, Robert Guiscard invested it by sea and land, and to prevent succours being thrown in, inclosed it with a semicircle of ships joined together by chains and booms, each extremity having a bridge of communication with the camp, which completed the line of circumvallation. This blockade lasted four years, during which, both parties exhausted every art of attack and defence practised in those ages, when the machines for demolishing fortifications were clumsy and feeble, and when famine, more frequently than force, compelled towns to surrender. The Barians, finding themselves worn out with hard fare and incessant alarms, and foreseeing that the obstinacy of their adversary would at length overcome their powers of defence, endeavoured to avert their ruin by cutting off the chief of the besiegers;

5                                                     with

with this intent, one Amerinus ftole out of the city by night, and drawing up to the quarters of Guifcard, attempted to kill him, by thrufting a poifoned lance through the wattles of his hut; but the weapon proved too fhort, and Robert, as we are told by his honeft biographer Malaterra, took care to have the wickered walls of his cabbin well plaftered over, to prevent fuch attacks for the future.

Earl Roger foon after joined his brother with a ftrong fleet, and helped him to carry on his affaults with fuch vigour, that the befieged were on the point of capitulating, when their hopes were revived by the appearance of an Imperial fquadron coming to their relief, under Jofceline d'Avranches, a Norman gentleman, who had fought his fortune in Greece, and ingratiated himfelf with the Emperor The Greek fhips were no fooner defcried, than Roger flipped his cables, and ran out to fea to give them battle. Jofceline was true to his truft, and bore down gallantly upon the Earl: the engagement was fharp, but very fhort; for the Greeks were no match for the Norman veterans. The Imperial veffels were taken, funk, or difperfed, and their admiral made a prifoner. Roger returned triumphant, and Bari opened its gates to the conquerors.

To fecure the allegiance of fo capital a town, a citadel was afterwards erected by King Roger; but it was fcarcely finifhed, when the Emperor Lotharius razed it to the ground. Upon the retreat of the Imperialifts, Jacinthus affumed the title of Prince, and refufed to fubmit to the King, who laid fiege to the city. Bari was then a populous

D d place,

place, and made an obftinate refiftance. The capitulation was honourable, but rendered invalid by a claufe, ftipulating, that all the Royalifts, taken during the fiege, were to be delivered up fafe and unhurt. When the King made his entry into Bari, a Norman captive, who had been deprived of his fight, and otherwife cruelly treated by the orders of Jacinthus, was led through the crowd to the feet of his fovereign, to claim juftice and vengeance. Roger, willing to feize any pretext for annulling the capitulation, affembled his council, declared the treaty void, and caufed Jacinthus, with his principal adherents, to be hanged.

Majone, prime minifter to William the Bad, was born at Bari, the fon of a notary; but the affection, we may prefume, this favourite retained for the place of his nativity, did not prevent William from treating it with the utmoft feverity. The Barians had joined in the grand rebellion againft him, had demolifhed his caftle and palace, and given the furniture as plunder to their foldiers; therefore, when the chief citizens fell on their knees before him, fuing for mercy, he anfwered all their fupplications with thefe words: " You did not fpare my houfe, how can you ex-" pect I fhould fpare yours?" They were ordered to diflodge within the fpace of two days, and their dwellings to be levelled to the ground. The city muft have rifen very fpeedily out of its ruins, as the Emperor Frederick eftablifhed an annual fair here in 1233, and in 1248, ordered the town to be deftroyed, to punifh the inhabitants for treafonable practices.

The

The firft perfon enfeoffed with the honours of Bari was Bohemund of Antioch, who accepted of thefe and other demefnes in lieu of his birthright. The fecond was Tancred fon of King Roger; Jacinthus had them next. The Princes of Taranto, defcended from Charles the Second, held them afterwards. Their heirefs carried this barony into the houfe of Baux, which was difpofleffed by Joan the Firft. During her reign, John Pipino Earl of Minervino, ufurped this fief for a fhort time. He was the fon of an officer of the revenue, who, having amaffed great riches by the management of the public money, or by treafures found at Lucera, where he fuperintended the expulfion of the Saracens, purchafed large eftates for his children. John was an empty vain-glorious man, deceived into a high opinion of his own confequence by the flattery of mifcreants and parafites, who flocked from all parts to fhare the prodigal bounty of this new-made nobleman. The fuccefs that attended an expedition againft Nicholas Rienzi, the famous tribune of Rome, completed his intoxication. The Orfini and Colonna factions, being overpowered by that demagogue, craved affiftance from Minervino, who always entertained a formidable band of foldiers ready for mifchief. Pipino embraced the opportunity of employing his troops, defeated Nicholas, and returned to Puglia mad with joy and pride. His infolence, rapacity, and exceffes now difdained all bounds; and half the neighbouring provinces were defolated by his lawlefs freebooters. The royal anger was at laft roufed, and a complete overthrow, near Afcoli, crufhed all

his

his glories; his adherents fled, and Pipino himfelf, abandoned and betrayed, was taken and hanged at a window of
the caftle of Altamura; his brothers fhared his unhappy
fate: and thus one generation faw the rife and fall of this
powerful family.

Ladiflaus granted Bari to the Orfini Princes of Taranto,
who afterwards enjoyed it almoft as a free fovereignty,
having extorted from Alphonfus the Firft the privilege of
exporting all manner of commodities without paying any
duties to the crown. This exemption brought in great riches,
and rendered them very formidable, as Ferdinand the Firft
found to his forrow, in his wars with the Barons. While
Aragon and Anjou were contending, James Caldora, a
famous Abruzzefe chieftain feized upon Bari, and his fon
Anthony affumed the title of Duke.

Upon the extinction of the houfe of Taranto, Bari re-
verted to the King, and was fettled by Alphonfus the
Second, upon the family of Sforza, in confideration of the
marriage of his daughter Ifabella with the Duke of Milan.
According to treaty, thefe eftates became the property of
Bona Queen of Poland, at whofe death this duchy returned to the crown; to which it has ever fince remained
annexed.

Our ftay at Bari was prolonged by my fellow-traveller's
being feized with a feverifh complaint, which at firft wore
an alarming appearance, but foon took a favourable turn:
however, he did not think it fafe to continue his journey

farther

farther south, as the weather was growing very warm; and therefore determined to return to Naples as soon as possible. I continued our original route on the 29th of April.

The first place I came to was Mola di Bari, a town containing six thousand souls, prettily situated on rocks, and very shewy from afar : what it may be on a nearer view I know not, as I rode past without stopping, my memorandums making no mention of any thing remarkable in it. I next passed by the Franciscan convent of Cape San Vito, delightfully seated among the olive groves, on a neck of land jutting out into the sea. Here travellers usually dine or sleep ; but as it had been represented to me as a very bad place of baiting, I rode a mile farther for dinner to Polignano, a small city, perched, like a bird's nest, on a crag rising perpendicularly out of the water. The bishop resides at Mola. The Caraccioli, Rodolvich, Toraldi, Stendardi, Boffa, and Lieto, have been successively lords of this place.

The soil of the whole tract I travelled through this morning is shallow and rocky, covered with olive trees, which are the principal object of the cultivator's care, as oil is the main support of commerce in this province. The rocks abound with pectinites of a large size.

While my dinner was preparing, I amused myself with looking at some peasants casting wooden balls with their feet; they are extremely dextrous at the sport, lifting the ball up with their toe, and tossing it a considerable length, along a high road as rugged and full of protuberances as the Glaciers of Switzerland.

4

In the afternoon, I had a pleafant ride of five miles, through noble olive woods, to Monopoli. This city, like moft others on the coaft, deceives one by its outward appearance into an opinion of extent and magnificence, which vanifhes on clofer infpection. The environs are neatly planted with fig, almond, and fome few lemon and orange trees. I faw but one garden that had any fhew of thofe evergreen fruit trees to boaft of. Olives are the grand concern. The extent of the plantations of this valuable tree is really aftonifhing. I was affured that the olive woods reach from Monopoli twelve miles, on three fides, without interruption. There are no great Barons in its immediate neighbourhood; and every burgher has his maffaria or farm, which he cultivates on his own account. This territory is faid to yield annually twenty thoufand falme of oil.

Monopoli is a dark difagreeable town, with narrow, crooked ftreets, and very lofty flat-roofed houfes. It is fuppofed to have been originally a ftation called Egnatiolum, and to have grown to the fize and dignity of a city, by the ruin of Gnatia. In the fift Norman partition, it fell to the fhare of Hugh. The Capeci were for fome time its poffeffors.

## SECTION XXVI.

NEXT morning I was on horfeback before fun-rife, intending to make a very long day's journey; and being apprehenfive, from the heavy feel of the air, that I fhould fuffer from intenfe heat in the noon-tide hours. My prognoftics were but too juft; for a hotter fun, and a more ftifling fultrinefs, could not be felt in the dog-days.

The foil of the country is a reddifh petrifaction, evidently the fame as the rocks upon the fhore. As I rode along, the huge piles of fea-weed, which almoft form a rampart on the coaft, appeared to be equally unaffected either by wind or waves I alighted feveral times to examine thefe heaps, and found different degrees of hardnefs in them. Some were quite moift and mucilaginous; others already petrified on the furface, but foft and pliable within; others again thoroughly pervaded by the ftony humour.

The fwarth on the fands is very poor, and produces few uncommon plants One is a beautiful poppy, of a bright yellow colour.

At a mile's diftance from Monopoli, the landfcape expands itfelf, and on the right hand difcovers a long range of woody hills. The olive grounds in the plain are remarkable for their great extent, thicknefs of foliage, and fize of trees.

They

They are pruned into the form of a cup, by cutting out the centric upright branches, in the same manner as gardeners trim gooseberry bushes. This treatment lets in an equal share of sun and ventilation to every part, and brings on an universal maturity.

Six miles farther are the ruins of Gnatia, the last stage but one of Horace's journey to Brundusium, and now called Torre d'Agnazzo. Little remains except part of the ramparts, which, near the sea, are entire as high up as the bottom of the battlements. Sixteen courses of large stones are still complete; and the thickness of this bulwark is exactly eight yards; an extaordinary breadth, which I ascertained by repeated measurements. The town seems to have been square, and its principal streets drawn in straight lines. On the most elevated part is a watch-tower; and probably this was the situation of the ancient citadel. Near it are some arches and vaults. The view towards Monopoli is extremely beautiful.

Want of water caused the destruction of Gnatia; a scarcity I had an opportunity of being made sensible of, and which naturally explains Horace's phrase of

———Gnatia lymphis
Iratis exstructa ———

The few pastoral inhabitants of these ruins have no temples left to melt incense in without fire, for the diversion or astonishment of passengers. But the art is not lost in the kingdom;

kingdom; and, whether preserved by tradition or revived by ingenuity, is still practised with success.

The stone employed in building along this coast, is cut with great ease in every part of the country. It is a soft whitish concretion, that hardens by being exposed to the air. The method used by the quarrymen is extremely simple: they clear away the soil from the level parts, and then hew out regular cubes, which leave vacancies in the rock exactly resembling ponds, baths, or reservoirs, with flights of steps all round leading down to the bottom. These holes are frequently filled up with earth, and olive sets planted in them.

The cystus, which grows in great abundance on these waste lands, exhaled so powerful an effluvium, when the sun had been risen some time, that I was overcome with it. One of the servants, already half dead with heat and fatigue, had the additional ill-fortune of being frightened almost out of his wits. As we were trotting along the burning sands, he on a sudden gave a loud shriek, and threw himself from his horse, crying out that he was a dead man, for either a scorpion, a tarantula, or a serpent had stung him on the instep. On pulling off his boot, I found that his terrors and pains were caused by the rays of the sun, which had penetrated through a hole in the upper leather, and raised a blister on the skin. The preposterous gestures and expressions of this lazzarone supported my spirits till we arrived at a small single house, consisting

of

of a kitchen, loft, and ftable, lately erected for the convenience of travellers, by the agents of the Order of Malta,
to which the land belongs. The kitchen was too hot for
me to breathe in, and the other two apartments as full of
fleas as Shakefpeare's inn at Rochefter; fo that my only
refuge was the narrow fhade of the houfe, which was con-
tracted every minute more and more, as the fun advanced
towards the meridian. Behind the houfe then I fat down,
to dine upon the fare we had brought in our wallet. Unluckily I had not thought of wine or water, neither of
which were now to be had tolerably drinkable; fo that I
was obliged to content myfelf with the water of a ciftern
full of tadpoles, and qualify it with a large quantity of wine,
that refembled treacle much more than the juice of the
grape. While I held the pitcher to my lips, I formed a
dam with a knife, to prevent the little frogs from flipping
down my throat. Till that day I had had but an imperfect
idea of thirft.

As foon as we had recruited our ftrength and fpirits, we
left the inn, and retired gradually from the fea, drawing up
towards the hills, through olive groves that afforded us a
very welcome fhade. Flocks of turtle doves fkimmed acrofs
the road; but, though they frequently fluttered near me, I
refpected the virtues afcribed to them by the poets too much
to think of fhooting at them :—young ones are efteemed a
great dainty. The mode of killing them is very fingular :
When the fun is vertical, and the fky clear, a couple of

fportfmen

ſportſmen drive into the olive grounds in an open chaiſe, and move ſlowly, but continually, round the trees, till they ſpy a dove ſitting upon the boughs. The poor bird, ſtruck with the unuſual ſight, or giddy with the rotation of the wheels, fixes its eyes upon them, and whirls its head round in imitation of their motion. When the eye of the turtle is thus faſcinated, one of the fowlers ſlips out of the carriage, and fires his piece. Little ſtone baſons full of water are alſo frequently placed for the doves to drink at, while the ſhooter lies in ambuſcade behind a buſh.

At the end of ſix miles we rode up to Oſtuni, a poor epiſcopal city, on a ſteep rocky brow, overlooking a whole foreſt of olive trees, and a long range of coaſt. In the fourteenth century it belonged to the Sanſeverini, and afterwards to the Zevallas *.

* On a green before the church of the Capuchin friars, the Duke delle Noci was killed in ſingle combat by the Duke of Martina in 1664, at which time the fury of faſhionable murder raged with great violence among the proud ungovernable nobles

A moſt famous duel was fought the ſame year between Don Francis Caraffa and Don Julius Aquaviva, who, after many bootleſs altercations, finding themſelves under an indiſpenſable neceſſity of deciding a family quarrel by the ſword, ſought for a proper place to engage in No Roman Catholic ſtate would allow of a public duel, becauſe ſuch combats are anathematized by the eccleſiaſtical canons, they therefore applied to the imperial city of Nuremberg, and obtained leave to draw regular bills, and to come to action, under the ſafeguard of that magiſtracy, in preſence of the nobility of the country Don Francis was diſabled by a wound in the arm, and the victory adjudged to his antagoniſt —The doughty knights embraced on the field of battle, and returned together very good friends to Naples. Such an adventure as this caſt a ridicule upon the practice, and co-operated with the growing effeminacy of manners in ſtifling the ſpirit of duelling

We now entered a more agreeable atmofphere, where the heat was tempered by a gentle breeze. The appearance of Oftuni was fo far from inviting, that I determined to travel to Francavilla that night. The road was ftony, and continually up and down hill, through a poor defert country, much covered with thin woods of unhealthy ftunted oaks. Thefe hills are the fouth-eaft extremity of a ridge that runs out from the Apennines, at a point many miles to the north-eaft of our road: we never came in fight of any mountains. From hence to the cape of Santa Maria di Leuca *, there is not a fingle eminence of any confequence; the whole tract is rather an uneven plain than a hilly country. Without rivers, and almoft without rivulets, yet from fome extraordinary quality in the foil, and the vapours of fubterraneous lakes, this province is furprifingly fertile and vegetative. The exiftence of underground refervoirs is proved by the fhallownefs of the wells, and by the pools that appear wherever the level is low. All the rain that falls is fwallowed up, before it can reach the fea, by large cracks in the rocks, called Voraggini, or Abyffes, marked down in the maps as lakes. In this corner of Italy every geographer, except Zannoni, draws, from the Apennines near Venofa to the Capo di Leuca, an uninterrupted diagonal chain of lofty mountains, upon which is written, *Branch of the Apennines.* This line is engraved of a fize that would, if

_____

* The ancient Promontorium Salentinum, which terminates the peninfula of Japygia, at the tip of the heel of the boot, to which geographers have likened the fhape of Italy.

it

it exifted, render the communication between Bari and Taranto, as difficult as the paffage of Mount Cenis or Sempion in the Alps. Had thefe geographers vifited the country they were about to delineate, or even enquired of the common carriers how they pafs this imaginary cordillera, they would foon have been made fenfible of their error; for fo little is the whole tract aforefaid raifed above the level of the fea, that, from the round Knolls of Oria, a centrical point between Taranto and Brindifi, there are few rifings high enough to prevent the eye from commanding a view as far as the fea, in each direction. Had they attended to the idea conveyed by Virgil, in his defcription of the diftant appearance of this peninfula, they might have fufpected fomething of the truth. That fenfible poet plainly indicates the lownefs of the Salentine fhores, in the third book of the Æneid, where his Hero relates the voyage fouthward, from that point of Epirus called the Acroceraunian mountains, now Monti della Chimera, which are not fixty miles from Otranto:

Provehimur pelago vicina Ceraunia juxta ;
Unde iter Italiam, curfuique breviffimus undis—
\* \* \* \* \* + ¬ ɪ
Jamque rubefcebat ftellis Aurora fugatis,
Cùm femel *obfcuros colles,* *humilen*que videmus
Italiam \* ——— ———

---

\* " We are carried on the waves near the Ceraunian cape, from which " point is the fhorteft paffage to Italy ——And now Aurora rofe blufhing, " after putting the ftars to flight, when fuddenly we behold the *dufky hills* " and *low fhores* of Italy "

Could

Could they fuppofe fo exact a defcriber would have called
Italy *low*, and fpoken only of *hills*, lighted up by the rifing
fun, if there had been any mountains in the Salentine territory, where, from the narrownefs of the land, they muft
have reached to the very edge of the water? Every one
that knows any thing of the Italian atmofphere, muft
recollect that fixty miles is not a fufficient diftance to hide
fuch mountains as the Apennines from the fight, if they
really did extend their branches fo near to Greece; and
that to navigators their tops would be vifible in the morning, long before the low country at their feet.

Towards dufk, we left the high lands, and traverfing a
well-cultivated champaign country, arrived at Francavilla,
where, by the Prince's orders, I was received and treated
with extraordinary refpect.


## S E C T I O N   XXVII.

I OUGHT to efteem the next day as one of the moft
brilliant of my life; for I received honours fufficient to
turn the head of a plain Englifh gentleman. As foon as I
was dreft, an audience was demanded by Don Domenico,
the Steward, who having formerly officiated in the capacity
of Clerk of the Chamber to the Princefs, was perfectly
qualified for the poft of Mafter of the Ceremonies. Being
admitted in his gala fuit of many colours and antique

cut,

cut, he expreffed his difappointment on finding he had the
honour of receiving but one *Nobile Signore* inftead of two,
as his mafter had notified. After I had explained the
reafon of my friend's abfence, he launched out into pathetic
compliments of condolance, and promifed me, that the
chaplain fhould offer up prayers for his fpeedy recovery.
And now the Rector of the College, the Father Guardian
of the Capuchins, and the Magiftrates, entered in great
form. The firft addreffed me in a fhort, polite fpeech,
which he uttered with fome embarraffment. My introducer
of Ambaffadors whifpered in my ear, that the Rector had
compofed a very eloquent harangue for *two* illuftrious
travellers; but on finding only one, had been obliged to
lay it afide, as he could not at a minute's warning adapt to
the fingular all the figures of rhetoric which were addreffed to the dual number. What I loft in his difcourfe,
was made up to me by the friar, who, with a nafal tone
and many bows, beftowed upon me every poffible virtue,
and ftruck out fuch wild metaphors, as quite enchanted his
auditors, and almoft threw me off my guard. He acquainted the company, that I travelled into foreign parts to
collect oil for the lamps of fcience in my own country;
that my mother wit was the wick, and my eloquence the
flame.——I was happy to difmifs the orators, and was ac-
companying them to the door, when my Mentor ftopped
me fhort, left I fhould make too great a conceffion.

I was

I was afterwards conducted to the chapel, where the town-muficians played, and a cloud of incenfe darkened the place during the whole fervice; after which Don Domenico led me out to fee the town, or rather to be feen, for we had a mob at our heels all the way. I was heartily fick of my glory, and fhould have fled from it, had I not been fenfible how great a mortification it would have been to my hofts.

Francavilla is large and regularly built; the ftreets wide and ftraight; the houfes fhewy, though in a heavy ftyle of architecture. Since the year 1734, when a confiderable part of the town was thrown down by an earthquake, the inhabitants are fo afraid of another vifitation, that they dare not raife their dwellings more than one ftory above the ground-floor. The main ftreet would be thought handfome even in a capital city. The avenues to the gates are well planted, and afford a pleafant fhade. The inhabitants, in number twelve thoufand, fubfift by the fale of oil and cotton, of which laft they make very fine ftockings. A great quantity of tobacco is raifed in the lordfhip, which, by a compofition entered into with the farmers of the revenue, is allowed to be cured and manufactured here into a fpecies of fnuff, in colour, flavour, and foftnefs, not a bad imitation of the Spanifh.

The Capuchins have a fpacious convent, and a new church, airily and fantaftically fitted up: the pulpit and

5

confeffionals

confeffionals are of inlaid wood, worked by the hands of a friar.

The college, directed by priefts of the Scuolepie, is a large edifice, with many handfome halls and galleries. They teach, as far as philofophy inclufively, to about half a dozen boarders, and a confiderable number of day-fcholars.

The principal parifh-church is new, gay, and well lighted; but fo ftuccoed, feftooned, and flowery, that the whole decoration is a mere chaos. The plan was drawn at Rome, but executed by a Puglian architect, who from caprice or blunder reverfed the difpofition of the parts, and opened the chief door at the head of the Latin crofs, a place ufually allotted to the altar and choir. This altera-tion is no improvement in the art, but, on the contrary, an experiment productive of very aukward effects. In a fide chapel is a dark portrait of the Madonna, which was the caufe of the foundation of the town.

In 1310, as Philip of Anjou, Prince of Taranto, was hunting in the forefts, which then covered the face of the country, a ftag was driven into a grotto, where the huntf-men difcovered this wonder-working image. It was re-moved with great folemnity to a chapel, and, in order to encourage people to fettle round it for its defence, Philip granted lands to all comers, with ten years exemption from taxes, and, as a pledge of the fincerity of his intentions, named the colony *Francavilla*, or Freetown; and gave it

an

an olive tree,. the emblem of peace and fertility, for its armorial feal.

The number of thefe devout paintings extant in the Neapolitan dominions, and faid by their legends to have been accidentally difcovered in caverns, woods, or wells, need not furprife us, if we recollect that the Saracens frequently over-ran thefe provinces. On the approach of the Barbarians, it is natural to fuppofe that the Greeks, who were undoubtedly the painters of fuch portraits, would hide what was moft precious to them, and moft obnoxious to the infults of the infidels. The hiding-places were forgotten, either from the long refidence of the invaders in the kingdom, or the deftruction of thofe who fecreted the holy treafures.

The Prince's manfion is a quadrangular caftle, furrounded by a dry ditch. The apartments are fpacious; but, as the owner has been abfent above fourteen years, every thing wears the face of neglect and decadency.

This and the adjoining manors were purchafed, about the middle of the fixteenth century, by the Imperiali of Genoa, from St. Charles Borromeo, archbifhop of Milan; who, if we may believe his biographers, diftributed in one day the whole purchafe-money to the poor of his diocefe, at that time afflicted with the joint fcourges of peftilence and famine.

The Marquis of Oria, grandfather to the prefent proprietor, refided conftantly on his eftate; and being an adept in rural œconomy, managed all his concerns himfelf, received

his

his rents in kind, and, by his great skill in disposing of his commodities to advantage, made every article turn to account. At present, very little remains unlet; the rents are paid as the crops are got in and sold, not at stated days of payment. All tythes belong to the Lord of the Manor, who is the lay impropriator, for the Church has only its glebe. Many gentlemen of a secondary rank hold their lands of the Prince, as under-tenants, by the payment of a fixed fine for their investiture, nearly in the same manner as our copyholders make surrenders, and hold estates by copy of court-roll. There are besides many owners of land, not of noble degree, who pay the tenth of all their crops to the Prince.

After my walk, I sat down to a pompous repast, but as the cook, who was never very skilful in his profession, and had been twenty years retired upon half-pay, chose to exert all his abilities on so grand an occasion, it was scarcely possible to get down any of his ragouts, and out of the reach of all guessing to name a single dish. I could not prevail on Don Domenico, or any of my company, to partake of the feast; so that I sat, like Governor Sancho, surrounded by all my officers, doctor, steward, chaplain, and musicians. In one point my case differed from that of the 'squire errant; for the physician, instead of conjuring away the plates, was very attentive in recommending and pressing me to eat of every dish, though I

observed

observed he durst not venture to fix a name upon any one of them.

After this long and tiresome meal, I was left to take my afternoon nap, and in the evening entertained with the tragedy of Judith and Holofernes, acted by the young people of the town, in a theatre belonging to the castle. Their rude accent, forced gestures, and strange blunders in language, rendered their dismal drama a complete farce. When the heroine murdered the general, the whole house shook with thundering bursts of applause; the upper part of his body was hidden by the side scenes; the lower parts lay on a couch upon the stage, and in the agonies of death were thrown into such convulsions, kickings, and writhings, as melted the hearts and ravished the souls of the attentive audience. Judith then came forward, and repeated a long monologue, with her sword in one hand, and a barber's block, dripping with blood, in the other. Never was tragedy-queen sent off the stage with louder or more sincere acclamations.

## SECTION XXVIII.

*May 2d.* I TOOK a ride to Oria, a city romantically situated upon three hills, in the centre of the plains. The castle and cathedral stand boldly on the highest points. This is a place of great antiquity, a colony of Cretans; on

its

its coins a minotaur*. Servilius, an officer of Octavius Cæsar, was here surprised by Mark Antony. In the lower ages it became part of the rich patrimony of the Baux. The Bonifazii were afterwards possessed of Oria; but about the year 1540 the last male heir of the family renounced his country and fortune with his religion, and retired to Geneva. The cause of this renunciation was the shameless conduct of his sisters, who, by living in public concubinage with the Viceroy and the Nuncio, brought disgrace upon their brother. The Marquisate now belongs to the Prince of Francavilla.

I continued my ride a few miles south, to another estate of the Imperiali, called Casalnuovo, through an open country, abounding with corn and cotton, prettily divided by rows of olive and almond trees. The cotton was just coming up, with two yawning lobes, exactly like the cotyledones of the common bean. It is of the shrubby kind, and, when full grown, resembles the raspberry plant. The pods of cotton are at top, and, when ripe, burst, and disclose a tuft of down, the wings destined to convey the seed through the air. The land intended for this crop is very neatly drest, and laid down in flat narrow ridges : the season for ploughing, between January and April The cotton is then sown, and, as soon as the shoots appear, the

---

* Nummi Hyrinæorum

ARG. 1. Cap Palladis gal noctua.=Minotaurus gradiens ΥΡΙΝΑΙ.
    2 Cap. Pallad.= Minotaurus ΙΛΝΙΑΥ
    3 Facies plena imb =Minotaurus ΛΝΙΑΥ.

field

field is hoed, and weeded with a small mattock. After a crop of cotton, it is ufual to take one of wheat, then one of barley or oats; afterwards the land is fuffered to lie fallow, or is ufed as a pafture for fheep during twelve months, and the enfuing year it is again fit for cotton. Thefe grounds are tilled in partnerfhip: the proprietor ploughs it the firft time; the tenant gives it four fubfe-quent ploughings, and furnifhes feed; the expence of the harveft is born equally by both, and the profits halved between them. Hoers earn a carlino a day, and a good ploughman four carlini, or five grana and his victuals.

Cafalnuovo is a confiderable town, without any buildings of note, except a large baronial manfion in the centre, begun by the late Marquis, and left unfinifhed at his death. The fuite of apartments is grand, but the fituation uncom-fortable, without garden or profpect. He chofe to remove to this place, becaufe the rocky foil affords a folid founda-tion for a houfe, and the air is remarkably wholefome; whereas Francavilla is the very reverfe, being built on a marfhy, unfound foil, where it is even difficult to find a bottom, and all the water has a brackifh tafte.

This town contains about four thoufand inhabitants, noted for nothing but their tafte for dogs flefh, in which they have no competitors that I know of, except their neighbours at Lecce, and the newly difcovered voluptuaries of Otahcite. We did not fee one animal of the canine fpecies in the ftreets; and woe be to the poor cur that fol-lows

lows its master into this cannibal settlement! I could not prevail upon my conductor to own whether they had any flocks of puppies, as of sheep; or took any pains, by castration or particular food, to fatten and sweeten the dainty before they brought it to the shambles. I have since procured some information on the subject from impartial persons, and find that the people of this neighbourhood are looked upon by the rest of the kingdom as dog-eaters; and that it is certain that, both at Lecce and Casalnuovo, many of the lower sort relish a slice of a well-fed cur. At both places tanners kidnap dogs, and tan their hides into an imitation of Turkey leather, with which they supply the gentlemen of the neighbouring cities, who are nice in their slippers. This demand for false Morocco occasions the slaughter of many dogs, and no doubt the custom of eating their flesh began among the needy tanners · hunger and experience have taught their countrymen to consider the discovery as a very beneficial one. At Bari and Francavilla, horse-flesh is said to be publicly sold in the market; and the tail left on, to shew the wretched purchasers what beast the meat belonged to. The wits among the populace nick-name these shamble horses *Caprio ferrato*, i. e. a shod Deer.

The Bailiff of the Manor informed me, that it contained six convents of men and two of women, and that the Belles Lettres flourished extraordinarily; for, besides himself, he could reckon up twelve men of great learning in the place,

place, who formed an academy; viz. two doctors of phyfic, two apothecaries, and eight men of the law. A tremendous junto for the poor Dog-eaters! There is neither trade nor manufactures here; the fruits of the earth are confumed on the fpot; if any remain above the confumption, they are fent to Taranto for fale.

On this fide ftood Manduria, a city of the Tarentines, deftroyed by Fabius Maximus in the fecond Punic war. Its coins are faid to have been dug up lately, but I never faw any; traces of the old name exift in fome fields called Il Campo Mandurino, and in a chapel dedicated to St. Pietro Mandurino. The Cafalnuovians being defirous of refuming the original appellation, have lately petitioned the King for leave to quit the name of Cafalnuovo, and to take that of Manduria in all public deeds.

At a fmall diftance from the town, the old walls are very difcernible, raifed feveral feet above the ground; they are double, except on the fouth fide, where the fortifications appear to have been left incomplete. The outer wall and its ditch meafure eight yards in breadth; behind this bulwark is a broad ftreet, and then an inner wall, which together meafure fourteen yards. The ftones are oblong, laid in courfes without mortar, and cut out of the ditch; the rocky ftratum, which comes to the furface with very little covering of mould, is a concretion of fea fand and fhells: thefe exuviæ of marine bodies, when decompofed by the action of the atmofphere, are converted into a moft fertile

tile soil. It is truly wonderful that such fruitfulness should exist in a country to all outward appearance as destitute of water as Arabia Petræa.

The greatest curiosity here is a well, mentioned by Pliny in his second Book[*]. In a field within the ancient inclosure, we descended several steps into a large circular cavern, lighted from above by a spacious aperture, the water comes from the north-west, and may be heard very distinctly under the rock, it issues out with force, and after running along a short channel, loses itself in a round bason by some subterraneous conduits. What excites the admiration of the neighbours, as it did that of their forefathers, is, that at no time the water ever rises or falls above a certain mark, if you throw in as much rubbish as will fill it half way up, this accession will nevertheless have no effect upon the level, even should you heap up the dirt above the mark, the water will not rise, but remain totally hidden; clear away the mud to the bottom, you will come to a hard smooth floor, without any signs of a chasm for the water to run off by. As too much curiosity, if indulged in examining the construction of this well, might endanger the loss of the only supply of good drinking water in the township, all experiment and removals are strictly forbidden. The rock is of a very porous nature, and the water carried off by a

[*] Juxta oppidum Mandurium lacus ad margines plenus, neque exhaustis aquis minuitur, neque infusis augetur.

G g

quick

quick filtration: as the ftream is no doubt formed by the overflowings of fome underground lake or river coming from the vaft refervoirs in the bofom of the Apennines, and has other paffages for its difcharge, the well is probably filled with the backwater only, and therefore the dirt thrown in muft of courfe prevent the water from entering the bafon *.

* Thefe eftates have fince efcheated to the Crown, by the death of Michael Imperiali, Prince of Francavilla, without heirs. No collateral heir beyond the third degree of confanguinity is capable of inheriting a fief in the kingdom of Naples.

# TARANTO, and its ENVIRONS.

---

## SECTION XXIX.

May 3d } I LEFT Francavilla, escorted by four well-mounted and well-armed guards in the Prince's pay. Every great Baron* keeps a certain number of trusty determined fellows to protect his vassals, convoy his rents, and prevent depredations on his game and forests; they travel by the side of his coach to defend his person and baggage; but as I was under no apprehension of an attack, I dismissed these attendants as soon as possible, and sending the servants on to Taranto to prepare my reception, sauntered slowly after them, that I might enjoy the pure morning breeze, and examine the country. Near Francavilla the soil is deep, and

---

* Our old English Barons had their Rod knights or Radmen, who held lands of them on the condition of attending their persons in their travels, and going wheresoever they pleased to send them

cultivated

cultivated with some degree of neatness; but I saw neither spring nor rivulet. These farms are bounded by extensive wastes, where the rocks are scantily covered with a mossy swarth. At Le Grottaglie, a large village belonging to Cicinelli Prince of Cursi, I arrived at the high plain of Oria, and by a steep descent entered the low one of Taranto, the separation is not gradual, but suddenly made by a barrier of perpendicular rocks, that run from the mountains quite across to the gulf. Le Grottaglie owes its origin to a concourse of inhabitants from many towns and villages laid in ashes by the Saracens; finding no other place of safety, the fugitives took refuge in these grottos and caverns, and by degrees recovering from their dismay, ventured out and built dwellings above ground. By one of those monstrous contradictions, of which the feudal system of Naples affords many examples, the criminal jurisdiction of this lordship appertains to the Archbishop of Taranto, while the civil is vested in its Prince. The people of this town are said to understand the business of a shepherd better than any of their neighbours, among whom their cream-cheeses are in great repute. The country abounds in corn and wine, but of late years they have treated their vines with so little care, that the wine is quite fallen in the public esteem; they make pottery-ware of a red colour, like that of the antique cups, but they fail in the art of tempering the clay, nor can they attain the same degree of lightness and transparency. After riding through a fine tract of orchards, I came in sight

of

The ⸱⸱⸱ of ⸱⸱⸱ An⸱ ⸱⸱⸱ from the ⸱⸱⸱ SIDE of the ⸱⸱⸱

*Brop s Imau*

of the Mare Piccolo, or Little Sea, beyond which rises the
city of Taranto: the banks that inclose the bay are so gently
sloped off as to create no very striking effect; there is a
tameness in the prospect not unlike the insipidity of the artificial lakes and elegant swells in our fashionable gardens in
England, totally different from the bold beauties of Italian
landscape. The country leading down to its verge is wild
but agreeable; a shallow soil and mossy turf, covered in
many places with tufts of aromatic shrubs, and clumps of
Carob trees that appear to be indigenous. Through this
heath runs the Cervaro, a small brook of whitish water, that
falls into the bay at the north-east corner, believed by some
authors to be the Galesus, because it correspond with the
distance of five miles from Taranto assigned by Polybius:
an additional proof might be alledged in the epithet *white*,
given to the Galesus by Martial, as agreeing with the present state of the rivulet, the waters of which are strongly
tinged with the chalky or marly particles of the soil it runs
over: this soapy quality may be supposed to have rendered
them peculiarly efficacious in purifying and bleaching the
fleeces that were washed in them. When Virgil applied
the distinctive term *Niger* * to this stream, he is thought to
have alluded to the thick pine groves that then shaded its
banks. Propertius, by the following lines addressed to the
Mantuan bard,

* Some commentators read *Piger*.

Fu

> Tu canis umbroſi ſubter pineta Galeſi
> Thyrſin et attritis Daphnin arundinibus *.

ſeems to inſinuate, that Virgil compoſed his Eclogues at Tarentum, or in ſome neighbouring villa; perhaps the ſame, where he ſays, he took leſſons of agriculture from Corycius the Illyrian pirate, tranſported by Pompey to theſe vallies.

> Namque ſub Oebaliæ memini me turribus altis,
> Qua niger humectat flaventia culta Galeſus
> Corycium vidiſſe ſenem †.

Whilſt I was combining the foregoing circumſtances in my mind, and endeavouring to ſatisfy myſelf that I was then actually ſtanding on the banks of ſo celebrated a river, an aged ſhepherd came up with his flock, and freely entered into converſation. I was glad of an opportunity of learning ſome particulars concerning the Tarentine ſheep, and the commonly received opinion that no white ones would now live in theſe paſtures, becauſe they ſoon would poiſon themſelves with the leaves of the *fumolo* (a ſpecies of hypericum criſpum, or St. John's wort of Linnæus's polyadelphia polyandria), though black ſheep may browze upon it with ſafety, for this reaſon, it is ſaid, no white ſheep are to be ſeen in the flocks, and no wool but of a black or dark brown colour.

* Thou ſingeſt, under the pine groves of ſhady Galeſus, the loves of Thyrſis and Daphnis on thy ſmooth reeds.

† For I remember to have ſeen the aged Corycius near the lofty towers of Oebalia, where dark Galeſus waters the yellow fields.

The old man smiled at my questions, and pointing to many white ewes in his flock, answered, that it was not in consequence of its colour, but of its species, that the animal suffered from those noxious herbs; the *pecore molli*, or delicate race of sheep, are so much more liable to perish by these and other accidents, than the *pecore rustice*, or *case*, a wilder and coarser breed, that the former kind is almost destroyed.

To explain this matter satisfactorily, it is necessary I should enlarge upon the subject, and recapitulate what we read of the flocks of the ancient Tarentines; the attempts made in latter times to revive the credit of the Puglian wool, with the causes which have defeated the intention, and rendered the scheme abortive. Columella informs us, that the Tarentines crossed their delicate breed with fierce foreign rams of a beautiful tawny colour, and that the fleece of their lambs had the strong glossy hue of the fire, with the downy silkness of the dam. To increase this lustre and softness, they used to buckle round the sheep a sort of leathern coat, which they took off occasionally, lest the beast should suffer from excessive heat, then bathed and soaked the wool in wine and oil, till it was quite saturated with the rich fomentation. Before shearing time, the sheep were washed in the Galesus, and at all seasons penned up in clean folds, and kept free from filth; they were never led out to feed till the sun had dried up the dew, as the spirting of the drops from the grass was apt to give them sore eyes. This

proceeds,

procefs, and the filence of the ancients concerning any particular whitenefs in the wool of Tarentum, prove how much
Sannazii, and other moderns, have confounded times and
ideas, in praifing it merely for its milky hue  The darknefs
of colour was by no means a hindrance to the imbibition of a
deep purple dye, which was the tint moft efteemed by the
Tarentines.

After the fall of Rome, a long train of wars and devaftation deprived this country of all its acquired advantages, and
even operated fo direfully upon its climate and productions,
as to vitiate thofe it held of the bounty of nature.  When
the manufacturers as well as manufactures were deftroyed,
the prime commodities of courfe loft their value, and it
ceafed to be worth the fhepherd's while, even had the niceit
arts of his calling been handed down to him, to take any
pains in preferving a purity of blood, or delicacy of covering
in his breed of fheep; thofe perfections had no longer any
admirers or chapmen, and confequently the race very foon
degenerated.

Frederick of Suabia took fome fteps towards retrieving
this branch of traffic, but the misfortunes of his family rendered all thofe projects vifionary.   The introduction of
filkworms from the Eaft by King Roger, proved a fatal
check to the demand for fine wool, and the heavy load of
taxes impofed upon this commodity by the Angevine Princes,
after they had loft Sicily, completed the deftruction of the
finer breed.   On account of their tender conftitution, they
required

required expensive housing and constant attendance to make them turn to profit, and therefore the Puglian shepherds, being from indigence unable to procure such conveniences, abandoned the delicate race, and attached themselves to a rougher variety, which are generally black or brown, hardy, and able to feed with impunity on many plants and species of grass that blind and weaken, if not poison, the Pecore gentili.

The breed was so debased in the fifteenth century, and the farmers reduced to such misery, that Joan the Second chose rather to remit the taxes laid upon wool by her brother, than attempt any method of amelioration, for which she wanted both skill and steadiness.

Alphonsus the First, who had greater views, and was blest with more peace and leisure than his predecessor, resolved to procure for his Neapolitan dominions some of the substantial advantages which his kingdom of Aragon had experienced from an improved breed of sheep, sent as a present to one of his ancestors from a King of England. To obtain this end, he caused a proper number of ewes and rams, the progeny of those English sheep, to be transported into Puglia. Ferdinand the First, ambitious of supporting his father's system, encouraged the woollen manufacture, by inviting workmen from all foreign parts where that trade flourished: but the duties imposed by these two Kings produced ultimately very pernicious effects, for they lay heavy upon the poorer class of farmers, and the sale of wool was not sufficient to indemnify them for losses sustained by bad years and accidents.

The

The oppreſſions of needy and ignorant Viceroys, who were obliged to anticipate and mortgage every revenue to ſupply the continual demands of the Spaniſh miniſtry, increaſed the evil to ſuch a height, that at laſt the white breed was entirely forſaken, and at this day the number of Pecore gentili is extremely inconſiderable within the diſtrict of Taranto. Very little nicety is now obſerved in the choice of rams, or in proper croſſes, by which means the wool is not ſo fine as it might be, though it be ſtill of a good quality. Better management and employment of the raw materials at home, might create an inexhauſtible fund of wealth for the ſtate. The fleſh of the Pecore gentili is more flabby, ſtringy, taſteleſs, and therefore cheaper than that of the Moſcia; and there is a penalty upon any butcher that ſhall paſs off the mutton of the former for that of the latter.

## S E C T I O N   XXX.

SOON after I left the ſhepherd, I paſſed near ſome rubbiſh which antiquaries call a remnant of the wall of the Japygians. It was forty miles long, and erected by that ancient people from ſea to ſea, in order to divide their territories from thoſe of the Meſſapians. I next reached a delicious vale, called Le Citrezze *, where a ſtream riſes in a baſon

about

---

* The Tarentines call this the Galeſus; D'Anville and Zannoni give that name to a river that diſcharges itſelf into the Mare Grand. The ſpring of

the

about three hundred yards from the sea. The waters occasion a perpetual verdure in the meadows, and groves of aged olive trees defend them from the scorching ray, and from all winds but the soft zephyrs that play upon the surface of the Mare Piccolo. I alighted to enjoy the charms of this sweet sequestered spot, and while my eyes ranged over the beautiful landscape, suffered my imagination to wander into a chain of melancholy reflections on the general vicissitudes in the fate of empires, and on the destiny of Taranto in particular. All was then still in that port, where the trading vessels of half the world rendezvoused. One single fishing boat disturbed the bosom of those waters, where the mighty navy of Carthage once displayed its flag. Of all the temples, gymnasia, theatres, and other monuments of glory and opulence, not so much as a single column rises upon the hill where Tarentum once stood: the paultry buildings of some mean convents, inhabited by the most insignificant of friars, mark its ancient situation; while the modern city, crowded into a narrow island, holds the place of the old citadel, and still resembles a fortress more than an emporium of trade. But in despite of this change in its fortunes, the appearance of Taranto is replete with wonderful beauties. At my feet,

the Citrezze is deep, and therefore answers Virgil's epithet of black The very little extent of its course corresponds with the ancient opinion of its being the shortest of all rivers, but still I cannot understand how so trifling a rill could be deemed a river, and be called Eurotas by the Parthenii from its resemblance to the river of Lacedemon, or how numerous flocks could wander on its banks, and be washed in its waters.

the

the Mare Piccolo rolled its gentle waves, ſtretching from eaſt to weſt, in the ſhape of an oval lake, divided into two unequal bays by a narrow promontory; olive woods clothe the fore-ground on both ſides, and the oppoſite hills appear rich in orchards and corn fields.    Over the city, the Mare Grande, or outer port, ſome ſhips at anchor, iſlands, capes; and be-hind, all the blue mountains of Baſilicata complete the proſpect.    A long bridge of ſeven arches joins the city to the continent on the north ſide; through them the tide flows with great impetuoſity, and nothing now but ſmall boats can be admitted by this paſſage, which was formerly the entrance of the harbour.    But even in the time of the Romans, I think it evident from what Appian ſays, that there were drawbridges, by which the garriſon of the citadel preſerved a command over the veſſels in port.    Had the mouth been quite free, the Tarentine fleet in the ſecond Punic war could not have been ſo completely blocked up, as to render all attempts to break through utterly fruitleſs. At each arch is fixed a frame for hanging nets to intercept fiſh as they run up into the little ſea with the flow, or fall back with the ebb; and upon this bridge is carried the aqueduct that ſupplies the town with water.

Tolita King of the Goths is ſaid to have been the firſt that erected an aqueduct on this north ſide; others attribute it to the Emperor Nicephorus.    It was built in the preſent form and direction in 1543.    The ſources lie twelve miles diſtant from Taranto in the mountains of Martina, where

many

many grooves and cuts in the heart of the rock collect the ftraggling rills and filtrations, and bring them together at a fpot called Valdenza; from thence the waters run to Triglio, where they fall into immenfe refervoirs, and then pafs under ground to the deep cifterns at Tremiti. At La Follia they rife to-day, and keep an open courfe for feven miles, till they enter an arcade of two hundred and three arches in very bad repair, overgrown with ivy, and oozing at every joint; the water is conveyed through hollow ftones, each of which has a fpout that fits into the next.

The fhape of Taranto has been likened to that of a fhip; of which the caftle at the eaft end reprefents the ftern, the great church the maft, the tower of Raymund Orfini the bowfprit, and the bridge the cable. It ftands upon the fite of the ancient fortrefs, but I believe occupies rather more room:—it was formerly joined to the continent by a narrow neck of fand, which occafioned William of Puglia to fay, That Tarentum would be an ifland, but for a fmall rifing ground.

Infula mox fieret modicus ni collis adeffet.

Ferdinand the Firft being apprehenfive of an attack from the Turks, ordered the ifthmus to be cut through, and the fea to be let in. Philip the Second caufed the paffage to be widened and deepened fo as to admit veffels, but it was afterwards choked up with fand and filth, and, by the ftagnation of its waters, became a great nuifance. The air of Ta-

ranto

ranto was grievously affected by it till 1755, when it was again cleared out by the King's directions. The streets are remarkably dirty and narrow, especially the Marina, which runs along the Mare Piccolo, and is, without dispute, the most disgustful habitation of human beings in Europe, except, perhaps, the Jewish Ghetto at Rome. The only tolerable street is a terrace above the steep rocks that hang over the Mare Grande, and prevent all access on that quarter. The cathedral, dedicated to Saint Cataldus, whom the Legend calls a native of Raphoe in Ireland, has little merit: it is a melancholy consideration, that the chapel of the patron has been decorated at the expence of almost every monument of the ancient city. The granite columns, taken from its ruinated fanes, are aukwardly crowded under the ill-proportioned roof of this church. The square near the bridge is the only opening of any extent, and the general resort of the citizens in summer, when they sit round the fountain to enjoy the soft evening breeze, and refresh themselves with the fanning of the balmy air. But modern Taranto cannot boast of that degree of salubrity at all seasons, which rendered the ancient city the delight of voluptuaries and valetudinarians. A failure of cultivation, and of attention towards keeping the passages for water free, causes some degree of malignity in its climate during the hot months; but there is great reason to hope these inconveniencies will be removed by the patriotic and judicious endeavours of the present Archbishop Monsignor Joseph Capecelatro, who

has

3

has abandoned the road that leads to the purple, and other objects of ecclesiastical ambition, in order to devote his life and talents to the welfare of his flock, and the improvement of his native country.

I was lodged at the Celestine convent, a neat house, built upon the ruins of a temple. The Prior received me with great politeness, and at supper treated me with the most varied service of shell fish I ever sat down to. There were no less than fifteen sorts, all extremely fat and savoury; especially a small species of muscle, the shell of which is covered with a velvet shag, and both inside and outside is tinged with the richest violet colour. I tasted of all, and ate plentifully of several sorts, without experiencing the least difficulty in the digestion.

## S E C T I O N   XXXI.

THE day no sooner appeared than my impatience hurried me out of the Porta di Lecce to examine the ruins of Tarentum, a city so often the subject of my most favourite reading, and so truly interesting by its glory and misfortunes. Not to leave any part unobserved for want of method, I directed my steps along the shore of the Mare Grande, which gradually draws off to the south, towards Cape San Vito. The slight remains of an amphitheatre did not detain me long, as the *opus reticulatum* proved it to be

Roman

Roman work; and at that moment my enthufiafm was all directed towards monuments raifed by the Tarentines, while they were a free Grecian ftate, not thofe they erected in fervile compliance with the fanguinary tafte of their conquerors. In vain did I run over fields and gardens, and examine with nice attention every ftone that had any thing of the venerable appearance of antique workmanfhip; to my utter aftonifhment not a fingle ruin occurred, fcarce a mark was left that fuch a city ever exifted on the fpot! Never was a place more completely fwept off the face of the earth than Tarentum. Its fplendid annals need be as well authenticated as they are by hiftorians, who had ocular or at leaft circumftantial evidence of its exiftence, for us to believe that a rival of Rome once raifed her proud towers, and arrayed her numerous armies, along thefe now lonefome hills. About two miles and a half from the gate, I difcovered veftiges of aqueducts, and had fome reafon to think I had found the point where the city-wall made a returning angle, and croffed the ifthmus in a north-weft direction, in order to join the Mare Piccolo, leaving an inclofure within, of the form of an equilateral triangle. But, as even ruins were wanting to affift me in my fearch, it was impoffible for me to determine the extent with any degree of certainty. The hints given in the writings of ancient hiftorians are too vague to lead us with any precifion to the true topography of the place.

4

I re-

I returned to town by the banks of the Mare Piccolo, a pleasant walk, and most delightful view.

Near the Alcantarine convent is a small hillock, wholly formed of the shells of fish employed by the ancients in the composition of their celebrated purple dye; and not far from it are the remains of some reservoirs and conduits appertaining to the works. My readers may not be sorry to meet with a description of the testaceous fishes that furnished the precious ingredient, and of the methods used in extracting and preparing it, taken from the accounts extant in the classic authors, and the dissertation of modern naturalists.

Purple was procured from two sorts of shell-fish, the Murex and the Purpura, both belonging to the Testacea, or third genus of Linnæus's sixth class.

From the former a dark blue colour was obtained; the latter gave a brighter tint, approaching to scarlet. The body of the animals that inhabit these shells, consists of three parts. The lowest, containing the bowels, remains fixed in the twisted screw at the bottom, for the purpose of performing the digestive functions: it is fleshy, and tinged with the colour of its food. The middle division is of a callous substance, and full of liquor, which, if let out of its bag, will stain the whole animal and its habitation. The third and upper part is made up of the members necessary for procuring food, and perpetuating the race. The Murex generally remains fastened to rocks and stones. The Pur-

pura,

pura, being a fish of prey, is by nature a rover, and one of the most voracious inhabitants of the deep. The proper season for dragging for this shell-fish, was in autumn and winter. To come at the liquor, the shell was broken with one smart blow, and the pouch extracted, with the greatest nicety, by means of a hook. If the shells were of a small size, they were thrown by heaps into a mill, and pounded.

The veins being laid in a cistern, salt was strewed over them, to cause them to purge and keep sweet, in the proportion of twenty ounces of salt to a hundred pounds of fish. They were thus macerated for three days; after which the mucilage was drawn off into a leaden cauldron, in order that the colours, by being heated therein, might acquire additional lustre and vivacity, as all marine acids do by a mixture with that metal. To keep the vessel from melting, eighteen pounds of water were added to a hundred and fifty pounds of purple, and the heat given horizontally to the kettle, by means of a flue brought from a furnace. By this process, the fleshy particles were carried off, and the liquor left pure, after about ten days settling.

The dye was tried by dipping locks of wool in it, till they had imbibed a dark blue colour. As the colour of the Murex would not stand alone, the dyers always mixed a proportion of Purpura juice with it. They steeped the wool for five hours; then shook, dried, and carded it; dipped it again and again, till it was saturated with the dye. The proportion requisite for staining fifty pounds of wool with the

the fineſt deep amethyſt colour, were twenty pounds of
Murex to a hundred and ten of Purpura.   To produce the
Tyrian purple, which reſembled the colour of congealed
blood, it was neceſſary firſt to ſteep the wool in pure un-
boiled Purpura juice, and then let it lie and ſimmer with
that of the Murex.   By different mixtures of thoſe two
dyes, varieties were obtained, according to the changes of
faſhion, which ran into violet till the reign of Auguſtus,
when it inclined to the Tarentine ſcarlet; and this ſoon
after made way for the Diabaſa Tyria, the moſt extrava-
gantly dear of all the tints.   We read of fleeces being dyed
upon the backs of the ſheep; but remain in the dark as to
the method and advantages of that proceſs.

The Greeks, who were never at a loſs for an ingenious
fable to cover their ignorance of origins and cauſes, attributed the diſcovery of purple to the dog of Hercules,
which, in a range along the ſhore, met with a ſhell-fiſh,
and greedily cruſhed it between its teeth.   Inſtantly an
indelible purple ſtained its muzzle, and by this accident
ſuggeſted the firſt idea of dying cloth.   The art was moſt
undoubtedly practiſed in times of very remote antiquity.
Moſes and Homer mention compound colours: the wife of
Alcinous is deſcribed as ſpinning wool tinged with marine
purple.

Below the ruins of theſe reſervoirs, the ſhore is thickly
ſtrewed with fragments of Etruſcan vaſes, ſimilar in colour
and deſign to thoſe depoſited in the cabinets of the curious.

Cloſe

Close by this place, the beach is covered with bits of plain red ones. A little nearer the city is the Argentaria, a bank so called from a tradition of the gold and silver smiths having had their shops there. It still deserves the name, from a number of medals, rings, chains, and other trinkets, that are constantly dug out of it.

## SECTION XXXII.

I DEVOTED the afternoon to a water party, taking with me one of the oldest and most intelligent of the Tarentine fishermen, to shew me the fishing and spawning places, and explain the different seasons and methods of catching fish. We took boat, and rowed up the southern shore of the Mare Piccolo, with an intention of measuring the whole circumference, which Strabo fixes at one hundred stadia, or twelve English miles and a half According to my calculation, the circuit of the western part is not more than half as great as that of the eastern one; and both together, by a rough estimate, are about sixteen miles. This increase may be accounted for by the destruction of all the parapets and walls of the old city, the wearing away of the banks, and overflowing of the low grounds. A tide is very perceptible, especially when the moon changes, and still more so at the solstices and equinoxes; but very feeble in comparison of the tides in the ocean: however, it serves to

keep

keep the waters of this land-locked bay sweet, and to bring in caravans of fish, that fatten and breed in its quiet pools. When the Scirocco blows hard, the waves are driven up with great violence, and navigation becomes perilous for small vessels.

The first objects of my curiosity were the beds of Cozzenere, or muscles, the greatest and most constant supply of the market. Their spawn is dropt in the mud. About the twenty-first of March, little muscles begin to rise up, and cling to long stakes driven by the fishermen into the water under the city wall, and in the castle ditch. There they thrive and grow in still water, while the washings of the streets supply them with rich and copious nutriment. In August they are as big as almonds, and are then drawn up with the poles, and sown on the opposite side of the Mare Piccolo, among the fresh-water springs.

About the middle of October they are again dragged up, separated, and scattered over a larger space. In spring, they are brought to market, long before they arrive at their full growth. This haste proceeds from the avidity of the officers of the revenue, who receive a duty of four carlini a cantaro for them, whether old or young.

When a long continuance of heavy rains swells the little streams that discharge themselves into this gulf, the waters become muddy, and these fish are then observed to grow distempered, rotten, and unwholesome. The cause of this malady lies in the noxious fragments of animal, putrid vegetables,

vegetables, oily, bituminous, and fulphureous particles, wafhed from the earth by the fhowers. They cut the tender fibres or fingers which the fifh ftretches out, miftaking them for wholefome food. The wounded parts fefter, and poifon the whole body. It is an obfervation made here, and confirmed by long experience, that all the teftaceous tribe is fuller, fatter, and more delicate, during the new and full moon, than in the firft and laft quarters. The difference is accounted for by the tides and currents, which fet in ftronger in the new and full moon, and bring with them large quantities of bruifed fifhes, infects, fruits, and other fattening nurture. I was affured that nothing caufes fifh to fpoil fooner than leaving them expofed to the beams of the moon; and that all prudent fifhermen, when out by night, cover what they catch with an awning. If they meet with any dead fifh on the ftrand, or in the market, they can always difcern, by its colour and flabbinefs, if it be *allunato*, moon-ftruck; and, except in cafes of great neceffity, abftain from it as unwholefome. Not having an opportunity of verifying this affertion, I give it as doubtful; for I know the Italians are apt to attribute to the baneful influence of the moon many ftrange effects, which philofophers of other nations do not afcribe to it. No Italian will lie down to fleep, where moonfhine can reach him.

The Cozze Pelofe, or velvet mufcle, is firft dragged for in the Great Sea, and then fcattered to breed on Sciaie, or heaps

of

of ſtones ſunk by the fiſhermen at every head-land of the Mare Piccolo.

Under the Piano, or eaſtern ſhore, are the oyſter-beds: no coaſt affords a more exquiſite ſort. In winter, large hampers of them are ſent over land to Naples. The ſeaſon is confined by law to a term between the 25th of November and Eaſter Sunday.

Brunduſium was the great ſupplier of oyſters for the Roman tables. From that port, the ſpawn was carried to ſtock their public reſervoirs at the Lucrene Lake, near Baiæ; and no mention is made by the ancients of the excellence of any Tarentine ſhell-fiſh except the ſcallop *. It is therefore not unlikely that oyſter ſpawn has been brought to Taranto from Brindiſi, and better preſerved than at the original bed, where the obſtructions in the mouth of the harbour have ruined all the fiſheries †.

The

---

* Pectinibus patulis jactat ſe molle Tarentum.     Hor. Sat.

† I received from my friend, F Ant Minaſi, the following Liſt of Shell-fiſh found in the Tarentine water, He drew it up according to the Linnæan ſyſtem from a large aſſortment of ſpecimens, which he was commiſſioned to claſs, before they were preſented by the Archbiſhop of Taranto to the Infant Don Gabriel. Had my learned correſpondent had an opportunity of viſiting thoſe ſeas, it is more than probable that his piercing and experienced eye would have diſcovered other ſpecies, if not occult, of fiſhes.

1  Chiton ſquamoſus et cinereus
2. Lepas balanus
3  Lepas anatifera
4. Lepas teſtudinaria—altera radiis 6, et altera 5.
5. Pholas dactylus cum cardine recurvato connexoque cartilagine
6. Mya pictorum

7  Solen enſis
8  Solen legumen
9  Solen ſtriolata
10  Tellina incaſalis
11  Tellina cornea
12  Tellina roſtrata
13  Tellina Punicea
14. Tellina fragilis

15 Tellae

The papyraceous Nautilus is sometimes, but very rarely,
seen spreading the wonderful mechanism of its sail and oars

| | | | |
|---|---|---|---|
| 15 | Tellina planata | 55. | Bulla aperta |
| 16. | Cardium aculeatum | 56. | Bulla Naucus |
| 17. | Cardium edule | 57 | Bulla hydatis |
| 18. | Cardium rusticum | 58 | Voluta cancellata |
| 19. | Mactra striatula | 59. | Voluta glabella |
| 20 | Donax trunculus | 60 | Buccinum echinophorum |
| 21. | Venus lata | 61. | Strombus pes pellicani |
| 22. | Venus Paphia | 62 | Strombus lentiginosus |
| 23. | Venus callypige | 63. | Murex saxatilis |
| 24 | Venus deflorata | 64 | Murex reticularis |
| 25 | Spondylus Gæderopus | 65 | Murex costatus |
| 26 | Chama antiquata | 66. | Murex cutaceus |
| 27. | Arca Noæ | 67 | Murex pusio |
| 28. | Arca barbata | 68 | Murex cornutus |
| 29 | Anomia ephissium | 69 | Murex erinaceus |
| 30. | Mytilus edulis | 70. | Murex pileare |
| 31. | Pinna nobilis | 71 | Murex triqueter |
| 32 | Argonauta Argo | 72 | Murex fulcatus |
| 33 | Buccinum galea | 73 | Trochus tessellatus |
| 34 | Buccinum maculatum | 74 | Trochus eritheus |
| 35. | Buccinum Tritonis | 75 | Turbo oculus |
| 36. | Echinus Cidaris | 76 | Turbo pratus |
| 37. | Echinus esculentus | 77 | Turbo thleus |
| 38. | Echinus saxatilis | 78. | Helix pe |
| 39. | Echinus mamillaris | 79. | Nerita beus |
| 40. | Echinus placenta | 80 | Nerita cum |
| 41 | Serpula anguina | 81 | Nerita rufa |
| 42 | Ostrea edulis | 82 | Haliotis Midæ |
| 43 | Ostrea Jacobea | 83 | Patella sinuata |
| 44 | Ostrea bullata | 84 | Patella lutea |
| 45. | Ostrea pusio | 85 | Patella rustica |
| 46 | Ostrea sanguinea | 86 | Patella tuba |
| 47 | Ostrea varia | 87 | Patella pustula |
| 48 | Ostrea lima | 88 | Patella Græca |
| 49 | Ostrea radula | 89. | Dentalium dentalis |
| 50 | Cypræa lata | 90. | Dentalium corneum |
| 51 | Cypræa tuberis | 91 | Serpula arenaria |
| 52 | Cypræa caput serpentis | 92 | Serpula vermicularis |
| 53 | Cypræa pediculus | 93. | Serpula contortuplicata. |
| 54 | Conus menachus | | |

in the fmooth bays of the Mare Grande; and fometime, fifhermen furprife trumpet-fhells of a prodigious bulk afleep, floating on the furface of the water in a fultry day.

Very fine branchy coral is found along the coaft eaft of the city. The places are kept a profound fecret. Marks are fet up on land, by which the Tarentines fteer their courfe, and fink their hooks and crofs-beams exactly in the middle of a coral bed, while ftrangers muft row about the whole day dragging, without a guide, or certainty of bringing up a fingle twig. There was, a few years ago, fuch abundance of coral near thefe fhores, that a boat's crew was once known to draw up in one day as much as fold for five hundred ducats (93 l. 15 s.). Large pieces may be had for about five ducats *per* rotolo, which at Taranto contains only thirteen ounces.

Under Cape St. Vito, once famous for an abbey of Bafilian monks, and in moft parts of the Mare Grande, the rocks are ftudded with the Pinna Marina This bivalved fhell of the mufcle tribe frequently exceeds two feet in length. It faftens itfelf to the ftones by its hinge, and throws out a large tuft of filky threads, which float and play about to allure fmall fifh : amidft thefe filaments is generally found, befides other infects, a fmall fhrimp, called by the ancients, Cancer Pinnotheres, by the modern Tarentines, Caurella. This little cruftaceous animal was imagined to be generated with the Pinna, and appointed by nature to act as a watchman, in apprizing it of the approach

K k

of prey or enemies; and that, upon the least alarm, this guard slipt down into the shell, which was instantly closed: but more accurate observers have discovered, that the poor shrimp is no more than a prey itself, and by no means a centinel for the muscle, which in its turn frequently falls a victim to the wiles of the Polypus Octopedia.    In very calm weather, this rapacious pirate may be seen stealing towards the yawning shells with a pebble in his claws, which he darts so dexterously into the aperture, that the Pinna cannot shut itself up close enough to pinch off the feelers of its antagonist, or save its flesh from his ravenous tooth. The Pinna is torn off the rocks with hooks, and broken for the sake of its bunch of silk called Lanapenna, which is sold, in its rude state, for about fifteen carlini a pound, to women that wash it well with soap and fresh water.    When it is perfectly cleansed of all its impurities, they dry it in the shade, straiten it with a large comb, cut off the useless root, and card the remainder; by which means they reduce a pound of coarse filaments to about three ounces of fine thread.    This they knit into stockings, gloves, caps, and waistcoats, but they commonly mix a little silk as a strengthener.    This web is of a beautiful yellow brown, resembling the burnished gold on the back of some flies and beetles.    I was told that the Lanapenna receives its gloss from being steeped in lemon juice, and being afterwards pressed down with a taylor's goose.

S E C-

## SECTION XXXIII.

THE seas of Taranto are as copiously stocked with the scaly and finny tribe, as with the crustaceous and testaceous. The quantity and varieties are very considerable; but fish caught in the lesser sea bears the highest price, as surpassing in delicacy and firmness that taken in the larger. This is contrary to what we experience in other countries, and must be owing to some peculiar quality in the water and situation, for, in general, fish found in still bays, and near the shore, is inferior in taste to that which is captured farther out, and in places where the currents beat it about, and seem to keep it firm and wholesome by constant motion *.

The

* I do not pretend to be acquainted with every sort of fish brought to this market, as at least a years stay on the spot would be requisite to acquire that knowledge, but it may be a satisfaction to many Readers to have a List of trivial names, such as it was roughly made out to me by the fishermen, and since compared with some imperfect catalogues I have had a sight of

| Tarentine Name | Latin Name | Tarentine Name | Latin Name |
|---|---|---|---|
| Aguglia | Sudis | Iero | |
| Anguilla | Anguilla | Lalappe | |
| Arciola | | Guonone | Gobio |
| Alice | Halex | Goh bo | Thrannys |
| Abruz | Rhombus | Iri | |
| Cefalo | Mugil | Lutrino | Rubello |
| Calladichell | Acus | Lucerna | Lucerna |
| Calamus | Polipo | Murena | Murena |
| Cheppia | Thrynu | Minchiarello | |
| Culmudi | | | Mullus |
| Dentice | Dentatus | Mola | |

*Tarentine*

The people of Taranto depend upon their fiſhery for
ſubſiſtence, and pay very heavy duties to the Crown, and
rents to private perſons, for the right of fiſhing. The
king receives from them annually three thouſand ſeven hundred and thirty-five ducats (700 *l.* 6 *s.* 3 *d.*) for rent, and
five thouſand four hundred and thirty ducats (1018 *l.* 2 *s.* 6 *d.*),
for the excluſive privilege. They purchaſe the beds for
ſhell-fiſh of monaſteries and individuals, at the yearly expence of ſix thouſand one hundred and ſixty-eight ducats
(1160 *l.* 13 *s.*); and beſides, all fiſh ſold to be carried out
of the city is ſubject to a toll, farmed out at five thouſand
ſix hundred and fifteen ducats (1052 *l.* 16 *s.* 3 *d.*) a year.
An old regiſter book called Il Libro Roſſo, kept with great
care and veneration in the cuſtom-houſe, points out the

| *Tarentine Name.* | *Latin Name.* | *Tarentine Name.* | *Latin Name.* |
|---|---|---|---|
| Mazzoni | Aſellus | Scorfano | Scorpio |
| Orato | Aurata | Samaghaſtro | Sargus |
| Occhiata | Melanurus | Seccia | Sæpia |
| Orva | | Sarde | Chalcis |
| Polpo | Polypus | Spigola | Lupus |
| Palamiti | Pelamydes | Sario | Saurus |
| Peſce ziffiro | Scarus | Sparitielli | Sparulus |
| Peſce ſpada | Xiphias * | Traulo | Lacerta |
| Ruonghi | Conger | Tonno | Thynnus † |
| Riccioli | Glaucus | Tremola | Torpedo |
| Storione | Acipenſer | Triglia | |
| Spina | | Vopa | Boops |
| Soliole | | Urigoli | Chelones. |
| Sarpa | Piſcis virgatus | | |

* This fiſh ſeldom makes its appearance ſo far north
† No Tunny fiſhery is allowed here, leſt that boiſterous fiſh ſhould be driven up into the
little ſea, and there diſturb and deſtroy the ſmall fry.

proper

proper feafon for each fpecies of fifh, the method of propagating them, the nets allowed, and the duty to be exacted. The directors of the cuftoms are very alert and rigorous in inforcing thefe regulations. They take care to clean the fpawning places, and weed the mouths of the rivers that empty their waters into the Mare Grande. They rent thofe ftreams of the Barons in order to complete the monopoly, and prevent any difturbance being given to the fifh at improper times.

To return to my tour, which the fifh had caufed me to lofe fight of, we paffed under the banks of the Piano, where the ancients kept their wines in grottos called Diulos. The mouths of thefe excavations are now almoft clofed up with rubbifh. Some perfons crept in lately, and found the floor ftrewed with fragments of Amphorc. During the canicular feafon, there iffues in the night-time from thefe caverns a moft impetuous piercing wind.

From the Piano we rowed to the mouth of the Cervaro, and from thence to the promontory of Penna, which divides the little fea into two unequal bays. As fomething like the foundations of piers may be obferved under water, it has been fuppofed by fome authors that a bridge formerly exifted, reaching from this cape to the Pizzone in the old city. It is poffible there may have been a loom laid acrofs for greater fecurity, or a paffage made for the convenience of the citizens; but it is clear from Strabo, that anciently the port was fhut up with a bridge in the very place where we now fee one. He fays that the harbour is * clofed up with a large bridge; a line drawn from the Penna would only fecure half of it, and no efforts of the Romans could have confined the Tarentine gallies, had not the garrifon of the citadel been in poffeffion of ftrong works and draw-bridges at the mouth of the harbour, which effectually commanded the paffage.

Not far from the Penna is the Citrello, a fpace of thirty-five yards by eight, where four ftrong fprings and feveral fmall ones of frefh water force their way up, and preferve their fweetnefs amidft the brine of the waves  Shoals of fifh may be feen fwimming over thefe *Occhi* or fountains, as it were to cool and cleanfe themfelves  Thefe boilers are only a continuation of the fpring that produces the brook of the Citrezze.

From hence we paffed under the bridge, where the current fets in very ftrong, and in boifterous weather the navigation is hazardous.  On the left hand, near the city wall, lies the fhipping in tolerable fafety, notwithftanding the great expanfe of the Mare Grande.  The force of the waves is broken by the iflands of Santa Pelagia and St. Andrew, the fhelves called Pietre Sizzofe, and the two capes which complete the circle.  Thofe iflands were known to the ancients by the name of Electrides or Chærades; and if we may judge by fome ruins ftill difcernible near the water, were certainly inhabited.  At prefent their only inhabitants are rab-

* Κλειφτι.

bits

bits that burrow in the fand, and under the bufhes, with which their whole furface is overgrown In 1594 Cicalà Baffa anchored at St. Pelagia for feveral days, to the great terror of all the people along the coaft. The intelligence he received of the country being alarmed, and troops marching to give him a warm reception, determined him to weigh a choi, and fail for Turkey, without attempting to land.

I rode next morning into the country to fee how far its actual fertility came up to the idea ancient authors have left us of it, and returned fatisfied, that nature is ftill ready to fhew the fame partiality, when called upon by the fame induftry and arts that tend to facilitate and improve her efforts. The early feafon of the year prevented my forming any judgment of the fruits of the earth. Columella, Pliny, and Macrobius fpeak highly of the pears of Tarentum, and praife its figs, cheftnuts, walnuts, and ambrofial almonds. At prefent the moft delicate of its figs is the Neapolitan, a fmall black fort that hangs on the tree till January.

The farmers take great care of their olive-trees; they manure and water the roots, plough the ground about them, and fow it with corn, but never with oats; the ftubble is cut off clofe, and fwept away, to make room for the fruit to fall, but is never fet on fire, for fear of damaging the trees; the boughs are not beaten, but the olives gathered

The vines, which are kept low and upon poles, are the moft healthy and vigorous I ever beheld; the wine is carried in fkins as in the days of paganifm, when it was a religious ceremony, as well as a gambol, to tumble over

2
the

the oiled leathern budget.    I tasted no wine at Taranto that pleased my palate, or deserved any commendation.    Horace's Amicus Aulon, which critics have transported to every hill within ten miles of Taranto, nay even so far as Castelvetere in Calabria, seems to have been about six miles from the present town to the east, at a part of the coast where a well-watered valley, full of orange and other fruit-trees, is sheltered from every rude blast by an amphitheatre of low eminences, most happily adapted to the growth of the vine.

The arable lands are well cultivated, and produce wheat, oats, barley, and cotton in great abundance, and of an excellent sound quality.    The cotton manufacture employs those poor Tarentines who are not able to follow the profession of fishermen    The wages of a labourer in the fields is a carlino a-day.    The usual method is to divide the crop equally between the owner of the land and the farmer that tills it ; but the extent of waste grounds is immense, and whatever pains may be bestowed upon corn land, nobody here has an idea of doing any thing to improve pastures or meadows ,—not a feed is sown, weed destroyed, or barren bush grubbed up.

The honey I tasted was so good, that I may affirm no degeneracy is perceptible among the modern bees of Taranto; and, that the poet might still compare their produce to that of the bees of Hymettus *.

* ——Ubi non Hymetto
Mella decedunt.————

## SECTION XXXIV.

A SITUATION, bleft with fo delicious a climate, and fo fine a haven, muft have attracted the early notice of the Eaftern navigators, who, like Columbus, Drake, and Cook, of modern times, failed from home in queft of new worlds and unexplored coafts. Some of them, no doubt, ventured up the Adriatic, in hopes of difcovering unopened fources of wealth, and commodious fettlements for the colonies, which excefs of population obliged the mother country to fend forth. Let us confider Taras in the light of another Cortez; but, inftead of making him the captain of a troop of bigoted affaffins, let us fuppofe him to have headed a fet of civilized, humane men, defirous of procuring a good eftablifhment in a ftrange country, but unwilling to cement the foundations of their new ftate with the blood of the natives. The wifdom and moderation of the adventurers gain the affections of the native favages, and a fenfe of mutual intereft unites them both into one body. The chief of the new-comers paffes in time for a being of godlike race, and his companions are too fenfible of the utility of the deception, not to encourage the belief. All leaders of maritime expeditions, and indeed all rulers of nations dwelling near the fea, were, in the oriental figura-

tive

tive language of thofe ages (whofe moſt ſimple expreſſions
are complete riddles for us), denominated Sons of the
Ocean, of Neptune, or of ſome other marine Deity. Veſ-
fels of a large ſize bore the name of ſome monſter of the
deep, or formidable quadruped of the earth. Europa's Bull
was a fhip of the firſt magnitude; Phryxus's Ram was one
of the ſecond rate; and we may preſume that the Dove,
fent by Jaſon to furvey the paffage of the Dardanelles, was
a light ſkiff, proper for diſcovery; the Dolphin on the
coins of Tarentum, with the naked man fitting upon its
back, was perhaps ſtruck in remembrance of Taras and his
ſhip. There ſeems to be very little reaſon for imagining
that Arion is repreſented by the figure with a lyre in its
hand. It was indeed on his paffage from hence to Leſbos
that he was thrown overboard, and taken up by a dolphin,
or a ſhip of that name; but we cannot ſuppoſe that the
Tarentines were very eager to perpetuate the memory of an
event that redounded ſo little to their honour.

About a century before the ſiege of Troy, a colony of
Cretans founded Uria, and obtruded themſelves upon the
Tarentines, who, after a long conteſt, were obliged to
admit them into their ſociety.

In the twenty-firſt Olympiad, ſo powerful a body of
emigrants arrived under Phalanthus from Laconia, that it
may almoſt be called a ſecond foundation. This general
was marked, from the fiſt moment of his exiſtence, for an
outcaſt and an adventurer. He and all his followers were
the

the spurious issue of the Spartan women, whose husbands, on marching against Messenæ, had made a vow not to return to their families till they had subdued their enemies. The war drawing out to a much greater length than they had imagined, these warriors began to be apprehensive lest the race of fighting citizens should become extinct, on the failure of that generation. In order to preserve their oath inviolate, and yet save the commonwealth from dissolution, they sent back all such as had joined the army after the first campaign, to keep the women company. The off-spring of these temporary unions were called Parthenii; and, when grown up, were driven out to seek their fortunes in distant climes. Being received into Tarentum, they acquired a superiority over the natives, new-modelled the government upon an aristocratical plan, enlarged the fortifi-cations, and transformed the city into a mere copy of Sparta. The very places were new-named, and among others, the Galesus took the name of Eurotas.

Most of the nobles having perished in a war with the Japyges, democracy was introduced. About the seventieth Olympiad, the Pythagorean philosophy gained a footing at Tarentum, and worked wonders in polishing the manners, opening the understanding, and enlarging the ideas of this people, who were naturally disposed to traffic, arts, and sciences. The improvements of its trade was the grand object that engaged the attention of its legislators. They knew full well, that to the fostering influence of commerce,

as

as much as to fuccefs in military exploits, Egypt, Phœnicia, and Greece owed the very tranfcendent degree of glory and power which they had attained. Every nerve was therefore ftrained to excite emulation in the citizens, to create a maritime force, to allure traders to the mart, and to render the city a centrical point of traffic for all parts of the mercantile world. The nature of its fituation feconded their endeavours; for no place lay more conveniently for the trade of Italy, Illyricum, Greece, Afia, and Africa, than Tarentum. We muft confider that, to moft of the ancient mariners, the Mediterranean was an ocean; Spain, a Peru; Tyre, and fome other ftates on the fea-coaft, what Britain and Holland have been fince, the great maritime powers: while Egypt and Perfia were the type of the prefent formidable inland monarchies. In all the long range of fhore from Rhegium to Sipontum, Tarentum was the only port where veffels fly for refuge in tempeftuous weather. Brundufium is not fuppofed to have exifted at fo early a period, and Croton was no better than a road where fhips could not venture to lie in winter. Every department of the Tarentine government had an eye to commerce; and even its religious games and feafts were inftituted to encourage barter, and attract ftrangers. In procefs of time, when abufes crept into the adminiftration of affairs, and giddy pleafure with unmeaning riot took the place of politic amufement, it was remarked that the Tarentine calendar contained more feftivals than there were days in the year.

The

The same thing may be said of modern Rome, where no day passes without bringing with it the feast of a patron, anniversary of the consecration of a church, or removal of some relic, if not several the same day, exclusive of general processions and solemnities  The different complexion of the two religions prevents the modern feasts from degenerating into as much gaiety and intemperance as those of Paganism.

With their wealth, the power of the Tarentines rose above that of all the colonies of Magna Græcia, their land-forces were estimated at thirty-two thousand foot and three thousand horse*, in constant pay; the number of citizens amounted to three hundred thousand†, and thirteen considerable cities acknowledged their dominion, at sea their fleets rode triumphant and unrivalled.  The most brilliant epocha of their history was during the government of Archytas, whose profound learning as a philosopher, and skill as a mechanician, were no clog upon his political abilities.  His virtues were of the noblest kind, exalted to as great sublimity of excellence as the plain morality of the the law of nature is capable of attaining.  He is said to have invented many useful instruments, and to have improved upon those already known.  He frequently led the Taren-

---

* The horse and rider so frequent on the coins of this republic allude, perhaps, to the great dexterity of the Tarentines in horsemanship.  They went to battle with two horses to each cavalier, who, when one fell or grew fatigued, vaulted upon the other

† The present city does not contain above eighteen thousand souls

tines

tines to battle, and always returned crowned with frefh laurels. To ftrengthen the finews of the Grecian confederacy, he appointed general affemblies to be held at Heraclea, a dependence of Tarentum, where every thing relative to the common intereft might be difcuffed and determined. He appears to have been murdered in fome civil commotion, and his body thrown into the fea.

With Archytas ended the true profperity of his country. In the one hundredth Olympiad, luxury and corruption had gained fuch power as to pervert all original good principles, both of morals and government; to enervate the minds and bodies of the citizens, and thereby to expofe the republic, feeble and defencelefs, to the infults of the hardy Barbarians that furrounded it. The liberal arts did not flourifh the worfe for this degeneracy; luxury and foftnefs of manners are as favourable to their advancement, as a rich mellow foil is to the vegetation of a beautiful flowering plant. Though the rude conquerors of the Tarentines have deprived us of the fight of their admirable performances in painting, fculpture, and architecture, we may ftill form an idea of the exquifitenefs of their tafte by their coins *. The number of learned men born at Tarentum,

or

---

* Nummi Tarentorum.

AUR. 1. Caput muliebre comptis capillis, delphines duo, ΤΑΡΑΣ.= Puer nudus equo infidens fupra volitante victoria, delphin, fydus ΣΑ.

2. Cap. puellæ cum monili ΤΑΡΑΝΤΙΝΩΝ = Puer nudus delphinum inequitans extensa dexterâ delphinum, lævâ tridentem tenens ΓΑΡΑΣ.

3. Cap.

or educated in its schools, is a sufficient proof of the esteem
in which science and polite literature were held.   Aristoxe-
nus

3. Cap imb laureatum =Aquila ΤΑΡΑΝΤΙΝ
4  Cap imb laur delphin ΣΑ ΤΑΡΑΣ =Hercules cum leone decer-
    tans, arcus ΚΝ
5  Cap. gal. ΝΙ =Noctua apertis alis insistens fulmini.
6. Cap. imb  pelle leoninâ tectum =Juvenis nudus delph ineq dext.
    extensâ diotam, lævi hastam tenens ΤΑΡΑΣ.
7  Cap imb tectum pelle leoninî =Bigæ aurigante Neptuno dext.
    habenas la. tridentem. ΤΑΡΑΝΤΙΝΩΝ
8  Cap. Jovis barbat laur. fulmen.=Aquila alis expansis fulm inf.
    ante avem Pallas hastâ minax ΤΑΡΑΝΤΙΝΩΝ
9. Cap. imb laur. Æ =Aquila fulm. inf ΤΑΡΑΝΤΙΝΩΝ ΑΡ.
10  Cap Minervæ gal ΤΑΡΑΝΤΙΝΩΝ =Victoria in curru i duob.
    delphinibus trac ΝΙΚ
ARG 1  Mulier æquo inf ΦΙ-ΦΙΛΗΜΕΝΟΣ =Homo delp. inf d. tripodem.
    i trid cap bovinum ΤΑΡΑΣ.
    2  Eques = -ΑΥΚΙΝΟΣ =Homo delp inf d trid l pallium noctua
        ΤΑΡΑΣ
    3  Cap nud diad =Mulier equo inf ΙΑ cornucopiæ, delphin.
    4  Cap mul diad =mul equo inf delphin dimidium capræ ΙΑ.
    5. Eques =Homo nud. delp inf ΤΑΡΑΣ
    6  Eques =Homo nud del inf facem tenens Σ
    7  Eques.=Homo delp inf tridentem ten subt unda Κ ΤΑΡ.
    8  Eques eripis ΣΑΛΑΝΩ =Mulier colum ten delp inf ΤΑΡΑΣ
    9  Eques g..ctus cum clypeo et hasta =Mulier delp inf velari d.
        bottum l colum ΤΑΡΑΣ ΑΝΟ
    10. Eques hominem calcins =Homo supra delp genu flex o nis d
        clyp te. i ΤΑΣ ΝΟΣ
    11  Duo equites, iter cum clava, alter cum lorica ΤΑΡ....Ω =
        Homo delp inf cum clypeo d victor olim, l duob icult l.
    12  Concha  Homo delp inf d facculum l tridentem ΤΑΡΑ
    13  Cap Palladis  Hercules inf ins duos serpentes suffoc ans ΤΑ
    14  Cap mul =Hercules leonem trucidans
    15  Cap Jovis =Delphin.
    16. Eques, victori equum ducente =Homo delp inf.
    17. Homo delp inf =Equus marinus.

                                    19 Cap

nus is, I believe, the only author of whofe works even a fragment has been preferved. He was a philofophical writer upon mufic, for which he feems to have felt extra-ordinary enthufiafm, as he afferts that the effence of the human foul is harmony.


## S E C T I O N   XXXV.

ABOUT three hundred years before Chrift, the Tarentine republic, confcious of the effeminacy and incapacity of its own citizens, began to employ foreign generals and mercenary troops to fight its battles. Being hard preffed by the Lucanians, the Tarentines called to their aid Alexander King of Epirus, who fecured them againft the enterprizes of thofe barbarians at the expence of his own life. Fifty-feven years after his death, Pyrrhus, alfo King of Epirus, came over to defend them againft the Romans. That ambitious people had levelled almoft all the barriers that

18. Cap. Minervæ = Noctua TAP
19. Cap. Cereris TAPAΣ = Eques haftam vibrans
20. Vir nudus equo inf. cap. rad. haft. vib. API = Vir delp. inf. d. vaf. f. temonem TAPA— TA HT
21. Eques haft. vib. — Vir delp. inf. cum victoriola hafta et clypeo.
22. Eques victoriam calcans — Vir delp. inf. ΞOP.

Æ R. 1 Cap. Herculis = Eques π T
2. Cap. mulieb. = Concha. delphin.
3. Cap. inib. = Delphin.
4. Figura delph. inf. d. cor. f. cornuc. = Concha
5. Caput barb. diad. Æ. = Pifcis

protected

protected the foft Tarentine nation, and nothing was wanting but a tolerable pretext for commencing hoftilities, which
could not fail to add thefe rich coafts to their other ufurpa-
tions.    Rome had never fhewn herfelf very fcrupulous or
nice in the choice of her reafons for affaulting a neighbour;
but, on the prefent occafion, Tarentum furnifhed her with
a caufe of war, which, if we may truft the very fufpicious
teftimony of the Latin hiftorians, would be deemed fufficiently weighty by the moft rigid cafuift.    A Roman fleet
bringing corn from Apulia, and paffing within fight of
Tarentum, was attacked by the inhabitants of that city,
the fhips deftroyed, and the crews maffacred.    The ambaffadors, fent to demand fatisfaction, were treated with
the utmoft indignity, and the refentment of the Romans
fet at defiance.    But if we pay proper attention to what we
read in Livy and Dionyfius Halycarnaffæus, we fhall difcover fomething that may clear the Tarentines; I will not
fay of the guilt of mifbehaving to perfons ufually accounted
facred, but at leaft of having been wantonly the aggreffors.
By a treaty entered into fome years before, the Romans
had engaged not to navigate to the north of the Lacinian
Cape, or interfere with the commerce of the Adriatic.    A
Roman conful had rejected with fcorn the mediation of
the Tarentines in behalf of the Samnites; and the emiffaries
of Rome had fomented infurrections among the fubjects
of Tarentum.    Whichfoever of the parties might have
juftice on its fide, it is but too obvious, that the weight of

power preponderated in favour of Rome; therefore the only refource of her foe was to feek defenders wherever money could purchafe them, fince the degeneracy of the citizens of Tarentum had deprived them even of the idea of becoming foldiers themfelves. Pyrrhus, the firft Grecian general of the age, was the perfon applied to. Allured by avaricious and ambitious motives, he landed in Italy, and defeated the Romans in two engagements; but finding the war likely to prove too heavy a burden for his fhoulders, and his government irkfome to the people he came to fight for, he feized a frivolous pretence, and failed to Sicily, which he alfo abandoned for fimilar reafons. He returned to Tarentum; but being defeated by Curius Dentatus near Beneventum, ftole away to Greece, and left his allies to make the beft terms they could with the victor. The Tarentines, roufed from their lethargy by defpair and the approach of danger, continued for fome time to make an obftinate defence. They even perfuaded the Carthaginians to fend a fleet to their fuccour; but being at length obliged to yield to the fuperior force of Rome, they experienced the mildeft treatment at her hands, were ranked in the number of her allies, and fuffered to govern themfelves by their own laws, under the control of a Roman garrifon.

We hear no more of the Tarentines till Hannibal penetrated into their country, and by the affiftance of Philemenes furprifed their city. Livius, the Roman Governor, remained in poffeffion of the citadel and entrance of the port,

by

by which means the Tarentine fleet was blocked up and rendered ufelefs. But the active genius of the African general was not to be cramped by apparent difficulties. He caufed the galleys to be brought afhore, placed upon carriages and rollers, and thus drawn over the ifthmus, through the city, into the outer bay, where he aftonifhed the enemy with the appearance of a formidable fleet. This naval armament, under Democrates, defeated the Roman convoy off Croton.

It is a doubt among antiquaries which is the place where the fhips were hauled over. The expreffions of Polybius appear to indicate the hollow of the prefent ditch or cut made by Ferdinand the Fuft, as it anfwers to the fpace between the wall and rampait erected by Hannibal, to prevent the Romans from fallying out of the citadel upon the town. Gonfalvo de Cordova did the very fame thing in the fame place. A fimilar expedient was practifed by Dragut, a Turkifh admiial, in efcaping from the Genoefe gallies of D'Oria, who had blocked him up in one of the bays of Greece.

The weaknefs and difunited councils of Carthage having obliged Hannibal to evacuate Italy, his allies were left at the mercy of a republic not always prone to clemency. But, before the departure of the African chief, Fabius Maximus had retaken Tarentum by the treachery of the garrifon, and plundered it of an immenfe treafure.

From

From this period Tarentum ceafed to be known in the world as a ftate of any political importance. The tide of commerce was infenfibly averted into other channels, and its hiftory, as well as its citizens, funk into an inglorious obfcurity; perhaps a happier fituation than it had ever enjoyed during the moft fhining periods of its annals. It retained a great amenity of manners, the effect of Greek inftitutions, mild climate, and fertile foil, where no very rough exertions were required to earn a fubfiftence, and where the very air feemed to breathe the foftnefs of its own character into the fouls of all the inhabitants. From the defcriptions and encomiums of Horace, we may judge how high an opinion the ancients had of its temperature.

A Roman colony was fent hither; but this city appears to have returned very fpeedily to the ftate of a municipium, governed by its own laws and ufages, under the obligation of furnifhing to the Roman navy a certain quota of fhips. The liberty it enjoyed muft have been very ample; for it was looked upon in the light of a Greek city, where Roman exiles might refide, as in a foreign country; a privilege it enjoyed in common with Naples.

In the Auguftan age, it ftill retained the Grecian manners and language; though, except Rhegium and Naples, all the reft of Magna Græcia had loft every trace of the features of its mother-country, utterly obliterated by an intercourfe with barbarians. In the fourth century after Chrift, Tarentum yielded to the fame baneful influence, and

and the language of Homer ceas'd to be the vulgar tongue; but Greek no doubt gained a superiority over Latin, during the tenth and eleventh ages, while Puglia obeyed the Emperors of the East. Its final banishment was the consequence of the Norman conquest.

The destruction of Tarentum's independence appears to have caused an early emigration of its citizens. Their numbers were so reduced about the time of Augustus, that the greatest part of the old inclosure was deserted, and most of the inhabitants settled near the castle. Here they laid out their forum, in which they placed a colossal statue of Jupiter, of a size inferior only to that of the Rhodian Apollo, and the only memorial left them of the splendour of their ancient commonwealth.

This situation near the citadel, was of particular advantage to the Tarentines, in securing them from the inroads of the Goths, who, being destitute of a maritime force, could make no attack but on the land quarter.

After the death of Constans the Second, in 668, Romuald, Duke of Benevento, conquered this province; and the Greek Patrician, who had hitherto resided at Tarentum, removed his tribunal to Reggio. On the decline of the Lombard power, the Grecian emperors recovered possession of this country, and kept it till Robert Guiscard drove them for ever out of Italy.

In the year 927, or in the preceding century (for the chronology of those times is miserably confused), the Sara-

cens

cens or Hungarians deftroyed the city of Tarentum; but its
fituation rendered it of too much confequence not to be
fpeedily rebuilt. It was probably on this re-eftablifhment
that the defertion of the old fite was completed. Nicephorus built the bridge, and made the Marina, for the
purpofe of fecuring the entrance of the haven, and affording
more fpace for building within the walls.

Duke Robert, the Norman, after the total expulfion of
the Greeks, created his fon Bohemund Prince of Taranto;
on the failure of whofe iffue, it was beftowed on Henry,
fon of King Roger; and afterwards on William, a baftard
of that King. From him William the Firft refumed it, as
being too great an appanage for an illegitimate branch of
the royal family. It was part of the fortune of Manfred of
Swabia, who long bore the title of Prince of Taranto. The
principality was next conferred by Charles the Second upon
his fon Philip, titular Emperor of Conftantinople, whofe
daughter, and at length fole heirefs, carried it into the
houfe of Baux. This family foon failed, and Raymund
Orfini, a younger fon of the Earl of Nola, obtained it.
He had raifed his fortune by his own adventurous valour;
and, taking advantage of the circumftances of the times,
affumed an almoft abfolute and independent fway over the coaft
of Puglia. Upon his death, his fon was ftripped of all his
poffeffions by King Ladiflaus, who, by marrying Raymund's
widow, made himfelf at length mafter of Taranto, the only
place that ftood out in defence of the infant proprietor.

Queen

Queen Joan the Second gave it to her husband, the Earl of La Marche; but he, being in distress for money to carry him out of the kingdom, when he fled from his wife, sold the principality to John Anthony Orsino Balzo, the right owner. This Prince, who was a very powerful Baron, made a great figure in the troubles that attended the first establishment of the Aragonian Kings, and became almost an independent sovereign. On his demise without issue, Taranto escheated to the Crown. Ferdinand the First made it a provision for his second son Frederick; after whose expulsion Taranto ceased to be feudal. It is now no longer even the shadow of that proud democratical republic, which dared to cope with Rome; nor is it the princely seat of a tyrannical feudatory. Poor and languishing, both as to trade and manufactures, it soothes its vanity with the consciousness of regal immunities, and immediate vassalage under the King.

The inhabitants neglect the culture of their fields, and turn all their attention to fishing; a profession hampered with fewer incumbrances, less continual labour, and affording greater certainty of success. Their lands are cultivated, their corn reaped, by Calabrians; their pastures covered with Abruzzese sheep and shepherds; while the modern Tarentines, as much at least as their poverty will allow them, seem to copy the gentle, indolent manners of their forefathers, citizens of *Molle Tarentum*. They are still passionately fond of amusements, and eager only in the

pursuit

purſuit of pleaſure.    Their addreſs is affable, and pleaſing
to ſtrangers ;  their pronunciation liſping, and ſofter than
that of the natives of the neighbouring provinces.    Here
women bring forth children with little difficulty ;  and treat
as a ſlight inconvenience thoſe dangers and pains, which
are ſo dreadful to their ſex in moſt other countries.    Here
it is impoſſible to cite an inſtance of a perſon's dying in
childbed.

# JOURNEY

## FROM

## TARANTO TO REGGIO.

---

## SECTION XXXVI.

ON the fixth of May, I hired a guide, and proceeded on my journey towards Calabria. About four miles from Taranto we croffed a river, fuppofed by fome geographers to be the Taras. It runs through marfhes and thickets of tall reeds, is deep, and much reforted to by wild boars, who in fummer defcend in droves to cool themfelves and wallow in the mud. If difturbed, they fwim acrofs, but foon return, unlefs it prove a very wet autumn, and then they retire up to the drier woods on the banks of the Bradano.

We

We rode all day along the sea shore, between the beach and an immense forest of low pitch-pines; the underwood, juniper. At the mouth of the Lieto, the sea runs a great way up into the land, and forms salt-ponds, which in summer exhale infectious vapours; in May, they were only beautiful objects in this wild and grand view of wood and water. The whole soil is sandy, and bears evident marks of its having been lately recovered from the sea, either by the voluntary recession of the watery element, or by the accumulation of earth hurried down in floods from the high lands. At the river Bradano * we left the province of Otranto, and entered that of Basilicata. It was also the boundary of ancient Lucania, and indeed of Italy; for in very early times that name was confined to the country south of this limit.

After a long but agreeable ride of twenty-four miles, we stopped at Torre di Mare, a poor place near a ruinous tower, built by the Angevine kings, as a safe-guard to the coast; but, by the retreat of the sea, now at such a distance from it, as no longer to serve that end. The waste round it is fenny, damp, and unwholesome. After dinner we ferried over the Basiento †, whereon Octavius Cæsar and Mark Antony had an interview, brought about by the generous mediation of Octavia. These triumvirs came with their troops to opposite banks of the river. Antony jumped

* Anciently Bradanus.
† Anciently the Metapontus, or Casuentum.

into

into a boat, and pushed off unattended towards the other side; but Cæsar met him, in another skiff, half-way, and, after mutual endeavours to shew excessive confidence in each other, Antony was persuaded to give up the point, and suffer Cæsar to accompany him to Tarentum, where they were to agree upon a plan for settling the Roman empire *.

Near the mouth of this river, some columns, rising out of the sandy hillocks. mark the situation of Metapontum. These pillars of coarse marble stand in two rows, which are about eighty feet asunder, ten in one row, and five in the other; their diameter five feet, their height fifteen, the interstices ten. Part of the architrave is all that remains of the entablature. They are of the ancient Doric order, tapering regularly with a large cyathiform capital †, and no base but a kind of plinth that belongs to the whole row. They are channelled into twenty sharp deep flutes, now much corroded by the salt spray, and the action of the air.

This style of architecture has something in it solemn and majestic, adapted to the dignity of divine worship, or the gravity of an assembly of senators. Were I to build a city,

* Alberti places this meeting on the Bradano, Juan Juvenis, on the Tara. But, as Appian expressly says it was on the river of Metapontum, it can be no other than the Basiento.

† I cannot convey to the reader a clearer idea of the shape of this cup-form capital (which is to be seen at Pæstum, Segesta, Selinunte, Syracuse, Girgenti, and St. Peter ad vincula in Rome), than by comparing it to a shallow bowl, covered with a thin square stone.

I should

I fhould appropriate this noble order to the great churches, town-hall, and exchange, whilft I embellifhed the palaces and theatres with the gay Corinthian. I do not allow the fame auguft appearance to the modern Doric, which is much lighter, and more properly enriched with ornaments.

Thefe are all the veftiges of Metapontum, a city once admirably calculated by fituation for attaining the fpecies of profperity that feems to have been the end conftantly propofed by its citizens, viz. opulence arifing from agriculture and exportation of corn. It ftood on the fkirts of a plain twenty-five miles in length, which, two thoufand years ago (when Metapontum was in the zenith of its refpectable, becaufe moft innocent, glory), was well peopled, full of towns and villages, attentively cultivated and fertilized, not defolated by the waters, as they were then confined to proper channels. The rich crops that waved upon its furface, were the bafis on which this colony of Pylians grounded their power and importance. The honour they attached to the profeffion of hufbandman, and the fruitfulnefs of their territory, are attefted by their coins*, marked with

* Nummi Metapontorum

AUR 1  Cap mulieb. fpics redim.  Spica figura viridis META
     2  Cap. Martis ?Θ =Dux fpicæ, apis META.
     3. Noctua ramo inf. = Spica & caduc. META
ARG 1  Hercules nud. ftans clav. ger. = Spica META.
     2  Cap Martis, canis ΛΓΤΚΙΠΠΟΣ =Spica avis—META.
     3  Homo nud. bovino capite d. pateram—s. Arundinem =Spica—cicada META.
     4  Cap. mul. fpic redim =Spica forceps ΛΟΑ—META.

5. Spica

with the head of Ceres and an ear of corn, and by the magnificent offering which they made at the shrine of the Delphic Apollo. This present consisted of an emblematical representation of Summer in massive gold, and was esteemed one of the richest offerings in the temple.

Pythagoras spent the last years of his life at Metapontum. After his decease, the house he had dwelt in was converted into a temple of Ceres, and resorted to with the greatest veneration by the Metapontines, who were truly sensible of the advantages they had derived from his instructions *.

This philosopher was one of the most exalted characters of antiquity, one of the few sages who did not confine their

5 Spica—META =Incertus
6 Cap. Palladis =Spica, clava Y
7 Cap. Jovis Ammonis =Spica tripus M
8 Cap. muliebri dia'em Spica META
9 Cap bovinum Spica META
10 Cap Martis HPAKAEIΩN =Duæ spicæ, apis META
11 Cap Cereris Spica—Ciconia META IIO
12 Galea =Crculus et cua tt læ META—radii ex granis hordei
13 Noctua ramo in 2 Spica, caduc META.

ΔR. 1 Cap Pallad Spica META AIIONA
2 Tripus lunat g in head =Spica META.
3 Cap inib corrut =Spica META
4 Cap Jovis =Spica META
5 Cap Apoll Spica META.
6. Cap Cereris =Spica META.
7 Aquila fulm in t =Spica META
8 Cap. Cereris Duæ spicæ META
9. Cap Minervæ Duæ spica META.
10 Cap Mercur alat 3 gr hord caduc META.

* Some authors write that he died, and that the temple was dedicated at Croton.

views to private and partial objects, but made their learning
of use to nations at large, whom they instructed, enlightened and directed in the paths of moral virtue and real glory.
Many ridiculous stories are related of his opinions and
doctrines, which give us the idea of a visionary or impostor;
but we should be cautious how we admit implicity anecdotes respecting the great men of distant ages, when we
find them clash with what is allowed to have been their
general line of conduct. Perhaps Pythagoras found it
necessary, in order to captivate the veneration and confidence of a credulous superstitious people, that he should
propagate strange and marvellous figments, and thereby
allure them to listen attentively to the lessons, and obey
the injunctions of a lawgiver. He was the legislator, the
reformer of Magna Græcia. To him and his disciples the
little states that composed it owe a celebrity which they
were not entitled to from extent of dominion or conquests.
Their ruin may be attributed to the neglect of his precepts;
or, indeed, in some shape to the very great success attending his institutions, which raised those republics to such an
uncommon pitch of prosperity, as intoxicated and finally
corrupted their citizens.

The Metapontines were warm partisans of Hannibal,
who, during many winters, made this city his head-quarters.
On the retreat of the Carthaginians, it was punished by the
Romans for that attachment with the loss of its liberty.
We are informed by Strabo, that this little commonwealth

I                                                    of

of farmers was deſtroyed by the Samnites. It remained in ruins, becauſe it could no longer hold out the ſweets of freedom, or the advantages of trade to entice inhabitants back to its deſolated walls; and the want of cultivators ſpeedily converted its once happy plains into a dreary deſert. At this day there cannot be a more melancholy ſight, or one more mortifying to the pride of man, than this wide-ſtretched tract of land, almoſt without an inhabitant; ſcarce diſturbed in any part by the plough, full of brown marſhes and ſtagnated pools: noiſome fogs and poiſonous vapours hang over them, and when ſet in motion by the power of the ſun, carry diſeaſe and death into the blood of the wretches doomed to breathe their venomous atmoſphere. Inſtead of a navigable river, in whoſe deep and capacious boſom whole fleets might moor with ſafety, the Baſiento now has the appearance of a ſtraggling torrent, impeded by ſand-banks that ſhift at every ſhower, and drive the waters back over half the plain, where they putrify*.

I ſlept a few off miles to the weſt at a farm-houſe, where my friends of Taranto had previouſly ſecured a comfortable lodging for me.

---

* When the ſhepherds are obliged to paſs the night in the open air during the bad ſeaſon, their method of guarding againſt the infection is as follows. A fire is lighted, on which they put a large pot of milk. As ſoon as it boils, they ſup up the hot liquor, cuſtom having ſufficiently hardened their throats and ſtomachs. This throws them into a profuſe ſweat, they then cover their heads with warm woollen caps, and lie down to ſleep with their feet cloſe to the fire.

SEC-

## SECTION XXXVII.

THE next day we travelled eleven miles in the plain, all one wild pasture; ferried over the Agri*, once a navigable river, now a rapid irregular torrent, and baited at Policoro, a very considerable farm lately belonging to the Jesuits, at present in the hands of the Crown. I believe these possessions do not yield to his Sicilian Majesty so great a revenue as they did to that intelligent society. Those fathers had a noble estate here, bounded by the sea, the rivers Agri and Sinno †; and the mountains, containing all kinds of land, pasture, wood, arable and salt-marsh. The buildings that were raised to contain the produce of so large a farm, to house the numerous herds and flocks, and to lodge the stewards and servants requisite for the conducting of such an establishment, are all laid out upon the great scale that marked every undertaking of that politic congregation. Not many years before the dissolution of their order, they had a stock of five thousand sheep, three hundred cows and oxen, four hundred buffaloes, four hundred goats, and two hundred horses, under the care of three hundred servants. At present things wear a different aspect, and seem verging to ruin rather than advancing towards greater perfection. During the hot season, when the air is

* Anciently, Acris                    † Anciently, Siris.

all

all on fire and very feverish, the Jesuits were wont to retire into the mountains to Latronico, another of their estates.

At the wood near the banks of the Agri, and about three miles from the sea, are some heaps of rubbish, that fix the situation of Heraclea *  And according to the most probable conjectures, near the mouth of the Sinno was Siris, the port of that city.  At present there is nothing but an open road, where ships may lie to take in a cargo of corn and other commodities, of which liquorice is one, a root that grows wild in great quantities along these swamps †, allowing for

* Nummi Heracleæ.
AUR  1  Cap. Palladis =Hercules leon strangul. IΦ HP \
     2  Cap  Palladis.=Hercules clava leon feriens HPAKΛHIΩN.
     3.  Cap  Muli. delph ΣA.=I ig. vir. nud. delph inf. d avem. f trident. FH. fubtus undæ.
ARG  1.  Cap Palladis cum monst mar. in galea.=Hercules nud. ftans d. clavam f. arcum & fpol. leon. ΠPAKΛHIΩN
     2  Cap. Palladis.=Hercules leon. ftrang clava. noctua fup hum. leonis FHPAKΛH
     3  Cap. Palladis =Noctua ramo inf HPAKΛHI
     4  Cap Pallad.=Hercules nud. ftans clav. nixus fpol. leon. tectus ΠM ΦIAΩ FHPAK.
     5.  Homo nudus delp inequ. d. diotam f. trident fub undæ FHP =  Eques nudus fupervolitante victor ΣY
     6  Cap Herculis.=Leo gradiens HL.
     7.  Cap leonis =Pharetra FHPA
ÆR  1  Cap imb hur ftella =Clava pharetra Arcus FH
     2.  Cap Pall laur & gal =Hercules ftans d pat. I clav. FHPA- KΛIΩN.
     3  Cap. Herculis=Clava pharetra FHPAKΛHIΩN.
     4.  Cap gal.=Tiophæum FHPAKΛI IΩN.

† The fale of this root is faid to produce 700l. a-year to the Duke of Corigliano.

O o                                     all

all the alterations that fo many revolving ages may have made in this abandoned fhore, it is a great matter of doubt with me, whether there ever was any good harbour here; or, even in the Agri, a much larger river, becaufe the fhape and expofure of the coaft reprobates that idea; efpecially as all ancient authors agree, that no bay between Rhegium and Tarentum was tenable after the autumnal equinox. It is therefore more than probable that fhips of burden feldom anchored in this place.

Siris * was a very ancient city, founded by Trojans, and renowned for its college of priefts fkilled in cabaliftic lore. It became a dependance of Heraclea, to which the principal inhabitants of Siris were obliged to remove. Heraclea was the point of rendezvous agreed upon by the whole Greek confederacy, where their general interefts and difputes were to be fettled. Upon its medals, many of which I purchafed of the peafants, is the figure of Hercules tearing open the jaws of the Nemæan lion. It is probable that Zeuxis, one of the moft celebrated painters of antiquity, was a native of this place rather than of any other Heraclea, as his moft capital performances were placed in the cities of Magna Græcia. The banks of the Sinno are famous in Roman hiftory for the victory gained by Pyrrhus over the Conful Levinus, in the

---

* Nummi Sirinorum.

Æ.R   1   Prora navis ϹϜΙΡΙΖ = Vas folium pamp. ΚΟΤΝ.
    2.   Cap. Mercurii petafatum. ΛΛ. = Aquila. corona ΣΕΙΡΙ.
    3   Cap. Mercurii pet. ϹΕΙ. = Vas.

I

year of Rome 473. This was the firſt encounter the Epirote had with the Romans. He purchaſed the honour of the day at the expence of the flower of his army, and thereby became ſenſible of the difficulties that awaited the proſecution of his enterprize. He was indebted for his ſucceſs to his own perſonal intrepidity, and to the panic which the firſt ſight of elephants ſtruck into the legions.

The neighbouring hills are compoſed of calcareous to-phus, replete with ſhells incruſted over, or petrified. Whole ſkeletons of the larger tribe of quadrupeds have been dug out of theſe ſtony ſtrata. At Rocca Imperiale, or near it, was the town of Lagaria, a colony of the Phoceans, noted in antiquity for a ſweet and ſoft wine much eſteemed by phyſicians as a cordial.

At Monte Giordano we entered the Upper or Hither Calabria. The inn wearing the face of dirt and poverty, I rode four miles farther to Roſeto, where my guide aſſured me he had an acquaintance that would be happy to accom-modate me with a room. The high lands approach very near to the ſea, and are tolerably cultivated : much of the land ſown with cotton.

At Roſeto, which is but a poor place, I was very hoſpi-tably received by a prieſt. The old man plied me with many queſtions concerning Naples, England, and America; and, in return for my readineſs in gratifying his curioſity, entered with great good ſenſe into a detail of the manners and cuſtoms of his own country, and informed me of many

particulars

particulars I was an entire ftranger to. I learned from him, that population is daily decreafing within the circle of his knowledge, from many caufes arifing out of the general government of the kingdom, of which he acknowledged himfelf an incompetent judge; and alfo, from many others that were within his fphere, and were daily felt by him. He attributed, but methinks without fufficient grounds, this progrefs of depopulation to the cuftom followed by the Calabrians, of never marrying beyond the limits of their own townfhip, which he thought perpetuated defects and dif-orders among them, and from a want of proper croffes in the breed, ended in barrennefs and the extinction of fami-lies. By thefe means all the peafants of a village are nearly related. The marriage-portion of a girl depends upon the wealth and numbers of the family, and generally confifts of a piece of vineyard, or a fingle fruit-tree, among which the mulberry holds the firft rank for honour and profit.

The common mode of letting farms of baronial or eccle-fiaftical eftates throughout Calabria, is by a leafe of two years, with many claufes and reftrictions. Proprietors of land of plebeian rank extend the term to fix years, and allow the tenant the liberty of cutting a ftipulated quantity of wood, on condition of his fencing off an equal portion to fpring up again.

The Barons are in general very far from confidering themfelves as the protectors, the political fathers of their vaffals, but encroach fo much on the commons and the

cultivated

cultivated grounds, for the fake of extending their chace, that the peafants have neither room nor opportunity to raife fufficient food for their fupport; they therefore fly to the mendicant and other orders of friars, and take the religious habit to procure a fubfiftence. The father of a family, when preffed for the payment of taxes, and finking beneath the load of hunger and diftrefs, *va alla montagna*, that is, retires to the woods, where he meets with fellow-fufferers, turns fmuggler, and becomes by degrees an outlaw, a robber, and an affaffin.

However, matters are not yet in fo defperate a fituation, as to preclude all poffibility of reftoring thefe provinces to a ftate of opulence and populoufnefs. If government were more attentive to the general good than particular interefts; if juftice were adminiftered with more honefty and impartiality by the fuperior magiftrates, and lefs rapacioufnefs by the fubalterns; if taxes were more equally and judicioufly impofed, and more tenderly exacted; if the aggrieved peafant had a refuge to fly to in the day of oppreffion, thefe fertile countries might emerge from their prefent ftate of defolation, and rich flourifhing towns might again rife along the now deferted fhores. The women are endowed by nature with fufficient fecundity, and bring forth their offspring almoft without a groan. It is a common thing for a woman, far gone with child, to go up to the foreft for fuel, and to be there furprifed with the pains of childbirth, perhaps haftened by her toil: She is nowife difmayed at the

solitude

folitude all around her, or the diftance from home, but delivers herfelf of the infant, which fhe folds up in her apron, and, after a little reft, carries to her cottage. It is a proverb much in ufe in the neighbouring provinces, *Che una ferva Calabrefe piu ama far un figlio che un bucato*, i. e. " A Calabrian maid-fervant prefers the labour of childbirth " to that of a wafh."

The Calabrians have fome very capricious notions deeply rooted in their minds. One is, that every child, whofe mother has been true to her marriage vow, muft neceffarily refemble the father. It is no doubt an eafy matter to per-fuade a peafant, who feldom confiders the lineaments of his face in a glafs, that the features of the infant are miniature copies of his; but if he were to become thoroughly con-vinced that no fuch refemblance exifted, he would never be perfuaded to pardon his wife, or look upon the child in any other light than that of a baftard.

It is thought a reproach to have been fuckled by any but one's own mother. This cafe feldom happens, for the wo-men recover with fo much eafe after lying-in, that few children are expofed to the neceffity of fucking a ftrange breaft

They repofe great confidence in judgments, and expect to fee every perfon that jeers at another's defects, afflicted with the fame; but have a milder idea of the penalty attending paffionate oaths and hafty curfes: if the party offending repent, they fuppofe all danger is blown over.

Inocu-

Inoculation has been attempted in one place only, near Reggio; but from ill fuccefs in fome inftances, and the fuperftitious averfion of the vulgar, thofe who have undergone the operation are held in utter contempt, and marked by fome opprobrious nickname.

If a perfon dies in the fields by a violent or accidental death, it is believed that his fpirit will appear in the fame place in white robes, and that the only way of laying it, is to fend out young boys to approach filently, and cover it with a volley of ftones. Not long ago a Dominican prieft, fitting in his white garment on a hill near Tropea, employed in taking a fketch of the country, was miftaken for the ghoft of an old mad woman who had dropt down dead fome time before on that identical fpot. The apparition brought out the youths of the neighbouring village, and the friar had his brains almoft knocked out before he could convince the little exorcifts of their error *.

## SECTION XXXVIII.

THE territory of Rofeto produces olives, capers, corn, faffron, and cotton. Good wine is faid to be made on the hills to the weft, but my hoft was not able to procure me any that was palatable. He told me that the

* All thefe particulars have been fince confirmed to me by perfons whom I know to be well acquainted with the ftate and manners of the country.

mountains

mountains abounded with very fine oak timber fit for ship-building, and that the woods were well stocked with game, which is a great annoyance to the farmers, whatever diversion it may afford the landlord.

By the Roman law, every person was at liberty to fish and hunt on the lands of another, unless formally prohibited by the owner; and, according to the Lombard institutions, no penalty was incurred by trespass without proof of damage. In the kingdom of Naples, the Emperor Frederick seems to be the first that forbade nets and snares, except when employed against bears, wolves, and other noxious animals. His passion for the chase dictated this law, which has been revived by many of his successors It is a doubt among the Neapolitan lawyers, what right the Barons have to an exclusive chase in their manors, where they cannot shew a precise grant in their investiture, or plead immemorial possession; and it has been the practice of the courts to discountenance their pretensions: much depends upon local custom. The use of guns is contrary to law, which the crown dispenses with at a regular price. A licence for fowling in the plains of Naples with bird-calls costs ten carlines a year; in the plains and woods, twenty-four; and sixty, with nets, in these and in the high lands. At a distance from the capital, it is only five, but the sportsman is not allowed either calls or nets, nor to enter inclosures and reserved baronial chases, if walled in. Overtures have been made to administration by several

under-

undertenants for the purchase of a general leave of shooting; but a difference in the price has prevented an agreement. The Cacciator Maggiore of the realm being a great Baron, we cannot be surprised if he coincide in sentiment with his fellow-nobles, and, in an aristocratical monarchy, be desirous of extending all restrictive laws; since we behold, in our land of liberal ideas and boasted freedom, the country gentlemen eagerly bent upon curtailing the privileges, and thwarting the inclinations, of the inferior class of citizens.

Calabria is too hilly to admit of hunting; all game is brought down by the gun, or taken in the net. The best kind of spaniel is the *Bracca focata*, a strong dog of a black or deep brown colour, with a tawny belly, and spots over the eyes. It is so excellent, that the king has taken particular pains to increase the breed.

The lower parts of the mountains abound with the Ornus, or small-leaved flowering manna ash, which grows spontaneously and without any culture, except that the woodmen cut down all the strong stems that grow above the thickness of a man's leg. Towards the end of July, the gatherers of manna make an horizontal gash, inclining upwards, in the bole of the tree. As the liquor never oozes out the first day, another cut is given on the second, and then the woodman fixes the stalk of a maple leaf in the upper wound, and the end of the leaf in the lower one, so as to form a cup to receive the gum as it extils from each flash.

P p

The

The old man told me, that vipers and martens were remarkably fond of manna.   He had himself frequently seen
the little quadruped at the tree; but never the reptile,
though many of his acquaintance had —The tyranny exercised over the peasants, on account of this native production
of their wildernesses, stands in the foremost line of their
numberless and abominable grievances.   All manna belongs
to the King, who gives it in farm to a set of contractors.
To gather it, a certain number of countrymen are furnished
by the feudatory, who receives five carlini for every man.
During the season, which continues about a month, these
fellows are not allowed to absent themselves a single day, or
undertake the least work of any other kind, however indif-
pensable for the preservation of their own little private harvest.   Their scanty wages are a poor compensation for this
involuntary service.   Their greedy employers give them
only three carlines* for every rotolo of manna; which
quantity, containing thirty-three ounces and a third, is sold
for twenty-four carlini and three quarters. if it be in tubular
pieces, the price rises one-third.   The peasants are punished
with the utmost severity, if detected in burning, destroying,
or damaging any of these trees, that cause to them so much
vexation; and are sent to prison, if the smallest quantity of
the juice be found in their houses.   They may eat as much
as they please in the woods; and most of them take this
physic once a year.

* In the Salernitan district, they pay the gatherers five carlini a rotolo.

Some

Some time ago eight hundred poor labourers of the province of Salerno, no longer able to fupport this oppreffive tafk, clubbed two carlini a-piece, and bribed a perfon of the court to prefent a memorial from them to the King, at Perfano; but, whether their agent deceived them, or the petition fhared the fate of fo many other petitions in all kingdoms, no manner of notice was taken of it; and their flavifh work returns every year, without any profpect of abolition or remittance. Indeed, throughout the realm, the fituation of the hufbandmen is truly deplorable; every thing is excifed, and the modes of collecting, wantonly cruel and pernicious. All live animals in Calabria are taxed. Six carlini are paid for an ox, four grains for a fheep; it is therefore no wonder if the graziers be in indigence, if the cottagers keep no beaft of any kind, and live upon cafual and unfubftantial nutriment, inftead of milk, cheefe, and other wholefome diet, which the rich pafturage of the country ought to afford them in as great abundance as that which the Flemings enjoy in their fat foil.

Arable land here is ploughed four times: the firft in May. But the labour is in general remifsly and languidly performed; and, inftead of laying down their fallows with hay-feeds, clover, or any of thofe rich artificial graffes which are fown in England to create fine meadows and paftures, the Calabrian farmer thinks he does his farm ample juftice, if he ceafes to plough it for two or three years, and leaves the good grafs, accidentally produced there, to

P p 2　　　　　　　　make

make its way, as well as it can, through the matted fibres of all manner of rank weeds. There is nothing to encourage the countryman to make any vigorous exertions, or try improvements in agriculture; which require both greater capital and courage than he is poſſeſſed of. He can foreſee no amelioration in his ſituation of life, from any efforts he can make: and woful experience has perhaps taught him to apprehend, that an increaſe of activity and produce would only draw on his ſhoulders an additional weight of taxes and oppreſſion.

I roſe before day, that I might have leiſure to examine the ſite of Sibaris, and reach Corigliano before ſupper; as there was no tolerable lodging to be expected ſhort of that place.

We rode paſt Trebiſaccio, a very ill-built town, on a hill, and within ſight of ſome others of no conſequence, ſituated on the right hand, upon little eminences prettily planted with olive and almond trees. One of them is called Amendolara, from the abundance of almonds; and is remarkable for being the birth place of Pomponius Lætus, a celebrated critic and hiſtorian of the fifteenth century. The component parts of theſe hills are a calcareous tophus, with ſea-ſhells, and other foſſile ſubſtances. The plains along the ſhore are very boggy, and interſected by a great number of ſmall rivulets, one of which is ſtrongly impregnated with ſulphur, and, as I was told, flows from ſome baths among the hills. The drier ſpots produce very rich

crops

crops of corn. Near the banks of the Racanello, we met great droves of buffaloes, belonging to the Duchefs of Caſſano: I think the number of beaſts exceeded a thouſand. Theſe rank, wet paſtures are very proper for the breeding of this ſpecies of horned cattle, which are of a heavy yet laborious diſpoſition, and delight in marſhes. During the broiling heats of ſummer, they lay themſelves down in the water, and leaving only the end of their noſes above the ſurface, defy the aſſaults of the myriads of inſects that ſwarm in theſe low grounds We repoſed, during the middle of the day, on the ſtraw of the great barn. Caſſano, a fief of the Serra Aragona family, is an epiſcopal city, about twelve miles from the fea: it has mineral waters, ſulphureous baths, and a very fruitful territory.

After dinner we croſſed the river Sybaris, now the Coſ-cile, and entered the peninſula formed by that river and the Crathis, where a few degraded fragments of aqueducts and tombs indicate the ſpot on which ſtood the city of Sybaris, noted to a proverb in ancient hiſtory for the luxury and effeminacy of its inhabitants.

No poſition could have been more judiciouſly choſen for commerce or agriculture, as long as an extenſive population and induſtry kept the rivers under controul. Irrigation is, in ſo dry a climate, the life of huſbandry; but unleſs ſtrong quays and embankments confine the waters to their due courſe, and prevent their coming down upon the country at improper ſeaſons and in ſuperabundant quantities, ruin and

I                                                                   peſtilence,

peftilence, inftead of riches and health, are the neceffary
confequences.   Attention to the management of thefe two
large ftreams enfured fertility to the lands, and deep, fafe
channels for trading fleets.   Many ages, alas! have now
revolved, fince Man inhabited thefe plains in fufficient
numbers to fecure falubrity.   The rivers have long rolled
lawlefs and unreftrained over thefe low defolate fields, leaving, as they fhrink back to their beds, black pools and
ftinking fwamps to poifon the whole region, and drive
mankind ftill farther fiom its ancient poffeffions.   Nothing
in reality remains of Sybaris, which once gave law to four
nations, reckoned twenty-five cities among its fubjects, and
could mufter three hundred thoufand fighting men.   I do
not think any remnants, now to be feen, date fo far back as
the old Sybaritan republic *.

Sybaris was one of the moft ancient of the fettlements
formed by the Greeks on the Italian fhore.   The natural
richnefs of its foil encouraged agriculture, which produced
abundance of articles of commerce ; and the convenience of
the fituation, between two confiderable rivers, naturally led
to a great exportation —From thefe fources wealth flowed
copioufly into the ftate, and with it brought fuch luxury
and degeneracy of manners, as have excited the aftonifhment
and indignation of all ancient writers.   Many anecdotes are

---

* The materials of the ruins being brick, argue Roman rather than Grecian workmanfhip.   I never met with bricks, in any undoubted Greek ruin,
throughout Magna Græcia or Sicily.

told

told us of the foft Sybarites; fome fcarcely credible, and all tending to fhew how much that people facrificed every confideration to the enjoyment of the prefent moment, and how eafy a conqueft they afforded their more needy and warlike neighbours But Sybaris, before its hour of misfortune, had numbered many of glory and dominion. It had founded the city of Pæftum on the Tyrrhene fea; its armies had been numerous and formidable; its authority refpected over a large range of country, and the wifdom of its councils admired by the furrounding nations. The walls of the capital inclofed a fpace of fix miles and a half, and its fuburbs extended near feven miles along the Crathis. What a noble fight! what beauties this country muft have difplayed, when the impetuous torrents were kept under command, and only let off cautioufly and regularly, to convey frefhnefs and fertility to the well-tilled thirfty fields!—when the banks of the river were adorned with warehoufes, wherein the merchant depofited his riches, and with elegant villas, and perfumed gardens, whither he retired to enjoy the fruits of his induftry!—when its fpacious plains teemed with harvefts, that, according to the teftimony of Varro, repaid the hufbandman an hundred fold, and annually loaded large fleets of veffels that crowded the mouths of its rivers!

After retracing all thefe circumftances in my mind, I looked round me, and could not help thinking myfelf in a dream, or that the hiftorians muft have been dreaming

when

when they wrote of Sybaris. Seventy days, as Strabo fays, fufficed to deftroy all this grandeur and profperity. Five hundred and feventy-two years before the Chriftian æra, the Crotoniates, under their famous Athleta Milo, defeated the Sybarites in a pitched battle, broke down the dams that kept out the Crathis, and let the furious ftream into the town, where it foon overturned and fwept away every building of ufe or ornament. The inhabitants were maffacred without mercy; and the few that efcaped the flaughter, and attempted to reftore their city, were cut to pieces by a colony of Athenians, who afterwards removed to fome diftance, and founded Thurium *. The coins of Sybaris are among the moft ancient known; being of the fort called *Incufi*, i e. convex on one fide, and concave on the reverfe. They bear a Bull, which I take to be an emblem of their fubdued river, fo long their friend and purveyor, but in the end an inftrument of their deftruction. The great works undertaken to drive back its waters, are probably expreffed by the head of the animal being turned back on its fhoulder †

* Modern authors place it at Terra Nova, four miles up the river, but Livy fays expressly it was on the fea fhore

† Nummi Sybaritarum.

ARG 1 Taurus ftans retroflexo capite ΥΜ = Altera pars incuffa
     2 Cap Palladis = Taurus ΣΥΒΑ
     3. Taurus = Vas incuffum
     4 Taurus . Quatuor Glob ΜΥ.
AR 1. Taurus cap reflexo ΥΜ = Incuffus

I have

I have often wondered why the moſt outrageous barbarians, the moſt blood-thirſty conquerors, have found more favour at the hands both of their cotemporaries and of poſterity, than the ſoft indolent Sybarites, who ſeem to have done harm to nobody, and whoſe faults originated in the affluent ſtate of their affairs, and the mild temperature of their climate, rather than in any miſchievous bent of character. I ſuſpect this virulence of abuſe ſprang, from the deſire their enemies, and the partiſans of thoſe enemies, had, of giving a plauſible excuſe for the cruelty with which the Sybarites were treated; perhaps alſo from a ſpirit of envy at their enjoyments; or from the common character, of philoſophical declamations. Theſe being the production of a ſet of men of great poverty, ſour tempers, auſtere morals, and much polemical iraſcibility, were more frequently employed to laſh the indulging voluptuary, than the bloody tyrant or ferocious raviſher; eſpecially as there was more danger in an attack upon the latter. Were the caſe otherwiſe, how ſhould we account for their ſpleen againſt theſe Epicures? for what compariſon is there between the culpability of a wealthy citizen, revelling in love and wine, pampered up with high ſeaſoned viands and delicious liquors, repoſing in eaſy carriages and beds of down; and the guilt of an exterminating conqueror, who embrues his hands in the blood of thoſe half-ſlumbering debauchees, that he may poſſeſs himſelf of their ſpoils,

and

and perhaps, in time, add their vices to his own native cruelty? Historians, and orators of all ages, have been guilty of this partiality. For my part, I cannot help feeling a degree of pity for the hard fate of the Sybarites, to whom we are indebted for the discovery of many most useful pieces of chamber and kitchen furniture. They appear to have been a people of great taste, and to have set the fashion, in point of dress, throughout Greece. Their cooks, embroiderers, and confectioners were famous over all the polite world; and we may suppose their riding-masters did not enjoy a less brilliant reputation, since we are told of their having taught their horses to dance to a particular tune. Alexis of Sybaris passes for being the inventor of fables or dialogues, in which the speakers are all rational beings;—the prototype of the Drama whereas Æsop and others had put their morality into the mouths of animals only.

After the destruction of Sybaris, Thurium became a considerable state under the discipline of Charondas, who died a martyr to the spirit of his own laws. Having fixed the pain of death upon any citizen that should enter the senate-house armed, and being reminded that in his hurry he had brought a sword with him into the assembly, he immediately plunged it into his breast, and sealed his decree with his own blood. Thurium flourished long even under the dominion of Rome, till falling to decay, it was judged

expedient

expedient to fend a colony thither; after which event it affumed the name of Copia*.

Herodotus, the father of hiftory, died at Thurium. Auguftus Cæfar was nicknamed Thurinus in his youth, either from his father's having governed this province, or from his family's deriving its origin from hence.

Suetonius made Adrian a prefent of a ftatue of Auguftus, with this name infcribed on the bafe. Cicero and Antony both reproached him with the lownefs of his origin, and afferted that his father, the firft of the race who had attained any honours in the republic, was, in the beginning, no better than a money-fcrivener; yet it is the common opinion, that this fortunate heir of Julius Cæfar fprang from a rich equeftrian family of Veletii.

* Nummi Thurinorum.
AUR 1 Cap Palladis cum monftro marino — Taurus cornupeta s.
ARG 1 Cap Pall = Taurus cornupeta pilcis ΘΟΥΡΙΩΝ
2 Cap Pallad clatum = Taurus cornup. vict fupervol cor impo. ΘΟΥΡΙΩΝ
3 Cap Pall laur = Taurus gradiens, pilcis — ΘΟΥΡΙΩΝ.
4. Cap Pall — Se mibos Θ
ÆR 1 Cap Pall gal = Taurus corn pilcis ΘΟΥΡΙΩΝ
2 Cap Apoll — Tripus ΘΟΥΡΙΩΝ
3 Cap Apoll = Lyra ΘΟΥΡΙΩΝ.
4 Cap. imb diad — Homo nud ftans ΚΡΟΤΩΝ ΘΟΥΡΙΩΝ

Nummi Copienfium
ÆR 1 Cap Pallad 4 globuli — Cornucopiæ 4 glob COPIA
2. Cap Herculis 3 glob — Cornuc 3 glob I C AIO COPIA.
3. Cap Mercurii petafat = Cornuc 3 glob Q. P. C. COPIA.

## SECTION XXXIX.

WE ferried over the Crati, a fine broad river, clear and
rapid.   The ancients were of opinion, that its waters
were medicinal, and had the faculty of tinging, of a fair or
yellow colour, the hair of all who drank them conftantly;
and that thofe of the Sybaris turned it black.   They deemed
it imprudent to drive cattle to drink at the Sybaris, as the
water was apt to excite dangerous fneezings and convulfions, being ftrongly impregnated with mephitic gas.

For the next three miles, our evening ride was up a moft
beautiful floping hill, thickly planted with orange, lemon,
citron, olive, almond, and other fruit-trees, which, by their
contrafted fhades of green, and the variety of their fize and
fhape, compofed one of the richeft profpects I ever beheld,
even in Italy, that country of enchanting landfcape.   I was
enraptured with the beautiful fcene, and almoft intoxicated
with perfumes.   The river Crati iffues out of a chafm in
the chain of mountains, forcing its boifterous way to the
Ionian fea, which, though four miles from the place where
I ftood, appeared, in that bright atmofphere, to lie clofe to
the foot of the hill, juft edged with a flip of verdant
pafture.   The little town of Corighano rifes boldly on the
peak of the richly clothed knoll, like the watch-tower and
fafeguard of all thefe natural treafures.   It is a dutchy belonging,

longing to the Saluzzi, a Genoese family, which has been for some years past annexed to the Seggio or ward of Porto at Naples. The buildings are rather better than those of the other Calabrian towns I had passed near, and contain about eight thousand inhabitants, who have an appearance of extreme poverty, and, like Tantalus, starve in the midst of plenty, though their lord has the reputation of being one of the most humane, as well as opulent, feudatories in the province. He has taken some pains to promote agriculture, and the breeding of horses and cattle; but his success has hitherto been inconsiderable.

It was a pleasing and refreshing circumstance to meet whole droves of mules and asses laden with oranges just plucked. They were carrying them to the sea-shore, to be embarked in small boats for Taranto and Gallipoli. The evening sea-breeze, strongly scented with the grateful effluvia, fanned me so delightfully, that with reluctance I entered the town, where I found the inn a very pitiful one, and infected with such disagreeable odours, as formed a woeful contrast with the perfumed air I had lately breathed. I never entered a Venta in Spain that was not preferable to this, for smell, cleanliness, and provisions. The route given me at Naples having made no mention of Carigliano as a sleeping-stage, I came, without any letter, to the Duke's agent, and therefore was refused a bed in his mansion. Upon this denial, I took up my lodging at the house of a dealer in oil. The master was absent, and we saw nobody but an old woman servant: the rest of the family kept themselves locked up. I was so ill accommodated, that, as soon as it was possible next morning to get ready, I rode down to the plains through a most delightful country, which I cannot pretend to describe in a manner to do it justice. On every side, fruits and flowers rose in clusters, freshened by the morning air; the round heads of the orange-trees glowed with the rays of the sun that was just rising, and darting his beams along the surface of the sea: the whole neighbourhood was enlivened by crowds of men and women singing as they descended the hill to their daily labour. Every production here is in the highest perfection it can possibly attain when unassisted by art. The husbandry of this province is slovenly, and the skill in gardening very superficial. Both betray a want of emulation and intelligence. Climate and soil do more than half the work, and the hand of dispirited man is sluggishly applied to the task; partial Nature empties the horn of plenty on his head, but from many fatal causes, her bounty contributes little to his welfare; whilst we see, in more northern and less happy regions, the active enterprising labourer able to extort favours from her, and, with the least gawdy of her riches, raise himself to comfort and independence

The road in the plain is very pleasant, under the shade of olive-trees or evergreen oaks, and through many tracks of very fine corn-fields; but at the end of six miles, it grows stony, steep, and rough, up to the very gates of Rossano,

which

which stands in a hollow, surrounded by fertile hills. There is nothing in this archiepiscopal city that claims much notice; the buildings are mean, the streets vilely paved and contrived. The number of inhabitants does not exceed six thousand, who subsist by the sale of their oil, the principal object of their attention, though the territory produces a great deal of good wine and corn.

The lower parts of the hills that encircle this town are composed of Breccia, or pebbles, particles of marcasites, mica, and lead, united together by means of a red bolar earth. There is no regularity in the strata, nor appearance of any gradual subsidence; the upper parts are a tophus full of petrified pectinites, and other exuviæ, of which the analogous shell-fish still exists in these seas. From the numerous fragments of lead, and some bits of silver ore picked up in the torrents, I conjecture that the mountains to the westward contain mines of those metals; though I have been assured by a judicious mineralogist of this country, that the accounts given by many writers of the Calabrian mines are vague exaggerations, and that nothing has yet been discovered but slender veins of ore, not likely to turn to any account in the working.

Rossano probably owes its origin to the Roman Emperors, who considered it as a post equally valuable for strength and convenience of traffic. The Marsans, a family of French extraction, possessed this territory, with the title of Prince, from the time of Charles the Second to that of Alphonsus the Second, when the last male heir was, by that

Prince's

Prince's order, put to death in Ifchia, where he was confined for treafon *.

Roffano afterwards belonged to Bona, Queen of Poland, in right of her mother Ifabella, daughter to Alphonfus the Second, and at her deceafe returned to the Crown. It was next in the poffeffion of the Aldobrandini, from whom the Borghefi inherited it.

So late as the fixteenth century, the inhabitants of this city fpoke the Greek language, and followed the rite of the Eaftern church. Here was formerly the moft celebrated rendezvous of the Bafilian monks in Magna Græcia. Of that body, the moft confpicuous member was Nilus, a faint of a very extraordinary character; for, during his whole life, he perfifted in refufing donations of lands, rents, and tenements, though he was the founder of many monafteries. Dominichino, by his admirable frefco paintings in the

---

* This illuftrious Houfe poffeffed extenfive domains in almoft every province, and made that ufe of their power and wealth, which is but too common in kingdoms diftracted by civil diffentions and litigated titles. The Marfans were principals in all difturbances, and took an active part in every commotion. Of thefe Princes, the moft potent was Marino, long the inveterate foe, but finally the dupe of Ferdinand the Firft, a King who was far from being fcrupulous in the means he employed to over-reach his enemies, or to rid himfelf of them when once in his power. In his treatment of Marino, the law of retaliation feems to plead his excufe, as that giddy nobleman had, fometime before his ruin, enticed the King to a conference near Teano, and there attempted to murder him. The plan failed in the execution, from the confternation and cowardice of the confpirators. Marfan was kept twenty-five years in prifon; and then, to complete the extermination of the whole rebellious baronage, was, with many other noblemen, fecretly executed, his fortunes for ever loft, and his family annihilated.

8

church

church of Grotta Ferrata, near Rome, has made his legend
more familiar to the dilettanti, than it is to the common
run of devotees; for this faint, being a Greek, is in no
very high repute in the Latin rubric: the numerous
founders and reformers of orders in fubfequent times, have
engroffed to themfelves almoft the whole ftock of homage;
and I believe very few Romans ever heard his name, though
he died in their neighbourhood. The Greek monks were
the prefervers of books and literature in the fouth of Italy;
for the Lombards defpifed and neglected the fciences.
Charles the Bald invited learned men from Greece to in-
ftruct his fubjects, and revive a tafte for learning among
them. Thefe priefts opened, in the convent of St. Nicholas,
near Otranto, a famous fchool, to which great numbers of
ftudents flocked, and received inftruction gratis. The monaftery even fupported thofe fcholars that wanted the means
of providing for their own maintenance. The aufterity of
life and profound learning of the Bafilian Cenobites, gained
them the efteem of princes and people, and procured them
eftablifhments in the kingdom to the number of five hundred. They maintained their ground to the fixteenth century, ufing the Greek idiom, but the Latin rite.

Pope John the Seventh, who was chofen in 705, was a
native of Reggio. Theologians blame him for his weaknefs, in yielding too much to the requefts of the Emperor
and the Eaftern prelates.

R r

## SECTION XL.

MY ftay at Roffano was very fhort; as the guide was eager to fet out, left we fhould be benighted before we reached Cariati, between which place and Roffano he affured me we fhould find very indifferent accommodations. We rode all the afternoon in a moft beautiful vale, cultivated with great neatnefs, and abounding with pulfe and vegetables of various forts. We paffed feveral rivulets that water and fertilize thefe fields. The Trionto alone * deferves the name of river, though not a navigable one, as fome geographers ftyle it. One of our horfes falling lame, we were obliged to take up our abode for the night at Mirti, a fingle houfe, or *Fondaco*. This inn was better than I expected, and the hoft very civil. He earneftly recommended to the fervants to leave nothing out of doors, as there was an encampment of Zingari, or gypfies, in the neighbouring fields, who would lay their hands upon any part of the baggage that was not watched with ftrict attention. His caution led me to an enquiry into the ftate of this ftrange tribe of vagabonds, of whom I had feen great numbers in Spain. The refult of his accounts, combined with thofe I have received from other hands, is as follows:

* Anciently the Traeis.

The

The gypfies of Calabria do not contract alliances with any other clafs of inhabitants, but marry among themfelves. It is not poffible to fay where they refide, as they have no fixed habitation, confequently poffefs neither houfe nor land; but wherever they think proper to make any ftay, pitch their tents. They fupport life by the profits of little handi-crafts, but more by thofe of fwopping affes and horfes, which they will do for the fmalleft trifle to boot; nay, one has been known to truck his afs with another for a glafs of wine. They generally work in iron, and make trivets, knitting-needles, bodkins, and fuch baubles. Their drefs is extremely fhabby; they fhave their chins, but indulge a great length of hair, which they feldom difturb with either comb or fciffars. As to their religion, it is a fecret they keep locked up in their own breafts. They feem to have no great veneration for the Virgin Mary; but are fuppofed to believe in Chrift. All the proof we have of their belief depends upon appearance, and an occafional conformity to the ceremonies of the Roman Catholic church in marriage, burials, &c.; but if the priefts ftart any difficulties, they manage the matter without their interference, and perform the functions according to their own cuftoms; which in many points refemble thofe of the heathens. At their weddings they carry torches, and have paranymphs to give the bride away, with many other unufual rites. It is in reality almoft an abfurdity to talk of the religion of a fet of people whofe moral character is fo depraved, as to make it evident they

believe

believe in nothing capable of being a check upon their paffions. They are univerfally accounted to be pilferers, cheats, faithlefs, fhamelefs, and abandoned to all manner of diffolutenefs. The following anecdote will fhew how little they are under the control of modefty, or fear of fhame. A gang of gypfies affembled at the fair of Marfico Nuovo, with an intention of robbing the fhops, for which purpofe a proper number of them were difperfed in the throng. To draw off the merchants by fome very extraordinary incitement to curiofity, was the next point to be confidered; and with this view they adopted an expedient that would have fhocked the moft hardened libertine. Some of their men and women went into the adjacent fields, and there proceeded to fuch indecent liberties, as foon brought moft of the people of the fair about them, and left their fhops a prey to the confederate thieves.

Contracts and plighting of faith are by them efteemed mere empty forms, and whenever the breach promifes more advantage than the obfervance, they never hefitate a moment. No cheats can be more artful or impudent. When they bring their affes to fale, they prick their fhoulders with very fmall needles fet in a piece of cork, which makes the poor animals bound like deer. The unfufpecting chapman thinks he buys the fleeteft of beafts, and perhaps finds, upon trial, that he has purchafed a dull, reftive, foundered grizel. The gypfies have a way of throwing down the mules and affes they wifh to buy, and thereby depreciating

their

their merit*. They tell fortunes, and play juggling tricks, as they do in all other countries where they are tolerated. In 1560, they were banished the kingdom as thieves, cheats, and spies for the Turks. In 1569, and 1585, the order was renewed, but not being enforced, had little effect.

A gypsy being brought to trial for larceny, declared, That his law allowed him to take from others as much every day as sufficed for his maintenance. These people make use of two languages, one Calabrian, with a foreign accent and pronunciation, the other, a peculiar one of their own; which, in sound, seems to bear a great affinity to the Oriental tongues, and is spoken when they have secrets to impart to each other.

One of the most intelligent of the crew being asked, Why his nation was a wandering one? replied, That they cannot remain in a place above a few days without being over-run with lice. This propensity to breed vermin proceeds from their excessive filthiness. They sleep like dogs in a kennel, huddled altogether, men, women, and children, taking up no more room asleep than if they were dead and buried, which crowding must cause a heat and fermentation extremely favourable to the multiplication of nauseous insects.

On the 10th of May we travelled along the shore, having high land on our right. The numberless beds of

* When they travel through a country where herds of horses and asses are suffered to wander without a keeper, they steal them, by casting over their necks a ball of lead fastened to a thong

torrents,

torrents, which we were obliged to crofs, made the road
very unpleafant.    The firft place we came to was Cariati,
a principality belonging to the Spinelli, one of the moft
opulent feudatory families, divided into feveral branches,
and poffeffed of very capital fiefs in Calabria *.    This city
is fmall, and thinly inhabited, on account of the weaknefs
of its fituation, and dread of the Turks, who, before a
treaty was concluded with the Porte, were continually
ravaging this coaft.    Its cathedral is a very heavy Gothic
ftructure, dedicated to St Peter, and the only parifh.    The
furrounding hills are gay, and pleafingly covered with fruit-
trees; the woods behind them produce manna of excellent
quality; much Turkey wheat is cultivated in the lands below, and extenfive paftures afford luxuriant and wholefome
fuftenance to a great ftock of oxen, buffaloes, fheep, goats,
and fwine.    In Calabria, all the oxen are white, large, and
long-horned, except thofe of the red breed, which have
been introduced from Sicily by the Princes of Cariati and
Geraci.    I never faw buffaloes of any colour but black;
and moft of the goats, fheep, and hogs are of that hue.
The laft fpecies have no hair, but are as fleek in the hide

* This family came from Somma, and is not mentioned in the chronicles
before the year 1224.    The man who laid the foundation of this wealth was
John Baptift Spinelli, confervator of the royal patrimony under Ferdinand
the Catholic, to whom he recommended himfelf by the vigilance with which
he watched the motions of the Viceroy Gonfalvo de Cordova.    Ferdinand, on
his arrival at Naples, diftinguifhed John very much, and gave, or enabled him
to purchafe, Cariati and' other confiderable eftates, fince augmented by the
prudence of his defcendants.

as an elephant. This country abounds with game of the lesser feathered tribes, such as doves, quails, and other birds of pasfage. Dormice are here accounted delicate game, as they were in ancient Rome, where they were kept in warrens, and fatted for the tables of the moſt refined epicures. The hair of these animals is here more generally grey than ruſſet. They are ſmoked out of their neſts in hollow trees, and caught with ſharp hooks. Their ſkins make very fine leather.——The ſea of Cariati abounds with fiſh. At a place called Terra Vecchia, eaſt of the city, are the ſlight remains of Paternum.

After dinner, we travelled four miles through arable lands of a ſtrong clayey ſoil, where the courſe of huſbandry is, to take a crop of wheat, and then to leave the field fallow two years for paſturage. We afterwards croſſed hilly olive grounds, covered with looſe ſtones, under which I found ſome ſtrata of compact grindſtone, and lumps of whetſtone, of a good quality. At the foot of theſe hills runs the Aquanile, which, both from name and poſition, I take to be the Hylias, anciently the limit between Sybaris and Croton. On its banks the Crotoniates gained the victory which made them maſters of the Sybaritan territory. They were led to battle by Milo the wreſtler, equipped like Hercules, with club and lion's ſkin, and crowned with the prize-wreaths he had won at the Olympic games.

My intention was to have ſlept at the town of Cio, which ſeems to ſtand on the ſite of Crimiſſa, a city founded

Ly

by Philoctetes, the friend, and, to his cost, the heir of
Hercules. But being assured that I should meet with
neither accommodations nor provisions at that place, I preferred remaining below in the plain, at a single house,
where my apartment was none of the best; but I had seen
worse, and the civility of the people made amends for
inconveniences. Ciro is a very poor place, containing
about six thousand inhabitants; it belongs to Spinelli,
Prince of Tarsia, who monopolizes all the silk made by his
vassals. The territory produces also very fine oil and corn,
execrable wine, but good water. This town, though by no
means in an unhealthy situation, affords a livelihood to six
doctors in physic. The evening was mild and still; I spent
it in a solitary walk along the beach of Cape Alice, the most
eastern point of the Calabrian coast, except the Lacinian
or Crotonian promontory. It was famous for a temple of
Apollo Halyus, of which I could not discover the smallest
vestige; the waves of the sea having covered, or the hand
of man removed, every stone of it. During supper, the
keeper of the neighbouring watch-tower came to pay me a
visit. A glass or two of wine restored that liberty to his
tongue which respect had restrained, and, after endeavouring to impress me with a high idea of his courage, and the
havoc he would make with his single gun in an army of
Algerines, he entertained me with several anecdotes of
his brother-warders, one of which I noted for its singularity. Part of the crew of a Barbary vessel had landed near

a man-a maritime tower, with an intent of plundering a village on the coaft; when their progrefs was impeded, and their fury diverted, by the watchman's fhooting their Reys through the head from the battlements. The Infidels flew to the foot of the tower, and attacked it with great fury. In fpite of the fire and other efforts of the defender, they had almoft reached the top; when the poor Calabrian, finding his ammunition gone, and his cafe defperate, bethought himfelf of a fingular engine of defence. He fnatched up fome bee-hives that ftood on the platform, and running round the parapet, fhook out the angry infects upon the affailants; who, ftung to the quick, and terrified with this incomprehenfible, miraculous attack, were glad to relinquifh the fcalado, and plunge into the water, to deliver themfelves from their cruel antagonifts. It is not every warder that can ftrike out fuch refources in generalfhip, and without them his poft is fcarce tenable, for the towers are but indifferently conftructed, or provided for refiftance. they are fquare and bulky, and not very lofty. The door is about half-way up, with a ladder, which is taken in at night, over this is a terrace, on which is placed a cannon, more for the purpofe of alarming the coaft, than finking the boats of an enemy. I was told at Rome, by an infpector of thefe forts, that, in the courfe of his vifitation, he came once to a tower, where the guard, in anfwer to the ufual queries concerning his fkill and care of the artillery, led him into the room under the battery, and pointing

S f

to

to a packthread fteeped in brimftone, that hung through a
crevice in the cieling from the touch-hole of the cannon,
informed him, that he had found out that to be the fafeft
and moft expeditious method of difcharging the piece.


## SECTION XLI.

THE next day we arrived at Cotrone for dinner;
having baited in the plain below Strongoli, a city on
a rugged mountain, fuppofed to be the ancient Petelia *.
Philoctetes firft fettled a colony at Petelia, which afterwards
became the capital of the Lucanians, and made a confpicuous figure, in the fecond Punic war, by its obftinate
refiftance to Hannibal.    Marcellus, the illuftrious rival of
that hero, perifhed in a fkirmifh near its walls.    Strongoli
belongs to a Pignatelli, who keeps a large ftud of horfes in
the wafte lands near the fea.    The Calabrian horfes are
pretty, fpirited and brilliant in their motions, but in general

* Nummi Petelinorum.
ÆR  1  Cap. barb galeat =Victoria gradiens d coron ΠΕΤΗΛΙΝΩΝ.
      2  Cap imb rad.=Tripus. T. ΠΕΤΗΛΙΝΩΝ
      3. Cap mul velat.=Jupiter fulminans ΠΕΤΗΛΙΝΩΝ.
      4. Cap Jovis=Jup fulm tripus. ΠΕΤΗΛΙΝΩΝ.
      5. Cap Jovis = Fulmen T. ΠΕΤΗΛΙΝΩΝ.
      6  Cap Apoll =Figura mulieb grad d ftyl ΠΕΤΗΛΙΝΩΝ duo
            glob
      7  Cap Herculis=Clava ΠΕΤΗΛΙΝΩΝ.
      8. Cap mul.=Canis. ΠΕΤΗΛΙΝΩΝ.

                                                        low,

low, and feldom free from vice. I know by experience that they can go through fevere fatigue, having rode a fmall one, in hot weather, five fucceffive days, at the rate of fifty miles a day. This breed is not attended to with all the care it deferves, for the prohibition of exportation renders the owners much more indifferent about the perfection of their horfes than they would be, if there were a demand from other countries, and a brifk fale allowed, to excite their emulation. Another caufe of neglect lies in the exceffive badnefs of the roads in this mountainous country, where mules, being much more hardy and enduring, are fitter for fervice, and confequently more marketable. They carry upwards of three cantara, through the moft difficult, dangerous ways imaginable, without ftumbling —The Barons have no exclufive feudal right to breed horfe, though fome of them arrogate to themfelves a monopoly by violence. We paffed the Nieto* in a boat. The air is unwholefome on the banks of this river, which divides the two Calabrias, but the herbage muft be incomparable, if I may judge from the delicacy and fweetnefs of the milk and cream cheefes, for which this canton is renowned.

Cotrone has fucceeded to the Greek city of Croton, but does not cover the fame extent of ground. I was affured that in fummer this climate is unhealthy; a misfortune that cannot proceed from local caufes, for the falubrity of

---

* Anciently Neœthus.

Croton was famous to a proverb among the ancients.   The Esaro, which flowed through the very centre of the old town, now runs in a shallow stony bed, at a considerable distance north of the gates.

Great works have been constructed, in the present reign, to form a harbour for this town.   Time will shew whether the exertions of ministry have been directed by skill and judgment ; and whether the obstacles, that heretofore prevented vessels from riding in safety before Cotrone, have been sufficiently removed and guarded against for the future. The entrance of the new haven is open to the north and north-east winds ; points of the compass from which very boisterous blasts rush down the Adriatic, across the Tarentine gulph, though perhaps less tremendous than the Scilocco and southerly winds.   As the hills and projection of the capes protect Cotrone from storms on the south quarter, I am surprised the engineers did not direct the mouth of the haven more easterly : the entrance would have been easier, and the vessels less disturbed while in port.   However, as I pretend to no technical knowledge in the engineering line, but speak from rude guess and cursory observation, I am willing to believe there were sufficient reasons for proceeding on the plan that has been adopted. Perhaps the weight of water rolled up the gulph might create a dangerous swell, or sands might in time accumulate at the passage, if the harbour lay open to the east.   But it is the opinion of many sensible observers, that greater

6

advan-

advantages might have been procured for the money, and that very great additional expence is requisite to complete the undertaking. I should no doubt have judged more favourably of an enterprize, which, like the hand of a Creator, forms a port, where the ancient mariners despaired of procuring secure anchorage,—had I not been informed that the venerable fragments of the old city, its suburbs and temples, had been dilapidated, to furnish materials for the piers and buttresses. This was a very trifling saving, in so expensive a concern; and appears a piece of extraordinary barbarism in ministers, that plumed themselves upon their excavations at Herculaneum, and the care with which they preserved the precious monuments of antiquity * Cotrone is fortified with single walls, and a castle erected by Charles the Fifth. Its private buildings are poor and sordid, the streets dismal and narrow: ill-humour, misery, and despondency were strongly depicted in the countenance of every inhabitant I met. There is very little bustle, little commercial hurry; cheese and corn are the principal commodities. For the stowage of corn, there are ranges of granaries in the suburbs; and the annual export is about two hundred thousand tomoti. The cheese is tolerably good; but has a great deal of that hot, acrid taste, so common to all cheese made with goats milk. The wine

* The harbour is capable of containing a considerable number of merchant ships, but none above the tonnage of a Polucca The mouth of the port is marked by two light houses

is not unpleasant, and appears susceptible of improvement, by better management in the making and keeping.

This being the actual state of the town, let us cast a view back upon its situation in those ages, when four republics, founded by Grecian refugees, gave the law to the shores of the Tarentine, Ionian, and part of the Tyrrhenian seas, when neither the Lucanians nor Bruttians had assembled together in sufficient numbers, amidst their mountainous recesses, to disturb or oppose the dominion of these colonies. I shall form no conjectures concerning Hercules or Myscellus, the supposed founders of Croton; but take for granted that it was occupied by navigators from Achaia, and that their posterity rose by virtue and valour to the highest eminence of fame among the sons of Greece. But this valour, this virtue, appear to have been called forth by the wholesome precepts and severe institutes of the Pythagorean school. Pythagoras, after his long peregrinations in search of knowledge, fixed his residence in this place, which some authors think his native one, at least that of his parents, supposing him to have been born in the isle of Samos, and not at some town of that name in Italy. This incomparable sage spent the latter part of his life in training up disciples to the rigid exercise of sublime and moral virtue, and instructing the Crotoniates in the true arts of government, such as alone can insure happiness, glory, and independence.

Under

Under the influence of this philosophy, the Crotoniates inured their bodies to frugality and hardships, and their minds to self-denial and patriotic disinterestedness. Their virtues were the admiration of Greece, where it was a current proverb, that the last of the Crotoniates was the first of the Greeks. In one Olympiad, seven of the victors in the games were citizens of Croton, and the name of Milo is almost as famous as that of Hercules. The vigour of the men, and beauty of the women, were ascribed to the climate, which was believed to be endowed with qualities peculiarly favourable to the human system. Their physicians were in high repute, and among these, Alcmeon and Democides rendered themselves most conspicuous. Alcmeon was the first who dared to amputate a limb, in order to save the life of a patient; and also the first writer who thought of inculcating moral precepts under the amusing cloak of apologues. This invention is more commonly attributed to Æsop, as he was remarkably ingenious in this species of composition. Democides was famous for his attachment to his native soil. Though caressed and enriched by the King of Persia, whose queen he had snatched from the jaws of death, he abandoned wealth and honours, and by stratagem escaped to the humble comforts of a private life at Croton.—The Pythagoreans are said to have discovered that disposition of the solar system, which, with some modifications, has been revived by Copernicus, and is now universally received, as being most agreeable to nature

and

and experiment. Theano, the wife of Pythagoras, and many other women, emulated the virtues of their hufbands *.

In thofe fortunate days the ftate of Croton was moft flourifhing. Its walls inclofed a circumference of twelve miles. Of all the colonies fent out from Greece, this alone furnifhed fuccour to the mother-country when invaded by the Perfians. By its avenging arms the Sybarites were punifhed for their fhameful degeneracy; but victory proved fatal to the conquerors, for riches, and all their pernicious attendants, infinuated themfelves into Croton, and foon con-

---

\* Nummi Crotonorum

AUR 1 Cap Mul.=Hercules fedens aquam verf KPOTΩNIAIAN.
ARG 1. Tripus ♀ᗞo    Incuffus
    2 Idem cum ave
    3 Tripus ♀ᗞo. avis = Aquila capite reverfo
    4 Facies plena diad cum monili = Hercules fed fup exuvias leon. d vas. fupri arcus clava & pharetra KPOTONIAIAN
    5. Fac. pl diad cum mon = Hercules tectus pelle leon aquam fundens ex vafe in tripodem—clava KPOTON. OΣ.
    6 Cap Apollinis diad = Hercules ftrang leon.
    7 Cap Apoll hur KPOTΩNIAIAN = Civitas murata fupri fulmen in muris victoria et eques
    8 Aquila fulm inf = Tripus, cornucop KPO
    9. Tripus Ƀ KPOIONIAIAN.—Aquila volans ung palmæ tanum tem
    10 Sæpia.=Tripus cum ave ♀ᗞo.
    11. Cap. Apoll = Lyra.
    12 Avis=Taurus ♀—v ftella cochlea
ÆR. 1 Herculis cap KPO = Tripus CY
    2. Cap. Jovis. = 3 lunæ et ftellæ.
    3. Cap. Cereris.= Tres lunæ KPO.
    4. Cap. imb.=3 lunæ KPO.

taminated

taminated the purity of its principles. Indeed, the very constitution of human nature militates against any long continuance in such rigid practices of virtue; and therefore it is no wonder if the Crotoniates fell by degrees into the irregularities they once abhorred. Not long after, the Locrians, who were less corrupted, defeated them on the banks of the Sagra, and reduced the republic to distress and penury. This restored the remaining Crotoniates to their pristine vigour of mind, and enabled them to make a brave, though unsuccessful resistance, when attacked by Dionysius of Syracuse. They suffered much in the war with Pyrrhus, and, by repeated misfortunes, decreased in strength and numbers, from age to age, down to that of Hannibal, when they could not muster twenty thousand inhabitants. This small population being incapable of manning the extensive works erected in the days of prosperity, Croton was taken by the Carthaginians, and its citizens transported to Locri. The Romans sent a colony hither two hundred years before Christ. In the Gothic war, this city rendered itself conspicuous by its fidelity to Justinian, and Totila besieged it long in vain. In one of the campaigns, during the war between Charles of Anjou and Frederick of Aragon, the latter not only drove his rival out of Sicily, but pursued his advantages into Calabria, where his fortunate admiral, Roger Lauria, obtained a complete victory over the Provençal party. The next step taken by the conqueror was to invest Cotrone, which made no long defence, but sent out commissioners

to

to propofe a capitulation. During the negociation, the Sicilians, taking advantage of the fecurity and negligence of the befieged, entered the city by furprife, and plundered it without mercy. The admiral infifted upon reftitution being made; but Frederick could not prevail upon himfelf to relinquifh a prize already won, and by this refufal to do juftice to Lauria's warranty, provoked him to join the Angevines, and become a moft formidable opponent.

A branch of the Houfe of Rufo was long in poffeffion of the fief of Cotrone. Henrietta, their heirefs, was deftined, by Alphonfus the Firft, to be the wife of his favourite, Inigo de Avalos; but fhe fell in love with, and married Antony Centeglia, who had been fent by Alphonfus to fettle the preliminaries of the match. Centeglia foon felt the weight of royal vengeance; was befieged in Catanzaro, and obliged to furrender at difcretion. The King confined both him and his wife in Naples, where they fpent many years in poverty and obfcurity. On the demife of Alphonfus, Antony efcaped to Calabria, and excited that province to revolt. The beginning of his enterprize was fuccefsful; but upon his being worfted and taken prifoner, all the hopes of his party vanifhed, and his family fank again into mifery.

## SECTION XLII.

IN order to vary the scene, I hired a boat to carry me round the capes, while my horses proceeded the shortest way to Catanzaro  By this plan I had an opportunity of seeing some places that lie out of the direct route by land.

We soon doubled Cape Nau, and darting through a shallow bay full of shelves and islets, landed at Cape delle Colonne, known in ancient geography by the name of the Lacinian Promontory, which, with the promontory of Salentum, or St. Maria di Leuca, forms the mouth of the Tarentine Gulf, seventy miles wide.   The land is very high, rocks, coarse granite, and breccia.   On a point impending over the waves, are some scattered stones, and a few regular courses of building, said to be the ruins of the school of Pythagoras, and of the temple of Juno Lacinia.   About forty years ago, two columns of this edifice were still standing   One has long been fallen, the other still remains standing upon a foundation of large stones cut into facets, and serves as a landmark for navigators.   Its order differs little from that of the columns at Metapontum, but some bricks, which appear intermixed with the stone-work, create a doubt in my mind, whether these fragments appertain to any building so ancient as the Crotonian republic.   It may have been rebuilt by the Romans, and the old columns made to serve

T t 2                                    again.

again.    This conjecture acquires weight by what hiftory tells
us of the Cenfor Fulvius Flaccus having ftripped the roof of
its marble flags, to cover a temple he had dedicated in
Rome.    The covering was fent back by order of the fenate;
but from a want of flaters able to replace it properly, the
edifice remained unroofed, and was probably deftroyed by
the weather.    Reidefel fuppofes thefe ruins to have been
part of Croton; but that is not poffible, as they are feven
miles from the Efaro, which we know divided the town
into two parts.    In my opinion, they are more likely to be
remains of the college of Juno's priefts, or of the ftalls for
her numerous herds and flocks, that ranged undifturbed
over the lawns and under the groves.    Few places of worfhip drew fo many pilgrims as this temple.    At ftated feafons, the roads of Italy and Greece were thronged with
parties of devotees marching, with expiatory prefents and
votive offerings, towards the fhrine of the goddefs.    Such
a conflux of facrifices fwelled the holy treafure to an incredible value.    Among heaps of ornaments of the moft
precious materials, was diftinguifhed a column of folid gold.
In a word, this wealth was the prototype of the golden
wainfcot, maffive lamps, and diamond crowns of Loreto.
But Loreto has been hitherto more fortunate, or better protected than Lacinium, which frequently excited the cupidity, and became the prey, of facrilegious conquerors.    This
temple was the fcene of a barbarous action committed by
Hannibal, if we are to believe the Romans, who, by de-
                                                                    ftroying

ftroying all records of Punic hiftory, have taken care to prevent our bringing any proof againft their affertions. They write, that Hannibal, finding himfelf under the neceffity of obeying the fummons of the Carthaginian fenate, affembled all his Italian allies in this temple, and there caufed fuch as refufed to embark with him for Carthage, to be maffacred by his African foldiers.

The view from this headland is very extenfive. I returned to my boat, and kept under the fhore till we had paffed three other capes, when night coming on, we were obliged to run into a cove on the fouth-eaft fide of Capo Rizzuto, the northern head of the Squillacean gulf, as Capo di Stilo is the fouthern one. My boatmen were very anxious to draw the felucca on fhore, and fhelter themfelves from danger under the gun of a watch-tower. They were much afraid left any Barbary rovers fhould be lurking among the iflands and creeks; though, from all their accounts, I could not find that they were often troubled with their vifits. The crew fet up an awning, and prepared fupper, perfectly fatisfied with the fafeguard of the tower, though ten Algerines would have been an overmatch for us and our protectors. I took a moon-light walk by the fea-fide, and fpent an hour very agreeably. When I returned to my company, they expoftulated with me on the rafhnefs of my venturing out alone; and feeing me laugh at their apprehenfions, nodded at each other, and agreed together, that I could not be fo bold, unlefs I had a

charm

charm about me.   This remark excited my curiofity, and
upon enquiry I learned that in Calabria there are certain
old women who fabricate talifmans on bits of parchment,
which they fell for eighteen ducats to the bravos that can
afford to lay out fo much money.   This charm is fuppofed
to render the wearer invulnerable; and as a preliminary
fecurity, a piftol is fired at it: but care is taken to qualify
the charge fo as to drive the ball but feebly againft the mark.
The purchafer, confident of fafety, lays the amulet upon his
breaft, attacks his adverfaries without fear, and generally, by
his daring appearance, ftrikes them with a panic*.

Before day-break we pufhed off our boat, and rowed over
to an ifland marked in every map as the habitation of
Calypfo.   Things muft have changed wonderfully fince the

---

* I have fince procured one of thefe pieces of witchcraft from a prieft, who
had obliged a penitent of his to give it up, as belonging to wicked practices
ftrictly forbidden by the church.

It was couched exactly in thefe terms·

+

+ Anna Pariote

Incanto la tua perfona ardente da parte di Chrifto
innipotente da parte del ciorno di natale per
le tre meffe chefi difino in cielo fi fcriffino
+lunedi fanto+marte difanto+mercodifanto+
Ciovedifanto+Vennardifanto+Sabatofanto da tutte
Magarie fia yuardata cirieleifon Chriftoeleifon
corpo di Chrifto falvate+Aglio+taglio et faglio
+lega mane piede e core a chi offennare mi uoli
Sangue di Chrifto commoglia metu+.

time of Ulysses, or the goddess have daily worked a miracle
in providing food, without which supernatural assistance the
shipwrecked hero had died of hunger: at present this rock
would scarcely maintain a sheep. Some thickets of lentiscus,
and other brushwood, are the only representatives of the
tall trees which the Ithican chief felled for the construction
of his vessel. Scholiasts have fixed Calypso's isle at Cape
Rizzuto, because it is directly east of Corfu, whither
Ulysses steered with a west wind; but unless Homer talked
of imaginary land, hidden from mankind, as the etymology
of the words Ortygia and Calypso imply, or, from the scarcity
of geographical helps in that age, was ignorant of the true
distances of places, it is difficult to reconcile matters to probability, I wont say truth, because a poet is not supposed to
be strictly bound to it. Corcyra or Corfu, the land of the
Phæacians, which is not a night's sail from Ithica, is scarce
one hundred miles distant from Italy, and therefore could
not require seventeen days sailing with a prosperous gale.
Homer, in the opinion of Strabo and the most enlightened
critics, had travelled much, and did not raise his epic building merely upon the shadowy basis of fiction,—the voyages of
Ulysses had been handed down by tradition, and to some
well-known stories he added poetical embellishments. Perhaps the sea has covered large tracts of land near this cape,
and the rocky islets we still perceive above the waters, may
be no more than the tops of the hills that rose upon the
beautiful plains where Calypso and her nymphs were said to

8

wander

wander. When, on confidering Homer's narrative with attention, I find Ulyffes is driven back into Charybdis by a fouth wind, gets again upon the wreck, and congratulates himfelf upon his paffing unnoticed under the jaws of Scylla, which was north of the whirlpool, I think it evident he was not carried into the Ionian, but the Mediterranean fea, or, perhaps the ocean, where he was hurried away before the wind during nine days and nine nights, till he reached the ifland of Ortygia. The Baleares in one, or the Fortunate Ifles in the other, afforded room enough for the goddefs's eftablifhment; and from thence he might very well be feventeen days before he faw Corfu rife like a buckler on the fea.

I found no charms on the ifland powerful enough to detain me; and therefore, after a breakfaft on prawns and limpets, caught and dreffed by my fteerfman, I put off, and doubling the cape, entered the Gulph of Squilacce. The rocks are compofed of pebbles, fand, and fhells, united together.

## S E C T I O N  XLIII.

THE fky was overcaft, and threatened rain, which made us keep clofe to the fhore. We rowed round the little harbour of Caftelle, probably the place formerly called Caftra Hannibalis, from which that able, but ill-feconded general, embarked for Carthage*. As we failed along, the man at the helm pointed out to me feveral inland towns of little note, but beautiful objects from the fea. Cutro was one, remarkable for having given birth to Galeni, a renegado, who, in the fixteenth century, rofe to great honour at the Ottoman Porte, and, by the name of Ulucciali Baffá, commanded the Turkifh fleet, was Viceroy of Algiers and Tunis, and became one of the greateft fcourges of Chriftendom. In the height of his profperity, he was defirous of beftowing a part of his wealth upon his aged mother, who lived in poverty at Cutro, but that fpirited old woman refufed to accept of the fmalleft token from a fon, who had forfaken the religion of his fathers, and profeffed himfelf the fworn enemy of Chriftianity.

Belcaftro was another town in view, diftinguifhed by the birth of Saint Thomas di Aquino, whofe father was Lord of this city. The good Calabrefe think the ftain of having produced ten thoufand Uluccialis, perfectly wiped away by the glory of having one fuch Doctor of the Church for their countryman †.

Cropani

* D'Anville places it near Squillace, from a perfuafion that Pliny and Solinus fix Hannibal's camp in the narroweft fpot of the whole ifthmus, but it appears to me they only meant, that the port from which he took his departure was fituated in the Gulph of Squillace, between which and that of St Eufemia, Italy is not quite twenty miles broad. The name of a tower called Torre d'Annibale, a little to the weft of this bay, is fome proof that d'Anville miftook the fenfe of the above-mentioned authors.

† This Dominican faint was full as good a gentleman as the founder, St Dominick de Gufman. The Houfe of Aquino derived its pedigree from the

U u

Lomba

Cropani was also in fight, once a flourishing town, but reduced by earthquakes to a ruinous village. The country about it, is a gay mixture of bean and corn fields, vineyards, and tufts of walnut and mulberry trees, a rich variety very unusual in a marine profpect. Several rivers, emptying their waters into the fea, make bold breaks in the hills, and produce charming accidents of light and fhadow.

On the banks of the Litrello, one of the many ftreams we faw, is a little village called Malifano, fixed upon by the Spaniards for the birth-place of a man who, in 1600, gave the Court of Madrid a great deal of uneafinefs. Parrino, one of the moft fervile flatterers among the court-writers, gives us, in his Theatre of Viceroys, the following curious account of this extraordinary perfonage: " This " year there came to Naples a famous impoftor, who pre-" tended to be the King of Portugal. This man was a " Calabrefe of Malifano, a village near Taverna, by name " Marco Tullio Cotifone, who went to Padua in a pil-" grim's drefs, and faid he was Don Sebaftian. He was feized " by order of the ftate, fent to Venice, and formally inter-" rogated. To the queftions put to him he made anfwer, " That the ftory of his death had been vamped up by the " Spaniards, that he had efcaped from the battle, and tra-

Lombard Princes of Capua, one of whom, in the tenth century, granted the county of Aquino in Terra di Lavoro, to his fon Adinolf. When it became again cuftomary to diftinguifh families by furnames, the defcendants of Adinolf affumed that of their earldom

" velled

" velled to Jerufalem, to fulfil a vow he had made in the
" moment of danger. As a proof of the identity of his
" perfon, befides the likenefs of features, fimilarity of fta-
" ture, and Portuguefe language, which he fpoke in perfec-
" tion, he fhewed one arm longer than the other, a
" remarkable and uncommon defect that had been ob-
" ferved in the King. What moft aftonifhed the fenate,
" was his quicknefs of repartee, judgment in political
" matters, dignity of behaviour, princely carriage, and
" the minute account he gave of the private propofals,
" anfwers, and negociations between that Prince and the
" Venetian Ambaffadors at Lifbon. However, as it was
" well known Don Sebaftian could not be alive, fince King
" Philip had redeemed his body of the Moors for an hun-
" dred thoufand ducats, the Senate fufpected this man to
" be, what in reality he was, an infamous forcerer; and
" therefore, after two years imprifonment, banifhed him
" out of their territories. The Portuguefe refiding in
" Venice clothed him, and forwarded him to Florence in
" the difguife of a friar; but there the Duke, who was
" attached to the Spanifh intereft, caufed him to be feized,
" and fent in chains to Naples. When he was brought
" into the prefence of the Viceroy Count de Lemos, who,
" on account of the heat, was ftanding without his hat, he
" haughtily bid him be covered. Being afked by the
" Viceroy, What authority he had for giving him fuch an
" order? he replied, That although the Count could not

" have

" have forgotten the bufinefs which had carried him twice
" to Lifbon in the time of the late King Philip, he would
" refrefh his memory with fome particulars of the affair.
" The minute detail he gave came fo near to truth, that
" the Viceroy was ftruck with amazement; but, upon re-
" collecting himfelf, declined all farther conference, and
" ordered him to prifon.  He remained there clofely con-
" fined till the arrival of the next Viceroy, when he was
" brought to trial.  His low birth was proved upon him,
" the fraud difcovered, and the impoftor condemned to the
" gallies.  While on board, he gained the love and refpect
" of all his fellow-flaves, and was conftantly treated by
" them as if he had really been the perfon he wifhed to
" pafs for.  He was afterwards fent to the fleet of Sicily,
" and there examined by the Duke of Medina Sidonia,
" who had vifited Lifbon during the reign of Don Sebaftian.
" The prifoner addreffed the Duke as an inferior, and
" afked him what became of an African boy he had given
" him twenty-two years ago?  Medina was confounded;
" and burfting into tears, retired from the galley, very
" much undecided what to think of the bufinefs.  The
" court, at laft, thought it fafeft to rid themfelves of
" him; and he was accordingly put to death on the ifland
" Delle Femine, near Palermo.  After he had been ftretch-
" ed on the rack, where he confeffed that he had carried
" on the cheat by the affiftance of the Devil; and, in fact,
" all thofe marks which had rendered his lies fo plaufible,
2                                             " difappeared

" difappeared from his body the moment he was dead." Giannone, who wrote under the patronage of an Auftrian prince, affects to treat this affair as a foolifh trick; but many authors give more credit to the flave's ftory. Parrino's abfurd recourfe to magic and diabolical illufion, is rather an argument in favour of this unhappy man's pretenfions; for if the court of Spain could have devifed better means of refuting his claim, it would certainly have employed them.

It was fo late before we reached the place fixed upon for our landing, that I preferred fleeping in the boat, to walking fix miles up to Catanzaro, in the dark, without a certainty of finding lodgings. A few hours, next morning, fufficed to examine every remarkable object in this capital of Nether Calabria.

Catanzaro was built in 963, by order of the Emperor Nicephorus Phocas, as a poft of ftrength againft the Saracens. Its fituation on an eminence, in the pafs between the mountains and fea, feems judicioufly chofen for the purpofe of repelling thofe Infidels, who, from Africa or Sicily, were wont to make good their landing at Reggio. Increafe of inhabitants and of fize caufed it to be deemed a proper refidence for the officers who compofe the provincial tribunal; and, in 1593, it arrived at the dignity of capital, formerly the right of Reggio. At prefent, Catanzaro contains twelve thoufand inhabitants, who live by the law, and the fale of corn, filk, and oil; of the laft they

export

export annually about ten thousand salme.  The water of this place has an unpleasant taste, and a great deal of earthy sediment: the wine is very rough.  The college of the late Jesuits is a handsome building, and possesses a good statue of St. Ignatius, by Fonseca; and a very fine picture, representing St. Bruno distributing bread to the poor.  The first feudal investiture of Catanzaro, was from King Roger, to his son-in-law Hugh de Molines, Earl of Molise.  The next, from the first Charles to Peter Ruffo, whose family was in possession down to the Aragonian reigns, when their estates went to Centeglia, and by him were forfeited.——Chaises can go no farther south than this stage; and indeed I do not comprehend how they can penetrate so far.  From hence to Reggio, the generality of travellers are conveyed in litters, by a route which crosses the country, and runs along the shore of the Mediterranean.

In the afternoon, I rode ten miles to Squillacce, through a level, well-cultivated country, abounding in corn, pulse, maize, mulberries, and olives.  The wages of a labourer are fifteen grana *per diem*; the soil, a fertile loam, full of broken shells.  My guide led me, with an air of triumph, to admire what he called a Temple of the old Saints of Calabria.  Upon inspection, it proved to be an edifice of Norman or Angevine times, with square towers at the corners.

## SECTION XLIV.

SQUILLACCE is built on the verge of a rocky mountain, sloping to the east, about three miles from the sea. I do not know why Virgil gives this city the epithet of *Navifragum*, "Breaker of Ships;" as there are no hidden or apparent dangers attending the approach of vessels. It is impossible this exact poet could be so careless, as to confound the attributes of the capacious bay of Scyllacæum, with the narrow pass of Scylla in the Faro of Messina. Perhaps those who explain the epithet by a tradition, that the first habitations of the place were built with fragments of the ship of Ulysses, may have stumbled upon a method of clearing up the difficulty.

In forming the body of Grecian commonwealths on the Italian shores, Athens furnished emigrants for Scyllacæum ; but this settlement never made any figure in the confederacy *. Rome sent a colony hither  In the year 982, the Emperor Otho the second was defeated under its walls, by the forces of the Greeks; who, from this victory, conceived delusive hopes of compelling Italy once more to resume their yoke. Montfort obtained this lordship in fee from Charles of Anjou ; but in the next reign it was given to the Marsans. This powerful house being overturned by the

* Num. Scyll.—ÆR. 1. Cap. Merc. Φ=Prora navis ΣΚΥΛΛΑΤΙΩΝ.

Aragonese,

3

Aragonese, the fief was bestowed upon that of Borgia, and is now vested in the Marquis Gregori, who, from being a commissioner of the victualing-office at Messina, rose to be Prime Minister of Naples, and afterwards of Spain. Though he knew how to secure the partiality of his sovereign, he was not able to conciliate the affections of the nation. A revolt in Madrid drove him out of the Spanish territories; and he has ever since resided at Venice, as Ambassador from the Court of Spain. The Neapolitans attribute many pernicious measures to his counsel, and detest him as the cause of their heaviest griefs and oppressions. We must wait for his death, and the subsiding of party-anger (the *recentia odia* of Tacitus), before we decide upon his criminality.

Squillacce prides itself on having given birth to Cassiodorus, a statesman of great abilities; and, considering the times he lived in, a very respectable author; beloved and honoured by Theodoric, and other Gothic monarchs. After passing through many high offices in the state, he fixed upon his native city for the retreat of his old age; and, in compliance with the then reigning fashion, took the habit of a monk, and spent the last years of his life in a cloister In his letters to Maximus, he has left us many tokens of his attachment to Squillacce; and enlarges, with feeling and triumph, on its beauties and advantages. I walked to the mouth of the river Alleli, where this patrician had made a reservoir, or fishery, into which, by means of a canal, he introduced the sea-water. But I could find no distinct

traces

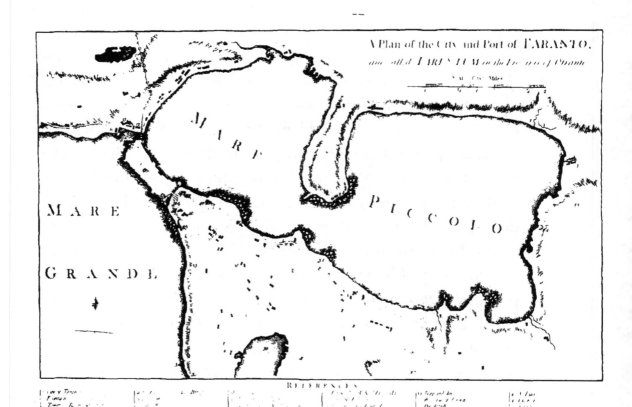

A Plan of the City and Port of TARANTO, and all'd TARENTUM in the Terra di Otranto

traces of any fuch work, which probably has been filled up by floods, or eaten away by the dafhing of the waves, during fo long a period as one thoufand two hundred years.

In the evening, I was difturbed by a violent noife; which, upon enquiry, I found was occafioned by the Marquis's bailiff kicking furioufly at the door of the neighbouring houfe. This is the ufual method of giving the laft fummons, without any farther hope of mercy, to a debtor or tenant that refufes to pay, and fhuts himfelf up in his houfe for fafety. If the defaulter be a friend, and indulgence intended in the profecution, the officer ftrikes the door with his hand only. In any fray, if one of the combatants run away and lock himfelf up, and his adverfary beat for entrance with his feet, it is underftood that he is incenfed beyond meafure, and means to give no quarter. even children, in their little broils, obferve the fame diftinction. This explains Horace's meaning *, when he fays, that Death beats with impartial foot the doors of palaces, and of cottages: he thereby implies, that he is inexorably bent on exacting the debt of nature, and not, as fome commentators fuppofe, that he makes ufe of the foot, merely becaufe his hands are employed in holding the fcythe and hour-glafs.

Other allufions in that Poet may be elucidated by reference to cuftoms ftill in force throughout Calabria.

---

* Pallida mors æquo pulfat pede pauperum tibernas
Regumque turres.————

His account of the hardy education and filial obedience of the Roman youth *, in former times, is still exact with respect to the young Calabrian peasant. After hoeing the ground all day, with no better fare than bread and water, seasoned with a clove of garlic, an onion, or a few dried olives, he does not presume to present himself before his mother, without a faggot of lentiscus, or other wood, which he throws down at the door, ere he offers to pass the threshold. A wise administration, under an ambitious monarch, might train up this race to be once more the conquerors of nations. Patience under penury, hardship, and hunger,—symmetry and strength of limb, and an ardent, fierce spirit, still exist in the mountains of the kingdom; but it would require a very fortunate combination of circumstances, with great judgment and resolution, to bring these qualities properly into action.

Horace's animated description of a mother longing for the return of her son †, may still be applied to the Calabrian matrons. If the feluccas do not appear at the usual

* ———Rusticorum mascula militum
Proles, Sabellis docti ligonibus
   Versare glebas, et severæ
    Matris ad arbitrium recisos
Portare fustes ———

† Ut mater juvenem, quem Notus invido
Flatu Carpathii trans maris æquora
   Cunctantem spatio longius annuo
    Dulci distinet a domo,
Votis omnibus hunc et precibus vocat,
Curvo nec faciem littore demovet ———

term of their annual voyage, the mothers and wives of the sailors offer up inceffant vows and prayers, call upon the beloved perfon by name, and remain at their windows, with eyes fixed on the Cape which the bark is to double. The inftant a boat is feen coming round the Point, the whole town refounds with joyful cries of "Barca, Barca!" The boys ring the bells, and, as foon as they can diftinguifh what felucca it is, run to the relations, to claim beverage for the good news.

Dionyfius of Syracufe, in hopes of difuniting the confederates of Magna Græcia, attempted to build a wall or rampire acrofs the ifthmus, but troubles in Sicily called him away before he could complete the work.

We paffed below Stenati, a town of one thoufand two hundred fouls, on a hill compofed of pebbles and mineral particles, glued together by a vifcous earth:—it contain fome fine fpecimens of mica fitu. As we advanced fouthward, the country fell off in beauty, and the foil in richnefs, from a mellow loam to a poor blue clay. The cotton fields have not the wholefome appearance of thofe farther north. The landfcape, however, revives near the banks of the Calipari or Elori, where Dionyfius defeated the allied Greeks. We flept at Monaftrace, a poor village, on an eminence. The road to it was good, except near the torrents, which, in great numbers, roll down from the mountains, and tear the plain to pieces. The defolate afpect of the country may be afcribed at leaft a

much to the fcarcity of cultivators, as to the badnefs of the
foil.

On the feventeenth, we came to Gerace, through a very
unpleafant tract of land along the coaft. A bare, ugly
ridge of hills clofes in the plain on the weft, and frequently
comes quite down to the beach. We croffed innumerable
ftreams, the banks of which were no doubt marked, in
ancient times, by many a bloody encounter between Greeks
and barbarians, or between the different Grecian ftates,
who were continually undermining their common fabric by
inteftine diffentions. It is now very difficult to afcertain
the precife pofition of ancient rivers and towns, but it
might certainly be accomplifhed with more accuracy than
has yet been done by any geographer whatever.

We left Stilo on our right, remarkable for a rich convent
of Carthufians; an Order which, in its very infancy, ftruck
a good root in this kingdom, by the favour of Roger, the
great Earl of Sicily, a very particular friend of their founder
St. Bruno. Thefe roots fpread vigoroufly, and grew to an
enormous fize, as to riches and extent of poffeffions; but
the fpirit of the times threatens them with a fpeedy lopping,
if not a total eradication. Not far from this place is a
mine of iron, now quite abandoned.

On our left was Cape di Stilo, a promontory which,
with Cape Spartivento, forms the bay of Locri. Caftel-
vetere, in a lofty fituation, three miles from the fea, occupies the fite of Caulon, of which fome veftiges are faid to
exift.

exift. I faw none that have any claim to fuch remote antiquity.——Caulon was one of the earlieft Greek fettlements, as its coins evince, being incufi; which was undoubtedly a mode of coining of very ancient date *. This city was demolifhed, and its inhabitants removed to Sicily, by Dionyfius, four hundred years before the Chriftian æra. Nearer the fea is La Roccella, a fief of the Caraffa family †,

\* Nummi Caulonorum.

ARG. 1 Figura virilis nuda diadem. ftans d fupra caput elati telum vibraturâ l extenfa, cui fuperftat icuncula genuflexa, fubtus cervus ΚΑΥΛΟ. = Incuffus

2. Eadem figura, &c fine epig = Cervus. laurus fup dorfum ΛΥΑΚ.

3 Vir nud fulmin l monilia ten. Φ = Cervus ΚΑΥΛΟΝΙΑΤΑΝ.

4. Vir tul n cervulus ΚΑΥ = Cervus. vas Φ ΚΑΥΛΟΝΙΑΤ.

5 Cervus ramus Ⱥ ΚΑΥ = Vir fulm cervulus ΚΑΥΛΟ

6 Vir fulm cervulus ΚΑΥΛ. = Cervus arbor ΛΥΑΥ

† This family came originally from the Caraccioli, and is equal to any in the realm in riches and confideration It is divided into two branches, one of which gives a fteelyard for its badge, the other, a bufh of thorns The laft emblem was adopted in confequence of a tournament held by Charles the Second, in the fuburbs of Naples. The fon of that Prince, who was King of Hungary, took great offence at the Caraffas, for giving a fhield barry, argent and gules, which are the Hungarian coat of arms; and infifted upon their being excluded the lifts, unlefs they altered their bearing To obviate all difficulties, the knights of this family cut fome branches out of a hedge, and tied them acrofs their bucklers, a diftinction which has been kept up by their defcendants Antonio Caraffa, furnamed Malizia, made himfelf very confpicuous as a politician, in the reign of Joan the Second. In 1680, Gregory was elected Grand Mafter of Malta. But the Caraffa that made the greateft noife in the world, was Pope Paul the Fourth, one of the moft turbulent, haughty priefts, that ever afcended the chair of St Peter fince the days of Gregory the Seventh, that famous trampler on all pretenfions of kings, and liberties of people Paul and his nephews were, during the courfe of a few years, the difturbers of Europe, and continually employed in exciting fovereigns and fubjects to fome bloody and fanatical act of violence At his death, he was declared an enemy to Rome; and all his ftatues and coats of arms were broken and thrown into the Tyber.

3

built

built on a rugged eminence overgrown with the Opuntia, or African fig. The natives eat the fruit, and plant out the flips as a fence to their gardens.

No author has clearly determined the fituation of the river Sagra fo renowned for the defeat of the Crotoniates by a handful of Locrians. Thofe who take it to be the Alaro, feem to come nearest the truth.

## SECTION XLV.

GERACE is poorly built, on a hill of coarfe granite rocks and ftiff clay; the road to it fteep and difficult, the vale below is well cultivated, and yet does not produce corn enough to anfwer the demands of the Geracians, though their number amounts but to three thoufand. They make good wine, which has the valuable quality of recovering its flavour and fpirit by proper keeping, long after it feems to have loft both. This city is fuppofed, by mofl writers, to ftand upon the identical fite of Locri, the capital of the Epizephyrian Locrians. Some antiquaries place the old town nearer the fea at Paghapoli, where many fcattered ruins ftill remain. The brick materials with which they were built, pronounce them of a later period than the happy days of Magna Græcia. One large well-preferved room diftinguifhes itfelf above the reft, but no part has any infcription, column, or ornament. I was at firft inclined to think,

that

that Locri had been situated in the plain, which afforded greater conveniencies for business, and that the citadel had been built on the hill of Gerace; but as Strabo says expressly, that the city stood on the brow of a hill called Esopis, the buildings along the shore can only have been suburbs, magazines, and habitations for fishermen. In those early days of navigation, every angle of a coast, projecting rock, island, or river's mouth, constituted a port, and therefore we must not be surprised, if we are often at a loss to discover any traces of the ancient harbours we read of. Locri had, no doubt, some safe retreat for gallies and row-boats, though nothing now appears but an open road. Without a few remarkable monuments to guide us, it is not easy to discover the true position of any ancient town on this coast. The difficulty arises from a progressive change of dwelling. Adventurers, on their first landing, provided for their security by seizing upon some elevated inaccessible rock, where they could bid defiance to the natives, as well as to any strangers that might venture to land on the coast. As soon as increase of numbers gave them sufficient powers for an attempt to enrich themselves by conquest or commerce, they descended from their mountainous fastnesses, and erected commodious cities in the fertile plains along the shore. The full tide of human prosperity lasts but a moment; and every state, when once it has reached the highest point of glory and power, must, by the natural course of things, be hurried back with the ebb to its original obscurity. The

2

viciſſitude was experienced by the Grecian cities of Italy. Deprived of liberty by the Romans, they ſoon ſaw the number of their citizens dwindle away; and then they found, that a too extenſive circuit of walls in an open country expoſed them to continual inſults by ſea and land. Unwholeſome vapours, the effects of depopulation and neglected huſbandry, completed their ruin; and the feeble remnants of their inhabitants retired for health and ſafety to the tops of the neighbouring mountains, where they built towns that reſembled aeries of birds of prey, rather than manſions of the human race. As peace and ſecurity return, as agriculture and trade meet with encouragement, we behold the inhabitants forſake their uſeleſs caſtles, and venture once more into the plains.

A colony from Locris in Greece founded the commonwealth of Locri in Italy, to which Zaleucus gave a code of laws, eſteemed by all the Greeks a maſter-piece of legiſlation. He was the firſt that committed his inſtitutions to writing, and fixed certain bounds to penalties and puniſhments, which, in all laws promulgated before his time, were left to the diſcretion of the judges. Like all the followers of Pythagoras, he ſupported the ſimplicity of his decrees by unalterable inflexibility, of which he is ſaid to have made his own family feel the effects, rather than derogate from the letter of the law. Jealous of innovation, he enacted, that whoever had a new law to propoſe, ſhould appear in the aſſembly of the people with a rope round his

neck,

neck, to be ftrangled immediately, if the propofals were rejected. The Locrians entered into an alliance with the Sicilian tyrants, and received the younger Dionyfius into their city when he fled from Syracufe. The villain repaid their hofpitality with the blackeft ingratitude. By artifice and force, he acquired an abfolute dominion over them, and exercifed it in a brutal manner, by infulting their wives and daughters, and plundering their property. Upon his departure for Sicily the Locrians vindicated their rights, and wreaked their vengeance on his wife and children. This commonwealth poffeffed an ample territory, and refpectable force, in proportion to the reft of the Greek ftates; but after it was fubdued by Rome, faded away like a plant wounded at the root, oppreffed and ruined by the cruelty and avarice of its governors*.

I cannot

* Nummi Locienfium.

AUR 1 Caput Jovis laur ΛΟΚΡΩΝ = Aquila leporem duc ΛΟΚΡΩΝ.

ARG 1 Cap Jov laur = Aquila lep duc ΛΟΚΡΩΝ
    2 Fulmen-caduceus ΛΟΚΡΩΝ = Aquila lep d fe
    3 Cap imb di d cud  Aquila fulm ol ramus Λ ΛΟΚΡΩΝ
    4 Cap barb. laur ⋈ = figura ftans Roluc coro inp on cap figur
      urbis fedent ΛΟΚΡΩΝ —ΡΩΜΑ ΠΙΣΤΙ
    5 Cap Palladis gal arcus ΛΟΚΡΩΝ  Pegalus

ÆR. 1 Cap Palladis gal = Racemus ΛΟΚΡΩΝ
    2 Caput mul fpica = Pallas ftans d haft f clypeum cornuc ftell
      ΛΟΚΡΩΝ
    3 Cap Viril laurcat = Pallas ftans d haft f cly Λ ΛΟΚΡΩΝ
    4 Cap Pall gal vir = fig mul fedens d. pat f fceptrum imp
      ΛΟΚΡΩΝ
    5. Cap Pall. gal  Pegafus ΛΟΚΡΩΝ
    6. Cap Mul. diad.  Aquila fulm inf corona ΛΟΚΡΩΝ

I cannot learn at what precife time the prefent name was given to the city, but as its Bifhop is called Hieracenfis in the eighth century, I fuppofe it became common about that period.　Gerace was always a place of ftrength.　In the courfe of a family quarrel among the Norman Princes, Guifcard was betrayed and taken as he attempted to furprife it; and had the Geracians been fuffered to follow their inclinations, would have loft his life; but Roger, though his enemy, refcued him out of their hands, and by this fignal fervice regained his brother's friendfhip.

This was one of the numerous baronies lavifhed by Charles of Anjou on the Montforts.　Under the Durazzian line, it was acquired by the Carraccioli, and is now held by the Grimaldi of Genoa, with the title of Prince.

In the evening I joined a crowd that was dragging a woman to church, in order to have the devil driven out of her by exorcifms.　She was a middle-aged perfon, and feemed to be in very ftrong convulfions, which every body prefent firmly believed to proceed from a demoniacal poffeffion. The prieft refufing to come, fome of the affiftants grew impatient, and pulled the woman about fo very roughly, that

7　Cap Jovis laur ΔΙΟΣ = Fulmen ΛΟΚΡΩΝ.

8　Cap Pall duo glob. = in coron. cornu. ΛΟ.

9　Cap. Cereris fpic coron fpica = Pallas ftans d. haftam f clyp cornuc ftella ΛΟΚΡΩΝ.

10.　Capiti Diofcur jugit. = Jupiter fed. d avem f. baculum cornuc. ΛΟΚΡΩΝ.

11　Cap Pall = Fulmen ΛΟΚΡΩΝ.

12　Cap. vir. laur = Mars ftans d. haft f. clyp. ΛΟΚΡΩΝ.

Belzebub

Belzebub thought proper to decamp. The patient rofe up, and though confufed and panting for breath, very foon recovered her fenfes, and ran away full fpeed to her own houfe. From which circumftances I inferred, there was more roguery in her cafe than real diforder.

All convulfions of the kind are attributed to affaults of malignant fpirits. Near fifteen hundred women, pretending to be tormented by thefe imps, go up annually to Soriano, to be cured of the poffeffion by looking at a portrait of St. Dominick, fent down as a prefent from the celeftial gallery. By thefe pretexts, they obtain from their tyrannical fpoufes leave to make this pleafant pilgrimage, and a pair of holiday fhoes, without which it would be highly difrefpectful to prefent themfelves before the holy picture. A prieft of that convent told me a ftory of a female demoniac, who, after going through the ufual courfe of cure, was fent to confefs her fins to him. As he was perfectly well acquainted with the common tricks, he ordered her to give him the true reafon of her acting that farce, and threatened her, in cafe of obftinacy, with a vifit from a real devil, who would torment her in good earneft. The poor woman, terrified to death at the menace, frankly acknowledged, that having been married by her parents againft her inclinations to a goatherd, who ftank intolerably of his goats and cheefes, fhe abhorred his approach, and feigned poffeffion to avoid cohabiting with him. Having thus wormed the fecret out of her, the prieft, in hopes of alleviating her misfortune, fent

Y y 2 for

for her hufband, and as he knew it would be in vain to attempt to argue him out of a belief of the devil's being in his wife, he planned a different mode of attack, and informed the fimple fellow, that he had difcovered what particular kind of fpirit it was; that this dæmon was remarkable for an outrageous antipathy to goatherds, and that no exorcifms could prevent him from plaguing them. The poor man, whofe firft profeffion had been gardening, and whofe fuccefs in the other line of bufinefs had not been very great, readily confented to return to his old way of labour, if that would keep Satan out of his houfe. The friar procured a garden for him, and a chapman for his flock, and foon had the happinefs of feeing the married couple well fettled, and perfectly fatisfied with each other.

We rode next day twelve miles, through a difagreeable low country, which, from the poornefs of its clayey foil, and the bad look of its corn, may be pronounced unfavourable to the purpofes of agriculture. The next fix miles were over hills of wretched afpect, compofed of hungry clay laid upon beds of round pebbles, minerals, fand, and fhells cemented together. After a weary ride through execrable roads, we ftopped at one of the worft looking villages I ever beheld. It is called Bianco, from the chalky hill it ftands upon, and confifts of houfes built of ftone and mud, covered with tufted boughs. The appearance of every thing about it was fo dreary, the looks of the villagers fo fqualid, and the evening fo ftormy, that I was glad to remain in my

2

fmoky

smoky crib, and comfort myself with some white-wine of a strong body and flavour, though rather too great a degree of roughness. My quiet was disturbed by the danger of my guide, whose hand was bitten by a viper, as he was climbing over an old wall. The symptoms were very quick and violent; but the landlord removed them by applying a red-hot iron to the wound, and thoroughly scarifying round it. He said the coldness of the weather had benumbed the serpent, and rendered the venom less virulent than it would have been in a hot day. He mentioned a relation of his, whose head had swelled to a prodigious size from his having sucked the place where a viper had bit one of his children; but the swelling went off with fomentations.

## SECTION XLVI.

*May 19th* WE descended the mountain at the hazard of our lives, by a miry narrow road, buttressed up with posts, over which are laid wooden bridges that quiver with the pressure even of a foot traveller. As it had rained very hard all night, our leader prudently preferred a longer way by the sands, to a short cut through the mountains. We crossed the isthmus of Cape Bruzzano, where the Locrians first landed, and remained four years before they moved northward. The low grounds are extremely rich in herbage, and produce spontaneously thick crops of

saintfoin,

tainfom, which are not turned to proper account; half the grafs is fuffered to rot on the ground for want of cattle to confume it.   Oleander, and many other beautiful fhrubs, line the banks of the torrents, near fome of which I found roots of the Calamus Aromaticus, Acorus, or fweet Flag, befides many other rare plants, but in the hurry of a journey, which had not botany for its fole object, their names have efcaped my memory.   I am confident a regular fearch in thefe waftes, would afford botanical obfervers a treafure of curious and medicinal vegetables.   I dined at Brancaleone, a fmall village; and afterwards rode to examine Cape Spartivento, the moft foutherly point of Italy.   It is furrounded by fmall iflands, and numerous rocky fhelves, on which the waves break with great fury as they are driven down the ftreights.   From this angle we ftruck into the mountains; and after much fatigue reached the city of Bova, where a letter procured me a very polite reception from one of the Canons.

Bova is placed on the brow of a hill, and being out of the way of trade and thoroughfare, can boaft of neither wealth nor agriculture.   Moft of the inhabitants are of Greek origin and rite.   I do not mean that they can trace their pedigree up to the old republicans of Magna Graecia, for all fuch filiations have been cut off, and confounded in the darknefs of many revolving ages.   Thefe people are of a much later importation, having emigrated from Albania only a few centuries ago.   I was defirous of obtaining every

                                               poffible

poffible information about them, and fhall bring into one point of view all I have learned at different times concerning their hiftory.

When we recollect, that a very large portion of the kingdom was once inhabited or governed by Greeks, and underftand that the Grecian rite has been in force in many parts of it, and ftill is fo in fome, we naturally incline to fuppofe a continued poffeffion, and the Greek church eftablifhed here by prefcription; but the fallacy of our conclufions will appear upon reflecting, that, when Chriftianity began in Italy, fcarce the fmalleft trace could be difcovered of Grecian laws, cuftoms, or language. Polybius, two hundred years before, fpeaks of them as old or former eftablifhments. Cicero mentions them as being already obfolete; and we learn from Strabo, that except three cities which retained fome faint idea of them, all the reft of Magna Græcia was become completely Roman in tongue, habits, and jurifprudence. The infcriptions found in the Neapolitan ftate clearly prove it. If any veftiges might be difcerned during the reign of Auguftus, they were certainly very foon after obliterated by the introduction of colonies, and a feries of domeftic wars. From thefe premifes it follows, that when a patriarch was eftablifhed at Conftantinople, there exifted no particular connexion between this country and Greece; but the Neapolitan provinces formed, with the reft of Italy, part of the immediate jurifdiction of the Bifhop of Rome. They followed the Latin rite till the eighth century, when Leo Ifauticus compelled the subjects of his Italian dominions to renounce all obedience to the see of Rome, and join in communion with the Constantinopolitan patriarch. The Norman conquerors, through zeal and policy, restored this province to the Pope's authority, thereby the better to annihilate all union with the Greek interest. In the fifteenth century, almost every trace of the Greeks was lost, except some faint traditions and resemblances of customs, when the following series of events brought a new colony into Italy.

George Castriot, Prince of Epire or Albany, better known among us by the name of Scanderbeg, the bulwark of Christendom against the Turks, received a considerable and timely succour from Alphonsus the First. In return, he ten years afterwards, in 1460, crossed the Adriatic, defeated John of Anjou, and established Ferdinand the First on the Neapolitan throne. That grateful King presented him with many large fiefs, and invited the Epirotes to settle in his dominions. The death of Scanderbeg removed every obstacle to the Turkish conquests, and John his son fled to Naples for refuge. He was received with open arms, lands were assigned to his followers, and exemption from taxes granted them, with many other privileges, of which some shadow still remains. These strangers fixed their abode in various provinces, but chiefly in Calabria, from a prospect of superior advantages, by being under the protection of Irene Castriota, married to San Severino, Prince of Bisignano.

nano. The Albanese continued to come over so late as the reign of Charles the Fifth, and their numbers increased very sensibly. At present, they amount to a hundred thousand at least, dispersed in a hundred villages or towns; but many of these settlements are wretchedly poor, and much decayed: those in the neighbourhood of Bova remarkably so. The villagers carry corn, cheese, and cattle to Reggio; but that being a poor mart, has but small demands, and little circulation of money. Their common language is Albanese. The men can speak Calabrese; but the women, who neither buy nor sell, understand no tongue but their own, which they pronounce with great sweetness of accent. This Albanian dialect is quite different from the modern Greek and Sclavonian languages, though they are spoken by all the nations round Albania. It is worthy of remark, that this jargon, which has been known in Europe upwards of a thousand years, should be so little attended to, that it still remains without an alphabet, and many of its sounds are not to be accurately expressed either by Latin or Greek letters. From this singularity we may infer, that it is a mixture of the dialects of those Tartarian hordes that overran Macedonia and Greece in the eighth century; to which medley the intercourse with Germans, Italians, and Crusaders, has added a variety of foreign terms. The roots of this language are unconnected with those of all other European ones, but it abounds with words borrowed from old and modern Greek, Latin, Sclavonian, Italian, French,

Z z

German,

German, and, what is very extraordinary and paſt account-
ing for, many Engliſh terms employed in their native ſigni-
fication, with ſome variation in the declenſion and pronunciation *.

The Greek rite is now obſerved in the province of Co-
ſenza alone, the Miniſtry and Biſhops having, by degrees,
perſuaded or compelled the other Albaneſe to conform to
the Roman liturgy and diſcipline.   The Latin Dioceſans
found it, no doubt, inconvenient to be charged with the
direction of a foreign nation, of whoſe cuſtoms, language,
and ceremonies they did not chooſe to confeſs their ignorance.   Moreover, a total want of inſtruction had plunged
the Epirotic coloniſts into ſuch a ſtate of barbariſm, that at
laſt there was not a prieſt to be found among them, who
knew Greek enough to perform divine ſervice in that
language.   To remedy theſe diſorders, and preſerve his
native worſhip, Monſignor Rodatà, Librarian of the Vatican,
prevailed upon Clement the Twelfth to found a college at

* Theſe words among others

| Aunt | Crab | Let | Rip |
|------|------|-----|-----|
| Boor | Door | Leg | Sea |
| Breeches | Dream | Lofty | Sheep |
| Breaſt | Feather | Loſe | Stir |
| Cow | Grumble | Milk | Sight |
| Cool | Gape | Muſhroom | Shame |
| Chimney | Hunt | Meal | Tickle |
| Chide | Hunger | Mud | Uncle |
| Cough | Knee | Open | Wood |
| Can | Leave | Run | You |

This Catalogue was given me by D. Paſquale Baffi, an Albaneſe.

St. Bene-

St. Benedetto Ullano, in Upper Calabria, for the education of the young Greeks who wished to dedicate themselves to the service of the church. He was himself consecrated an Archbishop *in partibus*, and sent to lay the first stone of this Italo-Greco-Corsinian seminary. Diplomas, immunities, and privileges were heaped upon the establishment, the property and jurisdiction of many villages purchased for it, sixteen thousand crowns expended upon the buildings, and a thousand ducats a year set apart for the provision of the Bishop. He acts as president of the college, but in his episcopal powers is subordinate to the Latin Prelate of Bisignano, without whose licence he cannot confer orders on his students. There is, besides, a parish-priest and a schoolmaster. The rest are boarders at twenty crowns a year. Two Dominican friars read lectures of moral philosophy and scholastic divinity; but whenever they touch upon the five famous propositions in dispute between the two churches, the zeal of their ancestors breaks out in the scholars, who seldom hear them inforced without betraying some tokens of disgust. Rodatà died too soon for the good of his settlement;—abuses crept in, and the temporal concerns of the house have, of late years, been egregiously mismanaged.

These Albanese are a quiet industrious people, and their women remarkable for regularity of conduct. In their dress they preserve the costume of Illyricum, from whence their forefathers came. The most beautiful women are

Z z 2                              generally

generally given in marriage to clergymen, and are exceedingly proud of their hufbands; for among them priefthood is the higheft nobility. When an ecclefiaftic dies, his widow never enters into a fecond engagement, becaufe none but a virgin can afpire to the hand of a prieft; and any other is beneath her acceptance.

## SECTION XLVII.

FROM Bova I travelled thirty miles along the fhore to Reggio. As foon as the morning mifts were difpelled by the rifing fun, I had a view of Sicily, where Ætna towered above all other mountains, with a flender line of fmoke flying from its top in a horizontal direction, as far as the eye could reach. We breakfafted at a farmer's houfe in a poor, but well-fituated village, called Amendolia. Here we defcended into the plain, and croffed the river Alice, the ancient boundary of the Locrian ftate. Immenfe quantities of anchovies frequent the mouth of this ftream and the adjacent coaft; it is therefore very likely, that either the fifh derived its Latin name Halec* from the river, or the river was called after the fifh. At Pentedattolo, a pretty village, I found the ftate of agriculture much better than what I had hitherto feen in this province. The

* The Italian name of both is Alice.

4                                                        ground

ground is managed with more skill and neatness, and consequently productive of greater crops. Its hemp is the best
in Calabria. The hills that border upon these flats, consist
of chalk and clay, mixed with rocks, formed of ferruginous
particles, talk, and small pebbles. The farmers were busy
with their harvest, but seemed to lose much time from a scarcity
of hands. Near Montebello, we passed over the last Point of the
Apennines, at the Capo dell' Armi, where the mountainous
ridge sinks into the sea, to rise again on the Sicilian shore
at Taormina, in an oblique line. The opinion which was
generally held by the ancients, that Sicily was formerly part
of Italy, torn from it by some violent concussion of the
globe, has been rejected by Cluver and others, upon their not
being able to trace any corresponding angles and congenerous
strata on the different sides of the streights. Their ill success
in this search arose from their mistaking the direction of
of the mountains. They denied the original juncture, because they found no traces of it between Capo dell' Armi and
the heights behind Cape Peloro; but, upon a more accurate
survey, they would have discovered that the mountains of
Taormina correspond, in composition and shape, with the
extremity of the Apennine, and that the high lands of Cape
Vaticano point towards the eminences north of Messina.

The soil of this promontory is light, and the stone white,
which is, no doubt, the origin of its Greek name, *Leucopetra*,
white rock —The aspect of the country is wild, and bare of
trees, but covered with lentiscus, the common fuel of the
neighbourhood

neighbourhood. The face of the rocks is divided by narrow streaks of pebbles inclining to the horizon. The road is excellent for horses, the prospects enchanting. The traveller has under his eye the beautiful Faro of Messina, and the fertile plains of Reggio, contrasted with a bold chain of mountains that stretches away to the north-east. On descending to the west, we entered upon a scene utterly different from what I had been long accustomed to. Instead of hills and marshy shores, with little population, or appearance of industry, I now came to a rich delicious garden, shaded by groves and avenues of poplars and mulberry-trees, divided by hedges of pomegranates, inclosing vineyards and orchards of orange, citron, and various other kinds of aromatic fruit. Vegetables of all sorts abound under the shade of these perfumed plantations; but hemp is chiefly cultivated, as being the most lucrative, though its emanations are supposed to be pernicious. Copious streams meander through these agreeable plains, and distribute life and vigour to every plant. On each side of the road are houses erected for the accommodation of silk-worms, upon a particular plan of construction. The windows are long, and not above six inches wide. This narrowness prevents too great a quantity of air being admitted at a time, which would overpower the tender insects. When the eggs are on the point of being hatched, these holes are shut, and a moderate fire kept up in the rooms. The worms, as soon as they come out, are placed upon beds of reeds, and there fed

with

with leaves of the mulberry-tree, which, in this diſtrict, is invariably of the red ſort. It is preferred to the white-fruited kind, as being a later ſhooter, and better adapted to the periods of the worm's life, which would be endangered from late changes of weather, if forced out of its ſhell at the time the white mulberry produces its leaves; beſides, it is the opinion of the ſilk-workers, that worms fed with the red mulberry, produce a more compact heavy ſilk, than thoſe that live upon the leaves of the white one. I am apt to think this a vulgar prejudice, unwarranted by experience, as the Chineſe, Piedmonteſe, and Languedocians prefer the white ſort. I was ſurpriſed to ſee the Calabreſe bring up their ſilk-worms ſo tenderly; for I ſhould have thought their climate warm and conſtant enough to allow them to leave the worms upon the trees, as they are treated in the ſouthern parts of China; but I was told, that many experiments had been made, without ſucceſs, to diſcover a method of preſerving them in the open air. In order to provide food for them in caſe of a blight among the mulberry-trees, other leaves have been tried, and bramble tops have been found the beſt ſuccedaneum. In the management of this produce, the Calabreſe are much inferior to the Tuſcans, who, though many degrees farther north, contrive to have two hatchings, or ſeaſons, in a year. Theſe ſilk-worm-houſes are the property of reputable families in Reggio, who furniſh rooms, leaves, eggs, and every neceſſary implement; take two-thirds of the profit, and leave the other for

the

the attendants. A succeffion of eggs is imported from Leghorn, and other places, to renew the breed, and by frequent changes keep up the quality of the filk. Great care · is requifite to prevent lizards from entering thefe apartments. If they get in while the worms are employed in their functions or transformations, they will deftroy great numbers, by running to and fro along the fhelves.——The natural and powerful enemy of the lizard, is the large black fnake fo common in Italy. The fight of one of them will fcare away all lizards, and therefore is very agreeable and ferviceable to the filk-dealers, who accept it as a happy omen, and fcream out, *Good luck! good luck!* whenever they fee one of thefe reptiles creep into their houfe. To fecure a good filk year, they offer a part of the produce to the faint of the parifh, who fometimes gets a fifth fhare from thefe zealots. Mariners, employed in exporting this commodity in barks, lay afide a bale of filk for their particular patron; but if there fall any rain to fpoil the cargo, the faint is fuppofed not to have fulfilled the reciprocal agreement, and accordingly lofes all claim to his portion.

All the pods muft be carried to public caldrons at Reggio, and there pay a duty for boiling and winding off. As the winders work by the pound, they perform their tafk in a more flovenly, carelefs manner, than they would do were they paid by the day. After the filk is drawn off, forty-two grana and a half per pound are exacted, even though the owner fhould keep it for his private ufe.

Nothing

Nothing can be more unfair than this tax, as the weight is set down while the merchandife is wet and heavy. The tyranny of excife is ftill carried greater lengths, for the poor wretches are forced to pay one grana a pound for the refufe and unprofitable pods, and two carlini a year for every mulberry-tree growing in their grounds. This odious, abfurd impofition was planned, by the Marquis of Squillace, contrary to every wife principle of adminiftration, and with many other vexations has checked this advantageous branch of commerce, difcouraged the farmers, and caufed hundreds of valuable trees to be cut down to fave the duty. In general, the profits of the filk trade in this country centre in the Barons and Revenue-officers The former by monopoly, and the latter by exactions, oblige the poor merchants to fmuggle for a livelihood, and, to the great detriment of the royal receipt, the excifemen find it their intereft to connive at the practice.

## SECTION XLVIII.

THE approach to Reggio is charming, for every cottage of the fuburb is fhaded with a beautiful arbour of vines, loaded with clufters of grapes, that produce a very good fort of wine.

Oranges, and their kindred fruits, arrive at great perfection in thefe plains, which are faid to be the firft fpot in

Italy where their culture was attempted, and from which it was extended over the country. They are found to be much hardier than was at first suspected, many large plantations thriving at the foot of the Apennines, twenty miles from the sea, where in winter there is often frost enough to congeal water. The Rheggians carry on a lucrative traffic with the French and Genoese in essence of citron, orange, and bergamot. This spirit is extracted by paring off the rhind of the fruit with a broad knife, pressing the peel between wooden pincers against a spunge, and, as soon as the spunge is saturated, the volatile liquor is squeezed into a phial, and sold at fifteen carlines an ounce. The caput mortuum is eaten by oxen, and the pulp serves to make syrup. There is a small sort of citrons set apart for the Jews of Leghorn, who come every year to buy them for three tornesi a piece. As they are destined for some religious ceremonies, the buyers take great care not to pollute them by a touch of the naked hand.

The olives of Reggio are huge and pulpy. They are much admired by those who relish a high flavour, but to those who have been accustomed only to eat the Provence sort, they appear too strong. The exportation of oil brings into Calabria-ultra half a million of ducats annually.

Before the Saracens were driven back to their original habitations on the Arabian and African sands, the environs of this city were adorned with stately groves of palm trees. Many of these trees were felled by the Christians out of a
whimsical

whimfical hatred to the plant, as if it had been an appurtenance of Mahometifm. The Infidels themfelves, on their
retreat, deftroyed all the male palms, except fuch as grew
within the walls. There are fome trees ftanding in the
city which annually produce feveral pounds of dates, but
moft of them fall off before they ripen, and are eaten by
the hogs. It has been remarked, that in feafons wherein
the Scirocco, or other foutherly winds blow for a long continuance, the dates ripen better and fooner than ufual.
Perhaps the great quantity of warm moifture and duft
fcattered over them by thofe winds, relolves the natural retir... nefs of the fruit, by caufing an uncommon heat and
fermentation. A fimilar precaution is obferved in figs growing near a dufty road. It is fuppofed that the fprinkling of
lees of oil would haften the maturation both of figs and
dates

Figs here have a fine flavour, thofe of Ielugafo and
Mammola are the beft. The gardeners of this province do
not follow the Levantine method of caprification, which is
performed by carrying an infect from the wild tree to the
cultivated one, in order to promote aggregation of the
duft or pollen that adheres to the feed and body of the fly,
as the wild fig alone bears male flowers nor do they
ripen the fruit as the Neapolitan cultivators do, by touching the eye of it with a feather dipt in oil. The Calabrian
figs come on very well without their help, though the
wild plant, abounding every where, affords opportunity for

caprification,

caprification, if required.   When the Calabrese are defirous of raifing fig-trees from feed, a method lefs in ufe than flipping, they gather a quantity of wild figs, ftring them upon pack-thread, and hang them over the cultivated ones on the tree, till both are half-dried by the fun.   In October they fplit the garden fruit, and rub it very hard upon a rope. When the rope is covered with feeds, they bury it a few inches under ground, and in a fhort time a plentiful crop of feedlings appears, which muft be grafted, as they are all wild, or at leaft of a mongrel breed.

The firft Platanus ever feen in Italy was brought from Sicily by Dionyfius the tyrant, and planted in his garden at Reggio.   The Mufa and Ananas grow very well out of doors here   The Prince of Scilla was, I believe, the firft in this part of the world that cultivated the pine-apple.   He treated it in the beginning with great charinefs and precaution; but, upon trial, found a bolder management fuit it better.

The hills, that fkirt the great chain of mountains, abound with chefnut-trees, producing very large and fweet fruit, which the inhabitants dry, grind, knead into a pafte, and ufe in lieu of bread

Between Reggio and Scilla a filver mine was opened by the prefent King of Spain; but the vein lying in a granite rock that dips confiderably towards the fea, as if dragged down by the finking of the ftreights, was not fufficient to cover the expences, and therefore abandoned.   I believe

this

this bad fuccefs may alfo be attributed to the unfkilful-
nefs and lazinefs of the miners. Large quantities of ore
were ftolen, and at laft all the works deftroyed, by the
negligence of the overfeers, who left the furnaces lighted
when they went away. The buildings took fire, and were
entirely confumed; and the whole ftock reduced, by the
violence and continuance of the flames, to a ftate of vitrification or calcination.

Reggio can boaft of neither beautiful buildings nor
ftrong fortifications. Of its edifices the Gothic cathedral is
the only ftriking one; but it affords nothing curious in
architecture. The citadel is far from formidable, according
to the prefent fyftem of tactics; nor could the city walls
make a long refiftance againft any enemy but Barbary
corfairs:—and even thefe they have not always been able
to repel; for, in 1543, it was laid in afhes by Barbaroffa;
Muftapha facked it fifteen years after; and the defolation
was renewed in 1593, by another fet of Turks. Its
expofed fituation, on the very threfhold of Italy, and front-
ing Sicily, has, from the earlieft period, rendered it liable to
attacks and devaftation. The Chalcidians feized upon it;
or, according to the ufual Greek phrafe, founded it, and
called the colony Rhegion, from a word that means a
break or crack; allufive of its pofition on the point where
Sicily broke off from the continent. Anaxilas oppreffed its
liberties. Dionyfius the Elder took it, and put many of
the principal citizens to death, in revenge for their having

refufed

refuſed his alliance. The Campanian legion, ſent to protect the Rhegians, turned its ſword againſt them, maſſacred many inhabitants, and tyrannized over the remainder; till the Roman ſenate thought proper to puniſh theſe traitors with exemplary ſeverity, though at the ſame time it entered into league with the revolted garriſon of Meſſina. This union with a ſet of villains, guilty of the ſame crime, proved that no love of juſtice, but political reaſons alone, drew down its vengeance on the Campanians *.

I en-

* Nummi Rheginorum.

ARG.  1. Facies leonis=Fig. vir. ſed. in cor. ΟΝΙΟƷÆ.

      2. Fac. leo.=Cap. mul laur. ΡΗΓΙΝΩΝ.

      3 Fac leo.=Cap. vitulinum. RECINON.

      4. Fac. leo.=Flos PH

ÆR  1 Cap. mul. averſa modio coron.=Jupiter ſed. d. haſt. tripus ΡΗΓΙΝΩΝ.

      2. Cap. Jovis laur.=Mulier ſtans d. patera ſerpentem paſcit. III. ΡΗΓΙΝ.

      3. Cap. Dianæ=Fig. vir ſtan. in brach. avem. d. ramum. ſ. baculum cornucop. ΡΗΓΙΝΩΝ.

      4. Cap. Dia.= Leo gradiens ΡΗΓΙΝΩΝ.

      5. Cap. Apoll. laur.=Tripus ΡΗΓΙΝΩΝ.

      6 Cap. Apoll. & Dian Jug.=Tripus ΡΗΓΙΝΩΝ.

      7 Cap Dian ᴘ =Tripus ΡΗΓΙΝΩΝ

      8 Cap Dian.=Lyra ΡΗΓΙΝΩΝ.

      9. Fac. leonis=Lyra. luna ΡΗΓΙΝΩΝ.

     1c Fac. leon.=Tripus ΡΗΓΙΝΩΝ

     11. Cap. Pall. gal. gryps in gal.=Minerva ſtans d. Victoriam. ſ haſt. & clyp. fulmen Π. ΡΗΓΙΝΩΝ.

     12. Cap. imb.=Fig. vir. nuda ſed. d. ſagittam ſ. arcum Π. ΡΗΓΙΝΩΝ.

     13. Cap. Apoll K. ΡΗΓΙΝΩΝ=Leon. facies.

     14. Cap. Apoll.=Vir nud. ſtans d ramum ſup. tripod. ſ. haſtam.

     15. Cap. viril. Jugata=Vir ſtans avem d. arborem i. ΡΗΓΙΝΩΝ.

16. Cap.

I enjoyed feveral delightful walks along the beach. Wherever a hole is made in the fands, though within a foot of the fea, frefh water bubbles up. The views on every fide are enchanting, equal to the charming ones of the Neapolitan gulf, and fuperior to all others that I have ever feen. Meffina rifes out of the waves like a grand amphitheatre; and the Faro, lined with villages and towns, feems a noble river, winding between two bold fhores.

Sometimes, but rarely, it exhibits a very curious phænomenon, vulgarly called *La Fata Morgana* *. The philofophical reader will find its caufes and operations learnedly accounted for in Kircher, Minafi, and other authors. I fhall only give a defcription of its appearance, from one that was an eye-witnefs. Father Angelucci is the firft that mentions it with any degree of accuracy, in the following terms:

" On

---

16. Cap Jug. Diofcura=Mercurius ftans d. ramum f caduc. III. PHΓINΩN.
17. Cap Jug Diofcur.=Vir nud. ftans d. avem & ramum f arborem. IIII PHΓINΩN.
18. Cap. vii. laur. idolum P.ΙΓINΩN =Cap. vir. laur. cliva. PHΓINΩN.
19. Cap Jug Apoll. & Dianæ=Mul. ftol. ftans d duas fpicas f bacul. luna. IIII. PHΓINΩN.
20. Fac leon =Corona RECI.
21. Fac. leon.=RECINON.

* The name is probably derived from an opinion, that the whole fpectacle is produced by a Fairy or a Magician. The populace are delighted whenever the vifion appears, and run about the ftreets, fhouting for joy,—calling every body out to partake of the glorious fight.

" On the fifteenth of Auguft, 1643, as I ftood at my
" window, I was furprifed with a moft wonderful, delect-
" able vifion.    The fea that wafhes the Sicilian fhore
" fwelled up, and became, for ten miles in length,  like a
" chain of dark mountains ;  while  the  waters  near  our
" Calabrian coaft grew quite fmooth, and in an inftant
" appeared  as  one  clear  polifhed mirror, reclining againft
" the aforefaid ridge.    On  this  glafs  was  depicted,  in
" *chiaro fcuro*,  a ftring of feveral thoufands of pilafters,  all
" equal in altitude, diftance, and degree of light and fhade.
" In a moment they loft half their height,  and bent into
" arcades,  like Roman aqueducts.    A  long  cornice was
" next formed on the  top,  and above it rofe caftles innu-
" merable,  all  perfectly alike.    Thefe  foon  fplit  into
" towers,  which were fhortly after loft in colonnades,  then
" windows,  and  at  laft  ended  in  pines,  cyprefes,  and
" other trees,  even and fimilar.    This is the *Fata Mor-*
" *gana*,  which, for twenty-fix years, I had thought a mere
" fable."

    To produce this pleafing deception, many circumftances
muft concur, which are not known to exift in any other
fituation.    The fpectator muft ftand with his back to the
eaft,  in fome elevated place behind the city,  that he may
command a view of the whole bay ;  beyond which the
mountains of Meffina rife like a wall,  and darken the back-
ground of the picture.    The winds muft be hufhed,  the
furface quite fmoothed ;  the tide at its height ;  and the

waters preffed up by currents to a great elevation in the middle of the channel. All thefe events coinciding, as foon as the fun furmounts the eaftern hills behind Reggio, and rifes high enough to form an angle of forty-five degrees on the water before the city,—every object exifting or moving at Reggio will be repeated a thoufand fold upon this marine looking-glafs; which, by its tremulous motion, is, as it were, cut into facets. Each image will pafs rapidly off in fucceffion, as the day advances, and the ftream carries down the wave on which it appeared.

Thus the parts of this moving picture will vanifh in the twinkling of an eye. Sometimes the air is at that moment fo impregnated with vapours, and undifturbed by winds, as to reflect objects in a kind of aerial fcreen, rifing about thirty feet above the level of the fea. In cloudy, heavy weather, they are drawn on the furface of the water, bordered with fine prifmatical colours.

# J O U R N E Y

## FROM

## REGGIO to NAPLES.

---

### S E C T I O N  XLIX.

THE heat I had experienced in Calabria determined
me to defer my voyage to Sicily till the enfuing winter. I therefore took my paffage for Gallipoli in a French
fhip ready to fail from the Straits; and on the twenty-fecond,
about funfet, we got under way. A heavy Scirocco, that
rofe in the night off Cape Spartivento, rendered the paffage
unpleafant, but carried us brifkly and fafely to our deftined
port, where we arrived on the twenty-fifth.

Gallipoli ftands on a rocky ifland, joined to the Continent by a bridge, near which flows a fountain of very

pure

pure water. From the remoteft antiquity this was a ftation
fo favourable to commerce, that every maritime power
wifhed to fecure it; and it is certainly a reproach to
Government, that nothing has been done to improve its
natural advantages :—at prefent it has neither harbour nor
fhelter for fhipping. Charles the Second demolifhed Gallipoli, for its adherence to Frederick of Aragon. The
Venetians treated it with great cruelty in the fifteenth
century; and, in 1481, it was pillaged by the Turks. To
preferve it from future calamities, Charles the Fifth repaired
and ftrengthened its fortifications; and, fince that period,
it has enjoyed the benefits of peace and trade, which have
rendered it the moft opulent and gaveft town upon the
coaft. Its inhabitants do not exceed fix thoufand in number; but they are eafy in their circumftances, lively, and
merry, and in general well-informed. Confumptions and
fpitting of blood are rather frequent here, occafioned by the
great fubtilty of the air, which is ventilated from every
quarter. The buildings are tolerable, and fome of the
churches have good paintings.

The cotton trade brings in about thirty thoufand ducats
a-year. Good muflins, cotton ftocking, and other parts
of apparel, are manufactured here, and purchafed by the
Provençals; for Gallipoli has no direct trade with the
metropolis. Silk and faffron were formerly objects of traffic, but heavy duties and oppreffion have caufed them to
be abandoned. The wine of this territory is good; but

from

from dryness of climate, and shallowness of soil, the vintage frequently fails in quantity; and then the Gallipolitans have recourse to Sicily for a supply. Oil is the great support of this place:—two-thirds of the produce of its olive plantations are exported to France, and the north of Italy; the remainder is sent to Naples, and other ports of the kingdom. It appears by the books of the Custom-house, that in 1766 *, eleven thousand four hundred and fifty-nine salme were shipped off for national markets, and thirty-five thousand four hundred and ninety-three salme for foreign ones. This quantity cannot be valued at less than a million of ducats; but the profits to the venders are much curtailed by a duty on exportation.

Neapolitan merchants, by means of agents settled at Gallipoli, buy up the oils, from year to year, long before an olive appears upon the tree. The price is afterwards settled by public authority, a mode of evaluation extremely favourable to the traders, and prejudicial to the land-owner, who is attached to the soil, and indeed seldom considered by Government. The Neapolitans sell their oil to the merchants of Leghorn; and, if faithfully served by their factors in Terra di Otranto, ought to double their capital

* I fix upon 1766, as being the year mentioned in Reidesel's evaluation, which I have good authority for correcting. His accounts are, one thousand three hundred and ninety-five lists, or thirteen thousand nine hundred and fifty salme, for home trade, and seventeen thousand three hundred and twenty-three lists, or one hundred seventy-three thousand two hundred and thirty salme, for foreign countries.

in two years. But, to balance this advantage, they run great risks, pay exorbitant interest, and have frequent bankruptcies to guard against.

About three miles due west, is a small island, level with the water, almost barren. Wherever the soil is deep enough, it produces short grass, renowned for giving a most exquisite flavour to mutton. This rock is a very convenient station for fishing, and is resorted to by flocks of sea-fowl.

On the twenty-seventh, I set out for Naples; making a little deviation from the direct road, to see Nardo and Otranto. Near Gallipoli, cultivation is in a flourishing state, though the rocks are very shallowly covered with earth. In this province, the rent of arable ground varies prodigiously, rather according to the degrees of population than those of fertility. For example,—Brindisi possesses a spacious territory, rich in soil and natural advantages, free from baronial tenures and burthens: yet the best of its land does not let at ten shillings an acre; while the rocky but well-peopled Salentine peninsula, hampered as it is with feudal claims and drawbacks, gives at least double the rent.

The olive-tree is here attended to with the nicest care, and no trouble spared to increase its fruitfulness, or revive prolific vigour in plants that begin to feel the decay of age. In winter, the peasants bare the roots of the old trees, lay upon them a thin coat of litter, and leave them thus,

during

during four months, to imbibe the reſtorative ſalts of the atmoſphere. Few of them have any principal bole; for all predominant ſhoots are early cut out, that every part may derive equal benefit from the influence of the ſun. Some huſbandmen only ſtir the earth near the tree; others plough all the interſtices, and raiſe profitable crops, though perhaps to the detriment of the olive plants In this province, the fruit is neither beaten off the tree, nor gathered; but remains till it falls through ripeneſs.

Don Giovanni Preſta has proved himſelf a zealous and valuable citizen of Gallipoli, by a long and attentive courſe of experiments upon the olive-tree, its fruit, and the method of making oil, with a view of increaſing its quantity, and improving its quality. The common mode of making oil, is to cruſh the olives to a paſte, with a perpendicular mill-ſtone running round a trough. This paſte is put into flat round baſkets, made of ruſhes, piled one upon another under the preſs. After a firſt preſſure, ſcalding water is poured into each baſket, its contents ſtirred up, and the operation repeated till no more oil can be ſkimmed off the ſurface of the tubs beneath. This method is liable to inconveniences; for the oil is ſeldom pure—keeps ill—and ſoon grows rancid. Don Giovanni employs other ways of extracting the liquor, which, though ſeemingly leſs effectual and more laborious, he thinks practice will prove to be full as expeditious as the mill, and much more advantageous to the vender, by the goodneſs of

3

the

the oil. He recommends a procefs, performed by pounding the fruit in a mortar. He throws a handful of the crufhed fubftance into a long woollen bag, which he rubs very hard upon a floping board; he then wrings it; afterwards adds hot water, and continues to prefs, as long as a drop of oil can be drawn from it This he fuppofes to have been the original mode of extraction, adopted by the difcoverers of oil; and, if performed by a fkilful, ftout workman, to be much more effectual than the common one. He has examined the different fpecies of olive-trees planted in his country, and appreciated their refpective merits. The kind moft commonly cultivated, and of oldeft ftanding in the province, is by him called the Salentine Olive,—by the peafant, Ogharola,—from the quantity of juice yielded by its fruit. A fecond fort, vulgarly named Faule, of which only a few are planted, bears a fmall olive kept for eating. The third is known by the names of Cellina, Scurancle, and Cafcia:—its olives give lefs oil than the Salentine kind, in a proportion of two to three; but the tree grows to a greater fize, refifts weather better, and is alfo more fruitful, —for which reafon it obtains the preference among the planters. He tried alfo a fourth fpecies; but of which only one tree exifts in his neighbourhood, and that a wild one Contrary to the nature of all other olives, its fruit grows white as it ripens —the ancients fpeak of fuch a kind. He has alfo procured fcions of the beft ftocks from Tufcany. I am forry to add, that as yet his efforts have been merely

fpeculative,

'fpeculative, for want of encouragement from thofe who alone can promote the public good to any extent. In Puglia, which abounds with cities and villages belonging to the Crown, and therefore more wealthy and independent than Baronial manors,—thefe trials may excite emulation, augment the cultivation of this valuable tree, and improve the manner of making oil, to the great emolument of King, planter, and merchant. I have little doubt but, with fkill, the olives of this province may be made to give as fine oil as thofe of either Provence or Lucca. In Calabria the cafe is more defperate ;—there feudal tyranny reigns paramount, and effectually clips the wings of induftry :—there the cuftom of the manor obliges all vaffals to grind their olives at the lord's mills *, though their number is not equal to the bufinefs. The unfortunate wretches behold their fruit rot, and their oil evaporate from the fermenting heaps, while they muft wait the preffing of the olives belonging to the Baron and his leffees, or to fuch proprietors as can afford to bribe the millers.

At the diftance of a few miles from the town, there is a good deal of woodland, where fportfmen find very good diverfion. Gentlemen hunt hare, fox, and fometimes wild boar, with hounds or lurchers, and fometimes with both. In autumn, fowlers ufe nets, fpringes, or birdlime; in winter, guns. All the country is free to whoever buys

* They pay for every grinding, or Macina, two carlini. A Macina confifts of eight bafkets, of thirty Neapolitan rotoli each.

the

the King's licence, except some few inclosures, where the Barons endeavour to preserve the game. Hawking has of late years been quite laid aside.

## SECTION L.

NARDO lies nine miles north of Gallipol; the road to it good and pleasant, with a fine view of the sea. In this little city are eight thousand inhabitants. The steeple of its cathedral is built in a very uncommon, but shewy stile of Gothic architecture. Luca Giordano and Solimeni have adorned the church with some agreeable paintings. This place was part of the Balzo estate. The Aquavivas were the next possessors:—they are thought to have come from the Marca di Ancona. In 1401, in consideration of their relationship to Pope Boniface the Ninth, Ladislaus erected their manor of Atri into a dukedom; an honour till then seldom granted to any but princes of the blood royal [*]. Claudius Aquaviva, a famous general of the Jesuits, who died in 1615, was of this family.

[*] Since that period, honours have been so lavishly bestowed, that, about the beginning of the last century, the single kingdom of Naples reckoned fifty Princes, sixty-three Dukes, one hundred and six Marquisses, in sixty Earls, fourteen Barons, who all held of the Crown *in capite*, and took their titles from their fiefs. At present, the numbers were, one hundred and twenty-four Princes, two hundred Dukes, two hundred Marquisses, and forty-three Earls.

The breadth of the peninfula, from Nardo, is about thirty-five miles: the road through an open country, interfperfed with fome coppices of a fmall jagged-leaved oak. We paffed near many villages; but I faw nothing in any of them worth my attention. As we approached the Adriatic, the landfcape grew dreary, from the great quantity of loofe ftone walls, by which the fields are divided. Near Otranto, the gardens, being full of orange-trees, have a more pleafing appearance. A rivulet, running into the fea, clofe to the walls, ftill retains its ancient name of Hydro.

Otranto is fmall, ftands on a hill, and contains only three thoufand inhabitants. Its little harbour is not fo bad, but it might induce more people to fettle here; as no port on the coaft lies fo convenient for traffic with Greece. The Adriatic Gulph is here but fixty miles wide. I climbed to the top of a tower, to get a fight of the Acroceraunian Mountains; but a vapour hanging over the fea, along the horizon, hid them from my view. in a clear morning, their fnowy tops are faid to be very vifible. The cathedral of Otranto is Gothic, and, according to the Puglian fafhion, has its fubterraneous fanctuary. The columns are of beautiful marbles and granite; the pavement, a rude fpecies of Mofaic, commonly called Saracenic. As it is to be met with in all churches founded by the Norman Kings of Sicily, the artifts who laid it were probably Saracens, or at leaft Greeks, their fcholars ——Thefe mofaics are compofed of pieces of porphyry, ferpentine, and cubes of gilt glafs,——

difpofed

difposed in ftairs, circles, or checquers. The compartments of the ftalls are bordered with them; and the fmall twifted columns, which fupport the pulpits and canopies, are ornamented with a fpiral ftripe of the fame work. It is a pity fo much durability, compactnefs, and beauty of materials, fhould have been lavifhed on fuch barbarous defigns.——Otranto was a Roman colony, as is certified by an infcription, almoft the only monument of antiquity left there *. In the tenth century, it was made an archbifhop's fee. In 1480, Laurence de Medici, to deliver himfelf from the attacks of the King of Naples, perfuaded Mahomet the Second to invade the realm; and Otranto was the unfortunate place where the Turks landed. It was invefted, ftormed and pillaged. Its Prelate was flain at the door of his church; eight hundred principal citizens dragged out of the gates, and butchered; their bodies left twelve months unburied, till the Duke of Calabria retook the city, and committed them to hallowed earth. About a hundred years after, a devout perfon affirmed, that thefe bones had appeared to him in a dream; and, upon the ftrength of his vifion, they became, for the vulgar, objects of almoft equal veneration with the relics of the primitive martyrs.

I was entertained in the evening with the mufic of fome of thofe itinerant performers, that play at Chriftmas in the ftreets of Rome and Naples. Their native country is Bafilicata, where the inhabitants of the Apennines learn

---

* Num Hydr.—Æ R Caput barb & laureat. ΓΑΡΟΝΤΙΝΩΝ = Τ ́ιdens, cum duobus delphinibus.

from their infancy to wield the mattock with one hand, and the flageolet or bagpipe with the other. In thefe favages of Italy, mufic is not merely an art of paftime or luxury, but a talent awakened by neceffity. Then ufual employment is hoeing out drains, to draw the water off the land; but as there is not every year, nor in all feafons, a fuperabundance of rain, they take up their mufical inftruments for a maintenance, and, in fmall parties, travel over Italy, France, and Spain. Some have penetrated even into America, and returned from thence with great comparative riches, earned by their paftoral melody. Their concerts are generally compofed of two muficians, who play on very long, large bagpipes, in unifon :—I mean as to the tone, becaufe one is always an octave higher than the other; while a third mufician founds a kind of hautboy, and, at the end of each ritornel, chants a rural ditty, to which the bagpipes play an accompaniment. The airs are all nearly alike, upon the model of the following Paftorale or Siciliana.

Largo

The trifling differences depend upon a greater or lesser vivacity in the performers, who are wont to embellish the common tune with variations, out of their own fancy. Every air, however, is composed of two characters: the ritornel is cheerful; the vocal part, flow and mournful. The instruments are all made by the shepherds themselves, in those forms and sizes which tradition has handed down to them, and experience has taught them to imitate.

My route to Lecce lay by the side of a large pond, that communicates with the sea. All around, for many miles, reigns one entire waste, productive of nothing but the holme oak, or *ilex coccifera.* These bushes were in full beauty, covered with the scarlet kermes, or false cochineal, which abounds in the same sort of country, in Andalusia and Languedoc. The Puglians seem ignorant that any use can be made of this shrub, except feeding their cattle with the leaves in winter, when other fodder fails. The villages on the road make a handsome shew, being built of white stone, but their churches are ornamented in a very barbarous stile. The face of the country is too rocky, and too bare of trees, corn, and grass, to be agreeable, and the prodigious number of stone walls would disfigure a much more fruitful one. Near the end of our ride, which was about twenty-four miles, the landscape became more lively, from a great quantity of gardens.

Le

Lecce, the capital of Terra di Otranto, the feat of its tribunal, and the fecond city in the kingdom,—is better paved and built than any town in the province. If its architects had been poffeffed of the fmalleft gleam of tafte, the buildings would have made a noble figure; for the ftone of the country is of a fine white, fo foft, when taken out of the quarry, that it may be moulded like wax, and will receive any form the flighteft ftrokes of the chiffel imprefs it with; yet, by remaining expofed to the air, very foon acquires a proper degree of confiftency. No materials, therefore, can be more defirable for ornamental mafonry, or more fufceptible of regularity and nicety of juncture. But the fronts of the principal edifices are crimped into fuch crowded uncouth decorations, that I lamented that the Grecian arts ever returned into this country: for the architecture of the Goths and Saracens, with all its oddities, is the very perfection of beauty and good fenfe, when compared with thefe Corinthian and Compofite extravagances at Lecce. The cathedral was erected by Tancred, before he afcended the throne; it is dedicated to Saints Cataldo and Nicholas, one of which is placed on a mutilated antique column in the great fquare. This fragment was brought from Brindifi, where its companion is ftill ftanding. Many of the paintings in the churches, and houfes of the nobility, are by Verrio, a native of Lecce, long employed in England,—where his ftaircafes and cielings are admired for their perfpective deception,

deception, and variety of figures, though deficient in correctness, choice, and other requisites of the art. He died in 1707.—The number of inhabitants does not reach thirteen thousand, very inadequate to the extent of the city. It has the reputation of being, to the rest of the kingdom, what Thebes was to Greece; and a native of Lecce is said to be distinguishable from his fellow-subjects, by the heaviness of his manner, and the dulness of his apprehension. I dare not be so rash as to pronounce upon this point; having had, during my short stay among them, very little opportunity of conversing with the Leccians, or appreciating their parts and learning. But I cannot suspect a city to be the seat of stupidity, that has an academy of Belles Lettres, and where some of the Muses at least meet with very sincere and successful admirers. Though the academy, from a want of royal protection, and proper directors, has of late confined its exertions to sonnets, and other absurd ebullitions of fancy; yet music is here cultivated with a degree of enthusiasm. Many of the nobility are good performers, and proud of exhibiting their skill on solemn festivals. The Leccian music has a very plaintive character, peculiar to itself. The Dilettanti sing stanzas to the following tune, which is a specimen of their style; and I have frequently heard Improvisatori chant their extempore verses to it [*].

* Don Luigi Serio of Naples is a very great genius in that line, and much superior to the celebrated Corilla, so well known to all the English that have been at Florence.

At or near Lecce, was the Roman colony of Lupiæ.
Some geographers confound it with Rudiæ, the birth-place
of Ennius, who flourished about two hundred years before
Christ, and composed several poems, of which only fragments have escaped the ravages of time.

Very soon after the establishment of the Normans, Earls
were enfeoffed with the manor of Lecce. The daughter of
one of them bore to the eldest son of King Roger a natural
son, called Tancred, who came at length to be King of
the Two Sicilies. Before his election to the crown, he
enjoyed the estate of his maternal ancestors, and was a great
benefactor to this city. His daughter Albinia transferred
the earldom to her husband Walter de Brienne, and the
heirefs of the Briennes married C de Engenio. Mary, the
last of that family was given in marriage by Lewis of Anjou,
to Raymond Orsino the fortunate adventurer, who afterwards became Prince of Taranto. On the failure of his
posterity,

posterity, Lecce fell, with the rest of their property, into the hands of the Crown.

From Lecce it is twenty-four miles to Brindisi, through an ugly tract of land, thinly peopled and poorly cultivated. The untilled part is over-run with beautiful shrubs. As we advanced, the country rather improved upon us, but still bore the marks of misery and depopulation.

## SECTION LI.

BRINDISI is a great city, if the extent of its walls be considered; but the inhabited houses do not fill above half the inclosure. The streets are crooked and rough, the buildings poor and ruinous; no very remarkable church or edifice. The cathedral, dedicated to St. Theodore, is a work of King Roger, but not equal in point of architecture to many churches founded by that monarch, who had a strong passion for building. The canons of this church retain the ancient custom of having handmaids; but as they take care to choose them of canonical age and face, we may suppose these locariæ to be only chaste representatives of the helpmates allowed to the clergy before Popes and Councils had reprobated them. These women are exempted from taxes, and enjoy many privileges. When they die, they are buried gratis, and the funeral is attended

3 D                                                                      by

by the Chapter with great solemnity; which is a mark of respect it does not pay to any relations of the canons.

Near the port stand the walls of a palace erected by Walter de Brienne, in a very bad taste. Its materials are grey stone, divided at regular distances with broad courses of black marble*. Little remains of ancient Brundusium, except innumerable broken pillars, fixed at the corners of streets to defend the houses from carts, fragments of coarse Mosaic, the floors of former habitations; the column of the light-house; a large marble bason, into which the water runs from brazen heads of deer; some inscriptions, ruins of aqueducts, coins, and other small furniture of an antiquary's cabinet. Its castle, built by the Emperor Frederick the Second to protect the northern branch of the harbour, is large and stately  Charles the Fifth repaired it.

The port is double, and the finest in the Adriatic. The outer part is formed by two promontories, that stretch off gradually from each other as they advance into the sea, leaving a very narrow channel at the base of the angle. The island of St. Andrew, on which Alphonsus the First built a fortress, lies between the capes, and secures the whole road from the fury of the waves. In this triangular space, large ships may ride at anchor. At the bottom of the bay the hills recede in a semicircular shape, to leave room for the inner-haven, which, as it were, clasps the city in its arms,

---

* These walls have been since pulled down, and employed in the facing of the new canal.

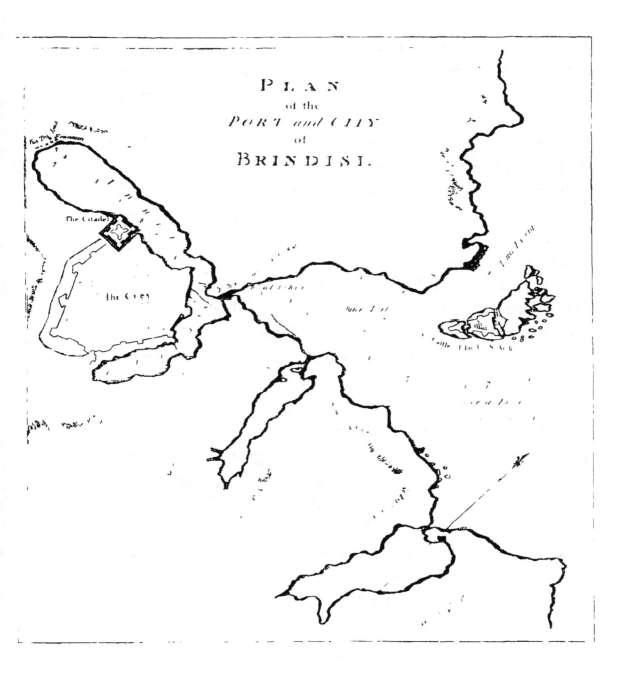

PLAN
of the
*PORT and CITY*
of
BRINDISI.

or rather encircles it, in the figure of a stag's head and horns. This form is said to have given rise to the name of Brundusium, which, in the old Messapian language, signified the head of a deer. I think it probable that this harbour was produced by an earthquake, which caused the ground to sink, and the waters to run into the cavity, for all the hills round it are on an exact level, and have parallel correspondent strata. Nothing can be more beautiful than this interior port, or better adapted to every purpose of trade and navigation. It is very deep, and extends in length two miles and a half, in breadth twelve hundred feet in the widest part. The hills and the town shelter it on every side. The north ridge is prettily cultivated and planted, but that to the south is bare of wood, and all sown with corn. In ancient days, the communication between the two havens was marked by lights placed upon columns of the Corinthian order, standing on a rising ground, in a direct line with the channel. Of these one remains entire upon its pedestal *. Its capital is adorned with figures of Syrens and Tritons, intermingled with the Acanthus leaf, and upon it is a circular vase, which formerly held the fire. A modern inscription has been cut upon the plinth. Near it is another pedestal of similar dimensions, with one piece of the shaft lying on it. The rest of the column was sold to the people of Lecce after the earthquake of 1756, which

* It is of the sort of green and white marble called Cipollino.

threw

threw it down, and destroyed great part of the city. The
space between these pillars answered to the entrance of the
harbour. The whole kingdom of Naples cannot shew a
more complete situation for trade than Brindisi. Here
goodness of soil, depth of water, safety of anchorage, and a
centrical position, are all united; yet it has neither commerce, husbandry, nor populousness. From the obstruc-
tions in the channel, which communicates with the two
havens, arises the tribe of evils that afflict and desolate this
unhappy town. Julius Cæsar may be said to have begun its
ruin, by attempting to block up Pompey's fleet. He drove
piles into the neck of land between the two ridges of hills;
threw in earth, trees, and ruins of houses; and had nearly
accomplished the blockade, when Pompey sailed out and
escaped to Greece. In the fifteenth century, the Prince
of Taranto sunk some ships in the middle of the passage, to
prevent the royalists from entering the port, and thereby
provided a resting place for sea-weeds and sand, which
so an accumulated, choked up the mouth, and rendered it
impracticable for any vessels whatsoever. In 1752, the evil
was increased, so as to hinder even the waves from beating
through, and all communication was cut off, except in violent easterly winds, or rainy seasons, when an extraordinary
quantity of fresh water raises the level. From that period
the port became a fetid green lake, full of infection and
noxious insects; no fish but eels could live in it, nor any
boat ply except canoes made of a single tree. They can

hold

hold but one perfon, and overfet with the leaft irregularity of motion. The low grounds at each end were overflowed and converted into marfhes, the vapours of which created every fummer a real peftilence, and, in the courfe of very few years, fwept off, or drove away, the largeft portion of the inhabitants. From the number of eighteen thoufand, they were reduced in 1766 to that of five thoufand livid wretches, tormented with agues and malignant fevers. In 1775 above fifteen hundred perfons died during the autumn,——A woful change of climate! Thirty years ago, the air of Brindifi was efteemed fo wholefome and balfamic, that the convents of Naples were wont to fend their confumptive friars to this city for the recovery of their health. This ftate of mifery and deftruction induced the remaining citizens to apply for relief to Don Carlo Demarco, one of the King's minifters, and a native of Brindifi. In confequence of this application, Don Vito Caravelli was ordered to draw up plans, and fix upon the means of opening the port afrefh. Don Andrea Pigonati was laft year fent to execute his projects, and by the help of machines, and the labour of the gally-flaves, has fucceeded in fome meafure. The channel has been partly cleared, and has now two fathom of water. It can admit large boats, a great ftep towards the revival of trade, but what is of more immediate importance, it gives a free paffage to the fea, which now rufhes in with impetuofity, and runs out again at each tide, fo that the water of the inner port is fet in motion,

in

and once more rendered wholesome. The canal, or gut, is to be seven hundred yards long, and drawn in a strait line from the column  At present, its parapets are defended by piles and fascines; but if the original plan be pursued, stone piers will be erected on both sides.  Don Andrea, who received me with great politeness and hospitality, has the success of this undertaking extremely at heart, and as he spares no pains, has money enough for his ends, and seems to be very well versed in his profession, it is to be hoped the patriotic wishes of his employers will not prove vain and delusory.  If the defence against the sea be sufficient, and a proper method be followed for turning off the load of sand which every tide brings in, and naturally tends to deposit where the current draws it, this work will remain an honour to the Minister by whose direction it was undertaken, and to the engineers who have superintended it, but it appeared to me, upon examining every thing very attentively, rather doubtful whether the work be properly secured against accidents, and whether a very considerable annual expence will not be necessary to keep it in order *.

When the canal shall be scooped out to a proper depth, and its piers solidly established, vessels of any burden may once more enter this land-locked port, which affords room

* I am sorry to find, by the last account, I have received from that country, that the piers have proved too weak to resist the violence of the sea, that much damage has already been done, and great part of the channel once more choked with sand

for a whole navy. Docks wet and dry may be dug, goods may be shipped at the quay, and convenient watering-places be made with great ease. If merchants should think it a place of rising trade, and worthy of their notice, there is no want of space in the town for any factory whatever. Circulation of cash would give vigour to husbandry, and provisions wou'd soon abound in this market. The sands at the foot of the hills, which form the channel, are to be laid out in beds for muscles and oysters. Some ecclesiastics are raising nurseries of orange and lemon trees; and other citizens intend introducing the cultivation of mulberry-trees, and breeding of silk-worms.

The Engineer would have done very little for the health of Brindisi, had he only opened a passage, and given a free course to the waters; the marshes at each extremity of the harbour would still have infected the air; he therefore, at the expence of about a thousand ducats, had the fens filled up with earth, and a dam raised to confine the waters, and prevent their flowing back upon the meadows. The people of Brindisi, who are sensible of the blessings already derived from these operations, who feel a return of health, and see an opening for commerce and opulence, seem ready to acknowledge the obligation. They intend to erect a statue to the King, with inscriptions on the pedestal in honour of the Minister and Agents.

The workmen, in clearing the channel, have found some medals and seals, and have drawn up many of the piles that

2                                                      were

were driven in by Cæsar.   They are fmall oaks ftripped of
their bark, and ftill as frefh as if they had been cut only a
month, though buried above eighteen centuries feven feet
under the fand.

The foil about the town is light and good.   It produces
excellent cotton with which the Brindifians manufacture
gloves and ftockings

## SECTION LII.

IT is impoffible to determine who were the founders of
Brundufium, or when it was firft inhabited[*].   The Romans took early poffeffion of a harbour fo convenient for
their enterprizes againft the nations dwelling beyond the
Adriatic.   In the five hundred and ninth year of Rome
they fent a colony hither.   Pompey took refuge here; but
finding his poft untenable, made a precipitate retreat to
Greece.   In this city Octavianus firft affumed the name of
Cæfar, and here he concluded one of his fhort-lived peaces
with Antony.   Brundufium had been already celebrated
for giving birth to the tragic poet Pacuvius, and about this
time became remarkable for the death of Virgil   The Bu-

---

* Nummi Brundufinorum

1 R   1 Cap Herculis and  pellem tect ═ Homo nudus d lp     d
      cap l lyr ten  ΤΑΝΑΗΣΙΝΩΝ
   2  Cap barb hur  glob ═ Homo nud d lp incg b lyra  glob
      b ΩΝ
   3  Cap barb hur pone vict cor  imp tridens  glob ═ Homo nud
      delp inc d Victor. f cornuc clava  glob PRI

barbarians,

barians, who ravaged every corner of Italy, did not fpare fo rich a town, and in eight hundred and thirty-fix, the Saracens gave a finifhing blow to its fortunes. The Greek Emperors, fenfible of the neceffity of having fuch a port as this in Italy, would have reftored it to its ancient ftrength and fplendour, had the Normans allowed them time and leifure. The Greeks ftruggled manfully to keep their ground, but, after many varieties of fuccefs, were finally driven out of Brindifi by William the Firft.

The phrenzy for expeditions to Paleftine, though it drained other kingdoms of their wealth and fubjects, contributed powerfully to the re-eftablifhment of this city, one of the ports where pilgrims and warriors took fhipping It alfo benefited by the refidence of the Emperor Frederick, whofe frequent armaments for the Holy Land required his prefence at this place of rendezvous. The lofs of Jerufalem, the fall of the Grecian empire, and the ruin of all the Levant trade after the Turks had conquered the Eaft, reduced Brindifi to a ftate of inactivity and defolation, from which it has never been able to emerge.

As I was now in the country of the Tarantula, I was defirous of inveftigating minutely every particular relative to that infect; but the feafon was not far enough advanced, and no Tarantati* had begun to ftir. I prevailed upon a woman, who had formerly been bitten, to act the part, and

---

* Perfons bitten, or pretending to be bitten, by the Tarantula

3 E                                                    dance

dance the Tarantata before me. A great many muficians were fummoned, and fhe performed the dance, as all prefent affured me, to perfection. At firft, fhe lolled ftupidly on a chair, while the inftruments were playing fome dull mufic. They touched, at length, the chord fuppofed to vibrate to her heart, and up fhe fprang with a moft hideous yell, ftaggered about the room like a drunken perfon, holding a handkerchief in both hands, raifing them alternately, and moving in very true time. As the mufic grew brifker, her motions quickened, and fhe fkipped about with great vigour and variety of fteps, every now and then fhrieking very loud. The fcene was far from pleafant; and, at my defire, an end was put to it before the woman was tired. Wherever the Tarantati are to dance, a place is prepared for them, hung round with bunches of grapes and ribbons. The patients are dreffed in white, with red, green, or yellow ribbons, for thofe are their favourite colours; on their fhoulders they caft a white fcarf, let their hair fall loofe about their ears, and throw their heads as far back as they can bear it. They are exact copies of the ancient priefteffes of Bacchus. The orgies of that God, whofe worfhip *, under various fymbols, was more widely fpread over the globe than that of any other divinity, were, no doubt, performed with energy and enthufiafm by

_____

* I fhall fay nothing more on the fubject of this univerfal worfhip, as it is treated in a moft ingenious and fatisfactory manner by Mr. D'Ancarville, who will foon favour the Public with his Work

the

the lively inhabitants of this warm climate. The introduction of Christianity abolished all public exhibitions of
these heathenish rites, and the women durst no longer act a
frantic part in the character of Bacchantes. Unwilling to
give up so darling an amusement, they devised other
pretences; and possession by evil spirits may have furnished
them with one. Accident may also have led them to a
discovery of the Tarantula, and, upon the strength of its
poison, the Puglian dames still enjoy their old dance, though
time has effaced the memory of its ancient name and institution: and this I take to be the origin of so strange a
practice. If at any time these dancers are really and in-
voluntarily affected, I can suppose it to be nothing more
than an attack upon their nerves, a species of St. Vitus's
dance. I incline the more to the idea, as there are numberless churches and places throughout these provinces dedicated to that saint. Many sensible people of this town
differ in opinion from Doctor Serao and other authors,
who have ridiculed the pretended disorder, and affirmed,
that the venom of this species of spider can produce no
effects but such as are common to all others. The
Brindisians say, that the Tarantulas sent to Naples for the
experiment were not of the true sort, but a much larger
and more innocent one; and that the length of the journey,
and want of food, had weakened their power so much, as to
suffer the Doctor, or others, to put their arm into the bag
where they were kept, with impunity. They quote many

example

examples of perfons bitten as they flept out in the fields
during the hot months, who grew languid, ftupid, deprived
of all courage and elafticity, till the found of fome favourite
tune roufed them to dance, and throw off the poifon.
Thefe arguments of theirs had little weight with me,
for they acknowledged that elderly perfons were more frequently infected than young ones, and that moft of them
were women, and thofe unmarried. No perfon above the
loweft rank in life was ever feized with this malady, nor is
there an inftance of its caufing death. The length of the
dance, and the patient's powers of bearing fuch exceffive
fatigue in the canicular feafon, prove nothing, becaufe every
day, at that time of the year, peafants may be feen dancing
with equal fpirit and perfeverance, though they do not
pretend to be feized with the Tarantifm. The illnefs may
therefore be attributed to hyfterics, exceffive heat, ftoppage
of perfpiration, and other effects of fleeping out of doors in
a hot fummer air, which is always extremely dangerous, if
not mortal, in moft parts of Italy. Violent exercife may
have been found to be a certain cure for this diforder, and
continued by tradition, though the date and circumftances
of this difcovery have been long buried in oblivion;—a
natural paffion for dancing, imitation, cuftom of the
country, and a defire of raifing contributions upon the fpec-
tators, are probably the real motives that infpire the Tarantati.
Before Serao's experiments, the Tarantula had been proved

to

to be harmlefs, from trials made in 1693 by Clarizio, and in 1740 at Lucera by other naturalifts.

The Tarantula is a fpider of the third fpecies of Linnæus's fourth family, with eight eyes placed four, two and two; its colour commonly a very dark grey, but varies according to age and food  The bulk of its fore-part is almoft double that of the hind part; the back of its neck raifed high, and its leg fhort and thick.  It lives in bare fields, where the lands are fallow, but not very hard; and, from its antipathy to damp and fhade, choofes for its refidence the rifing part of the ground facing the eaft.  Its dwelling is about four inches deep, and half an inch wide; at the bottom it is curved, and there the infect fits in wet weather, and cuts its way out, if water gains upon it.  It weaves a net at the mouth of the hole.  Thefe fpiders do not live quite a year.  In July they fhed their fkin, and proceed to propagation, which, from a mutual diftruft, as they frequently devour one another, is a work undertaken with great circumfpection.  They lay about feven hundred and thirty eggs, which are hatched in the fpring, but the parent does not live to fee her progeny, having expired early in the winter.  The Ichneumon fly is their moft formidable enemy.                                                                   3

## SECTION LIII.

ON leaving Brindisi, I passed by the well at the head of the haven, which supplies the town with water. The view from this point takes in the port, column, a large palm-tree, churches, and castles, all objects of great picturesque beauty.

At a few miles distance, the Trajan way is easily traced as it crosses a hollow. It is raised to a level upon arches, built in the reticular or losengy manner. Most of this day's journey to Monopoli, although forty-three miles long, was near the coast, through a wild country covered with varieties of ever-green shrubs. The small portion of ground in cultivation is sown with beans; but there is a cruel enemy that every year destroys the best part of the crop: this is the Orobanche or Broom Rape, a parasite weed that shoots up with beans, and other leguminous plants, mixes its roots with theirs, and, by drawing out all the nutriment, causes them to droop, pine, and die. The Pughese call it La Sporchia. All their efforts to eradicate it have hitherto proved ineffectual; but I suspect they have gone very superficially to work.

At

of the        of                    Au              ken from the                    of the

At Bari I took the inland road by the ancient Via Egnatiana, which Horace travelled upon. We slept at Bitonto *, a fine town of sixteen thousand inhabitants, much easier in their fortunes, and more polished and improved in their manners, than those that dwell in the cities along the coast; its markets are well supplied, and an air of affluence reigns in the place. The country between it and Bari, which is nine miles distant, is very much inclosed, and, though stony, fertile in corn, almonds, olives, wine, and fruit of all kinds. I found there was a general cry of famine throughout the country, but it was a want of snow, not of bread, that was complained of. Near this city an obelisk was erected by the present King of Spain, with four fulsome inscriptions in praise of himself, his father Philip, his soldiers, and the Count of Mortemar, who was honoured with the title of Duke of Bitonto for having defeated the Austrians on this spot in 1734. The engagement was a very trifling one, but as it cleared the kingdom of Germans, proved of essential service to the Spaniards. If the King wishes to transmit this event to posterity by a monument, he must build something more durable, for the present one is already disjointed, and crumbling to ruin. A most disagreeable stony road brought us to Ruvo, through a fine country. The pomegranate hedges in flower, and the holm oak loaded with

* Numina Botont.

A R 1 Cop Pallid = Architecton ON
1 Nocturr m on —I ulnach O TONTINO.

2                                                  komes,

kermes, enlivened the profpect, which otherwise would have been very dull. Near Quarata, another monument is to be feen, commemorating a victory gained there in 1503 by thirteen Italians over an equal number of French. They fought in lifts upon a formal challenge, in confequence of fome contemptuous expreffions made ufe of by the latter. Each of the vanquifhed party was to forfeit one hundred ducats, his horfe, and armour. The conteft was not very obftinate; one Frenchman was killed; the reft made prifoners, and led away to Barletta, becaufe they had not brought their ranfom with them. The Italian authors extol this action as a moft glorious atchievement: the French accufe their adverfaries of having difplayed more trick and cunning, than valour, in the combat.—I here quitted the Roman way, and rode fifteen miles weftward to Caftel del Monte. The country I traverfed is open, uneven, and dry. The caftle is a landmark, and ftands on the brow of a very high hill, the extremity of a ridge that branches out from the Apennine   The afcent to it is near half a mile long, and very fteep, the view from its terrace moft extenfive   A vaft reach of fea and plain on one fide, and mountains on the other, not a city in the province but is diftinguifhable, yet the barrennefs of the fore-ground takes off a great deal of the beauty of the picture   The building is octangular, in a plain folid ftyle, the walls are ruled with reddifh and white ftones, ten feet fix inches thick; the great gate is of marble, cut into very intricate ornaments, after

the

the manner of the Arabians; on the baluſtrade of the ſteps lie two enormous lions of marble, their buſhy manes nicely, though barbarouſly, expreſſed, the court, which is in the centre of the edifice, contains an octangular marble baſon of a ſurpriſing diameter. To carry it to the ſummit of ſuch a hill muſt have coſt an infinite deal of labour. Two hundred ſteps lead up to the top of the caſtle, which conſiſts of two ſtories. In each of them are fifteen ſaloons of great dimenſions, caſed throughout with various and valuable marbles; the cielings are ſupported by triple cluſtered columns of a ſingle block of white marble, the capitals extremely ſimple. Various have been the opinions concerning the founder of this caſtle; but the beſt grounded aſcribe it to Frederick of Swabia *. I dined and ſpent the hot hours with great comfort under the porch, which commands a noble view of the Adriatic.

In the evening I deſcended the mountain, and rode nine miles to Andria. a large feudal city, eaſt of the Roman road. Andria ſtands on the edge of the incloſed country, and its environs being rather hilly, are far from unpleaſant, though without any running water. This town was built

* A Neapolitan gentleman found, in one of theſe rooms, a baſſo relievo repreſenting this Emperor and his Chancellor Peter de Vineis, of which he had a copy taken in plaſter. This ſettles the matter beyond a doubt. I did not diſcover this ſculpture, nor hear of it till long after my return to Naples, but I ſaw another baſſo relievo of ſome warriors in Norman habits meeting a woman dreſſed after the Greek faſhion —As this ſtone appears to have been inſerted into the walls ſince their firſt building, and bears the date of 1520, it caſts no light on the hiſtory of the place.

by

by Peter the Norman, and acquired its name from the antra or caverns in which the first settlers abided. Conrad the Fourth was born at Andria, where his mother, the Empress Iole Queen of Jerusalem died in childbed of him; and here also lies buried Isabella of England, another wife of the Emperor Frederick. Beatrix, daughter to Charles the Second, had Andria for her portion on marrying Azzo D'Este Marquis of Ferrara. This Prince dying, she took for her second husband Bertrand Del Balzo, progenitor of the Dukes of Andria, who were long at the head of the Neapolitan Nobility. In 1370, Francis Del Balzo, by a quarrel with the powerful House of Sanseverino, and his obstinate resistance to the royal mandate, drew upon himself the vengeance of Queen Joan the First, who confiscated his estate. On the accession of Charles the Third, he was reinstated. This family failing, Fabricio Caraffa purchased the Dutchy of Andria in 1525 for one hundred thousand ducats.

From hence I travelled twelve miles to Canosa, over a pleasant down, where the Roman road remains entire in many places, paved with common rough pebbles. Canusium, founded by Diomed, and afterwards a Roman colony, became one of the most considerable cities of this part of Italy for extent, population, and magnificence in building. The æra of Trajan seems to have been that of its greatest splendour, but this pomp only served to mark it as a capital object for the avarice and fury of the Barbarians. Genseric, feric, Totila, and Autharis, treated it with extreme cruelty The deplorable state to which this province was reduced in 590 is concisely, but strongly, painted by Gregory the Great in these terms. " On every side we hear groans! on every " side we behold crowds of mourners, cities burnt, castles " rased to the ground, countries laid waste, provinces be- " come deserts, some citizens led away captives, and others " inhumanly massacred." No town in Puglia suffered more than Canosa from the outrages of the Saracens; the contests between the Greeks and Normans increased the measure of its woes, which was filled by a conflagration that happened when it was stormed by Duke Robert. In 1093, it was assigned, by agreement, to Bohemund Prince of Antioch, who died here in 1111. Under the reign of Ferdinand the Third this estate belonged to the Grimaldis On their forfeiture, the Affaititi acquired it, and still retain the title of Marqui, though the Capeci are the propri- tors of the fief.

The ancient city* it d in a plain between the hills and the river Ofanto, and covered a large tract of ground. Many brick monuments, though degraded and stripped of their marble casing, still attest its ancient grandeur. Among them may be traced the fragments of aqueducts, tombs, amphitheatre baths. military columns, and two

* Numm Canuf

AR 1 Cap. Juv imb =1 ques gal hallat KANΥΣΙΝΩ.

triumphal

triumphal arches, which, by their position, seem to have been two city gates. The present town stands above, on the foundations of the old citadel, and is a most pitiful remnant of so great a city, not containing above three hundred houses. The church of St. Sabinus, built, as is said, in the sixth century, is now without the inclosure. It is astonishing, that any part of this ancient cathedral should have withstood so many calamities. Its altars and pavements are rich in marbles, and the six Verde Antico columns that support its roof, are the largest and finest I ever saw of that species of marble. In a small court adjoining, under an octagonal cupola, is the mausoleum of Bohemund, adorned in a minute Gothic style. Round the cornice runs a string of barbarous rhymes; and upon the door are other inscriptions, with an embossed representation of warriors kneeling before the Madonna. In 1461, the Prince of Taranto, among the many acts of barbarity practised by him in Canosa, broke open this sepulchre, and disturbed the ashes of a hero whose memory should have been held sacred, at least by a soldier: for Bohemund was a warrior of most exalted fame, the sharer and the rival of his father Guiscard's glory; who, by his victories, was enabled to shake the throne of the Eastern Emperors. when, by the intrigues of his mother-in-law Sigelgaita, and the partiality of his uncle Earl Roger, Bohemund found himself deprived of his Italian inheritance, he turned his arms against the Saracens, and formed a new sovereignty for himself in Palestine. As

1

Prince

Prince of Antioch, he became one of the firmest ramparts of the Crusado against the Infidels.

The prowess of these Norman conquerors was so much greater than that of their cotemporaries, their bodily strength and feats of arms were so wonderful, that it is probable they were the originals from whom the writers of romance drew their heroes. Giants cloven to the saddle; armies routed by a single warrior; castles and bridges defended by one person alone, knights travelling over the world in search of kingdoms, princesses, and adventures, are no more than the real events of the lives of William Fierabras, Robert Guiscard, Earl Roger, and their companions. Malaterra, their cotemporary, friend, and historian, furnishes ample materials for a complete romance, with the addition of a few enchanters and dragons. In the first Sicilian campaign, William slays a gigantic champion in single combat. At Melfi, to shew the Greek herald what he could do, Hugh Tudextifem seizes his horse, and kills it with a blow of his fist. In another affair, Fierabras springs from his bed, where he lay sick of a fever, rallies his troops, kills the general of the enemies, obtains the victory, and returns to his couch. We read frequently of Robert's being obliged for food to sally out of his castle by night to surprise and carry off the cattle in the neighbourhood, and once he called out the commander of a fort to parley, caught him by the middle, and rode off with him in sight of his whole garrison. I do not know which to admire
most,

moſt, the franknefs of the prince who dictated his own ſtory, or the honeſt plainnefs of the hiſtorian who wrote, that Earl Roger was once ſo poor as to be obliged to ſteal horſes, and plunder travellers for a ſupport. At the ſiege of Reggio, Roger hews a mighty giant down with his two-handed ſword. In a ſally he makes from a caſtle in Sicily, where he and his wife were beſieged by the Saracens, his horſe is killed under him; but the hero cuts his way through their battalions, and, left he ſhould be thought to have left the field out of fear, marches off with the ſaddle upon his ſhoulders. In 1063, Serlo defeats an army of thirty thouſand men with only thirty-ſix knights armed cap-a-pee. What a fund of marvellous fictions would not ſuch facts give birth to! How many ſupernatural circumſtances might not a bard create out of the ſingle one of Roger's defeating the Mahometans at Miſilmeri, taking all their carrier-pigeons, ſmearing them with the blood of the ſlain, and letting them fly to announce the diſaſter at Palermo, which he was marching to inveſt. The idea of theſe extraordinary men certainly remained long impreſſed on the minds of the Italians, whoſe lively imagination muſt have embelliſhed tradition with ſo many additional wonders, that the old romances had little more to do than to commit to writing, and drefs up in rhyme, the common tales of every evening affembly. In theſe the eaſy brilliant genius of Arioſto revelled, and ſtruck out the moſt delightful, but moſt eccentrical defcriptions ever ſeriouſly attempted by a poet.

## SECTION LIV.

I LEFT the bridge of Canofa early on the 7th, and travelled up the fouth-fide of the river for twelve miles, without meeting with any object worthy of remark. The city of Minervino, feated on an eminence, was the only place I faw during the ride,—the country bare and difagreeable, till I entered the heart of the mountains, where I found a more woody and pleafant landfcape. I dined at Lavello, a fmall city belonging to Caracciolo Prince of Torella. Some Roman infcriptions, and many Jewifh epitaphs of the ninth century, are the amount of its antiquities. The æra of its foundation is unknown. Mention is made of it in the Lombard Chronicles, Sicard the eighteenth Duke of Beneventum having been affaffinated at Lavello. Conrad the Fourth was encamped under its walls, when he was feized with the diforder that carried him off, poifoned, as is faid, by his brother Manfred. Hiftorians fpeak of a ftrange kind of poifon adminiftered on the occafion, viz powder of diamonds mixed with fcammony, which being given in a clyfter, brought away the Emperor's bowels by piece-meal. This Prince was then in the zenith of his glory, having routed his enemies, punifhed the rebels with feverit , and effectually crufhed their power. Had he been allowed to live longer, the

House

House of Swabia would not have been so easily overturned, for though bloody and cruel to excess, Conrad was possessed of the bold manly qualities requisite for fixing his dominion on a permanent basis

From Lavello I passed over rugged mountains to Venosa, which stands on a high level of nine miles in circumference, surrounded by precipices, that form on every side a natural ditch and fortification. The whole mass has been raised by the force of subterranean fires, as the nature of the soil, and a forum vulcani, or solfatara, distant a mile from the city, clearly evince. This solfatara is not encircled by hills like that of Puzzuoli, which it resembles in every other particular, of colour, sulphureous productions, and internal rumblings. Numberless streams flow out of its sides, and, what is extraordinary, vary much in their colour and mineral qualities.

Venosa was a very considerable place in ancient times, and a steady useful friend to Rome in her struggles with Hannibal. The remnant of Terentius Varro's army fled hither from Cannæ, and obtained of the generous Venusians both protection and supplies of all sorts. When the Normans subdued Puglia, Dreux had Venosa for his share of the spoil The San Severinos enjoyed it afterwards; then passing through the family of Balzo, the honour devolved upon a son of Raymund Prince of Taranto. A brother of Pope Martin the Fifth, was for a few years invested with **this** fief, but on the Pontiff's demise, was deprived of his

Neapolitan

Neapolitan grants.  Caracciolo, Prince of Torella, is the present proprietor.

Nothing is now to be seen at Venosa that can recal an idea of its ancient magnificence, except pieces of marble containing parts of inscriptions, fixed in the walls of houses and churches  The Gothic edifice belonging to the Maltese order, and dedicated to the Holy Trinity, affords the greatest quantity of fragments, and even entire monuments, torn by the hands of its barbarous founders from ruinated theatres, baths, and temples.  This church was erected upon the foundations of a temple consecrated to Venus, from which goddess the city is supposed to have taken its name.  The Benedictine monks were in possession of this abbey till the reign of Boniface the Eighth, who endowed the Knights of Saint John with it.  Its architecture offers nothing singular or beautiful in the Gothic line  Solidity appears to have been more studied by the Norman architects who rebuilt or repaired it, than elegance or lightness, which became the principal objects of those builders that succeeded them.  The remains of Dreux, Robert Guiscard, and Albarade his wife, whom he divorced to marry a Lombard Princess, repose under its roof.  From the number of Hebraic monuments, which bear the same date with those of Lavello, I infer that the Jews flocked to this country about the time that the Saracen power was predominant in Puglia.  The piece of antiquity of highest reputation, and upon which the inhabitants of Venosa pride themselves

themselves

themselves most, is a marble buft placed in the great fquare on a column. This they fhew as the effigy of their fellow-citizen Horace; but the badnefs of the defign, and the mode of drefs, render this opinion very problematical I take it to be the head of a faint. The refpect paid to fo diftinguifhed a genius does honour to the tafte of the Venofians; but I am aftonifhed they have not canonized their poet, for the vulgar at Naples have made a faint of Virgil.

I made an excurfion fix miles along the Tarentine road to vifit the Bandufian fountain, celebrated by Horace in the thirteenth Ode of his Third Book, and fo long a point in litigation among critics and commentators. The common opinion placed it at his Sabine farm; but Abbé Chaupy has inconteftibly proved, that it can be no other than a fpring near Palazzo, in the principality of St Gervafio. I difcovered it by the defcription given by Chaupy; and was forry to find him fo faithful a painter of the prefent deplorable ftate of this once charming fountain No fhady groves now hang over its banks to fhut out the burning mid-day fun; its gelid waters no longer tumble down the rocks in beautiful cafcades, but, choked with dirt, and loft in bogs, are forced to feek their way under ground to a vent at the foot of the hill.

I returned to Venofa, and paffed the night at Barile, at the bottom of Mount Voltore, which I propofed to afcend the next day. Barile is a large burgh, fituated on a hill, that appears to owe its exiftence to an eruption, as the foil is entirely volcanical, and the stone, employed in buildings, a dark-coloured compact lava. A line of circumvallation of thirty miles, marks the extent of this cast-up soil. The inclosed space is covered with every species of stone, earth, and mineral, usually found on or near ignivomous mountains. Medicinal waters break on all sides, and are prescribed by physicians in many cases. The summit of Mount Voltore is like that of all volcanoes, broken on one side, and hollow in the middle. In the crater are two lakes of great depth; one near a mile, the other almost two in circumference. The water is clear, sweet, and cool, at least near the surface; but I was assured that it is insupportably strong, both in taste and smell, if drawn up from a considerable depth.

A change of weather obliged me to leave the mountain in a hurry, and make the best of my way to Lavello*.

On the 10th, I passed the whole day in crossing the plains of Puglia to the bridge of Bovino, almost suffocated with dust, and parched up with heat. We dined at

---

* Had the weather been more favourable, I should have stopped at Melfi, remarkable for being the first place that was seized by the Normans, and appointed a common rendezvous for all the chiefs of the league. Hither they brought their booty, and threw it into a common stock. Hither they retired on any reverse of fortune. In 1052, Nicholas the Second called a Council of one hundred prelates at Melfi, and confirmed the Normans in the possession of their usurped dominions. Upon this condition Count Robert resigned all the rights to the Crown of the two Sicilies. Frederick of Swabia held a Parliament here for the purpose of promulgating the constitutions compiled by his Chancellor Peter de Vines.

Ordona, near the ruins of Herdonia, a place of importance in the Punic war; at present some brick walls, vestiges of baths, aqueducts, and gates, are all that remain. About a mile off is a farm of the late Jesuits, called L'Orta, a stupendous pile of buildings. From Ariano, we turned off to Benevento, where we arrived through an unremitting deluge of rain, with incessant claps of thunder and flashes of lightning. Every gutter became a brook, and every brook a river; so that we were obliged to make great haste to get there, before they should swell to such a height as to stop our passage.

## S E C T I O N   LV.

BENEVENTO is situated on the slope, and at the point of a hill between two narrow vallies, in one of which runs the river Sabato, in the other the Calore; below the city they unite into one stream.

We entered through the arch of Trajan, now called the Porta Aurea, which appears to great disadvantage from the walls and houses that hem it in on both sides; however, it is in tolerable preservation, and one of the most magnificent remains of Roman grandeur to be met with out of Rome. The architecture and sculpture are both singularly beautiful. This elegant monument was erected in the year of Christ 114, about the commencement of the Parthian war, and

after

after the submission of Decebalus had entitled Trajan to the surname of Dacicus. The order is composite; the materials, white marble; the height, sixty palms; length, thirty-seven and a half, and depth twenty-four. It consists of a single arch, the span of which is twenty palms, the height thirty-five. On each side of it, two fluted columns, upon a joint pedestal, support an entablement and an Attic. The intercolumniations and frize are covered with basso-relievos, representing the battles and triumph of the Dacian war. In the Attic is the inscription —As the sixth year of Trajan's consulate, marked on this arch, is also to be seen on all the milliary columns he erected along his new road to Brundusium, it is probable that the arch was built to commemorate so beneficial an undertaking.

Except the old Metropolis of the World, no city in Italy can boast of so many remains of ancient sculpture, as are to be found in Benevento. Scarce a wall is built of any thing but altars, tombs, columns, and remains of entablatures. The most considerable are in the upper town, which I take to be the site of the old one. The cupola of St. Sophia rests upon a circular colonnade of antique marble, in the same manner as those of Santa Maria near Nocera, Saint Sebastian, and St. Agnes at Rome,—and other buildings erected under Constantine and his family, when the arts were declining. In the court is a fine relievo of the Rape of the Sabines the other remarkable fragments are, the Death of Meleager,—a Measure of Corn,—some sepulchral busts,

busts,—a large boar, covered with the stole and vitta for sacrifice, which antiquaries call the Caledonian Boar, left by Diomed as a badge to his colony of Benevento,—and, Hercules stealing the Hesperian Apples. This last piece struck me very much, from the resemblance it bears to our common mode of depicting the Fall of Man. A woman lies at the foot of a tree, and a huge serpent is twined round the trunk, stretching out its head towards the fruit, which a man leans forward to pluck. The club he holds in his hand, and a Greek inscription [*], mark him out for Hercules [†]. A volume might be filled with inscriptions collected here, relative to every subject, on which the ancients, who recorded every trifle, were wont to set up a lapidary memorial. The christians have also contributed a considerable variety of monuments. I remarked one, in particular, representing a man rising out of the waters, and pursued by a fish: this alludes to the story of Jonas, and was sometimes carved upon the tombs of the primitive christians, to express mysteriously their belief in the resurrection.

The cathedral is a clumsy edifice, in a stile of Gothic, or rather Lombard, architecture. This church, dedicated to the Virgin Mary, was built in the sixth century, enlarged

---

[*] ΗΡΑΚΛΗ ΣΩΤΗΡΙ Η ΙΟΥΝΙΚΣ ΤΑΝΟΤΑΡΙΟΣ ΑΥΓΟΥΣ ΑΝΕΘΗΚΕΝ.

[†] Some ingenious writers have endeavoured to prove, that the fable of the Hesperides is built upon the scriptural account of our First Parents, and this *Ex Voto* to Hercules, shews that there are good grounds for the comparison

in the eleventh, and altered confiderably in the thirteenth, when Archbithop Roger adorned it with a new front. To obtain a fufficient quantity of marble for this purpofe, he fpared neither farcophagus, altar, nor infcription; but fixed them promifcuoufly and irregularly in the walls of his bar-barous ftructure. Three doors (a type of the Trinity, according to the rules eftablithed by the myftical Vitruvii of thofe ages) open into this facade. That in the centre is of bronze, emboffed with the life of Chrift, and the effigies of the Beneventine Metropolitan, with all his fuffragan Bifhops. The infide offers nothing to the curious obferver but columns, altars, and other decorations, executed in the moft inelegant ftile that any of the church-building barba-rians ever adopted. In the court ftands a fmall Egyptian obelifk, of red granite, crowded with hieroglyphics. In the adjoining fquare, are a fountain, and a very indifferent ftatue of Benedict the Thirteenth, long archbifhop of Benevento.

The writers of the Beneventine hiftory unanimoufly claim Diomed, the Etolian chief, for the founder of their city; and confequently fix its origin in the years that immediately fucceeded the Trojan war. Other authors affign it to the Samnites, who made it one of their principal towns, where they frequently took refuge, when worfted by the Romans. In their time, its name was Maleventum, a word of uncer-tain etymology: however, it founded fo ill in the Latin tongue, that the fuperftitious Romans, after taking the

8 compleat

conqueft of Samnium, changed it into Beneventum, in order to introduce their colony under fortunate aufpices. Near this place, in the four hundred and feventy-ninth year of Rome, Pyrrhus was defeated by Curius Dentatus. In the war againft Hannibal, Beneventum fignalized its attachment to Rome, by liberal tenders of fuccour, and real fervices. Its reception of Gracchus, after his defeat of Hanno, is extolled by Livy; and, from the gratitude of the Senate, many folid advantages accrued to the Beneventines. As they long partook, in a diftinguifhed manner, of the glories and profperity of the Roman empire,—they alfo feverely felt the effects of its decline, and fhared, in a large proportion, the horrors of devaftation that attended the irruption of the northern nations.

The modern hiftory of this city will appear interefting to thofe readers, who do not defpife the events of ages, which we ufually and juftly call dark and barbarous. They certainly are of importance to all the prefent ftates of Europe; for at that period originated the political exiftence of moft of them. Had no northern favages defcended from their fnowy mountains, to overturn the Roman coloffus, and break afunder the fetters of mankind, few of thofe powers, which now make fo formidable a figure, would ever have been fo much as heard of. The avengers of the general wrongs were, no doubt, the deftroyers of arts and literature, and brought on the thick clouds of ignorance, which, for many centuries, no gleam of light could penetrate; but it is to be remembered, also, that the Romans themselves had already made great progress in banishing true taste and knowledge, and would very soon have been a barbarous nation, though neither Goths nor Vandals had ever approached the frontier.

The Lombards came the last of the Scythian or Scandinavian hordes, to invade Italy. After fixing the seat of their empire at Pavia, they sent a detachment to possess itself of the southern provinces. In 571, Zotto was appointed Duke of Benevento, as a feudatory of the King of Lombardy; and seems to have confined his rule to the city alone, from which he sallied forth to seek for booty. The second Duke, whose name was Arechis, conquered almost the whole country that now constitutes the kingdom of Naples. His successors appear long to have remained satisfied with the extent of dominion he had transmitted to them. Grimwald, one of them, usurped the crown of Lombardy, but his son Romwald, though a very successful warrior, contented himself with the ducal title. The fall of Desiderius, last King of the Lombards, did not affect the state of Benevento. By an effort of policy or resolution, Arechis the Second kept possession; and availing himself of the favourable conjuncture, asserted his independence,—threw off all feudal submission,—assumed the stile of Prince,—and coined money with his own image upon it, a prerogative exercised by none of his predecessors, as Duke of Benevento. During four reigns, this state maintained

3 H itself

itfelf on a refpectable footing; and might long have continued fo, had not civil war, added to very powerful affaults from abroad, haftened its ruin. Radelchis and Siconulph afpired to the principality; and each of them invited the Saracens to his aid. The defolation caufed by this conflict is fcarcely to be defcribed. No better method for terminating thefe fatal diffentions could be devifed, than dividing the dominions into two diftinct fovereignties. In 851, Radelchis reigned as Prince at Benevento; and his adverfary fixed his court, with the fame title, at Salerno. From this treaty of partition, the ruin of the Lombards became inevitable: a want of union undermined their ftrength,—foreigners gained an afcendant over them,—irrefolution and weaknefs pervaded their whole fyftem of government. The erection of Capua into a third principality, was another deftructive operation: and now the inroads of the Saracens,—the attacks of the eaftern and weftern emperors,—anarchy and animofity at home—reduced the Lombard ftates to fuch wretchednefs, that they were able to make a very feeble refiftance to the Norman arms. The city of Benevento alone efcaped their fway, by a grant which the Emperor Henry the Second had made of it to the Bifhop of Rome, in exchange for the territory of Bamberg in Germany, where the Popes enjoyed a kind of fovereignty. From the year 1054 to this day, the Roman See, with fome fhort interruptions of poffeffion, has exercifed temporal dominion over this city. Benevento has given three Popes to the chair of St. Peter; viz. Felix the Third, Victor the Third, and Gregory the Eighth; and, what it is much prouder of, reckons St. Januarius in the lift of its Bifhops.

## SECTION LVI.

I TOOK a walk in the evening to the field of battle, where Charles of Anjou defeated Manfred, and in the way would gladly have perfuaded my conductor to fhew me the fpot where the famous walnut-tree grew, round which the witches were fuppofed to affemble and keep their Sabbath. He denied having any knowledge of the place, though he confeffed he believed that many old women of the neighbourhood were very well acquainted with it, and that feveral of his friends had heard the noifes the forcereffes make in the air, as they ride along on their broomfticks. This refort of witches, which was believed by all writers upon dæmonology, and is ftill fo among the peafants hereabouts, is founded upon a very old tradition. The Lombards, whofe creed differed little from that of other nations of Celtic origin, had a great veneration for trees, and were wont to perform, under a particular hallowed one, fuch rites, as were enjoined them by their ancient inftitutions. At Benevento, the place of meeting was under a large walnut-tree; and it was cuftomary to hang on the branches the

Figure

figure of a viper, with two heads, coiled up. A ring of this kind was found some years ago. This symbol, which is expressive of the vital principle, is among the oldest emblems invented by man, and may be traced through the religion of all nations, from Japan to Iceland. When St. Barbatus converted the Beneventine Lombards to Christianity, he caused the tree to be cut down; but the Legend gravely informs us, that the Devil found means to raise suckers out of the root, round which he and his sultanas from Lapland, and other seminaries of magicians, flock by night to celebrate their infernal orgies.

The plain, where the battle was fought, lies about two miles down the river. Neither commander seems to have displayed any great military skill, but to have rested the event upon the valour of his troops. Charles, indeed, had an advantage in the known treachery of the Neapolitan Barons in the Swabian army; as most of them had been gained over by his promises, or the Pope's spiritual threats. Manfred seeing the traitors refuse to charge, rushed with his faithful adherents into the thickest of the fray, where he was slain. His body remained above a day undiscovered, till a peasant, who was well acquainted with his person, found it, and laying it across his ass, called out in derision, Who will attack Manfred? The French officers sued in vain to their chief for leave to deposit the corpse in holy ground. Pignatelli, the Pope's Legate, insisted upon its being thrown into a ditch: every soldier in the army cast a stone upon the

the grave, and thus raised a barrow over it. But this fanatical Prelate, whose revenge nothing could satisfy, caused the bones to be taken up, and scattered on the banks of the river Verde in Abruzzo, where no friend or humane person might find them, and again commit them to earth. Thus ended Manfred.—No Prince has been more virulently traduced by the Guelph writers, whose interest and hatred combined to set his character in as bad a light as possible, in order to strengthen the claim of his opponent, and to support the high pretensions of the church. Some Ghibellines have attempted to do him justice. It would be no difficult task, with the documents that may be obtained from the chronicles of the thirteenth century, to draw up a fair state of the question, and vindicate Manfred from many of the heavy charges brought against him. An ingenious Author, in his historic doubts concerning our King Richard the Third, has pointed out the way of proceeding in such a reintegration of character. Those unfortunate monarchs resembled each other in many particulars, but undoubtedly the Neapolitan greatly deserves the preference. Manfred was beautiful in his person, accomplished in all arts then becoming a gentleman, affable, magnificent, liberal, great in his views, and anxious for the welfare of his people; inflexible and impartial in the distribution of justice, learned, for the times he lived in; and a protector of those who cultivated science. On the other hand, I must not dissemble his contempt for religion,—but I impute the fault to the complexion of the times in which he lived,—when the temporal dictates of the Pope were so artfully interwoven with the spiritual dogmas of the church, that whoever dared to dispute the former, was apt to reject the latter,—at least was supposed so to do. I believe him to have indulged a passion for the fair sex; but, had he been permitted to live longer, age would no doubt have brought on repentance, and he might have died in as good repute as Charlemagne, Lewis the Fourteenth, or any other great and amorous monarch. Manfred was ambitious,—and, to obtain a crown, infringed the laws of inheritance: but a defence of his conduct, on that point, would look like a satire on his numberless fellow culprits, from Cæsar down to Kouli Khan,—and I must have better proofs than any yet alleged, to convince me of his having been a murderer and a parricide. If we had not examples, in all ages, of the like weaknesses in other great men, I should be astonished to find Manfred such a believer in astrology and omens. He gave an instance of this credulity, as he was marching to battle, by being so shocked at the falling of a silver eagle from his helmet, that he turned pale, and cried out, "This is a sign from God!"

On leaving Benevento, I crossed the Calore, and travelled to Montesarchio, up hill most of the way, by a very fine road. Three bridges, built of immense blocks of stone, are the only remains of the *Via Appia*. The soil varies, but is in many places volcanical: one small hill is an entire lump

of

of lava. Montefarchio, a large town belonging to the Prince of Troja, stands at the head of a plain surrounded with lofty mountains on every side, except the north-west corner, where the chain is broken. This plain is of an oblong shape, and has, in my opinion, been originally the crater of a very large volcano, and afterwards a lake. The sediment of the waters may have levelled and filled up the bottom; and at last a shock may have broken down some part of the environing hills, and let out the water. Torrents washing down the soil of the mountains, may have continued to raise the level, and cultivation completed the drainage. This seems to me, from its size and position, to be the place where the Roman Consuls, and their army of thirty thousand men, were enveloped and captured by the Samnites, who possessed themselves of the high ground,—blocked up the pass that leads eastward to Benevento,—and, as soon as the Romans had entered the valley, closed up the way from Capua, by which the legions had entered. I know it is usual to call the narrow dell below Arpaia, or that which leads to Durazzano, by the name of the Caudine Forks, and dissertations have been written to prove and explain this idea. But these valleys are so short and narrow, that I cannot conceive how so many thousand armed men, in marching array, could be squeezed into the space. It is clear that the vanguard must have marched out at the head of the defile, before the rear could arrive at the bottom, which would effectually have frustrated the

scheme

ſcheme of the Samnites. The flatneſs of the plain of Monteſarchio is not a ſufficient reaſon for rejecting my ſuppoſition, becauſe earth waſhed from mountains, ruins of houſes, and fall of wood—muſt, in the proceſs of ages, have raiſed the ſoil conſiderably, and changed the whole face of the country. At the Forchia d'Arpaia, the ancient Caudium—the paſs is ſtill ſo narrow, the hills on each ſide ſo bold and ſteep, that even now it would be eaſy to throw in ſuch an abattis as could not be forced, though defended only by a handful of men.

From hence the deſcent is rapid to Arienzo, by a beautiful winding valley, well ſhaded with hanging woods of cheſnut-trees ,—the road excellent. Arienzo is a large burgh, in a low but delightful ſituation, ſurrounded with vineyards and gardens. It belonged to Ltendart, one of Charles the Firſt's generals,—then to Boffa,—and now to Caraffa, Duke of Madaloni.

Here I left the hills, and travelled to Accira, a neat city, walled round after the old manner, in a very flat, wet ſituation  Large drains prevent the river Lagno from being ſo deſtructive to its territory as it was in the time of the Romans, when its poſition was bad to a proverb. This fief was firſt held by a branch of the Aquino family, which failed in 1292. Otho of Brunſwick received it from his wife Joan the Firſt, and ſold it to Orſino  In Charles the Third's reign, Protogiudice had it, and, under Joan the Second, it paſſed to Origlia: Alphonſus the Firſt inveſted

Cardines

Cardines with it.—Acerra is called the country of Punch-nellos, becaufe that comic character, which is to the Neapolitan ftage what Harlequin the Bergamafque is to the other Italian ones, is always underftood to be a native of this little city. Punchinello is the wit, the droll of Neapolitan comedy,—fpeaks the provincial jargon, and has the exclufive privilege of faying good things and double entendres. He is fuch a favourite, that, in carnival time, the ftreets of Naples are crowded with mafks in his drefs, all acting inimitably a part, for which they are fo exactly formed by nature. From Acerra to Naples, the road is fandy, through one continued wood of vines and poplars.

END OF THE FIRST VOLUME.

# INDEX

OF

## Remarkable PLACES, PERSONS, and THINGS

Cates

# INDEX.

# INDEX.

**

# DIRECTIONS for placing the PLATES.

*Juſt Publiſhed,*

Handſomely printed in Quarto,

# TRAVELS through SPAIN,

In the Years 1775, and 1776.

In which ſeveral MONUMENTS of ROMAN and MOORISH ARCHITECTURE are illuſtrated by accurate DRAWINGS taken on the Spot.

By HENRY SWINBURNE, Eſq.

Printed for P. ELMSLY, in the Strand.

CPSIA information can be obtained
at www.ICGtesting.com
Printed in the USA
LVHW021439100723
752005LV00021B/528